POLTERGEISTS

POLTERGEISTS

*An Introduction and Examination
followed by
Chosen Instances*

★

SACHEVERELL
SITWELL

*with decorations by
Irene Hawkins
and silhouettes by
Cruikshank*

DORSET PRESS
New York

Published 1959 in the United States
by University Books, Inc.
by arrangement with Sacheverell Sitwell

This edition published by Dorset Press,
a division of Marboro Books Corporation,
by arrangement with
Lyle Stuart, Inc.
1988 Dorset Press

ISBN 0-88029-166-4

Printed in the United States of America
M 9 8 7 6 5 4 3 2 1

To
the Genius of

GEORGE CRUIKSHANK

and
in particular
his etchings for
Grimm's *Household Tales*
and the
Peter Schlemihl of Chamisso

THE DRUM
(The Narrative of the Demon of Tedworth)

In his tall senatorial
Black and manorial
House where decoy-duck
Dust doth clack—
Clatter and quack
To a shadow black—
Said the musty Justice Mompesson
'What is that dark stark beating drum
That we hear rolling like the sea?'
'It is a beggar with a pass
Signed by you.' 'I signed not one.'
They took the ragged drum that we
Once heard rolling like the sea;
In the house of the Justice it must lie
And usher in Eternity.
. . . . .
Is it black night?
Black as Hecate howls a star
Wolfishly, and whined
The wind from very far.

In the pomp of the Mompesson house is one
Candle that lolls like the midnight sun,
Or the coral comb of a cock; . . . it rocks . . .
Only the goatish snow's locks
Watch the candles lit by fright
One by one through the black night.

Through the kitchen there runs a hare—
Whinnying, whines like grass, the air;
It passes; now is standing there
A lovely lady . . . see her eyes—
Black angels in a heavenly place,
Her shady locks and her dangerous grace.

THE DRUM

'I thought I saw the wicked old witch in
The richest gallipot in the kitchen!'
A lolloping galloping candle confesses.
'Outside in the passage are wildernesses
Of darkness rustling like witches' dresses.'
Out go the candles one by one
Hearing a rolling of a Drum!

What is the march we hear groan
As the hoofèd sound of a drum marched on
With a pang like darkness, with a clang
Blacker than an orang-outang?
'Heliogabalus is alone,—
Only his bones to play upon!'

The mocking money in the pockets
Then turned black . . . now caws
The fire . . . outside, one scratched the door
As with iron claws,—

Scratching under the children's bed
And up the trembling stairs . . . 'Long dead'
Moaned the water black as crape.
Over the snow the wintry moon
Limp as henbane, or herb paris,
Spotted the bare trees; and soon

Whinnying, neighed the maned blue wind
Turning the burning milk to snow,
Whining it shied down the corridor—
Over the floor I heard it go
Where the drum rolls up the stairs, nor tarries.

EDITH SITWELL

THE CAULD LAD O' HILTON
(Poem written by a Poltergeist)

Wae's me, wae's me,
The acorn's not yet
Fallen from the tree
That's to grow the wood,
That's to make the cradle,
That's to rock the bairn
That's to grow a man
That's to lay me.

The method of this book is as follows. We begin with an Introduction dealing with many Poltergeist stories in general. This is followed by the Examination of particular cases, after which the Chosen Instances are printed. A story, therefore, which is discussed in the Examination will appear, narrated at full length from the original sources, among our Chosen Instances. These are printed in the same order in which they are commented upon in the Examination, so as to facilitate reference. The Index at the end of the book will furnish any other necessary links between our remarks and the actual narratives.

SACHEVERELL SITWELL

CONTENTS

FOREWORD	*page* 17
INTRODUCTION	25
EXAMINATION	77
CHOSEN INSTANCES	155
1. The Epworth Phenomena	157
From letters of his family published by John Wesley, and his own account.	
2. The Haunting of Willington Mill	189
From the Diary of the owner, Mr. John Procter, reprinted by permission of the Society for Psychical Research.	
3. The Drummer of Tedworth	214
Reprinted from 'Saducismus Triumphatus' by the Rev. Joseph Glanvil (1682).	
4. The Haunting of Hinton Ampner	230
Reprinted from the narrative of Mrs. Ricketts, by permission of the Society for Psychical Research.	
5. Strange Phenomena in a Calvados Castle	268
From 'Haunted Houses' by Camille Flammarion (T. Fisher Unwin, 1924).	
6. The Poltergeist of the Germans	288
Reprinted from 'The Night Side of Nature' by Mrs. Catherine Crowe (1849).	
7. Report on the Enniscorthy, Derrygonnelly, and other Poltergeist cases by Sir William Barrett, F.R.S.	328
Reprinted by permission of the Society for Psychical Research.	

CONTENTS

8. The Great Amherst Mystery   *page* 359
   Reduced from the book of that name by Mr. Walter Hubbell (Brentano, New York, 1888).

9. The Case of Mr. G—— in Sumatra   380
   Reprinted by permission of the Society for Psychical Research.

10. The Worksop and Wem Poltergeists: A Report by Frank Podmore   387
    Reprinted by permission of the Society for Psychical Research.

INDEX   417

FOREWORD

One or two of the stories of Poltergeists may be familiar to readers. This will be the case, more especially, with the Drummer of Tedworth, with Epworth Rectory, and with the Cock Lane Ghost. But we have been at pains to gather together as many other typical instances as possible. Of their total mysteries we can attempt no general explanation. All we can say is that they fall into certain well-defined types. And this, in itself, brings us but little nearer to a solution of their secrets. That there are haunted houses will be agreed to by all but a minority of sceptical readers. If we allow for much exaggeration and distortion, there remain phenomena which it is impossible to explain.

In the course of writing this book it has been difficult, sometimes, to define the Poltergeist, to draw the line that divides it from ordinary hauntings and from stories of witchcraft. But the lore of witchcraft is closely concerned with these manifestations and, if we want proof of this, we need only quote the famous case of the Curé of Cideville.[1] This begins in March 1849, and came before the Courts in January and February of 1851. The scene is Cideville, near Yvetot in Normandy. A shepherd, G——, of a near-by hamlet, was well known as being the wizard or white witch of the neighbourhood. In March 1849 M. Tinel, the Curé of Cideville, visited a peasant who was ill in bed and advised him to send away G—— and call in a reputable doctor. G—— was present at this interview, though concealed, and swore to be revenged. The Curé had two pupils in his house, Lemonier and Bunel, boys of fifteen and twelve

[1] The Cideville case is reported in de Mirville's *Des Esprits*, Vol. I, Chapter XI; in *Footfalls on the Boundary of Another World*, by Robert Dale Owen, London, 1860; and in *Cock Lane and Common Sense*, by Andrew Lang, 1894. See also, *Proceedings of the Society for Psychical Research*, Vol. XVII; *La Table Parlante*; and *Fragment d'un Ouvrage Inédit*, by the Marquis de Mirville, Paris, 1852.

FOREWORD

years old. It was G——'s boast that he would turn these pupils out of the Curé's house. A few days later G—— was arrested for illegal medical practice and sent to prison for some months. He suspected, and perhaps rightly, that the Curé was responsible for this.

G——'s vengeance now began, taking shape through an adept of his, a peasant named Thorel, forty years old, stupid and illiterate, and fond of boasting. The villagers had already decided in their minds that Thorel would be the instrument of G——'s vengeance upon the Curé. But, here, an interesting point arises. In order to accomplish his aims, it was necessary for the sorcerer to touch his victim. This G—— could not do, as he was in prison. On the other hand Thorel had opportunity to do so. On November 25, 1850, Thorel succeeded in touching both boys, in a crowd, at a sale of wood. Next day, November 26, Lemonier, the elder boy, while studying, heard light blows of a hammer, which, henceforth, recurred daily, about 5 p.m. (*a*); the Curé heard them, and to his request, 'Plus fort', the knockings became louder (*b*); within a day or two, as in so many of these cases, they would play popular tunes, on request (*c*); while, at the same time, tables moved about, knives and shoes flew round the room, and there was pandemonium in the house (*d*); Lemonier was struck continually by a black hand, attached to no body (*e*); he was dragged by the leg (*f*); and haunted by a human phantasm in a blue blouse (*g*).

Thorel invented a pretext to visit the Curé's house, and the Curé made him beg Lemonier's pardon, thus acknowledging his own belief in Thorel's evil powers. The boy immediately recognised Thorel as the phantasm in the blouse. Thorel knelt down, asked the boy's pardon, at the same time violently pulling at his clothes. This amounted to the casting of a further spell. The other boy, Bunel, supported Lemonier in his evidence and mentioned that, on November 28, he heard first a rush of wind (*h*), and then hammerings, followed by all the other phenomena.

Thorel was, at this time, boasting in the village that could he but touch one of the boys again, the furniture would move of itself and the windows would be broken. Lemonier was still haunted by the phantasm, and nails were driven into the floor by the Curé at places where the phantom had been seen. One nail became red hot, and the wood round it smoked. Lemonier said this nail had struck the man in the blouse on the cheek. On Thorel's next visit an identical mark was found on his face (*i*). Meanwhile, true to Thorel's promise, the furniture was moved and the windows were broken. Much excitement had already been aroused and many persons came to the Curé's house to watch. One witness, M. Cheval, saw furniture moving of itself (*j*); he slept in Lemonier's bed, and the pillow blew from under his head (*k*); he lay down between the two boys, holding their hands, and placing his feet on theirs; the coverlet of the bed rose in the air and floated away (*l*). Another witness saw a desk rise up, pause in the air, and then fall down (*m*). A farmer, Le Seigneur, walking with the boys in the fields, 'saw stones come to us, without striking us, hurled by some invisible force' (*n*).

A curious scene followed in front of the Maire, when Thorel tried in his presence to touch the Curé, who fled to the end of the room and struck at the shepherd with his stick. Thorel then brought a case for libel and assault against the Curé, and forty-two witnesses were cited. The Maire of Cideville swore in Court that before the disturbances began, and three weeks after G—— was released from prison, Thorel had boasted to him of what he would do to the Curé. In the end, Thorel was non-suited; his counsel suggested an appeal, but nothing more is heard of the case. The pupils were sent to their homes, and it is said that disturbances continued for some time in the house of the younger of the two boys. During the trial, the Maire of Cideville deposed to having heard, indirectly, that Thorel had once said to one of two companions: 'Every time I strike my cabin (a shelter on wheels used by shepherds) you will fall', and, at each stroke, the victim felt something seize his throat, and fell. Another account says that the Maire, himself, was witness to this incident. This piece of peasant witch-lore must be many hundreds of years old and should have analogies in savage countries. Of the whole trial, Andrew Lang says, with truth: 'A more astonishing example of survival cannot be imagined, of survival, or of disconnected and spontaneous revival and recrudescence.' The same thing, we

FOREWORD

believe, might be said of most of these Poltergeist stories; of the Drummer of Tedworth, which, again, as with the case of Rambouillet, see p. 302, is an instance of hauntings induced, by revenge, on the part of a countryman, an 'idle drummer', at Tedworth; a pedlar, in the latter story; or of Epworth Rectory, where the Rev. Samuel Wesley had offended the 'cunning men', or local wizards.

We have given this summary of the Cideville case because it might almost be called the pattern book of Poltergeist hauntings, containing as it does every category of the phenomena, except that of fire. With this one exception, that objects in the house are not mysteriously set alight, every other variety is present. Thus, for (*a*) see the Epworth and Enniscorthy cases, and also many others included in this book; (*b*) see, in particular, the Epworth case; (*c*) the rapping of tunes is nearly universal in these cases, but see Epworth, Tedworth, and Dr. Eliakim Phelps; (*d*) this is the ordinary stock-in-trade of the Poltergeist; (*e*) see the Ringcroft and Shchapoff cases, among others; (*f*) this phenomena is reported, though we do not quote the passage, in the haunted villa at Coimbra; (*g*) this can be found, too, in other cases; (*h*) the sound of a loud wind was heard in the Epworth case, where it was noticed that 'the wind commonly rose after any of these demonstrations and increased with it, whistling loudly round the house', at Hinton Ampner, and in a house in Mayor's Walks, in Peterborough, in 1891, where several witnesses stated that 'the noises were almost always preceded by a low humming sound, as if made by a rushing wind'; (*i*) this is to be found in innumerable cases of witchcraft; (*j*) once more, this is universal in Poltergeist cases; (*k*) see the Great Amherst Mystery; (*l*) see the Enniscorthy Case, the story of William Morse, in Newberry in New England, in 1679, reported by Increase Mather in his 'Remarkable Providences', and the case of Councillor Hahn; (*m*) see the A. J. Clarke case; (*n*) this is the ordinary phenomena of stone throwing, attested to upon innumerable occasions. I am afraid such details may be wearying, but this is a remarkable concatenation. We might paraphrase the remark of Andrew Lang in *Cock Lane and Common Sense*, that in this case the peasant Thorel 'might have been familiar

FOREWORD

with the whole extent of psychical literature, for he scarcely left a single phenomenon unrepresented'. He continues: 'Is there a method of imposture handed down by one generation to another?' and ends with the remark: 'Our only conclusion is that psychological conditions which begat the ancient narratives produce the new legends.' This is eminently sensible and is, probably, as far as it is possible to go towards any explanation of these extraordinary stories. It would not be difficult to draw up a coincidental table of phenomena, and the details of this would range to nearly every country in the world. But, in the end, we should be no nearer to a solution of these mysteries.

In writing this book my thanks are due, more especially, to the Committee of the Society for Psychical Research, who have given permission to quote the story of Mr. Gröttendieck from Volume XII of their *Journal*; the stories of the cases at Worksop and at Wem from Volume XII of their *Proceedings*; and Sir William Barrett's accounts of the Derrygonnelly and Enniscorthy cases from Volume XXV of their *Proceedings*. Further, they have allowed me to reprint the Diary of Mr. Joseph Procter, of Willington Mill, from Volume V of their *Journal*; and the narrative of Mrs. Ricketts, of Hinton Ampner, from Volume VI of their *Journal*. For permission to reprint this last, I have also to thank the present Marquess of Bute. I am, as well, much indebted to Messrs. Ernest Benn, of Bouverie House, for their permission to quote Chapter III, 'Strange Phenomena in a Calvados Castle', from *Haunted Houses* by Camille Flammarion, originally published by T. Fisher Unwin in 1924. The Epworth Case has been printed from the original authority; and the Drummer of Tedworth has been transcribed from *Saducismus Triumphatus*, second edition, 1684, by the Rev. Joseph Glanvil. I have, also, to thank Miss Edith Sitwell, and her publishers, Messrs. Gerald Duckworth and Co., for her poem, *The Drum*. The chapter on 'The Poltergeist of the Germans' has been reprinted from *The Night Side of Nature* by Mrs. Catherine Crowe, 1849. 'The Great Amherst Mystery' has been copied from the book of that name by Walter Hubbell, New York (Brentano's), 1888.

FOREWORD

For the T. B. Clarke Case, in 1874, I have consulted the *Proceedings of the American Society for Psychical Research*, Volume VII, pp. 193–425.

I must, also, express my indebtedness and obligation to the Rev. Montague Summers for his histories of the witches; but in particular to his *Geography of Witchcraft*, 1927: *The History of Demonology and Witchcraft*, and *A Popular History of Witchcraft*. *The God of the Witches*, and *The Witch Cult in Western Europe*, by Miss Margaret Murray have been not less valuable. I must mention, as well, *Witches and Warlocks*, by Philip W. Sargeant, 1936. A special note of thanks is due to the *March of the Poltergeist*, a bibliography of cases by Hereward Carrington and Nandor Fodor, LL.D., in Bulletin I of the International Institute for Psychical Research, Limited. The books by Harry F. Price on various aspects of Spiritualism have been invaluable, and references are given to them, where required. *The Haunting of Cashen's Gap*, by Harry F. Price and R. S. Lambert, is the invaluable modern instance. The much derided 'talking mongoose' is, as it were, a modern text book of hauntings, and will be found of quite exceptional interest. *A Disturbed House and its Relief*, by Ada M. Sharpe, describes curious experiences, including loud explosive sounds 'like bombs', that continued for three years, 1905–8, in a house at Tackley, Oxfordshire. Two old Icelandic stories, of which we give a brief summary, are to be read in *Icelandic Folklore and Fairy Tales*, by John Arnason, London, 1862. I have also consulted *Demonology and Witchcraft*, by Sir Walter Scott, 1832, a little book which is full of good stories, and has additional point in that it was illustrated by George Cruikshank. *Cock Lane and Common Sense*, 1894, and *Dreams and Ghosts*, 1899, two books by Andrew Lang, contain much information and the reports of many cases. I have consulted, of course, innumerable earlier books during the writing of this study. The standard work upon the Epworth Case, which is to be read, also, in older books, is *The Epworth Phenomena*, by Dudley Wright, London, 1917. There are old, or contemporary, accounts of many other cases, the Stockwell Ghost, the Telfair-Mackie case at Rerrick, in Scotland, the Cock Lane Ghost, and so forth. For the New England Poltergeist

FOREWORD

stories it is necessary to consult the works of the Mathers: *Magnalia Christi Americana, or an Ecclesiastical History of New England*, 1702, by Cotton Mather, and *Remarkable Providences* by Increase Mather, 1684. The trials of the Salem witches are, so to speak, in combination with these, for the Poltergeist cases were, of course, classed as witchcraft. Two more Poltergeist stories, which are not further mentioned in our text, and of which no plausible explanation was ever found, are noticed in *Cock Lane and Common Sense*, by Andrew Lang, 1894. These are the Saint-Maur Case, concerning the house of M. Poupart, in 1706; and that of Amiens, which was witnessed and described by a Dominican friar, Père Charles Louis Richard, in 1746. Disturbances continued, in the house at Amiens, for no less than fourteen years, and in both cases all the usual phenomena were present. I must, also, mention *Bealings Bells*, by Major Edward Moor, F.R.S., 1841, which is an account of mysterious bell ringing in a house in Suffolk, together with a collection of many other similar instances.

Unfortunately, circumstances have prevented my reading *Narrative of the Stampford Ghost*,[1] by the Rev. Caleb Colton, 1810, an account of extraordinary phenomena in the house of Mr. John Chave, Stampford Peverell, near Tiverton, Devon, which would appear to be one of the most interesting of all the Poltergeist stories. In conclusion, one of the most alarming of all these mysteries, which we are unable to quote here, is to be found in Chapter V, 'A Haunted Rest House,' of *Ju-Ju and Justice in Nigeria*, by Frank Hives, John Lane, 1930. This should be read in conjunction with the narrative of M. Gröttendieck, reproduced here in, as it were, an Oriental or African supplement to these tales. This story from Nigeria brings us, indeed, to the threshold of new worlds of superstition. The hut of the Ju-Ju man is as sinister as any witch's cottage. We must believe, if it is credible that there are powers of evil, that Benin or Dahomey were their kingdoms.

Those lands of black magic have many possessions that the

---

[1] Since the above was written I have had an opportunity of reading *Narrative of the Stampford Ghost*, but it is involved and litigious and, in fact, disappointing.

FOREWORD

north has never known, or has forgotten. They have the secrets, benevolent and malevolent, of their blood, things which are not lightly to be dismissed or scorned. It may well be that the secret to some varieties of these hauntings will be found among the traditions of native wizards and medicine men. Finally, if I have omitted to thank any other authors, old or new, to whom I am indebted, this is a last opportunity to express to them my obvious, and manifold, obligations.

SACHEVERELL SITWELL

INTRODUCTION

We begin this book with a pair of ghost stories, told in simple language. Both of them are in the words of young girls, one of them written down at the time, the other much later in life. Here is the first of them.

Oct. 7, 1873. 'I forgot to tell about the last night Mother spent at Weston; where the house is supposed to be haunted by Mrs. Heber, walking in high-heeled shoes.

'A little time after Mother had been in bed, she heard a most extraordinary noise of rustling silk. She got up, lighted her candle, and looked in every corner of her room, behind the tapestry and everywhere, and finding nothing, got into bed again. She had not been long in bed before she heard the sound of a file, filing away very near. "Well," she thought, "if there are thieves in the house they shan't get in here," so she shut and barred the shutters and got into bed again, when she heard along the passage the sound of little high-heeled boots walking to and fro. Mother then became anxious, as she thought whoever the thieves were, they would disturb grandpapa, so she got up, armed with an umbrella and made straight for the room where the steps had sounded last, and opened the door, with her umbrella aimed ready to poke the thief in the face, when to her surprise she found the room empty. As she was wondering at this, Aunt Puss's door opened a little bit and Aunt Puss's face peeped out. "Oh, my dear," said Aunt Puss, "what can all this noise be? Isn't it dreadful!"

'"Well," said Mother, "I don't know, but anyone, ghost or thief, it will be disturbing Papa." However, as the source of the noise could not be found, Mother had to go back to bed, but Mrs. Heber kept on, all night long, treading up and down the passages, with her little high-heeled boots, and driving away all chance of sleep, so Mother got up, lighted her candle,

INTRODUCTION

and read an interesting book till morning. The next day, Aunt Puss had the whole house hunted through from top to bottom, to see if there were any traces of the thieves, but none could be found.'

That is the first story. And here is the other.

'I slept in the same room with Fraulein Khayn, a companion of my mother's. My bed stood against the wall and hers not far from mine, with only a small passage between. Another passage remained open between the windows and the bed of Fraulein Khayn. On a table between the windows stood a water pitcher, a silver basin, and a nightlight. The only door of the room was at the foot of the bed and was closed. Towards midnight I was suddenly awakened by someone who lay down beside me in bed. I opened my eyes and saw that it was Fraulein Khayn. I asked her why she wanted to come into my bed. She answered, "For God's sake let me be and go to sleep quietly." I wanted to know what had caused her to leave her bed and come to mine, for I saw that she was trembling from fright and was almost speechless. When I pressed her, she said: "Don't you see what is going on in the room, and what is on the table?" and drew the cover over her face. I got on my knees, and reached over her to draw away the curtain and see what was going on. But I heard and saw absolutely nothing. The door was closed; candles, basin, and silver pitcher were on the table. I told her what I saw and she became quieter. A few minutes later she arose to shove the bolt on the door, but it was already locked. I went to sleep again, but the next morning she looked wretched and quite distracted. I wanted now to know why and what she thought she had seen in the night; but she answered that she could not say. I knew that she believed in ghosts and visions, and that she often claimed to have seen apparitions. She often said that she was a Sunday child, and that those who were born on other days did not have the clear sight that she had. I related the occurrence to my Mother, who was already accustomed to Fraulein Khayn's experiences. Often she had frightened and disturbed my Mother. I have often wondered why this experience did not make me fearful.'

The first of these stories comes from the diary of the writer's

INTRODUCTION

Aunt. It is a gentle beginning to what, we hope, will prove frightening in the end. When it was written down, the diarist was just under fifteen years of age. The scene of the story is the present writer's home, an old manor house in Northamptonshire. The ghost of Mrs. Heber is a tradition in the family, though she makes but rare appearances. But the rustling of her silk dress, the tapping of her high-heeled boots are the conventional part of the story. They are the sham eighteenth century of Mignon or Manon Lescaut, to music of Ambroise Thomas, or of Massenet. The eighteenth century had just, then, in the 'seventies, begun to be sentimentalized over. What is of more interest is the other sound heard by my grandmother and by her sister. 'She had not been long in bed before she heard the sound of a file, filing away very near.' This, as we hope to show in the course of this book, and to prove by numerous instances, is the machinery of haunting. What it means, how, or why it is done, we know not. And we can offer no explanation. But this is its signal, or the manner of its coming. Anyone who reads further into the narratives here collected and examined will feel certain of this. So far as we know, where this particular house is concerned, this is the solitary instance. There is no other story of that sound. It is interesting only because of its close resemblance to details in every one of the experiences that we cite. Nor, although I have lived in my home for twelve years, have I ever determined the actual rooms involved, so complicated is the system of little staircases and passages. That is, perhaps, fortunate. For there is, then, no definite ghost room.

The old gentleman referred to as 'grandpapa', and whom it was feared the noises would disturb, was the present writer's great-grandfather, a veteran of the Peninsular Wars, and one of the last survivors of the Battle of Waterloo. He died, in fact, in 1874, the year after this incident. But the whole diary will shortly be published in full. As a writer, it is only fair to say that this religious Aunt possessed remarkable literary qualities of naïveté and clearness, the mid-Victorian scene being rendered by her with the careful touch of some Dutch seventeenth-century painter, only with religious beliefs as naïve as those of the primitives. Her diary, indeed, might be the complement

INTRODUCTION

to Kilvert's journal. Both writers have the same qualities of truth and realism. We may feel certain, and we can say this from personal knowledge of the diarist, that she will in no way have exaggerated, or altered in detail, the story that she heard from her Mother.

The second of the pair of narratives of our opening is taken from the memoirs, written forty years later, by the Empress Catherine the Great of Russia.[1] It refers to a visit paid by her and her mother to the latter's godmother, the old Duchess of Brunswick, during the exceptionally cold winter of 1740. Catherine, at that time, was eleven years old. She was the eldest daughter of a particularly poor and obscure German princeling, Christian August of Anhalt-Zerbst, paying a visit to rich relations, for the Court of Brunswick, after those of Munich and Dresden, was the most luxurious in Germany. We have thought the story worth notice because of the interest of the person whom it concerns, and because as a simple ghost story it is so typical. Nothing happens in it, and there is nothing seen. We may feel certain, in our own minds, that it was no more than the nightmare imaginings of Fraulein Khayn. And yet is it so simple? Or so unfrightening? It did not make Catherine the Great fearful, but, then, she was one of the most extraordinary of women. 'Don't you see what is going on in the room and what is on the table?' What was it that Fraulein Khayn dreamt, or imagined that she could see? It may well have been no less than the murder of the Czar Peter III, who was to be the husband of her charge; or it could have been another murder, that of her charge's son, Paul I, or, indeed, more recent murders of that family, not singly, but in quantity. A dead body was lying on that table; and had it been either the husband or son of Catherine, the sight may well have been more frightening than that of other murdered corpses. For Peter III and Paul I, both of them, were of terrifying appearance. Merely the suggestion of their extraordinary features would be enough to frighten.

Now the stories told by these two little girls have this in common. Both at the time, and for long afterwards, if they lay

[1] *Catherine the Great*, by Katherine Anthony, London, Jonathan Cape, 1928, pp. 24, 25.

INTRODUCTION

awake at night, listening—and there is no mortal being who does not do this—each will have remembered this story of her childhood. So far these are but ghosts, not old wives' tales, not yet the Poltergeist. But, already, we are in the night world. The hauntings have begun. And, soon, those deeper mysteries will come. Catherine remarked in her narrative that she often wondered why this experience did not make her fearful. This can only have been because she was, herself, the pivot or centre of a life of such outrageous extravagance and intrigue. Always, let us remember, if you lie awake at night, you are reassured by the picture of daytime. But, in this pair of children, there is a contrast over which it is impossible not to delay for a moment. In the first instance, it is the picture of mid-Victorian prosperity and peace, of the flowers in the conservatory, the birds in the aviary, the comforts of breakfast or tea table, rescue work, and the certainty of a life to come. Of such is that diary, but rendered in minute naïveté and detail. And how different is the other little girl!

No ghost story of her childhood, told in her own words by Catherine the Great of Russia, could but call to mind the metamorphosis of this extraordinary being. The Court of Brunswick, as she wrote this, may have seemed to her as distant as the Middle Ages, but what of her own first years in Russia? What of the Empress Elizabeth, daughter of Peter the Great and, like her father, a giant in stature? Written down, it is probable, in her state bedroom at Tsarsköe Selo, with its pilasters of purple glass and walls of porcelain, in a palace the whole façade of which had its every statue, pedestal, and capital gilded with pure gold leaf, lying close to halls of amber and of lapis lazuli, what a contrast there was between this classical world of her own creation, carried out to her orders by architects from Italy and by Cameron, the Jacobite, and the barbarian Russia of her youth. Yet it had ghosts enough; or material for such. We need but think of her lovers. The elegant and supine Poniatowski, last King of Poland: Orlov and Zubov: Potemkin, in whom were present Peter the Great and the talents of a Diaghilev. How was it that, falsifying all history, this obscure princess, from Anhalt-Zerbst, procured the murder of her husband and left her throne to the son she

INTRODUCTION

hated, the child of her lover Saltykóv, the Romanovs being, indeed, not Romanov at all, with no blood of Peter the Great, but descended from Saltykov and left by Catherine the throne of all the Russias. We could dwell for much longer in that world of fantasy, having the wish above all things, where time and place are concerned, to see its liveries and the bright colours of its ornaments and dresses against the snow, but this is not the moment. And so we come back again to Fraulein Khayn, whose nightmare, long ago at Brunswick on that winter night, may so well have had prophetic details in its horror.

So far, as we have said, these are but ghosts. We have copied down a pair of ghost stories; one of them, the first that came to hand, with a hint in it of things that are to come; the other, a story taken note of long ago, because of the interest of its narrator. The first may have been heard treading in the passage a few feet away from me as I write this. But now we move from the simple ghost story to the Poltergeist. This is no simple haunting. Every few weeks the newspapers have some story which tends in this direction. Never a year passes but there are these reports.

The object of this present book is to gather together for discussion the few best authenticated cases of the Poltergeist. Such a collection of their principal appearances has never, perhaps, been made before. For it is our ambition in the light of their total to make some contribution, however humble, towards the explanation of what is, beyond disputing, one of the most curious of human mysteries. Of a certainty it is human. There can be no question as to that. And for that exact reason it is interesting. We live in an age in which the recent exploration of the subconscious has but just been undertaken. It has been praised, and we think rightly, as being of a comparable importance to the discoveries of a Columbus or Magellan. At the same time that dreams and visions have been analysed and explained, that the old magic of their interpretation has been revived and placed upon a scientific basis, made, in fact, into an exact science, there has been a great increase in the study of every folk-lore and folk legend from all over the world. Old wives' tales are studied in all seriousness and

INTRODUCTION

searched for meaning. The same stories, or their variants, are found, inexplicably, in lands far apart, or even in different continents. One great body awaits investigation. But it has to be cleared, first of all, of so much nonsense and superstition. We refer to the trials of the witches in every Christian country; but chiefly in England, France, Scotland, and Germany, and in the Puritan settlements in North America, and more than at any other time, during the seventeenth century. Whether or not this is the definite survival, as has been argued by Doctor Margaret Murray[1] in her most interesting book, of an ancient pagan religion, there are, at least, most curious secrets to be gathered. To this world of twilight, or even dark midnight, we relate the Poltergeist. This is where the Poltergeist belongs; but not quite, for it has affinities, also, to the séances of spiritualism.[2]

---

[1] *The Witch-cult in Western Europe*, Clarendon Press, 1921; and *The God of the Witches* (Sampson Low), 1926.

[2] In his book, *Cock Lane and Common Sense* (Longmans, Green & Co.), 1894, p. 36, *et seq*: Andrew Lang remarks that: 'Enough is known to show that savage spiritualism wonderfully resembles even in minute details, that of modern mediums and séances, while both have the most striking parallels in the old classical thaumaturgy.... Thus, either the rite of binding the sorcerer was invented for no obvious reason, in a given place, and thence reached the Australian blacks, the Eskimo, the Déné Hareskins, the Davenport Brothers and the Neoplatonists; or it was independently evolved in each of several remote regions; or it was found to have some actual effect—what, we cannot guess—on persons entranced.... We find savage mediums tied up in their trances, all over the north, among Canadian Hareskins, among Samoyed and Eskimo, while the practice ceases at a given point on Labrador, and gives place to Medicine Lodges. The binding then reappears in Australia, and in the ancient Greek spiritualistic ceremonial.' Of the Medicine Lodge, Andrew Lang remarks: 'The Lodge answers to what modern spiritualists call the "cabinet", usually a place curtained off in modern practice.' The Lodge seen by the Jesuit, Père Lejeune, in 1637, was composed of stout posts, connected with basketwork, and covered with birch bark. 'It is tall and narrow and resembles a chimney. It is very firmly built, and two men, even if exerting their utmost strength, would be unable to move, shake, or bend it.' The Red Indian sorcerers told Père Lejeune that they did not shake the Lodge, but that a great wind entered 'fort promptement et rudement'. The sorcerer was a small weak man. Lejeune, himself, noted the strength of the Lodge, and saw it move with a violence which he did not think a man could have communicated to it, especially not for such a length of time. Indians swore to him that the tabernacle was sometimes laid level with the ground, and

INTRODUCTION

What, then, is a Poltergeist? It is not an ordinary ghost. The literal meaning of this German term is a spirit that throws things about. These are, in the primitive sense, those cases of stone or pebble throwing which come fairly often into the papers. Never a year goes by but there are reports of them. The scene is often, but not always, a lonely farmhouse. But at its best, as this book will show, the Poltergeist goes far beyond the mere volleying of little handfuls of stones. Within limits, and this is important, for it is, indeed, the limits that prove the case, there is almost nothing that the Poltergeist cannot do. Knocking and rapping are the second weapon in its armoury. Small objects rise up into the air and fly slowly, always slowly, across the room; or are thrown from an unoccupied room through an open door into the presence of witnesses. These flying missiles even move upon curved lines. They do not fly straight. And, when they land, they do not roll. Neither, if they strike anyone, is he hurt by them. Sometimes

again that the sorcerer's arms and legs might be seen projecting outside, while the Lodge staggered about—nay, more, the Lodge would rock and sway after the sorcerer had left it. One Indian swore that he had seen a sorcerer rise in air out of the structure, while others, looking in, said that he was absent. These tales are to be found in Père Lejeune's *Relation de la Nouvelle France*, 1637. A later missionary, Père Arnaud, visited the Nasquapees in 1853 and describes how: 'The conjurers shut themselves up in a little Lodge, and remain for a few minutes in a pensive attitude, cross-legged. Soon the Lodge begins to move like a table turning, and replies by bounds and jumps to the questions which are put to the conjurer.' This account, which is to be found in Hinds' *Labrador*, Vol. II, p. 102, dates from just after the sensational spirit rappings in 1847-8, in the home of the Fox sisters at Hydesville, and later, at Rochester, N.Y., which phenomena were, in fact, the beginning of modern 'table turning'. Kohl, in his book, *Kitchi-Gami*, p. 278, writing of 1829, tells a story of the medium being seen to crawl into his Lodge, beating his tambour: 'The entire case began gradually trembling, shaking, and oscillating slowly amidst great noise.... It bent back and forwards, up and down, like the mast of a vessel in a storm. I could not understand how these movements could be produced by a man inside, as we could not have caused them from the exterior.' Meanwhile, two voices, 'both entirely different', were heard from within, just like the voices heard by Père Lejeune two hundred years before, which spoke Montagnais and Algonquin from within the Lodge. It may be only, as we say on another page in this book, after study of wizard and shamanistic rites in many remote parts of the world that the secret of some of the Poltergeist mysteries will be found.

INTRODUCTION

the stones, or other objects, if picked up are too hot to hold. And then in the end, but not always, a young girl, or a boy living in the house, confesses, the haunting ceases, and the mystery is supposed to be at an end. But, in reality, it is ending just at the moment when it is becoming interesting.

But there is another thing. The Poltergeist has, in many cases, the faculty of starting fires all over the house. In one instance, the Great Amherst mystery, lighted matches were seen falling from the ceiling. Clothes which have been locked away in cupboards, or packed into trunks, burst into flames. The house is burnt down. This was the case only a few months ago, at that haunted rectory in Norfolk of which Mr. Harry Price, the expert investigator, has promised an account.[1] It is, of course, easy to argue that the naughty child, or whoever is suspected, has been guilty of arson. But is it so simple as that? Is it not some power which has got beyond control and in its own interests, we grant that, burns down the haunted house just when its secrets are in danger?

The theory is that these manifestations have their centre of energy in the person of a child, who performs them, both consciously and unconsciously, being gifted, for the time being, with something approaching a criminal cunning. More usually it is a young girl; but always, girl or boy, it has some connection with the beginnings of puberty. After a time the power passes from them, with the quieting, as it might be, of their sensual or animal psyche. Sometimes, but not always, the person thus gifted is of low or abnormal intelligence. And it should be remarked, apropos of this, that in some backward countries idiots are looked upon as holy, and our instinct tells us that, had they in reality any powers to justify this superstition, we should expect of them just what the Poltergeist can perform. The holy idiots of old Russia and of Moslem lands, were their histories known in detail, would, we may feel certain, give us the instances of this. On the other hand, there are stories of Poltergeists where it is impossible to fix upon the culprit, where neither child nor imbecile person can be suspected. In perhaps nine cases out of ten a child is the explanation, but

[1] Borley Rectory, Suffolk, burnt down during the night, February 27th–28th, 1939.

INTRODUCTION

not always. And the contradictions, or exceptions, make the whole subject still more interesting.

But we can say more than this, although little, or nothing, is proved by it. At spiritual séances, among so much else that is but trickery and falsification, it has been found that during the trance of the medium, just before and during the play of phenomena, a change takes place in the temperature of the room. It is just at the moment when mysterious rappings come from tables, walls or cupboards; when the ectoplasm pours in loathsome mass from the lips, the ears, the navel of the medium, taking on rudimentary or elemental forms, a face that is like a bloated fœtus, a human hand, but of black and fœcal digits. There can be, also, telekinesis, the supernormal displacement of objects. There have even been seen teleplasmic limbs, pseudopods, fifth limbs of ectoplasm. 'From near the medium's foot, which was invisible, I saw an egg-shaped body beginning to crawl towards the centre of the floor under the table. It was white, and where the light was reflected, it appeared oval. To the end nearest the medium was attached a thin white neck like a piece of macaroni. It advanced towards the centre, and then rapidly withdrew to the shadow.'[1] In a complicated experiment arranged by Mr. Harry Price, lights, with which there was no possible contact, have burned for no reason.[2] A few years ago, in Northern Italy, the medical profession studied the case of a woman who, during her sleep, shed forth a mysterious light from her chest. She was admitted to the hospital, at Pirano, suffering from asthma, and the nurses at that institution declared that she 'glowed at night'. Three doctors sat up to watch this phenomenon. On one occasion, 'at 10.35 p.m. without any sound, there suddenly appeared a glow of bluish-white light, which appeared to come from the patient's chest and lit up her neck and face so as to show her features. The light threw no shadow. At the same time the woman stirred uneasily in her sleep and moaned. The phenomenon lasted for only a second.'[3]

[1] This was witnessed, in the case of the medium Stella C., by Dr. E. J. Dingwall. Cf. *Stella C., An Account of some original Experiments in Psychical Research*, by Harry Price, London, 1925.
[2] The case of Stella C., on 24 May 1923.
[3] Cf. Harry Price, *Fifty Years of Psychical Research*, London,

INTRODUCTION

We may feel certain there will have been a drop in temperature, during that moment, in the immediate vicinity of the sleeping woman. At one séance in London, conducted with every scientific safeguard and precaution, the mercury fell no less than 11 degrees Fahrenheit, accompanied by violent telekinetic movements of the séance table. The sudden changes in temperature appeared to synchronize with violent telekinetic displacements. One commentator remarks on this subject that: 'It is not an extravagant hypothesis which finds an explanation for supernormal physical phenomena in the withdrawal of heat from the circle of sitters, such heat being turned into some other form of energy, possibly of a kind not yet investigated by science.'[1] In the case of this particular medium, her powers had early manifested themselves, when she was a child. 'Curious happenings occurred in her vicinity, happenings which we know now must have had a psychic origin, though she was quite unaware of their importance or significance. For example, she would be sitting reading at a table on which stood a vase of flowers, when suddenly a strong cool breeze would sweep across, taking in its path the flowers, which bent under the strain. The flowers were thought to induce the breeze. This would happen when there was no wind, or in a closed room. On very rare occasions she noted a brilliant flash of light at the precise moment when she entered her bedroom; as she opened the door the flash occurred. Occasionally, small objects would jerk themselves out of her way as she approached; and raps would be heard in various parts of the room in which she was present, especially on her bedstead.'[2] Such cold air currents, or psychic winds, have been experienced, we should add, with many mediums. So much so that, in fraudulent cases, a chemical powder has been thrown into

Longmans, Green & Co., 1939, pp. 90, 91; and F. Vitali, *Sul Fenomeno di Pirano*, Roma, 1934. The name of the 'luminous woman' is Anna Monaro.

[1] Dr. R. J. Tillyard in an article, 'Science and Psychical Research', in *Nature*, for July 31, 1926.

[2] All the phenomena in this paragraph occurred in the case of Stella C.; cf. *Stella C., An Account of some Original Experiments in Psychical Research*, by Harry Price, London, 1925; and the chapter devoted to Stella C. in *Fifty Years of Psychical Research* by Harry Price, London, Longmans, Green & Co., 1939.

the air, under cover of darkness, possessed of freezing properties, in order to induce the chill feeling upon wrists and forehead which is a recognized sign that contact has been made and that the mysteries have begun.

In the case, both of the medium, Miss X., and in that of the luminous woman of Pirano, there are analogies to instances of religious ecstasy. These are the sort of stories to be read of St. Thérèse of Lisieux, or even of Joan of Arc. The incident with the vase of flowers is typical of St. Thérèse; that, of the light in her bedroom, of St. Joan. You could interpolate either anecdote into their lives, and they would fit in, exactly, with the context. In both cases, of course, this gift, if we can call it that, will have been developed and sharpened by deep emotional experiences of religion, and by ascetic practice. All three of them, for we include the medium, Miss X., will have been so patently virgin, by the very nature of these psychic adventures, that we are tempted to wonder whether such things can ever befall any person, man or woman, who does not fulfil those, apparently, essential conditions.[1] Such, also, where the Poltergeist is a child, is the invariable rule. It is a trance or ecstasy of the psyche that only in holy India has been prolonged beyond childhood, and only there because the study of those mysteries has, for thousands of years, amounted to a religion in itself. St. Thérèse of Lisieux, who is so recent in history, could be called the pattern of the saintly life in all that it can achieve of genuine mystery and wonder. It is impossible, even for the sceptic, not to grant to her a magnification of those powers which are accepted, by science, however grudgingly, in the séance room. The curious happenings during the youth of Miss X. would have been accepted in times of faith as a mark of special favour, a consecration or setting aside of their recipient for a life of religion. In the careful hands of priests and nuns she might have ended as a minor saint, a beatic, for the Catholic religion has the wisdom to realize the dangers into which such special gifts can deteriorate.

The mystery of those currents of cold air, those psychic winds which are in sign of an intensification of magical excitement, or ecstasy, can be carried still further. For it is our

[1] For an exception, see p. 74 (the case of Mme Shchapoff).

INTRODUCTION

theory that this feeling in the pores of the skin is really and truly in sign of an enchantment. This is the true communication, as well, of music, poetry, or painting. No one who has not felt it has understood their secret language. More than this, that cold wind is the trance in which inspiration has descended. It is in that chill wind upon the wrists and temples that the muse has come down to earth. We could believe that the writing of poetry, in the persons of its priests or mediums, will have been signalized by some atmospheric change as material as a fall in temperature. And this is yet more easily to be credited in the case of music. For music must affect the skin. While music plays, it should be impossible to move. In Hindu mythology, at the sound of Krishna's flute all earth's beings felt his music in the pores of their skins. All instruments of music played of themselves. The beasts of the forest listened, ravished, unable to move, attentive and with closed eyes, others motionless and weeping. Such an effect of music was held sacred in antiquity. It was a trance, a sacred trance. And the act of listening, while you feel this music in the pores of your skin, can be explained if we repeat that sentence which refers to other magical effects: 'It is not an extravagant hypothesis which finds an explanation for supernormal physical phenomena in the withdrawal of heat from the circle of sitters, such heat being turned into some other form of energy, possibly of a kind not yet investigated by science.'

The lives of the saints, just as much as the trials of the witches, should be studied for the magical evidence that they contain. Not only, we would infer, in a study of their miracles, but for the lesser phenomena which were the accompaniment to their careers. There were saints, however, like the flying saint of Copertino, in Southern Italy, before whom credulity would stop short. He invokes direct comparison with Home, the medium, just for his feats of levitation which, in the exaggeration of that southern public, surpass all sense and reason. At the same time, it is nearly as difficult to believe that all of it is fabrication. His recent date (he was born in 1603 and died in 1663), even in the superstitious miasma of the Neapolitan provinces, where he lived and died, calls for some modicum of fact. He cannot, we may conclude, have never, at

INTRODUCTION

any time of his career, performed any feat whatever of this peculiar nature. Making allowance, a thousand times over for exaggeration, something must remain. And it is interesting, again, that he is described in contemporary accounts as a person of low intelligence, able to read but poorly.[1]

Our study of this curious subject now takes us off at what may seem, at first, an abrupt tangent, but, in the course of the argument we shall hope to establish its relevance. For the precise topic under discussion is levitation, or the possibility of that, and this brings us to dancing. It was remarked in the case of the two greatest male dancers in history, Auguste

---

[1] In his eighth year St. Joseph of Copertino had an ecstatic vision while at school, and this was renewed several times; so that the children, seeing him gape and stare on such occasions, gave him the sobriquet, Bocca Aperta! At an adult age he was refused by the Friars Minor on account of his ignorance. He then became a lay brother with the Capuchins, but his continual ecstasies unfitted him for work, and he was dismissed. After this, he joined the priesthood. It was then that his miracles began. Frequently he would be raised from his feet and be suspended in the air. For thirty-five years he was not allowed to attend choir, go to the refectory, walk in procession, or say Mass, but was ordered to remain in his room, where a private chapel was prepared for him. These strictures were put upon him owing to the excitement caused by his appearance, and the anticipation of some feat of levitation on his part. He fasted continually, and kept seven Lents of forty days each year. Another 'flying saint' was the Neapolitan, St. Alphonso Liguori, a character of unusual intelligence and saintliness. His levitations came late in life, although he was crippled by rheumatic fever to the extent that his chin, in its drooping position, had inflicted a serious wound upon his chest. The characteristic tilt of his head is to be noticed in his portraits; and we are told that he could only drink through a tube. In spite of this weak constitution, St. Alphonso Liguori lived to the age of ninety-one years, dying in 1787. A full account of St. Joseph Copertino is to be found in the Acta Sanctorum. Lives of him were published in 1678 (fifteen years after his death), in 1722, and in 1753. He is reputed to have flown upon seventy occasions in all; he hovered for a quarter of an hour over the high altar; flew over the heads of the congregation in the presence of the Spanish ambassador; and, upon occasion, flew with other persons whom he caught up by the hair, or round the waist. His flights were always preluded by a loud shriek; and he would shriek, and fall into ecstasy, on hearing sacred names. The present writer has seen paintings of St. Joseph in flight, over the heads of an elegantly dressed seventeenth-century congregation in a church of classical architecture, which pictures are to be found in the churches of Lecce, in Apulia, a town famous for the beauty of its baroque buildings.

INTRODUCTION

Vestris and Nijinski, that besides their extraordinary technical ability they had the gift of appearing to remain longer in the air than any other dancers. With Nijinski, there are numberless accounts of how he seemed to stay still for the fraction of a second at the height or summit of his leap. It was like a breaking of the laws of gravity, and, then, slowly, slowly, he came down again. His descent was twice more slow than his springing into the air, a delayed descent, a lowering of his body to the ground in slow motion trajectory. It is, of course, one of the contradictions of human nature that made this most miraculously endowed of classical dancers move into a direction in which he had no chance to exhibit himself in his supreme gifts. The classical figures of a Petipa, or a Perrot, were intended for him so much more than the clumsy movements of *Le Sacre du Printemps*. His supreme gift, something similar or akin to levitation, was possessed also by Vestris, and by no other male dancer of whom there is record. When questioned about this, Nijinski is said only to have made the comment that it was simple.

But the whole question receives confirmation of its truth in a curious manner. Besides Vestris and Nijinski, only Marie Taglioni had this gift. It was noticed in her by all her contemporaries. But the special evidence to which we refer comes from a manuscript journal that we have seen. It is the diary of a young English girl, written in the late 'sixties, or early 'seventies. The diarist was a fanatical admirer or devotee of Taglioni, with whom she was in close association, seeing her nearly every day over a period of months. Taglioni had long before retired from the stage, and was occupied in giving lessons to a few pupils, of whom the diarist was one, but the subject taught by her was deportment and ballroom dancing, more than ballet dancing, which she would not teach, save in exceptional cases. This young girl wrote down in her journal, day by day, everything that she remembered of Taglioni's conversations, together with impressions of her. The leaves are interspersed, moreover, by the diarist's clever drawings, in coloured chalks, in which Taglioni is to be seen, surprisingly enough, to those who only know her in the lithograph portraits of her youth, as an old lady in a crinoline. This diary should, most certainly, be printed with its accompanying drawings. But its supreme interest to our context is that Taglioni mentions this gift of which we have been talking. She, too, describes it as simple, and says that she could teach it to others, provided that they had the necessary qualities in them. It was a question of breath control, of learning to hold the breath in a particular way which lightened the body. Taglioni claimed, even, to have taught the secret to one of her pupils, the unhappy Emma Livry, who was fatally burned when only twenty-one years of age, while dancing at the Paris Opera, in 1862. The secret perished with her and Taglioni, we are to conclude, never found another pupil worthy of having it imparted to her. This transcendental gift in dancing has, then, its serious explanation and this knowledge brings us nearer to that whole corpus of magical or sense-defying faculties with which we are dealing.

We have come to a region which is as definitely established, though unexplained, as that of the water diviner. This territory, too, is that of the healer, the thaumaturge. That such persons exist, and have peculiar powers, is beyond dispute. Their special aptitude, a thing the possession of which, or not, in themselves, is never taken consideration of for a moment by young men before they decide to take up a medical career, must be something physical or which no explanation can be given. But, like mediumship, it tempts to trickery, and, once exposed, or once mistaken, it is too easily assumed that all the original powers are disproved. In the case of a certain well-known healer, a French peasant living in the Midi, it has been described to me how he will not let you tell him of your ailment but runs his hands over your body until he comes near to the torn muscle, the twisted tendon, or whatever it may be. A curious rattling or crackling sound is set up between his fingers, which might be trying the notes of some stringed instrument, and the sinews and muscles of your leg or arm. This becomes much louder when he reaches the exact spot, and then, with a sort of rending or tearing sound, and much excitement, he takes away his hands and the cure has been effected. But his hands are perfectly white, the fingers swollen, and this chalky pallor extends up his wrists into his open shirt sleeves. For a few moments he is in intense pain. The inference must be that he has the faculty literally to remove or take away the pain. Having manipulated what was out of place, or twisted, into its position, the pain passes into him and, after a short while, dies away. Upon this occasion, he refused to accept any payment. And his promise, that the trouble would never come back again, has held good.

It is in the light of such other human mysteries that we come back to the Poltergeist. The throwing, or displacement of objects, the knockings or tappings, are not more mysterious. In several of the stories that we print, more particularly in the haunting of Epworth Rectory, and in the Drummer of Tedworth, the 'spirit' would play the most complicated games with his audience, tapping out any number required, or even a tune. You could rap with your own hand and 'he' would reply; or, even, ask aloud and be answered with the exact number that you had requested. In fact, 'someone' must have been listening; even if it was only a sleeping child, genuinely asleep, but also lying, if you will, in a psychic or mediumistic trance, self-imposed, a sort of chrysalis sleep, with hidden instincts working and, among other things, not so much an exaggerated sense of hearing, for there might be thick walls between, but a state of receptivity for messages. In the mood, in fact, for thought transference. But, also, with what might be termed its own executive at work, able and willing to carry out its pranks. Someone, put into a trance, or mesmerized, will do as he is told, stand up, lie down, and so forth. What we are to suppose in such a case as this, is that not only has the sleeping child that amount of unconscious obedience, but, also, its own powers to carry out these mysteries. The rappings, so often, come from the wooden frame of the bedstead, in horrid or obscene prophecy of the latent powers in puberty. It is primitive and horrible, like the gorilla drumming on his stomach to communicate with his mate. At Epworth Rectory, it was always the one child, Hetty Wesley, who was asleep, but with confused breathing and a flushed face. And the 'luminous woman' of Pirano stirred uneasily in her sleep, and moaned. Such are the clues to these mysteries; but we are very far from an explanation of them.

INTRODUCTION

They are not ordinary hauntings. Those, indeed, are so largely a question of credulity. These are mysteries, which may be trickery or deception, but may not. But, before we proceed so far, we must look into what association or environment can produce. For it is generally to be assumed that the Poltergeist is in the present and not the past. It is, so to speak, so obviously alive and kicking. And yet, in two of our cases, Willington Mill and that which is reported by Lord St. Vincent, the hauntings hint back. Their direction is backward, into the deadness of time. Are we not to believe that happenings of a dreadful nature must affect the dead walls? The lingering, pent-up malice of an old infirm woman, confined for fifteen or twenty years, perhaps longer, in one room of a house, can this be of no significance to the child who, afterwards, must inhabit that stained room? Would you, you yourself, who read this, civilian or soldier, like to be billeted in a bedroom in a lunatic asylum? And would it not be worse if the asylum were empty and you were its one occupant, without even the company of those unhappy beings? For we are to think that the old woman, the hag or beldame, of our theory, will have been of that type of madness which is called 'possessed', the home or tenement of an evil spirit, prompting her to malice and all wickedness. She, again, will have been something of the holy idiot, half in another world. But what world? Not, assuredly, that of which there could be pleasant dreams, in anticipation.

So many horrid settings could be found for the play of environment. Those persons who have read the Penge mystery will appreciate my meaning. It will be remembered that this horror of the 'seventies concerned a lonely house, 'The Woodlands', Cudham, in a remote part of Kent, among the orchards, and that this was the home of two brothers, the Stauntons, one of them married to a half-imbecile woman, who had a little sum of money. The other brother, we say this in parenthesis, is described as an artist and it would be easy to imagine the charm, the Birket Foster prettiness of his country watercolours. It had become the purpose of this pair of brothers, and of the other wife, to bring about the death of this weak-minded woman. They set about, therefore, to starve her

INTRODUCTION

systematically to death. To make things worse, she had a baby. They boarded up the windows of her room and never allowed her to come downstairs. Her baby was in a wooden box upon the floor. Quite soon it died. Her brother-in-law would come to her door and taunt her. 'Well, Harriett! Are you hungry yet?' On occasion he was heard shouting up the stairs to her: 'If you come downstairs I'll break your damned back like a cat's.' This comes in the evidence of a maid, who, in 1940, could be still alive, and who had to sleep in the room with her. Eventually, they became frightened. She was evidently dying. They drove her to the station, and took her by train. When she came out from the train at Penge, she collapsed upon the platform. They had her carried by porters and moved her to a lodging, where they called a nurse. The evidence of this nurse, as to the horrifying condition of her body—'It appeared to be covered all over with a down or fur' (she was covered from head to foot with lice, and with sores from her scratching)—brought it about that both brothers and the sister-in-law were arrested after she had died, a day or two later, and they were charged with having brought about her death from criminal negligence. They were acquitted of actual murder, but sentenced to long terms of imprisonment. We are not told what has been the fate of 'The Woodlands'. Doubtless, if it is still standing, the name of it has been changed. But think again of that terrible darkened bedroom where Harriett Staunton lay dying, tortured by thirst and hunger, and where her baby died. The maidservant, in an interview with the papers, describes the ravings of this tormented woman. 'She was like a mad skeleton,' is one phrase she used. Is there anyone, of their own free will, who, knowing this, would sleep there without a qualm?

Think, again, of the house of Dr. Buck Ruxton, who lived in Lancaster, and murdered his wife and her nursemaid, cutting up and dismembering their bodies with a care to minute detail that has no parallel in the history of crime. One after another, he placed their dead bodies in the bath, whence the blood could flow, and must have worked hour after hour before his work was done. We could not envy the happiest pair of lovers in the world their experience in that haunted house.

INTRODUCTION

And, apropos of curious houses, what of this? It may seem remote and far away, but it happened. The scene is Tambor (which may be the same as Tambof, between Moscow and the Volga), and the year is 1868. The person concerned is Maxime Koutzmine Plotitsine, a rich tallow merchant from Morshansk (a town between St. Petersburg and Moscow), upon the river Tsna. He had settled in Tambor and built himself a wooden house. Three of his peasant women, gardeners or outdoor servants, were arrested because they had not paid their taxes. Plotitsine incurred suspicion because of his repeated attempts to obtain the release of these women from prison, offering a bribe of forty thousand francs and inventing any and every excuse to procure their release. But, as well, Plotitsine was already, himself, the subject of comment. The Governor of the province sent police to the house of Plotitsine. He was arrested with his sister, a peasant, and one of his adopted sons.

When the police knocked at the door it was opened by someone excessively tall, very pale or sallow faced, and with an exaggerated high-pitched voice, one of the servants of the house. His bulk will have been swollen, his hands soft and flabby, his hips like a woman's. Plotitsine, himself, was in a backroom of the house and, together with eleven other persons, was taken into custody. In all, searching the house and the farm buildings and cottages, twelve more adepts, and not less than twenty-four women, some of them described as beautiful young girls, were removed by the police. They were put on trial, and all sent to Siberia. Their secret was this, that they belonged to the sect of the Skopiṭi, religious fanatics who emasculate themselves. Plotitsine, and his sister and his adopted son, all self-mutilated in this fashion, had been the centre of a cult and had persuaded these peasants and peasant girls to this sacrifice. The rites of the Skopiṭi, about which no authentic description is to be found, are said to be celebrated in religious frenzy.[1] It would be Plotitsine, himself, who performed the operation with a red hot knife, as climax, or coda, to the orgiastic festival. For some years they had kept their secret and increased their number; but when the peasant

---

[1] More details of the Skopiṭi can be read in the present writer's *Roumanian Journey* (Batsford & Co.), London, 1938.

INTRODUCTION

women were arrested, it was Plotitsine who was terrified, for they had been operated upon. At all costs they must be brought back from prison.

Long, ago, that wooden house in Tambor will have been destroyed. Almost certainly by fire, for the wooden houses of Russian towns seldom have a life of more than a few years. But, while it stood, and while its former inmates were in prison in Siberia, the house will have kept something of its recent history. Men who have turned eunuchs, women who have become odalisques, suffer extraordinary and uncanny changes. We cannot but think of this large body of men and women, as many in number as the inhabitants of a small monastery or convent, moving slowly and listlessly, as is their wont, within the precincts. How extraordinary their interrupted love affairs: your lover become your brother; your adored mistress become your blameless sister! And the sexes flow together, and are intermingled, and pass by. The men are like old women. In a few months, when their strength comes back to them, if they recover, it is a bovine, or oxlike complacency. The women are like neuter men. We would have seen them in a summer thunderstorm; or, looking more yellow, in the winter snow. Sitting round the samovar, grouped together, monks and nuns. On winter nights they had their religious gatherings, with a feast, now and again, for some new sacrifice. Plotitsine and his daughter and his adopted son owned this neuter race that they had started. He was the priest and the rich man and the landowner. The others were but neophytes, if becoming more curious every day. And they will have knelt and prayed together, like groups of waxworks, like tableaux of prayer or meditation, still groups sewing, or at domestic work, ever more listless, almost stopping still.

And now the Poltergeist—in a clever sketch or parody. The curious Phelps case, in the village of Stratford, Connecticut, in 1850–1.[1] It is the home of the Rev. Dr. Eliakim Phelps,

[1] An account of this case is to be found in *Bulletin* I of the International Institute for Psychical Research, Ltd., Walton House, Walton Street. The author, Hereward Carrington, Ph.D., has, in his possession, the original accounts of this case, mostly taken from *The New Haven Journal and Courier* of the time. It is, also, mentioned by Podmore in his *Modern Spiritualism*; in *Modern Spiritualism* by E. W.

INTRODUCTION

Presbyterian minister. He had married, late in life, a widow with four children; two girls, of sixteen and six, and two boys, of eleven and three years of age. It is suspicious, or remarkable, that Dr. Phelps, himself, believed in clairvoyance and had treated diseases by means of mesmerism. He seems, too, to have brought the trouble upon himself. Early in March of that year he was in touch with a gentleman from New York who came to him, at Stratford, in order that they should hold séances and try to obtain replies, through rapping, to questions that they asked. These attempts were, apparently, successful. A few days after this, on 10th March, when they came home from church, this is what they found. The furniture was thrown about, all over the house, as if the whole building had been ransacked. But the disturbance centred round one particular room. In this, they found eleven figures, made out of clothing, and arranged so as to form a tableau—a portrayal of a scene of prayer. Ten out of the eleven figures were female; all were in attitudes of extreme devotion; some with their foreheads nearly touching the floor; others kneeling about the room with open Bibles before them which, so we are told, indicated different passages sanctioning the phenomena then going on. In the centre of the group there was the figure of a dwarf grotesquely dressed, and above this a figure suspended as though flying through the air. Dr. Webster, a friend of Dr. Eliakim Phelps, describes this in two letters written to the *New Haven Journal*. He says: 'From this time on, the rooms were closely watched, and figures appeared when no human being could have entered the room. They were constructed and arranged, I am convinced by no visible power, with a *tout ensemble* most beautiful and picturesque. The clothing of which the figures were constructed was somehow gathered from all parts of the house, in spite of the strict watch which was kept to see that nothing of the sort could possibly happen. In a short space of time so many figures were constructed that it would not have been possible for half a dozen women, working

Capon; and in *The Spiritualist*, for August 1878, and *The Spiritual Magazine*, for 1875. It should be added that this number of the *Bulletin* of the International Institute for Psychical Research, Ltd., contains an invaluable bibliography of the Poltergeist, ranging from A.D. 530 to 1935.

INTRODUCTION

steadily for several hours, to have completed their design and arranged the picturesque tableau. Yet these things happened in a short space of time, with the whole house on the watch. In all, about thirty figures were constructed during this period. Some of them were so life-like that, a small child being shown the room, thought his mother was kneeling in prayer with the rest!'

The house was violently disturbed for a period of eighteen months. Objects and pieces of furniture were thrown about; panes of glass broken; mysterious written messages appeared on the walls, and on pieces of paper; and there was almost continual rapping, which gave intelligent, but often blasphemous answers to the questions asked. Chairs moved across the room, in front of spectators; objects were thrown through the windows; letters dropped from the ceiling; and, upon one occasion, a vegetable growth sprouted out of the carpet pattern. The evidence continues: 'Again, on one occasion, Dr. Phelps, writing at his table, and alone in the room, turned away for a moment, and on turning back to his table, found a sheet of paper, previously blank, was now covered with strange-looking writing, the ink being still wet.' Another eye-witness, Mr. H. B. Taylor, reports: 'In my presence the elder boy was carried across the room by invisible hands and gently deposited on the floor. A supper table was raised and tipped over when the room was completely empty of people. In one instance the boy's clothes were cut to ribbons.... On March 13th, in the presence of several persons, articles moved through the air, and a brass candlestick fell from the mantelpiece and continued to dash itself against the floor until broken. A shovel and tongs set moved out from the fireplace and proceeded to hop about in a dance in the middle of the floor. A heavy dining-room table was raised in the air, and a lamp moved across the room and set fire to some papers. On a later occasion, the boy was found hung to a tree, and the elder girl, while sleeping, had a pillow pressed over her head and tape tied round her neck which almost strangled her....'

Professor Austin Phelps, a son of Dr. Phelps by a previous marriage, says: 'On one occasion, when Dr. Phelps was alone, walking across the room, a key and a nail flew over his head

INTRODUCTION

and fell at his feet. That same evening, in the presence of the whole family, a turnip fell from the ceiling. Spoons and forks flew from the dinner table into the air; and one day six or eight spoons were taken up at once, bent double by no visible agency, and thrown at those in the room.' Another witness, Mr. Beach, reported in the *New York Sun* for April 29th, 1850, that he was present with several others when, in the room of the elder boy, who was sitting up in bed, a matchbox was seen to fall to the floor from the mantelpiece, landing with a noise like a bar of iron. The box then began to slide towards the bed and, when it moved to a position under it, the boy cried out that he was being burned. Mr. Beach reached quickly under the bed, and found a small piece of paper, which was in flames, about the size of half a dollar. He also says that on one occasion, while the mother and daughter were alone with him in the room, where he was observing them carefully, the daughter's right arm stiffened suddenly, and she cried out, 'I am pinched.' Her sleeve being instantly turned back, disclosed a severe fresh pinch mark on her arm.[1]

Another witness, Mr. Horace Day, gives this odd piece of evidence: 'On the occasion of my visit Mrs. Phelps hurriedly entered the room, reporting her son missing. I was struck by the curious fact that only the father seemed much alarmed. Later, Mrs. Phelps led the group to the backyard, where the boy was found in the hay mound, in a seemingly comatose state, from which he recovered in about an hour.' And we are told: 'Dr. Phelps had striking phenomena when alone with Harry, his son, under conditions where the boy could be strictly watched. The boy's clothes were on some occasions torn to ribbons!' Dr. Phelps, himself, in an interview with Mr. Charles W. Elliott on August 21st, 1851, says: 'The

[1] This particular incident invites comparison with the feats of the Roumanian Poltergeist girl, Eleonore Zugun, whose case was only recently investigated, and who produced exactly this phenomena, even in London, in 1926-7. Cf. 'Some Account of the Poltergeist Phenomena of Eleonore Zugun', by Harry Price, in the *Journal of the American Society for Psychical Research*, August 1926. According to Mr. Harry Price, and this is a most interesting point, the phenomena, in her case both telekinetic and stigmatic, ceased abruptly after the first appearance of her menses. Now, in his words: 'at the age of 26, she manages her own hairdressing business in Czernowitz, Roumania!'

phenomena have been entirely inexplicable to me. I have followed the slow movement of objects through the air, observing carefully their direction, their slow movement, and their curving flight, and am convinced that they were not moved by any human agency ... the noises are most violent when all the family are present, especially when they are seated at table.... I place no value in any of the messages, and if they are from spirits they are from evil spirits.... I am satisfied that the communications are wholly worthless, in that they are frequently false, contradictory and nonsensical, the spirits often accusing each other of lying and constantly inflicting injury on persons and property.... Fifty-six articles were picked up at one time which had been thrown at someone's head. Thirty figures were seen, and twenty window panes broken.... The phenomena for the past several weeks have been subsiding, and have now ceased entirely, I hope!' Actually, their time of activity was from March 10th, 1850, to October 1st, 1851.

'Some of the papers', we are told, 'containing records of the phenomena were found torn to bits or destroyed by fire when in locked drawers, with only the ashes remaining. The contents of the pantry were placed in a heap on the kitchen floor, accompanied by loud noises. Loaves of freshly baked cake were transported to various parts of the house, and clothing removed from locked closets and drawers, and scattered through the rooms.' Mr. Charles W. Elliott states again: 'In the presence of W——, who reports for the *New Haven Journal*, and that of three other witnesses, the following incident occurred. They were standing in the hall, outside the chamber of the eldest girl, from which loud raps were proceeding. Hearing the girl cry out, they quickly opened the door and found that her face had a deep red mark on it, where, she said, she had been struck. While the girl's hands were being held in an effort to quiet her, a huge porcelain jug was hurled against the door with far more force than the frail child could possibly have used, even had her hands been free. The jug was broken to pieces, and a half-inch indentation made in the door, showing the violence with which the jug had been thrown. One curious fact was that the line of flight was not direct from

INTRODUCTION

where the jug had stood, but in a semi-circle.' And, finally, we have the report of the Rev. John Mitchell that, when he accompanied the family to and from the house, articles of furniture had been displaced and writing had appeared on the walls and on clothing, in their absence. He had seen objects thrown, heard noises and screams, and received scurrilous answers to questions through the raps. He was convinced that these did not occur through trickery on the part of any member of the family, and that they were inexplicable...'

Let us now examine the case of Dr. Eliakim Phelps and his household. The reverend gentleman, himself, may be said to have put the disturbances in motion. As soon as they began, Mrs. Phelps was, obviously, no doubter. On the occasion when she announced the disappearance of the boy, Mr. Horace Day was 'struck by the curious fact that only the father seemed much alarmed'. Later, the mother led the way directly to the backyard where the boy was lying. Another time, 'the boy was hung to a tree, and the elder girl, while sleeping, had a pillow pressed over her head and tape tied round her neck which almost strangled her.' Who can doubt but that they did this to themselves? Thus far, trickery and imposture.

The incident when the elder girl called out that her arm had been pinched invites comparison, as we have said in a footnote, with the feats of Eleonore Zugun, but there is, as we shall see, an almost monotonous similarity in certain other details or situations between this story and other classical cases of the Poltergeist. We refer, at this moment, to the episode, just quoted, when witnesses 'were standing in the hall outside the chamber of the eldest girl, from which loud raps were proceeding'. They quickly opened the door and found her lying in bed. It is, so often, when the young girl is lying harmlessly in bed that the most startling of the phenomena are likely to occur. Compare (though, in that case, she was sleeping) Hetty Wesley in the haunting of Epworth Rectory; or, in the Drummer of Tedworth, 'the two little modest girls in the bed, between seven and eleven years old as I guess'.

By this time Mrs. Phelps, we would infer, may have been almost actively helping the phenomena. She would at least be disappointed if they failed to occur. It amounted, we would suggest, to the point that, had she come into the room and found one of the tableaux of figures waiting ready, and a single figure of them out of its place and fallen to the ground, she would be capable of lifting it up and restoring it to its intended position, smoothing down and ruffling its clothes, repairing that 'most beautiful and picturesque effect' so much admired by Dr. Webster. To that extent, we would surmise, she was in league with the Poltergeist, somewhat proud of it, anxious for it to shine. This is mere conjecture, but we feel that it is justified by the circumstances.

Who, then, was this Poltergeist? Was it Harry, his son of eleven, found hanging, and in the hay mound in a seemingly comatose state? Or the eldest daughter, sixteen years old, pinched and struck mysteriously, and discovered with the pillow over her head and tape tied round her neck which almost strangled her? It can have been either, or both of them. Thus far, as we say, went trickery and imposture. For much else of the phenomena seemed to centre, equally, in both of them. The boy's clothes were torn to ribbons; the girl had that experience in her bedroom. When the whole family were together, 'the noises were most violent, especially when they were seated at table'. Spoons and forks flew about the room; the shovel and tongs danced upon the floor. 'That evening'—this is a delightful touch—'in the presence of the whole family, a turnip fell from the ceiling.'

The rappings answered back with obscenity or blasphemy. And the writings that appeared on walls and on articles of clothing are mysterious, too. We are not told what the words were. This was the Poltergeist in its most unpleasant mood, such a guest, exactly, as the 'talking mongoose' in the farm in Cashen's Gap. The machinery of these illusions, to regard them from the standpoint of a Maskelyn and Devant, is difficult to understand. Their writing and spelling should have been studied carefully. And should all this trickery be unmasked as the work of Harry and his sister of sixteen, does it, we may ask, make the mystery less mysterious? Not so phenomenal, but just as unpleasant, and just as difficult to explain. The curving flight of objects thrown through the air

INTRODUCTION

is symptomatic of the Poltergeist, its greatest mystery, the king of its tricks, and one which has never yet been understood.

We have left, till last, the tableaux, or lay figures. We are not told precisely, but may feel certain in our minds, that their scene was the dining-room. This would be the room for family prayers. The figures were first found, we should remember, eleven of them in number, on a Sunday morning when the family came back from church. It was the first, and most terrific, of the phenomena; a new departure altogether in these stories, and a thing for which there is no precedent. There can, of course, be no question whatever that they were the work of human hands. The first intention seems to have been pietistic, as if it were a form of good work. Some of the figures had open Bibles before them, pointing to passages 'which sanctioned the phenomena then going on', whatever this may mean. It is a pity these references are not given us. They imply, at least, a considerable degree of Bible scholarship, such as a clever girl of sixteen might have had. Also, ten of the eleven figures were female. Only one—put in as an afterthought?—was the figure of a man. This, again, looks like a woman's handiwork. A boy or man would not be so adept at the dressing of these dummies. They started, we say, in a mood of piety, but the eternal unpleasantness, the obscenity of the Poltergeist, its wish to frighten, came in 'at the centre of the group, where was the figure of a dwarf grotesquely dressed'. As for the statement that half a dozen women working steadily for several hours could scarcely have completed this tableau, an inspired worker can do wonders. And it should be noted that the statement says, quite naturally, 'half a dozen women'. It was the handiwork of women, human or spiritual, not men.

This is an episode which makes one regret the infancy of the camera. It was a scene which, so easily, only a few years later, could have been photographed, the figures, even, being as though posed for a picture, able to keep still indefinitely, though one feels that the next trick of the Poltergeist would have been to make them move. We are told, with regard to subsequent tableaux: 'Yet these things happened in a short

INTRODUCTION

space of time, with the whole house on the watch.' It may be imagined with what relish the Poltergeist among them must have taken on its work of watchman. Thirty figures, in all, were found, so it would seem that this entertainment was intermittent, only put on for particular occasions. The first of the tableaux, with eleven figures, may have been the most elaborate of all. There is no denying that the thought of it is frightening. In part, of course, because of the period of the clothes. But, in particular, we should have liked much closer detail of the figures; whether any of them were in caricature, whether some were meant as portraits? Who were the ten women and one man? And how were they made? Were they just hung upon clothes horses, towel rails, chairs and fenders? How did they stand or kneel? How did their foreheads nearly touch the floor? But we are confirmed in our feeling that these figures may have been most finished and in detail by the 'beautiful and picturesque effect' referred to, and by the figure of the dwarf, grotesquely dressed. It is a thousand pities that Edgar Allan Poe, who died only a year before this, in Baltimore, could not have seen them and left us his account.

This whole episode would seem to be a perversion of the children's game of dressing dolls. The daughter, for we are certain it was she, was making a 'presepio', for it was Sunday, and the whole conception is akin to the 'presepio' of Neapolitan or Bavarian churches, but a 'presepio' gone wrong, and turned diabolist. How can she have done this in so short a space of time, whether she went to church with the family, or stayed at home and worked while they were praying, must remain the greatest mystery. She had a bedroom, a 'chamber' of her own. She could creep downstairs and work all night. It may be that, on a Sunday, the dining-room was not used till luncheon, until they had returned from church, and that, did we know more details, the other appearances of these dolls or dummies were calculated, equally, to be got ready in secrecy, and revealed when she knew a room would be opened which had been shut, or locked, till then. In conclusion, it would be very interesting to hear if there is no parallel to be found in the lives of any of the minor saints. For this could be called a convent fantasy. We are thinking of the skeletons of saints to

INTRODUCTION

be seen in rococo churches in Bavaria and the Tyrol, at Ottobeuren, and, best of all, in the church at Hall, near Innsbrück. The bones are made to kneel or stand; they have been dressed by the nuns in court clothes of Spanish fashion; they are jewelled, and their skulls wear crowns and diadems. This, again, is doll-dressing perverted. We have said that the tableaux or dummy figures of this Phelps case are unique and have no parallel in any story of a Poltergeist. But we would be prepared to say with certainty, though from conjecture, merely, that something similar could be discovered in the annals of the nuns and that, among them, it was taken as miraculous, accounted a miracle, and has become a legend, like a fairy story.

For effects upon this transcendental scale there must be genius, or predisposition. And, before we come to detail, it should be said that not only persons, but places, must be suited. We have, already, discussed environment, in its historical sense of scenes of crime, or violence. A backward, or lonely neighbourhood is another asset. The two most remarkable mediums of modern times, the brothers Willi and Rudi Schneider, came from Braunau, an old town which was the birthplace, too, of Adolf Hitler, the perfect type of a medium, if ever there was one, who is described in the newspapers, upon every dramatic or terrible occasion, as 'walking like one in a trance', or 'stepping from his aeroplane, like a person absorbed', and giving vent, alternatively, to the hysterical climaxes of the true Poltergeist. We could readily believe that this remarkable person, did he feel so inclined, could displace objects and move them about in oblique and curving flight; could rap out equivocal answers; or cause lighted matches to drop down from the ceiling. But, coming back from generalities, we stress again the lonely or the backward neighbourhood. A perfect instance is at Cashen's Gap, the home of 'Jeff', the 'talking mongoose'. Ringcroft, in Galloway, is another specimen, a backwater of Scotland, which, even now, is far behind the times. And the same thing could be said of Epworth Rectory, which is in Lincolnshire, in the Isle of Axholme. Several old customs linger in the island, and its inhabitants still pride themselves on their distinctness. At

INTRODUCTION

Haxley, near Epworth, there used to be the Haxeyhood, a custom kept up on Twelfth Day (January 6th). It is thus described. A roll of tightly corded canvas was contended for by the rustics in a sort of game of Rugby football, with plough boggins (as they were called), in red jackets, acting as umpires. The next day there was a morris dance, in character, including a 'farmer', and a harlequin who was called 'Billy Buck', while a plough was run round the village cross. This curious custom is said to have had some connection with the tenure of land by the Mowbray family, not much later than the Norman conquest. During the Civil Wars, only seventy years before the haunting of the Rectory, the isle of Axholme was described as a nest of Royalist rioters who defied authority. A Dutch engineer, Vermuyden, had lately, upon command of Charles I, installed a system of sluices and brought over Dutch and Flemish workmen, the King having made an agreement that Vermuyden should hold a third of any lands recovered. During the course of these riots the sluices were freely opened to flood the country and, in the end, after a regular battle, a military force had to be stationed here to protect the enclosures. We learn, moreover, and this is an important point in the hauntings, that Epworth Rectory was burnt down by the turbulent islanders, in 1709, on account of Mr. Wesley's Hanoverian principles. His cattle, also, were maimed by the islanders. Finally, in order to have the Wesley family's own opinion of the Isle of Axholme, it is recorded that Hetty Wesley, the suspected Poltergeist of the story, described Wroot, a village a mile or two away, in her own words, as 'a place devoid of wisdom, wit or grace'.

Cashen's Gap, in a remote part of the Isle of Man, in our own time is nearly as lonely as this. It is the Ringcroft, in Galloway, of the present day. Working upon these principles, we should look for Poltergeists, and probably find them, in the Forest of Dean and in lonely parts of Herefordshire. But the classical instance of the importance of a remote and lonely district in the history of superstition in these islands occurs in the case of the Lancashire Witches, during the reign of James I. For principal scene, there was Malking Tower, in the Forest of Pendle, a place that was dreaded by all the surround-

INTRODUCTION

ing neighbourhood.[1] The word 'Malking' means 'hare', a form commonly taken by the evil spirit in these stories; and, if any more sinister meaning is needed, there is the affinity between Malking and Grimalkin, a word that could not better describe, in its sound, the serenading of cats in the moonlight upon those haunted walls. Malking Tower was the home of Elizabeth Southernes, usually known as Old Demdike, and given honourable appellation, where the honour of witches is at stake, as a 'rampant hag'. Thomas Potts, the chronicler of the Lancashire Witches, describes it as 'a vaste place, fitte for her profession'. The other chief witch, besides Old Demdike, was Anne Whittle, known as Old Chattox. Both women were eighty years of age; Old Demdike, 'a very old woman, about the age of four score years'; Old Chattox, 'a very old, withered, spent and decreped creature'. The former had been blind for two years and was led about by her granddaughter, Alison; the latter was nearly blind.

Most of their machinations were concerned with cats or hares. For instance, after making a clay or marl puppet, or poppet, of someone she wished to kill, Old Demdike, in her own evidence, met with her spirit Tibb, in the form of a black cat (from Malking Tower), who bade her go back and do as the others were doing. She refused, and the imp pushed her into a ditch, upsetting her pail of milk. Later, Tibb appeared again in the form of a hare, and followed her along the road for a quarter of a mile without speaking. After the arrest of Old Chattox and Old Demdike, there was a great meeting of the witches of the whole neighbourhood, held at Malking Tower, on Good Friday. Its object was to discuss what could be done about those of their number who were in gaol, at Lancaster Castle, and it is fascinating to think of this meeting. More arrests were made; the whole coven was broken up, and the trials began.

The daughter of Old Demdike, Elizabeth Device, was put upon trial. She is described by Potts as having 'a left eye that,

---

[1] The Forest of Pendle lies in the hills of south-eastern Lancashire, at that time a very wild part of the county, in which Roman Catholicism lay a long while dying, a circumstance that must be taken into consideration when the trials of the Lancashire Witches are concerned.

INTRODUCTION

from birth, stood lower than the other, the one looking down, the other looking up; a preposterous mark in nature!' She confessed nothing until her own natural daughter, Jennet Device, a 'yong maid about the age of nine years', gave evidence against her. Then her cursings and ravings became so fearful that she was removed from Court and her daughter was set up on a table to continue her evidence. Alison Device, the granddaughter of Old Demdike, who led her about, was already a suspected witch. In fact, Old Demdike and Old Chattox had initiated all their descendants and relations into the cult. It was, most obviously, a regular and established witch's coven. The best, or most typical description of such women comes from a famous contemporary writer upon witches: 'One sort of such as are said to bee witches are women which be commonly old, lame, bleare-eied, pale, fowle, and full of wrinkles; poore, sullen, superstitious and Papists; or such as knowe no religion; in whose drowsie minds the divell hath gotten a fine seat; so as, what mischief, mischance, calamitie, or slaughter is brought to pass, they are easily persuaded the same is doone by themselves; imprinting in their minds a constant imagination. They are leane and deformed, shewing melancholie in their faces, to the horror of all that see them. They are doting, scolds, mad, divellish, and not much differing from them that are thought to be possessed by spirits. . . . These miserable wretches . . . go from house to house and from doore to doore for a pot of milke, yest, drink, pottage or some such releefe; without which they could hardlie live; neither obtaining for their service and paines, nor by their art, nor yet at the divel's hands (with whome they are said to make a perfect and visible bargaine) either beautie, monie, promotion, welth, worship, pleasure, honor, knowledge, learning, or anie other benefit whatsoever.'[1]

The boundaries between ghost and witch and Poltergeist are ever in dispute. No history of the one subject can but take into account the other two. That is why, and for its own good self, that we have delayed, or even gone out of our way to Malking Tower in the Forest of Pendle. Lovers of the picturesque (and that includes the horrible) cannot fail to give

[1] Cf. *Discoverie of Witchcraft*, by Reginald Scot, 1584.

INTRODUCTION

to it a high place in their imaginations. But here, at this present, there is neither time nor place for more. We must leave out of our account the second coven, twenty years later, of the Lancashire Witches, a prime figure among whom was Jennet Device, the former 'yong maide, about nine years old'.

Nor can we more than touch upon the Essex Witches, a subject no less interesting. In this part of England, as Miss Margaret Murray points out, animal familiars were especially prevalent and figure largely in all the cases. According to this authority, their appearance is nearly limited to the eastern counties of England. Her stricture is, perhaps, a little exaggerated, for the animal familiar appears frequently, also, in the Lancashire Witches and in cases of the Scottish Witches. It is necessary for us to bear their presence, real or not, continually in mind when we read of Epworth Rectory, of Willington Mill, or of their descendant at Cashen's Gap. Also, where the Essex Witches are concerned, we should draw attention to the situation of St. Osyth, which was a centre of these disturbances, for it fulfils every criterion of distance and remoteness. The trials at St. Osyth, which are referred to again on page 101 of this book, took place in 1582, and the locality, at that time, must have been absolutely upon the edge of the world. It is on an extremity of flat land, between the Naze and Mersea Island, about ten miles from Colchester. This lowland, or English polder, could scarcely have been more remote. It was in this setting that the chief of the St. Osyth Witches, Ursley Kempe (cf. page 103), had her dominion; and we read, also, of Ales Hunt and her sister Margerie Sammon, the daughters of old Mother Barnes, a famous witch. They had 'two spirites like Toades, the one called Tom, and the other Robbyn', which had been given to them by their mother. The stepdaughter of Ales Hunt, a little girl of eight, called Febey Hunt, swore that her stepmother had two little things, one black and one white, 'the which shee kept in a little lowe earthen pot with woll colour white and black and saith, that shee hath seene her Mother to feede them with milk'. Another witch, Annis Herd, according to her daughter, aged seven, had six avices or black birds as imps, and another six who lay in a box lined with

INTRODUCTION

black and white wool. Thirteen, or according to some authorities, seventeen or eighteen of these witches, were executed. And, in our own day, trippers on their way to or from Clacton-on-Sea can stop in a little cottage in St. Osyth, and for the sum of threepence see the skeleton of one of these witches of St. Osyth, lying in a grave at the end of the garden, under a wooden cover that is lifted up to show her bones with great rivets of iron driven through her knees and ankles. It is the skeleton of a gigantic woman, who must have been six feet two, or three, inches in height.

We must regret, also, that we have no space here in which to write of the Scottish Witches. The trials of witches in Scotland are as interesting, if not more so, than those of any other part of Europe, more especially because of the copious evidence of the witches, themselves, that there existed the land of Elfhame, a magical country, like that of which we read in Goblin Market, by Christina Rossetti, with its sinister and wicked charm. The folk traditions of the aboriginal Pictish inhabitants, a very small race of men who lived in excavated caves and hollows upon the bleak moorlands, must largely account for these beliefs. Those primitive inhabitants may have resembled, racially, the Laplanders; and more than one authority has pointed out the Lapps, even to-day, wear the conventional clothes, and the peaked caps, of faery lands, or Elfhame. What a fascinating subject, and how sad it is that we must leave it, without the time to examine Doctor Fian, Major Weir, or, most interesting of all, Isobel Gowdie, the Auldearne Witch, who gave her evidence voluntarily, and without torture, in 1662! There is, perhaps, no such complete picture of the witches, or of the old 'Dianic' cult, as Miss Margaret Murray would have it, as in this instance. And we cannot part from the Scottish Witches without a mention of the Forfar Witches of 1661, who met in Forfar churchyard, when at their revels. 'Andrew Watson hade his usuall staff in his hand, altho he be a blind man yet he danced alse nimblie as any of the companye, and made also great miriement by singing his old ballads, and that Isobel Shyrrie did sing her song called Tinkletum, Tankletum; and that the divill kist every one of the women.' These revels had their tragic ending

INTRODUCTION

at the stake. The witches' fires burned very late in Scotland, until the reign of William and Mary, and even of Queen Anne; several witches being burned quick (or alive) on the Gallow Green at Paisley in 1697, and others, on the top of Spott Loan in 1705; the last of these Scottish executions taking place at Dornoch, in June 1722, during the reign of George I. This last of the witches was charged with having used her daughter as her 'horse and hattock', causing her to be shod by the devil, so that she was lame and crippled in both hands and feet. It was in the chill of the early morning that this old and senseless woman was brought out to the stake and tar barrel, brought to burn her, upon Dornoch sands; and while preparation was being made, she sat warming her hands at the bonfire in which she was so shortly to be consumed. The grandson of this woman, son of the bewitched mother, and lame and crippled in her likeness, was known to, if not seen by, Sir Walter Scott, who in his *Letters on Demonology and Witchcraft* says of him, writing in 1830, that he 'was living so lately as to receive the charity of the present Marchioness of Stafford, Countess of Sutherland in her own right'.[1]

We come, now, to the witches of New England in the Puritan settlements of the seventeenth century, for here was a flourishing centre for the Poltergeist. In these colonies of Dissenters a complete reproduction of the current civilization of the English countryside, in so much as they had been used to it themselves, in their denial of all luxury and idle extravagance, is to be noticed in the trials of the Salem Witches. This is the fourth 'locale', or breeding ground, of the witches in the

[1] There is a curious story that one of the last of the race of the Great Auks was burnt as a witch in Scotland early in the nineteenth century. No doubt, like the penguins, it had a human walk and human manners, and this brought it from the wild cliffs where it was caught to the funeral pyre. We cannot resist, at this point, the temptation to tell an appropriate story from southern Italy. Some fifteen years ago when I was at Amalfi, the fishermen at a neighbouring village brought ashore a large turtle in their nets. They carried it to the piazza and put it in the fountain. The fishermen and their wives gathered round it. No one had seen such a large turtle before. Soon, it began to weep. Great tears ran down its face, and it sobbed like a child. The fisherwomen began to cry too. No one knew what to do to help it. The idea of putting it back in the sea never occurred to them. And so, with most of the inhabitants weeping over it, and crying bitterly itself, the turtle died.

INTRODUCTION

history of the English speaking peoples and we will delay upon it, if only for a few moments.

The village of Salem, some fifteen miles from Boston, Massachusetts, had been founded as early as 1626. The incidental detail that emerges from the printed accounts shows life in Massachusetts, during the last years of the seventeenth century, as being in no way distinguished from that of the most typical Puritan settlements in England, only with the difference that, if anything, a deeper degree of strictness could be enforced, here, in the New World, where the Puritans had their liberty and could live as they willed. The date of the persecution of the witches at Salem is 1692, some seventy years after the settlement had been founded. There were, by then, persons old enough to have the designation of crony or warlock attached to them. Old women are called Goody Wildes, or Osborne, or whatever name it may have been; while the devil, whether or not it really was, as they alleged, the Rev. George Burroughs, who was afterwards executed, appeared as the tall black man of convention with the high-crowned hat.[1] Abigail or Deliverance Hobbs are names typical of this far off country place; while there is, unfortunately, not space here to more than mention Increase or Cotton Mather, the former being Acting-President and, later, Rector of Harvard University. That fact seems to make a curious connection between fiction and reality, so remote and distant do the early Puritans seem to be, and so much the more removed are they from the ordinary conception of them when it is realized that the Mathers were implicit believers, they were, in fact, prime instigators of the witch trials. Such, we might say, is the medieval ancestry of the great American University. And this descent may be thought to bring it nearer to the true humanities than had it been founded in an age of pure reason. The hysterical seizures, in court, of those implicated in the Salem trials, their 'grievous torments and tortures', their 'hideous clamours and screechings', the fact that when they cried out the print of teeth would be seen on the flesh of the complainers, all this is so near to the children in the case of

[1] It seems curious and improbable that the Rev. George Burroughs was a graduate of Harvard University.

INTRODUCTION

Dr. Eliakim Phelps, and also to the feats of Eleanore Zugun. These are Poltergeist symptoms, to be at once recognized as such.

The psychic disturbances which had their culmination at Salem in 1692 had been preceded by other hysterical happenings in New England, of which the account is to be read in *Remarkable Providences Illustrative of the Earlier Days of American Colonisation*, by Increase Mather, a book which has an odd title if we consider that the date of its publication was 1684. His son, Cotton Mather, quotes other examples in *Magnalia Christi Americana, or an Ecclesiastical History of New England*, published in 1702. From these two books we resume the following. The first of these books contains a long and involved account of hauntings in the house of William Morse, in Newberry, in 1679. The house and farm buildings were the centre of extraordinary disturbances, beginning with 'a noise upon the roof of the house, as if sticks and stones had been thrown against it with great violence'. After this preliminary, the Poltergeist began its tricks in full blast. Chairs, nails, distaffs, weather boards, were hurled about, and a state of pandemonium ensued that might remind those of our readers who were lucky enough to see it of that well-known music hall turn, 'Fun in a Bakehouse', performed by the Boganny Troupe. The son, a small boy, became soon 'the principal sufferer in these afflictions'. 'On the 18 December, he sitting by his grandfather, was hurried into great motions, and the man thereupon took him, and made him stand between his legs; but the chair danced up and down, and had like to have cast both man and boy into the fire; and the child was afterwards flung about in such a manner, as that they feared that his brains would have been beaten out. . . . The lad was soon put to bed, and they presently heard an huge noise, and demanded what was the matter? and he answered, that his bedstead leaped up and down; and they went up, and at first found all quiet, but before they had been there long, they saw the board by his bed trembling by him, and the bed-clothes flying off him; the latter they laid on immediately, but they were no sooner on than off; so they took him out of his bed for quietness.'

INTRODUCTION

The boy seems, after this, to have developed all the symptoms of acute hysteria. He was pinched and beaten; his tongue hung out of his mouth; he was thrown into the fire; he made, for a long time together, a noise like a dog, and like a hen with her chickens, and could not speak rationally. 'Particularly, on December 26, he barked like a dog, and cluck't like a hen.' They then removed him to a neighbour's house; and it is significant that 'the boy was growing antick as he was on the journey, but before the end of it he made a grievous hollowing; and when he lighted, he threw a great stone at a maid in the house, and fell on eating of ashes . . . on the 19th of January, in the morning, he swooned, and coming to himself, he roared terribly, and did eat ashes, sticks, rug-yarn.' It is also an important point that the pious Increase Mather mentions the Drummer of Tedworth in connection with this case at Newberry; for a chain of circumstantial evidence convinces us that, just as the Drummer of Tedworth was known to Increase Mather and, perhaps, to William Morse, so both of these cases and their sum total, together, were well known to the Wesley household at Epworth Rectory; that haunting, in its turn, was well known, and commented upon, by Mr. Procter at Willington Mill; and the Epworth haunting, again, was known to Mr. Irving of Cashen's Gap, the owner of the notorious 'talking mongoose'.[1]

The other New England Poltergeist, described in *Remarkable Providences*, by Increase Mather, concerns a person named Nicholas Desborough, of Hartford, Connecticut. This refers to the year 1682. The said person, we read: 'was strangely molested by stones, pieces of earth, and cobs of Indian corn falling upon and about him, which sometimes came in through the door, sometimes through the window, sometimes down the chimney; at other times they seemed to fall from the floor of the chamber, which yet was very close; sometimes he met them in his shop, the yard, the barn, and in the field at work. . . . There was no great violence in the motion, though several persons of the family, and others also, were struck with the

---

[1] We are to presume that all of these cases, those in New England more especially, as reported by Increase and Cotton Mather, will have been known to the Rev. Eliakim Phelps.

INTRODUCTION

things that were thrown by an invisible hand, yet they were not hurt thereby. . . .' Increase Mather continues with another case, at Portsmouth, in New England. On June 11, 1682, 'being the Lord's Day, at night showers of stones were thrown both against the sides and roof of the house of George Walton: some of the people went abroad, found the gate at some distance from the house wrung off the hinges, and stones came thick about them, sometimes falling down by them, sometimes touching them without any hurt done to them, though they seemed to come with great force, yet did no more but softly touch them; stones flying about the room, the doors being shut; the glass windows shattered to pieces by stones that seemed to come, not from without, but from within, the lead of the glass casements, windowbars, et cetera, being driven forcibly outwards, and so standing bent. While the secretary was walking in the room, a great hammer came brushing along against the chamber floor that was over his head and fell down by him. A candlestick beaten off the table. They took up nine of the stones, and laid them on the table, some of them being as hot as if they came out of the fire; but some of those mark't stones were found flying about again, in this manner about four hours' space that night.' The predominant interest in this narrative is the mention of some of the stones being warm. This occurs, too, as we shall see presently, in the case of Mr. G——, in Sumatra. And it is to be observed that there is a marked similarity in language between 'while the secretary was walking in the room, a great hammer came brushing along the chamber floor that was over his head' and the picturesque phrase that we shall find in the haunting of Epworth Rectory, as retailed by the Rev. Samuel Wesley: 'My man who lay in the garret heard someone come slaring through the garret to his chamber, rattling by his side, as if against his shoes, though he had none there.' In other words, we may feel certain in our minds that the works of Increase and Cotton Mather were known and read by the Rev. Samuel Wesley and his family, a thing which is not at all improbable in those Puritan circles.

Before we leave these New England cases, it is necessary to relate, for the sake of those persons who love picturesque

INTRODUCTION

detail, that the Rev. Montague Summers in his able and learned resumption of these cases,[1] quotes to us the evidence concerning Bridget Bishop, who was executed as one of the most notorious of the Salem Witches, that she was the mistress of a hostelry, which stood on the high road between Salem and Beverley, and that she was wont to deck her person in 'a black cap and a black hat, and a red paragon bodice, bordered and looped with different colours', which gave much offence to the Genevan housewives who were clad in 'cinder grey or subfuse brown'. Her hostelry even contained a shovel board for the entertainment of passing guests. We are given, in this, the true picture of New England during the late seventeenth century, with its figures of Quaker, of Puritan, of Calvinistic cut; and we are to think of the new built streets filled with these variously distinguished sects of the Reformed Religion. Evidence against Bridget Bishop, who must have been in many ways the lightening of this sombre and dour scene, tells us that 'two men, John Bly and William Bly, being employed by her to take down the Cellar wall of the old house wherein she formerly lived, they did in holes of the said old Wall, find several Poppets, made up of rags and Hogs-bristles, with headless Pins in them, the Points being outward; whereof she could give no account unto the Court, that was reasonable or tolerable'.

As we have implied before, there is never far to look to find the Poltergeist. A case occurred so near home as to be upon a farm belonging to my brother, in Derbyshire, not further, indeed, than a mile or a mile and a half from our home. The hauntings were some forty years ago, but I have been told of them all my life. The scene, we can say this, had a name as good as Malking Tower. It was a lonely farm, which has to be reached across the fields and does not lie upon any road. The name of it is Toadpool Farm. And this name, already sinister enough, is, perhaps, bettered if the first syllable, as has been suggested, is the Saxon 'tod' or death, in fact, a suicide pool, or a pool in which someone was drowned. All round the farm,

[1] Cf. *The Geography of Witchcraft* by Montague Summers, London, 1927, pp. 207–313.

INTRODUCTION

in the fields, there are the mysterious mushroom rings. It is, or was, enchanted ground, but with an evil meaning. The hauntings took place during two successive tenancies; the earlier of the tenant farmers being dead, long since, and his successor still alive, but in an asylum. The usual stone-throwing took place; showers of pebbles fell from the roof, or rattled against the windows. There were tappings and rappings. And, for greater mystery, in the time of both tenants, the cart-horses in the stables were found in the morning ready harnessed, or ready saddled. The odd point in this story is the continuance of the hauntings under two successive tenants. The same children, therefore, or maidservants, cannot have been in the house. But, unfortunately, it was forty years ago and it is too late, now, to discover further details. The background is a little similar to that of Willington Mill—when we come to that—in the sense that it is rural or bucolic, but with railway lines and coal mines near by. The great slag heaps, or clinker, as it is known locally, raise their artificial hills in every direction, covered, in summer, with the pink flowering flax. The great Staveley Ironworks are in the distance. Near by is Foxton Wood, with a dam one hundred feet deep, a favourite place for suicides, and, beyond the wood, a fine Jacobean manor house, now become a farmhouse, but once the dower house of Lady Frescheville, the wife of the Cavalier. This manor house, which, too, in its remoteness should be haunted, has the name of Hagge Hall. Toadpool Farm and Hagge Hall, what better or more appropriate names could there be!

Our miscellany of the Poltergeist takes us from Toadpool Farm to what would seem to be an ideal setting, Iceland, a hundred and fifty years ago. The loneliness, the inbreeding, the long winters, the old Norse legends, the absolute lack of recreation, such are congenial surroundings for this entertainment. It is the world of Bishop Pontoppidan, the Norwegian prelate who wrote of the sea-serpent. Two stories of what was evidently a Poltergeist are to be found in a book of Icelandic folk-lore by John Arnason, of which an English translation was published in the 'sixties. The first of them, which dates from as far back as 1750, is mentioned in letters written from

INTRODUCTION

Sheriff Hans Wium to Bishop Haldoor Brynjolfsson. It was called the devil of Hjalta-Stad; and the Sheriff describes approaching the haunted farmstead and hearing the 'iron voice' speaking. This was accompanied by any amount of knocking and rapping, and by the displacement of furniture and of heavy wooden doors. It would seem that the 'iron voice' was really ventriloquism and that a young man, who was ever afterwards given a nickname suggesting that he was the culprit, must be held responsible. The story is, though, no less mysterious for that. The second case, in the house of a minister at Garpsdal, is less convincing and was spoilt by visible phantoms, who are seldom interesting in these stories and mark, nearly always, the deterioration of the theme. None the less, these Icelandic tales must be mentioned in any collection of this sort, if only because every circumstance was so appropriate to their existence.

There is another sort of haunting which we have not mentioned, consisting in the inexplicable ringing of bells. There is a curious and rare old book upon this subject, with the name of *Bealings Bells*, the author being Major Edward Moore, F.R.S., 1841. Bells had been rung in his home at Great Bealings, in Suffolk, without any possible explanation, for fifty-three days. His pamphlet does not seem to suggest any human being in his household as possible agency for these forces, but it is evident that his suspicions were aroused. He has collected no fewer than twenty other instances of this inexplicable bell-ringing. Many other examples could be quoted, of which the most interesting is the case reported in the *Atlantic Monthly* for 1868. This took place in the house of Mr. H. A. Willis at Boston, Massachusetts, and was due to Mary Carrick, an Irish girl of eighteen, who had but just arrived in the U.S.A. and had come to the house as a servant. The bells, as at Great Bealings, rang every half-hour throughout the day and evening, when totally disconnected. Sometimes the whole peal would ring, always excepting one bell. At other times, it was two or three particular bells; but, always, with no possibility of contact. But, besides this, there were other Poltergeist phenomena; the usual breaking of crockery, clothes strewn and thrown about, and the jumping of a stone slab,

INTRODUCTION

weighing forty-eight pounds, into the air without any possible reason.[1]

For the sake of convenience we class with this the extraordinary story known as the T. B. Clarke case, of which the account may be found in the *Proceedings of the American Society for Psychical Research*, Volume VII. The date of these happenings is 1874. The narrative takes the form, almost, of a judicial examination. It is a brave attempt to sift the evidence and arrive at the truth, but the continuity of the story suffers, inevitably, in the process, so that it is even difficult to be certain of what did occur. It is a very odd story. The person on whom suspicion rested was Mr. T. B. Clarke himself. There would seem to be suggestions, or inferences, that he was not entirely to be trusted. On the other hand, there was a Chinese cook in the house, who is scarcely mentioned in the evidence, but to whom attention might just as well have been directed. We shall see that, at a critical moment, our own suspicions would have fallen upon him. It is not easy to be certain of what so many persons were doing in that small house, but its occupants included a young Englishman who gave reliable evidence; and it is to be remarked that all concerned were educated persons. The most startling of the phenomena were the extraordinary movements of a heavy chair, which, according to the Englishman, and to others in the case, was of a sudden spun round with a wild velocity, just as though some superhuman force were spinning it, only to come to an equally sudden and abrupt end to its gyrations. It had stopped in the flicker of a second and was standing squarely on its four legs, as though nothing strange had happened to it the moment before. The Englishman was himself levitated, or slightly lifted in this chair, and describes the curious sensation (which we should compare with the evidence of the boy Randall, in the Enniscorthy case, p. 336). The chair seems, too, to have come round corners and spun wildly round the room, but without hitting anything. More phenomena quickly developed. Among much else, a heavy cupboard on the landing would descend the

---

[1] This case is also reported in this present book in the article on Poltergeists by Sir William Barrett, quoted from *Proceedings of the Society for Psychical Research*, Vol. XXV. Cf. page 345.

INTRODUCTION

stairs, and not content with its trajectory down one flight of steps, would take the corner and negotiate the rest of the descent. All the occupants of the house were, by now, in a state of nervous alarm (except the Chinese boy, of whose reactions we are not informed. All that we know is that when asked his opinion of Mr. Clarke, after the phenomena had ceased, he said 'Always the samee foxee', implying no great love for his master. This was twisted into partial evidence, so to speak, against the trustworthiness of Mr. Clarke, but it reflects, also, upon the Chinaman). At the height of this weird performance, when all the persons concerned were in one room together, or grouped upon the landing, a loud and piercing scream was heard, coming from no ascertainable direction, but near at hand.[1] It is described in all the evidence as the voice of a woman. The rumour of these hauntings had drawn attention to the house, and it is admitted that the small boys of the neighbourhood had been giving catcalls and whistling outside, earlier in the evening. It was, by now, however, two o'clock in the morning, not an hour at which small boys would be outside in the street. My own conviction, for what it is worth, is that this terrible scream came from the Chinese cook. It was described as a woman's shriek, and the Chinese have always shrill voices. Perhaps it may have been the Chinese boy in a nightmare; but it is so much more likely that it was the deliberate act of someone who was enjoying the disturbances. We would say, then, that this Chinese boy was the Poltergeist in the case. But it is an interesting and enthralling story to read, the distribution of the characters and the restriction of setting, together with the form of inquiry and answer in which it is printed, giving to it the illusion of a play.

Another odd story, but we are now approaching the end of our miscellany, concerns a haunted railway telegraph tower, at Dale, Georgia, upon a railway on the main line of the Atlantic Coast railroad. The occurrences took place in 1911.[2] A telegraph tower would seem an improbable environment. Three young men were working in it, a concatenation which

---

[1] This may have been an auditory hallucination, cf. page 75.
[2] This case, too, is quoted in this present book from Sir William Barrett's article. Cf. page 353.

a little suggests the two and, at one time, three young men who shared the haunted bedroom at Enniscorthy. Again, objects were moved about; doors would not open, or would not stay closed; and when all had fled in terror, a large chair came in pursuit of them and was hurled out through a window. This case has, to some small extent, an echo of the case of Councillor Hahn (see p. 307). It would seem, that is to say, to need the unconscious collaboration of two or more individuals.

There is another strange episode, the scene of which was a carpenter's shop at Swanland, near Hull, in 1849. The account of this is to be found in the *Proceedings of the Society for Psychical Research*, Volume VII. Mr. Myers, the famous authority on Spiritualism, made a close examination of one of the eyewitnesses, Mr. Bristow, in 1891. This was, it will be noted, after a lapse of forty-two years. Three workmen, in the carpenter's shop, 'were pelted with bits of wood, now moving in a straight line and striking a door, noiselessly as a feather, and again as though borne along on gently heaving waves'. This phrase of an eyewitness might apply to the movements of objects in the house of Mr. Mompesson, or in the Ringcroft case in Galloway. It is the common, or distinctive, feature of the Poltergeist at play. Mr. Bristow, after those forty years, still regarded the occurrence as a magical or inexplicable happening.

This is Mr. Bristow's story, taken from Volume VII of the *Proceedings of the Society for Psychical Research*. 'On the morning when the phenomena took place I was working at the bench next the wall, where I could see the movements of my two companions and watch the door. Suddenly one of them turned round and called out: "You had better keep those blocks of wood and stick to work, mates!" We asked him to explain, and he said: "You know quite well what I mean; one of you hit me with this piece of wood", and he showed us a piece of wood about an inch square. We both protested that we had not thrown it; and I for one was quite certain my other companion had never stopped working. The incident was being forgotten, when, some minutes afterwards, the other companion turned round like the first, and shouted at me: "It is you, this time, who threw this piece of wood at me!"

and he showed me a piece the size of a matchbox. There were two of them accusing me, now, and my denials counted for nothing, so that I laughed and added: "Since I did not do it, I suppose that if someone was aiming at you it is now my turn." I had hardly said this when a piece hit me on the hip. I called out: "I am touched. There is a mystery somewhere; let us see what happens."

'We searched inside and out, but could discover nothing. This strange and embarrassing occurrence gave us much to talk about, but in the end we set to work again.

'I had hardly started when some Venetian blinds, held above by beams let into the wall, started shaking with such a clatter that it seemed as if they must be broken to bits. We thought at once, "Somebody is up there." I seized a ladder, rushed up and craned my neck, but to find that the blinds were immovable and covered with a layer of dust and cobwebs. As I descended and found myself with my head on a level with the beams, I saw a small piece of wood, two fingers thick, hop forward on a plank, and with a final bound of two feet pass close to my ear. Dumfounded, I jumped to earth, and then I said: "This is nothing to laugh at. There is something supernatural. What do you say?" One of my companions agreed with me, the other still maintained that somebody was making fun of us. During this little dispute a bit of wood from the entrance end of the workshop flew and hit him on his hat. I shall never forget the sheepish look on his face.

'From time to time a piece of wood, just cut, and fallen upon the floor, jumped up on the benches and started a dance amidst the tools. And it is remarkable that in spite of innumerable attempts, we could never catch a piece in movement, for it cleverly eluded all our stratagems. They seemed animated and intelligent.

'I remember a piece which jumped from the bench on to an easel standing three yards away, whence it bounded on to another piece of furniture, then into a corner of the shop, where it stopped. Another traversed the shop like an arrow at the level of three feet above the ground.

'Immediately afterwards a piece took a flight with a wavy motion. Another went in a slanting line and then alighted quickly at my feet. While the chief of the works, Mr. Clarke, was explaining the details of a drawing, and we were both holding our fingers out in such a way that between our fingers there was a distance of rather less than an inch, a pointed piece of wood passed between our two fingers and hit the table.

'This state of things continued with more or less intensity during six weeks, and always in broad daylight. Sometimes there was comparative quiet for a day or two, during which one or two manifestations occurred, but then followed days of extraordinary activity, as if they wanted to make up for the time lost. In one of these periods, while a workman was repairing a Venetian shutter on the bench next to mine, I saw a piece of wood about six inches square and one inch thick rise up and describe three-quarters of a large circle in the air and then hit the shutter with some force just at the spot at which the man was working. It was the largest piece of wood which I have seen in the air. Most of them were no larger than an ordinary box of matches, though they were of various shapes, the last flying piece that I saw was of oak and about $2\frac{1}{2}$ inches square and 1 inch thick. It fell on me from the far corner of the ceiling, and described in its course a screw line like a spiral staircase of about 20 inches diameter. It is necessary to add that all these objects, without exception, came from the interior of the shop, and that not one came in by the door.

'One of the strangest peculiarities of the manifestations consisted in this, that the pieces of wood cut by us and fallen on the ground worked their way into the corners of the shop, from where they raised themselves to the ceiling in some mysterious and invisible manner. None of the workmen, none of the visitors, who flocked here in great numbers during the six weeks of these manifestations, ever saw a single piece in the act of rising. And yet the pieces of wood, in spite of our vigilance, quickly found their way up in order to fall on us where nothing existed a moment before. By degrees we got used to the thing, and the movements of the pieces of wood, which seemed to be alive and some cases even intelligent, no longer surprised us and hardly attracted our attention....

'Except in some special cases, the projectiles fell and hit

INTRODUCTION

without any noise, although they came at such a speed that in normal conditions they would have produced a fairly loud clatter. Nobody ever saw a missile at the time it started. One would have said they could not be perceived until they had travelled at least six inches from their starting point. . . . The missiles only moved when nobody was looking and when they were least expected. Now and again one of us would watch a piece of wood closely for a good number of minutes and the piece would not budge; but if the observer stopped looking at it, the same piece would jump at us. . . . Sometimes the direction taken by the projectiles was a straight line, but more often it was undulating, rotatory, spiral, serpentine, or jerky.'

In his book, *Haunted Houses*, M. Camille Flammarion tells two more stories, the points of which must be resumed by us for this introduction. The first of them is a case of stone-throwing at Marcinelle, in Belgium, in 1913. Immense quantities of small stones, or pebbles, were hurled with great force through the windows of a detached house, which had no buildings near to it. It was noted that the stones, which all came from the same direction, perforated the window-pane with the greatest regularity, never erring in their aim, and piercing, but not shattering, the glass. 'I have seen', an eye-witness said, 'a stone arriving in the middle of a large window-pane, and then came others in a spiral round the first point of impact, so that the whole of the glass was broken up methodically. I even saw, in another window, a projectile caught in the fragments of glass of the first hole it made, and subsequently ejected by another passing through the same point.' This case was never given a satisfactory explanation.[1] It is one of the most curious of all instances of stone-throwing; but no less remarkable (we will return to M. Flammarion in a moment) was the story reported in the *Giornale di Sicilia* for June 7, 1910. According to this, in the first week of that month a certain Signor Paolo Palmisano 'saw stones falling slowly without doing any damage, and says that one of them, near the place where the young deaf and dumb daughter of a

---

[1] Needless to say, there was a servant girl, fifteen years old, in the house, and the phenomena were connected with her. They would only take place in her presence, and ceased with her absence.

INTRODUCTION

peasant was sitting, detached itself from the wall, and after describing a slow semi-circle in the air, buried itself in the wall of another house'.

But we return to M. Flammarion, for his other story is of contingency to much that we have said. It is the account of a house at Fives, near Lille, in 1865. Here, once more, no explanation was ever forthcoming, though the police were called in to watch the house. A curious figure was traced on the bed of one of the rooms, which was formed with hats. At other times, large figures of eight were traced out with stockings and socks; and a dozen steps were covered with overcoats and surmounted by a hat. Upon the bed, a similar design was made with a rolled up, hooded cloak and a game basket. This sounds like the ghost in the home of Dr. Eliakim Phelps at work. It is, indeed, the only parallel that we can find to those figures and manikins (compare p. 46); but, at Fives, there was not the same practised hand. We may be positive that some young girl in the house will have been directly, or indirectly, responsible!

And, finally, to end our collection, there is the story of the house of M. Shchapoff. We find this in Andrew Lang's *Dreams and Ghosts*, and in the *Proceedings of the Society for Psychical Research*, Volume XII. M. Shchapoff was a Russian squire living near Orenburg, in 1870. He had a wife, twenty years old, and a baby daughter. He had been away from home upon a journey and came back to find the most extraordinary disturbances in progress. It is hardly necessary for us, after so many examples, to state their nature, but they included certain unusual features. Objects and pieces of crockery flew from, or towards, her, instead of pursuing an aimless trajectory. There was another contradiction, in the sense that a heavy object would strike like a straw or a feather, while things of the lightest weight struck like strokes of a hammer. Fires broke out, and Mme Shchapoff was badly burned. Most peculiar of all, while she was lying in bed, where, as we might have expected, she was especially tormented, a little pink hand was seen to come up from the floor and pull away her counterpane. This is the 'little hand', the 'little white hand and arm pressing up your arm, and presently vanishing', seen more than two

INTRODUCTION

hundred and fifty years ago at Ringcroft, in Galloway.[1] The phenomena, which were of a terrific nature, and which cannot but be helped for us by their setting in provincial Russia, near to us in time but as remote as seventeenth-century Scotland, continued for many months, but seem to have come to an end after the occasion upon which Mme Shchapoff had been so badly burned. They then ceased, and we are told that she died in childbed in 1878. But the prime interest of this case is that this is the only instance known to us in which the woman medium was a mother. In all other cases they are at the age of puberty, delayed or premature. This is, therefore, an exceptional story in that respect, just as it is among the most dramatic and extraordinary of the whole series. And it can bring us to the examination of those Poltergeists of which the cases are printed in full at the end of this volume.[2]

[1] Phantom hands appeared also in a case quoted by M. Flammarion in his book *Haunted Houses*, the scene being a school at La Cape, Porte-Sainte-Marie, in France. This particular haunting continued for no less than sixteen years. 'The little white hand, and an arm from the elbow down,' appear, also, in the Rerrick case, of 1695, as reported by the Rev. Alexander Telfair.

[2] Rappings, given out by the 'spirit' in this case, laid the blame for the disturbances on a peasant belonging to a neighbouring miller, with whom M. Shchapoff had a dispute about a mill-pond. There are, therefore, local wizards, or countrymen, in this case, as with the Drummer of Tedworth, at Cideville, with Angélique Cottin, and at Epworth Rectory.

EXAMINATION

It can be the same house, or any house, but in a lonely place. And loneliness does not mean a lack of living beings. For, where nothing human exists, there could not be the incidents that we are about to relate. They are human, unmistakably human, in the form of their manifestations; though this does not diminish the mystery. For that, indeed, is the mysterious problem. These things are earthbound: they are of the earth: nothing out of the heavens prompts them in their tortuous ways.

It would begin with a waiting, or an apprehension. In this you are an unwilling partner, for it plays with you. And, then, perhaps, the rapping will begin. But this is its primal, or conspicuous presence. It is a deaf and dumb language, no more than that. It is the red anchorite, above you in his study, and treading on the boards. Or a knocking in the wainscoting. I hope that anyone who reads this will think, at once, of the red anchorite in his attic. For this might be in his red brick house. But it is any house; or not a house at all. The canal, with its strewing of dead leaves, runs below the windows. Or it is an hotel bedroom; or a cabin on board ship. Or the empty, bare plough land; or a green field, in the dead of night, when you can hear the whirring of the world.

Now which of these alternatives is to be preferred to all the others? All are upon the earth, and earthbound. They may be far from the starlight, but they cannot get away from man. You can be more lonely in one room in a red brick town than in the sandy desert, or in the mangrove swamp. But it is the lonely, looking for company, who break down their prison bars and can transcend reality. We carry all the gods of the world in our bellies, made in our own image. They are the mists or vapourings of our sub-pyschic selves, inchoate assemblances as disparate and indescribable as some great minster or abbey of the misty north. This Gothic, which frightens or appals, which may stand blackened in some manufacturing town, has become a dead or dying monster. Its very fabric stains the fingers with smoke and soot. It is no longer like the work of men's hands; or, at most, it is the slag heap, the clinker of the mines, molten, one moment, when the sun sets or rises, and, afterwards, a putrefaction, a rotting carcass, lifting and falling on the sea of fog. Its earthy sublimity, its soil of slime, where you could skim the waters, puckering their skum of filth, banking the grimy bubbles, such is this river Styx, flowing by the gasworks and beside the tramlines. This is the soul of the town and is, as well, its refuse and its night soil.

This is the strata from which such emanations rise. They come from the underworld, from caverns or cesspools covered up or hidden. These things creep underground; they are blind like the mole, sightless and pale from their imprisonment, with long rodent fingers, cold, and as a dead man's hand. Yet, all these monsters live within ourselves. Faiths and religions fall out of the skies and keep, grave deep, in shallows of the sands. They were never more than the motes and chains that float before the eyes. The true underworld, the miasma of the mind and soul, is the heaven or hell where nothing ever dies. More shades walk here than all the buried dead. Every religion, and all superstition, serve one another and are sealed in compact. But, at this moment, our meeting is with the lesser shades. Noble lives, passed in true religion, do not concern us here. It is the scullions, or scavengers, the stragglers and camp followers, those who strip dead bodies, who have come upon the earth. They have grown up behind us, in our footsteps. They gather, like a choking weed, and no care can keep them down.

All fanaticism, all magic formula, are but a part, small beyond infinity, of the subterranean world. Wherever there is mystery we have made excuses, and, since all is mysterious, the underworld is all legend and no facts. But, as well, there is a meaning. The little details have a theme, or pattern. The abracadabra spells into real words. They are in memory of something and have been worn into their jargon. And those who used them have, on purpose, made it worse. Such are the hands that make a haunted place more frightening. This is the renegade soul, armed against itself. And the underworld in which we find ourselves is a pit of treachery and lying. Nothing is truthful in this hell, this place of waiting. All are armed against each other; or, in desperate need, have banded for a purpose and will be enemies, once more, when they have gained their ends.

And now it can begin. For there are so many ways and such a multiplicity of means. It can start, for this has happened, with a little white hand and arm pressing up your arm; and presently it vanishes. There was never anything seen, except that hand you saw. Such are the words in this account of it. After this, stone-throwing began. It went on all over the house; but it could not be discovered whence the stones came. And then, at several times, was seen a young boy about the age of fourteen years, with grey clothes and a bonnet on his head, who presently disappeared; and, in the evening, a person as it were a young man, red-faced, with yellow hair looking in at the window. In fact, it was the Poltergeist.[1]

The very word has a wild ring in it, which fits its action. The narrator goes on: 'Then I came out with a resolution to leave the house, and as I was standing speaking to some men at the barn end, I saw two little stones drop down on the croft at a little distance from me, and then, immediately, some came crying out of the house that it was become as ill as ever within; whereupon I went into the house again, and as I was at prayer, it threw several stones at me, but they did no hurt. Later, it began as before, and threw more frequently greater stones whose strokes were sorer where they hit. Besides the throwing of stones there was beating with staves, gripping of people by the hair, dragging of them up and down the house by their clothes. The bar of the door would move through the house as if someone were carrying it, while it was plain that no one was doing so. While prayers were being offered, it whistled, groaned, and cried "Bo, bo" and "kick, cuck"! It continued throwing stones, whisling and whisting, with all its former words. When it hit any person and said, "Take you that till

[1] The Poltergeist of Ringcroft, in Galloway, in 1695.

you get more," that person was sure, immediately, of another blow; but, when it said, "Take you that," the person got no more for a while.'

And then, a few days later, it stopped and never came again. The person who was medium must have gone away from this place or it is more likely that, for no reason, and without the knowledge of its earthly instrument, who, in all probability, was unaware, when in a normal state, of his or her black powers, this faculty or magical endowment had left the body in which it dwelt. No reason can ever be given for this: either for its presence, or for its discontinuance. It enters into a body, inhabits it, and leaves it. While it dwells there it is master of the soul, just as though a surrender or a deed of purchase had taken place. Superstition was not mistaken when it told of a bargain with the devil, for, in such a case, evil is predominant. Its instrument has mischievous or wicked purposes. It is far-fetched in malign intention, and deals in trickery and subterfuge. No trouble is too great for it to gain its ends, which are always of terror. It will practise deceits worthy of a master conjurer in their ingenuity. Sleight of hand, and every kind of cunning, are its tools. And the medium is nearly always a child, or adolescent, as though this were the age at which those powers are rampant. It is, more especially, the time of puberty, when the physical body and the soul are troubled, as if the suspense of this transition from childhood into normality, this chrysalis or metamorphosis condition, made of it a temporary habitation till the finished form emerged. This could be delayed, or kept in suspension, while the psychic trance continued. Such must be the explanation, but it gives no reason, nor tells the cause, nor cure.

In one of the most famous cases upon record, that of Epworth Rectory, in Lincolnshire, which was the home of the Wesley family, the testimony is such as exactly to support these contentions. An account can be found in the words of John Wesley himself, who, if somewhat credulous, could certainly be depended upon to be truthful. He was not present at the time of the hauntings, a circumstance which it is natural to deplore, but he took down the depositions of his father and mother, and of his numerous family of brothers and sisters.

EXAMINATION

The youngest of these, it is important to note, were little children. There are all the usual concomitants of such cases, with, as well, some exceptional and peculiar features. The servants and the farm hands were the first to be troubled. Strange knockings and rappings were heard, and upon one occasion an animal like a hare bounded at wildest speed out of the kitchen. Nothing improbable about this, in itself, but this detail has a contributory importance. As for the rappings and knockings, they manifested themselves with an exceptional strength when the family were at their prayers. They took on certain regular patterns, as of a hand beating out a tune. If anyone knocked back, one, two, three, they would reply in exact copy. They would learn instantly, and repeat, the most complicated measures of this sort, as though to give tangible proof that they were present and looking on.[1] The raps would come from the wainscoting, or from a chair, or table. But, in particular, they took exception, as it were, and were determined to interrupt or divert attention, whenever old Mr. Wesley read out the prayer for the King. And then it was remembered that, some years before, Mrs. Wesley, who, we may be certain, was then, as always, with one of her innumerable children upon the way, and, perhaps, in an unusually nervous condition owing to this, had expressed an objection to this prayer because of her Jacobite sympathies. To her husband's intense sorrow she refused to associate herself in the prayer and it became, for some years, the cause of estrangement between them. The spirit, then, was aware of this former complication in their lives. It was petty minded and took its delight in raking up this forgotten quarrel.

The other escapades of the Poltergeist seemed to concern themselves with frightening the children when they were in their beds. This took the form of violently heaving underneath their mattresses, dragging pieces of furniture to and fro, or causing small objects to fly through the air and hit different persons, or to clatter upon the walls. But it was always preceded by a most curious noise coming from somewhere, apparently, upon the outside wall of the house, near the roof,

---

[1] The Poltergeist would repeat, in particular, this special knock of the Rev. Samuel Wesley, 1 — 2 3 4 5 6 — 7.

and always in that special place. This is described as being like a winding or cranking, like the turning or winding of clockwork, of a windlass or of some machine, continuing as a rule for the space of some quarter of an hour together, and its pranks or manifestations could not begin, it was to be supposed, until this power had been stored, this clock wound up, or the process, whatever it may have been, had been brought to the necessary pitch of readiness. When that had been done, and the cranking stopped, it was then just a question of what form the haunting would take. But it was certain, at least, that it was ready to begin.

During all of these evening or nocturnal visits, when the spirit was abroad in the children's bedrooms, it was noticed that Hetty, the youngest daughter, stirred much in her sleep and that her face was flushed.[1] Her breathing was troubled, and yet the most obstreperous attention of the Poltergeist, the heaving, shaking, pinching, or hitting of her body, would never wake her. She continued in her slumber, but her disturbed and noisy breathing and the flushing of her face, even when the energies of the spirit had relaxed, or had not yet assumed their most violent forms, were the symptoms that she was under its spell or control, that she was, in fact, the special victim chosen for its workings. Of course, the truth, which never occurred to their credulity, was that she was not only its instrument, but was the Poltergeist herself. Was she, we may wonder, the child who was alive, but yet unborn, before her mother's estrangement from her father? Such things have a very definite effect upon the psychosis. There is, often, evidence that it takes more than one person to make a Poltergeist.

It is possible that it may have been the mother and daughter together who were responsible for these extraordinary happenings. Not as deliberate accomplices, but in subconscious intention, working in with each other, without surface knowledge and with nothing approaching planning or discussion, to the perfecting of these mediumistic pranks. Their subconscious intelligence, their souls, for this is one meaning

[1] It is nearly impossible to determine the age of Hetty Wesley at this time. She may have been as young as fourteen, or as old as nineteen.

of that word, had, therefore, if this were true, a definite, but dumb, contract between them. And such a compact almost presupposes a third person who drew up the terms, and for whose benefit it was put to work. The contracting of this silent alliance must have had a go-between, or a power whom both parties implicitly obeyed. For, in its workings, it was a treaty of mutual balance; neither mother nor daughter, it is evident, would do anything to invalidate the tricks or wonders of their cherished master.

If it worked alone, inhabiting only the shell of the child, even then it possessed a special knowledge, a kind of spiritual blackmail, upon the mother. And the particular direction of this occult power is always towards the secret or concealed weaknesses of the spirit, those of its failings in which the spirit becomes flesh. It implements the obscene or erotic recesses of the soul. The mysteries of puberty, that trance or dozing of the psyche before it awakes into adult life, is a favourite playground for the Poltergeist. Pregnancy, it would only be natural to suppose, might produce the same subconscious receptivity. And the failing, or dying, of those same powers can bring on that identical mood with all the fluctuating changes or metamorphoses of soul and body. But, in each one of these psychical situations there is some factor which is neither quite soul, nor all body. In children and young persons, where it is in association with delayed or premature puberty, the conditions and symptoms are those of too much sleep; in older persons, the dying strugglings of their potency produce a condition which is like that of sleeplessness. Nervous delusions, exaggerated suspicions, worrying over trivial details, these are exactly akin to the mental and spiritual results of insomnia. The psyche, then, is difficult to awake and, once aroused, takes long in dying. But it is a nervous force, over and above its material functions. Energies play, like lightnings, round the sleepy or lethargic body in which it lives.

These activities, of which there is so much evidence, have never received their proper share of attention owing to the fact that they have been treated with complete credulity, or, once the trick has been exposed, interest has lapsed and no further investigation has been undertaken. And yet it is when the supernatural has been disproved that these cases become really interesting. Some outer thing is really inhabiting a human body and imparting to it powers of deceit of which only a half, or, it may be, none of its normal intelligence at all, is aware. But, as well, it has often powers which cannot be explained away as mere trickery or sleight of hand. And it has always, and in every case, a devilish ingenuity that is entirely different from the naughtiness or mischief of any ordinary child. The bias is never directed towards doing something funny or amusing; it is always meant to instil terror. It is the dark background to the mind upon which it preys.

But the Poltergeist of Epworth Rectory was lacking in one of the finer instruments of panic. It never spoke. For, often enough, the spirit has a voice. The Poltergeist of Ringcroft, in Galloway, which was our first instance, has already been described in some few of its remarks, and in its cries of 'Bo, bo' and 'Kick, cuck', which were heard during prayers. This manifestation, it should be remarked, took place in 1695, and Galloway was then, or still is, for that matter, one of the most remote parts of Scotland. Later on, the Reverend Alexander Telfair, who published the account from which we have quoted, describes how it woke up Andrew Mackie, one of the household, who was asleep, with the words 'Thou shalt be troubled till Tuesday.' All in the house heard this. He asked it, 'Who gave thee a commission?' It answered 'God gave me a commission, and I am sent to warn the land to repent, for a judgement is to come if the land do not quickly repent.' It commanded him to reveal this upon his peril, and added that if the land did not repent, it would go to its father and get a commission to return with a hundred worse than itself and would trouble every family in the land. Here, again, there can be no doubt whatever that the actual Poltergeist was one of the children of the family. It had, in fact, learnt to ventriloquize. This, though, does not make the mystery any less unpleasant. Many years of training, as well as a special aptitude, go to the making of a ventriloquist. In fact, the Poltergeist in its play with a ventriloquist's dummy, is as complicated a trick as if the medium, who had never been taught, became an adept at playing the piano. There have been cases, too, in

EXAMINATION

which a child, or a young girl, will reel off long strings of sentences in some foreign tongue, and it has been proved, upon more than one occasion, that this is no less than some miraculous feat of memory, dating, perhaps, from hardly more than a single experience of hearing someone speak in whatever foreign language it may have been. But there is always, to the majority of persons, something weird and unpleasant about ventriloquism, a point of view which is helped by the extreme ugliness, the wildly unfunny humour, of the dummy's appearance. He is, always, the type of the wooden head child, a variety which is to be seen in ordinary life and that approximates to the idiot boy. Who, then, can have taught the Poltergeist to speak? Who was the master of this art of ventriloquism?

In the case of the Wesley family there is one other significant feature. Upon one occasion, the second time when anything was seen, a little animal described as looking like a badger ran out from underneath one of the children's beds. Was it, we wonder, the bed of Hetty, who was sleeping with the confused breathing and the flushed face that were so often noticed? The children, themselves, seem to have attributed it all to that little animal, for they even called the spirit by a nickname, 'Jeff'. This, as other writers have pointed out, has some extraordinary points of resemblance with the 'talking mongoose' which, in that lonely farm of Cashen's Gap, in the Isle of Man, was the minor, but mysterious sensation, of a few years ago. In that case, the mongoose even referred to itself under the name of 'Jeff'.[1] It had made a particular friend of the daughter of the house and the circumstances in that peculiar story do not preclude the possibility, they, indeed, point to the fact, that the daughter was a ventriloquist. In this, as in the case of Mrs. Wesley and her daughter, the mother may, or may not, have been unconscious assistant to her child. It has been pointed out that the farm was in an extremely lonely place, such as Epworth,[2] or Ringcroft, in Galloway, and these frightening

---

[1] And one of the ghosts at Willington Mill was known to the neighbours as 'Old Jeffrey'. Cf. *The Night Side of Nature*, by Mrs. Catherine Crowe, 1852, p. 351.

[2] For the lonely situation of Epworth Rectory, see p. 55.

events were, certainly, a stimulus and an excitement. Someone who possessed this faculty, consciously or unconsciously, would be reluctant to give up their powers of entertainment. And yet, how curious never to come out into the open! They were careful of their secret as any escaped murderer. And there are, and must be, as many reasons for this.

As to the levitation of objects, many successes, it is evident, could be won with the help of a piece of black thread, for instance. But, at the same time, there are circumstantial stories which point to the actual possession of some power over inanimate objects. But the spirit in every case, as, indeed, the talking mongoose said, often enough, in not over-refined language, is suspicious. It will not work in front of doubters, or of persons whom there is not a good chance of convincing. And it is, surely, unnatural according to our view of these phenomena, to blame it for this. Why should it display the most precious of its gifts to an unappreciative audience, who are lying in wait to rob it of its birthright! The trick, like one of the masterpieces of a famous chef, should only be displayed upon select occasions, where every circumstance is congenial. Not every public is worthy of its greatest pains. Not only this, but unless all the factors are propitious, we may conclude that the wonder will not work. For it is probable that it requires the participation of all concerned. A judicious mingling of confirmed believers and of a few persons who are certain to be converted must be its ideal audience. And, in a lonely farmhouse or parsonage, with a family who are already completely in its control and under its subjection, a family, moreover, who must regard these events, however disturbing, as an entertainment, as a solace against the dullness of their lives, there could be no limits to the scope and variety of its play. In such a case it becomes like a virtuoso performing to a chosen gathering of his friends. Nothing is discordant or jarring in this perfect circle. On the other hand, the arrival of a stranger might mar the harmony of these select proceedings. And the temperamental musician—and who has more of a temperament than the Poltergeist?—might refuse to perform any more.

In particular, the scientific investigator might be expected to act as an absolute deterrent. Why, and for what reason,

EXAMINATION

should the spirit perform its tricks for such? The steadfastly incredulous are, in this respect, akin to those unhappy persons who dislike music. Conversion is out of the question; and the Poltergeist, moreover, must be credited with its own reasons for not wishing to become a mere laboratory experiment. Its powers are reserved for very special occasions and the object behind them, for there is, of course, an object, must be far removed from any wish to be made a discussion, and a mere explanation, in the cold light of day. Like owl, or bat, or nocturnal spider, the Poltergeist must prefer the dark.

Its powers, then, seem to be fixed or loaded in the person of someone in the house, preferably a child in the most impressionable months of its life. It numbs, or altogether subdues, the surface consciousness, so that the tasks to which it is put are ignored or forgotten by the medium, who may yet lend all his or her powers of ingenuity, and more than his or her normal share of that, to the perfecting of this trickery. It learns the arts of conjuring, of sleight of hand, or even of ventriloquism. It can show the most wakeful apprehension while in this subnormal trance. The evil spirit prompts it to every description of deceit and fraud. But these adjuncts of guilt are not to be taken in presumption of nothing but trickery and lying. They are the mere external trappings; and it would be as sensible to disparage the whole art of acting because it relies on scenery and costume for its immediate effects. Where the whole method is evil, and worked for evil ends, it is only natural to expect that it will make use of any and every weapon that lies to hand. For it is an art of deceit, and the smaller trickeries that are so easily unmasked are no more than the clothes and scenery of the play. When stones, or pennies, are thrown against the window, when furniture is dragged about in a room overhead, and there can be no more doubt as to the child who did this, then, indeed, the mystery is far from solved. For it would have been easy to guess this much at the beginning. It is from now, onward, that the true mystery begins.

These few, simple trickeries are in proof of what is here. For the real feats of the Poltergeist are only done when the ground is carefully prepared. This lonely farmhouse or parsonage must have that air of expectancy in which anything may happen. Nothing, and nobody, can be entirely trusted. Little tricks or deceits are continually in play. There is no knowing who is in the plot. And the person, or persons, could plead entire ignorance and tell the truth in that. Their dual personality is hidden from them; or, if they are aware of it, there is no explanation they can offer. A mother, as we have seen, could aid or abet her daughter. Is it unreasonable, in such a case, to think that the child may have learnt from its parent? There may be a long tradition behind many such spirits in the seventeenth century. In the recent case that we have mentioned, the Manx background may have been more than fortuitous. For the mother was of Manx origin, and the child who was, and may still be, pivot of the action had a Manx name, Voirrey, which has its own special significance and its bearing, so to speak, upon the action, since Voirrey is the Manx form of the name Mary.

But let us, for the sake of our own information, recapitulate the haunting of Epworth Rectory in the very words, in the verbatim report, gathered from his family and noted down by John Wesley, for this evidence has its bearing upon what is to follow. It is in the light of this report that we shall proceed to another and parallel encounter. This, for instance, comes at the beginning of the story: 'After 9, Robert Brown—the servant—sitting alone by the fire in the back kitchen something came out of the copper hole like a rabbit, but less, and turned round five times, very swiftly. Its ears lay flat upon its neck, and its little scut stood straight up.' And, upon about the same date—it is the Rev. Samuel Wesley speaking: 'My man who lay in the garret heard someone come slaring through the garret to his chamber, rattling by his side, as if against his shoes, though he had none there; at other times walking up and down stairs, when all the house were in bed, and gobbling like a turkeycock.' And now we come to the interruption of the prayers, and this is given in John Wesley's own words: 'The year before King William died my father observed that my mother did not say Amen to the prayer for the King. She said she could not, for she did not believe the Prince of Orange was king. My father vowed he would never cohabit with her till she did. He, then, took his horse, and rode away; nor did she hear

EXAMINATION

anything of him for a twelvemonth. He, then, came back and lived with her as before. But I fear his vow was not forgotten before God.'[1] This episode must have taken place in 1701 and since the Wesley parents had no fewer than nineteen children, of whom some fourteen died in infancy, it is safe, perhaps, to conclude that this will have been the only year, out of twenty and more years of married life, in which Mrs. Wesley had a respite from the labours of childbearing. Now the Poltergeist of Epworth, as we have seen, became particularly violent during family prayers, and especially during the prayer for the King. John Wesley had the decided opinion that this fact must have some connection with the quarrel, long before, between his father and mother.

This is his description of how it afflicted the children: 'They were much affected, though asleep, sweating and trembling exceedingly.' Soon after, it made a terrific disturbance in the Rector's study, which he entered, alone, resolved to meet it upon its own ground. 'When I heard the noise, I spoke to it to tell me what it was, but never heard any articulate voice, and only, once or twice, two or three feeble squeaks, a little louder than the chirping of a bird.'

The time at which the manifestations began was nearly always 9.45 in the evening. 'Emilia heard the usual signal of its beginning to play, with which she was perfectly well acquainted: it was like the strong winding up of a jack.' It is described, in other places, in the narrative, as 'resembling the loud creaking of a saw; or rather that of a windmill, when the body of it is turned about, in order to shift the sails to the wind'. Or we are told: 'it is like a carpenter planing deals.' The phenomena would, then, immediately begin; and an expressive phrase described their gradual quietening down again into silence, for we read, of its knocking, that 'at its going off, it is like the rubbing of a beast against a wall'.

Now the haunting of Epworth Rectory is, in some senses, a simple case, because the agent or agents are known, and for the reason that the disturbances continued for such a limited time,

---

[1] The Rev. Samuel Wesley had been presented to the living of Epworth by Queen Mary, to whom he had dedicated a poem on the life of Christ. The Rev. Samuel Wesley deserted his wife in 1701–2.

during the space, only, of the two months of November and December 1719, after which they ceased entirely, and appear never to have begun again. The most remarkable points in the evidence, taking it as a whole, are the rapping during family prayers, and the curious inarticulate sounds, two or three feeble squeaks, heard only once or twice, a little louder than the chirping of a bird. These, so to speak, were the creakings of the machinery, the attempts at its highest functions, which is voice transference, or the simulation of that. We must note, also, the 'gobbling like a turkeycock', when 'someone came slaring through the garret'. There are, also, the two animal apparitions, the little creature 'like a rabbit, but less', that leapt out from the kitchen copper, with its ears lying flat upon its neck, and its little scut standing straight up, and the little animal, like a badger, that ran out from underneath one of the children's beds. The children, indeed, blamed all that happened upon this animal, whatever it may have been, if, in fact, it had any existence, at all, except in their imaginations. Every form of the manifestations was 'Old Jeffrey' to their minds; it was Old Jeffrey who knocked during prayers, and who, every evening at 9.45, gave them his signal to begin. More especially must we note the vivid descriptions given of the noise of this process of preparation for what was to come.

In the light of these details we will transfer ourselves, as quickly as may be, to the scene of a Poltergeist, which, if less famous, is in all respects even more remarkable than that of Epworth Rectory. This is the haunting of Willington Mill, an appropriately lonely spot in Tyneside, between Newcastle and North Shields. Willington Mill was famous, locally, as a haunted house, and, in due course, all memory of the extraordinary happenings that took place there might have been allowed to die. It is most fortunate, therefore, that the diary kept by the owner of the house, Mr. Joseph Procter, should have turned up, many years later, in the possession of his son, Mr. Edmund Procter, who allowed it to be published in the *Journal of the Society for Psychical Research*, in their volume for 1892. The diary is, unhappily, not complete and the son, at that time seems still to have entertained some hope of discovering the missing portion. We are ignorant of whether he succeeded or not. In any case, nothing further would seem to have been published upon this matter. As it stands, though, this little-known diary, which has never been given to the general public, is one of the four classical instances of the Poltergeist in these islands, the others being the Narrative of the Drummer of Tedworth; the haunting of Epworth Rectory; and our contemporary instance of the haunting of Cashen's Gap, the 'talking mongoose', in fact, of only a year or two ago. But, of these four, that of Willington Mill is in some ways the most interesting, as it is certainly the most closely and accurately observed.

For the hauntings continued with hardly an interruption for the space of some twelve years until, eventually, the family could stand it no longer, the health of the children was prejudiced, and they had to leave. The owner of Willington Mill was Mr. Joseph Procter, a Quaker gentleman, a person noted for his probity and truthfulness and, so we are informed by his son, a staunch and incorruptible teetotaller. His business was that of a farmer and mill-owner. He entered into possession of Willington Mill in 1835 and vacated it, under the pressure of these peculiar circumstances, in 1847. It may be remarked in parenthesis that, at the date the diary was published, in 1892, his son, who would be between fifty and sixty years of age, could remember, as a child, the last few years of these phenomena, and had a sister alive who corroborated his evidence. Innumerable other details he knew, of course, from hearsay, these stories being, it was natural, the most interesting thing that had to do with his family. In fact, his childhood can have consisted of little else than these extraordinary happenings and the tales or echoes of what had gone before.

The diary is written in plain, truthful language that reflects this Quaker family in all the simplicity of their daily lives. They lived here frugally but comfortably and far removed, at least, from poverty. It was a large house of three storeys, the top floor of attics not being put to use, for the building was large enough for their requirements without it. The attics were, therefore, left empty. The house was old-fashioned, but not actually old in date, having been built soon after 1800, or a mere thirty years before they entered into occupation. During

EXAMINATION

twenty-five of these years, since 1806, the house had been lived in by a Quaker family of the odd name of Unthanks, cousins of the Procters. Previous to their arrival the house had the reputation of being haunted, but nothing peculiar had been heard by them during their occupancy. Antiquity, however, is not necessary for these things. The farmhouse at Cashen's Gap was built, or altered, out of recognition by its present proprietor, who installed in it that elaborate system of deal panelling which has given to the whole farmhouse the resonance of a sounding board and fitted it peculiarly for the simulance, or transference, of sounds. Antiquity is no necessity; what is needed are congenial circumstances, and in the rare perfection of these the phenomena will flourish. The diary begins with the earliest manifestations of something peculiar. It was first noticed by the children's nurse, who complained of curious sounds in the attic overhead, of the dragging of heavy objects and the noise of footsteps. She was made ill and sleepless by their frequency and had, before, long, to be dismissed and another taken in her place, who soon became a victim to the same experience. Within a short time these bangings and knockings were heard all over the house by all its occupants; but its centre of action, or starting point, was the garret, on the third floor, over the front door.

Another very curious thing happened at about this time. The mill at the back of the house had in its yard a wooden cistern on iron wheels to bring water for the horses. When in motion, this cistern made a very peculiar noise which could be heard at a considerable distance. Now it was the duty of Mr. Thomas Mann, the foreman of the mill, to come up, every night, in order to work the mill until 2 a.m. Upon the night in question, going out to fill the barrow with coals, about one o'clock, he heard this machine, as he thought, going along the yard. It was creaking excessively, from want of oil, as might be supposed, and was then drawing near the yard gates, towards which he pursued after it. The cistern was a heavy affair that required a horse to drag it along, and he could only think that, while the family slept, someone was trying to remove and steal it. So he followed after it, when, to his astonishment, there was the engine, just where it should have been, standing quiet

EXAMINATION

and idle in its shed. And as he came up to it, the noise ceased and all was silent. He afterwards searched round the premises with a lantern but descried nothing. This odd occurrence, which it is difficult to explain, took place at the very start of the hauntings and might never have been mentioned by the man to his master, had not the rumour gone round of the still stranger events within the house itself. For, by now, the spirit was causing heavy objects to fly all over the place, and was indulging in a perfect plethora of knockings and rappings. The diary, at this point, becomes almost monstrous. It is a long recital of these phenomena, continuing month after month, but growing gradually in intensity. Within the next year or so it had become a never failing and expected occurrence, a part, almost, of the everyday life of the house. But, at about this time, also, it made a most peculiar whistling noise heard generally once or twice, but on infrequent occasions, during the night, from across the yard. This sound was of a most peculiar nature, so that Mr. Procter would imitate it to his family, and the owner of the diary, his son, could well remember his father's doing so. Others of the family, also, had heard it; and we may be reminded, at this point, of the 'whisling and whisting' of the spirit of Ringcroft. How interesting, then, it would be to have heard, if not the original, at least the imitation of it which Mr. Procter could produce for many years afterwards, long indeed after he had been forced to leave Willington Mill. It may be thought that we are suggesting that he was, himself, the agency in this. But we mean nothing of the kind. His diary is much too genuine a document to bear this interpretation and, indeed, he seems by this point, though he endured with the Poltergeist for many years longer, to have been beginning to get a little frightened himself. It was a house in which anything and everything might happen. There is, probably, no other case upon record in which the phenomena continued with such a show of vigour for so long an extent of time. In all they lasted, as we have said, for not less than twelve years, and with a steadily increasing violence, growing, also, in the scope of their activities. The children were, by now, becoming old enough to take notice of what was happening. Perhaps their evidence is not so convincing. Children so easily imagine things, or exaggerate the truth until it becomes untruth. Also, after a time, with legendary events that have been firmly impressed upon them, as children, by their nurses and parents, it is difficult to remember what really happened, and what one was told did happen. A person, for instance, who at the age of three, saw Queen Victoria, is more likely to describe her to you in the words of his nurse or parent, repeated to him over and over again, it is probable, than in the words of a genuine personal experience. So, in a case such as this, the family legend of the haunted house hardly allows of an authentic description of fact, especially when the children were of so young an age. By now, also, it must have become a kind of entertainment to them, a freezing of the blood that through constant repetition had some elements of pleasure in its pain.

After all these years, therefore, of persistent haunting the credible becomes merged, a little, into the incredible. A diaphanous, or transparent figure is seen standing in the window of the haunted attic; and the ghost or Poltergeist, or whatever it may have been, comes down the stair and walks boldly into the rooms. Upon one occasion, Mrs. Procter who, through terror, had her sister to sleep with her in a great old fashioned tester bed with curtains, heard the dreadful footsteps upon the stairs, and it came into her room. She and her sister through the heavy curtains saw a body interpose itself between themselves and the rushlight that they kept burning all night upon the table. This body masked or obscured the rushlight, as any living body would do that stood between you and the candle flame. And then, after an interval, it went away, leaving the door wide open, which, when the daylight came and they had courage to look out from the sheets that they had pulled over their heads, was locked, or even bolted, as it had been, that night, at the time when they went to bed.

At about this period, also, it began to be articulate. It was heard, upstairs in its garret, repeating some meaningless phrases that sounded like 'Never mind—Come and get'. It made a noise, as well, like the winding up of the clock that stood upon the landing of the stairs. It gobbled like a turkey-cock; that peculiar whistling sound was heard again; and by an

EXAMINATION

incredible parallel with the Poltergeist of Ringcroft, it was heard by one of the sons, a small boy of five or six years old, to say, 'Chuck, chuck', and to make the sound of a child's lips when it takes its mouth away from its mother's breast. What, then, can be the import and significance of this? The gobbling, as of a turkeycock, the chuck, chuck, that connect it with the hauntings of both Epworth Rectory and of Ringcroft, these peculiar points of identity must be in the nature of some clue, some explanation of the mystery.[1]

By this time, in supreme manifestations of its powers it could create animal apparitions. A small creature, like a monkey, was seen upon several occasions in the children's rooms; and the owner of the diary, one of the younger children, remembered well, after the lapse of some fifty years, his actual experience of seeing this animal, to the reality of which he was prepared to take his oath. He gives, in fact, his definite assurance that he saw it, in the statement, written by him, that accompanies the publication of his father's diary, in the *Journal of the Society for Psychical Research*. Moreover, his sister, who was still living, described, without being able to give any explanation of it, an animal that she and her sisters saw in the garden, described as being like a white cat, only larger and with a long, pointed snout.[2] The happenings were,

---

[1] 'Jeff', the 'talking mongoose', used to call out 'Charlie, Charlie, chuck, chuck, chuck.' Cf. the evidence of Mr. Charles Northwood in *The Haunting of Cashen's Gap* by Harry Price and R. S. Lambert, p. 99. This, again, is a most curious coincidence.

[2] What follows is the account of an interview between Professor Sidgwick and Mrs. Hargrave, on Jan. 3rd, 1884, taken from his notes made at the time : 'Mrs. Hargrave, one of Mrs. Procter's sisters, saw on one occasion an apparition similar to that seen by Dr. Drury. She described it as the figure of a woman in a grey mantle, which came through the wall of her room from the next. There was a light in the room; her sister who was with her was asleep. The feet of the figure appeared to be about three feet from the floor. It came close up to the bed. She also saw in the daytime a large white cat in the garden. It was larger than a real cat and with a long snout. It appeared to go through the closed garden-door or through the wall into the engine-house, where Mr. Procter, being in the mill-yard, saw it go into the engine-house and disappear as if it had gone into the fire. The cat was also seen by her in one of the bedrooms, going through a closed door. She often heard the noises which so many others in the house heard; e.g. she would hear sounds as of someone coming downstairs with wooden

EXAMINATION

in fact, becoming more incredible than ever. But it is necessary, either to disbelieve the whole lot of them and dismiss them as lies, the worthy Mr. Procter being, therefore, one of the most permanent and long-winded liars upon record; or else it is to be admitted that some exceptionally curious things had happened, and that, in the light of these, some exaggeration was natural, but that, granted the long continuance over so many years of these ideal conditions, this perfect receptivity for the Poltergeist, not a few of these embellishments of the imagination may have been so completely in the atmosphere of what had gone before and was authentic fact, that they amounted, on the whole, to no improbable magnification of the truth, that they followed, indeed, exactly the direction into which events were leading and were the fitting culmination, the logical finale, to this chain of incredible circumstances.

But there came a period, in the end, when these things were no longer to be borne. The nerves of everyone in the house were affected, and the health of the children had to be considered. At last, therefore, in 1847, the Procter family removed from Willington Mill. The son writes that he well remembers his parents' description of their last night in the haunted house. The whole night, it would seem, was a turmoil, a crescendo of noise. Boxes and heavy packing-cases were dragged to and fro across that attic floor and it sounded as if

shoes and rapping every rail with a stick, also as of the clock being wound up. For about three months she slept in the room on the third floor over the nursery, and though she heard the noises for three months, said nothing about them, till her youngest sister, now Mrs. Wright, heard a loud noise and talked to her about it. Mrs. Hargrave also often felt her bed shaken as if some one was standing at the bottom of it and striking blows against a board placed to keep a child from falling out. She also used to hear dancing and noises in a room which was used as a schoolroom (the schoolroom being ascertained to be empty), and shaking of the window frame in the room below. When the children were playing in the room upstairs, Mrs. Hargrave and her sister, playing with them, used to see a door banged in their faces, the windows being shut and there being no draughts to cause it.

'Mrs. Hargrave also referred to many of the incidents related in Mr. Procter's narrative in connection with other members of the family, and gave Professor Sidgwick an account of the description of the haunting by the clairvoyante "Jane" (for which see Mrs. Sidgwick's paper "On the Evidence for Clairvoyance", *Proceedings S.P.R.*, Vol. VII, pp. 54, 82-4, 86, 87).'

trunks were being corded and made ready for leaving. The Poltergeist, in fact, was going with them. It was, in Mr. Edmund Procter's words, a pantomimic or spiritualistic repetition of all the noises incident to a household flitting. In fact, though, it did not accompany them. They were troubled by it no more. It had brought them to the edge of the precipice and was making pretence, upon that final night, of leaping over the edge of it and plunging down, down with them. Or was it no more than the Poltergeist's sardonic humour, its cynical speeding of the departing guest? It may, even, have been attempting, in all earnestness, to follow them. And yet, in spite of this, it would seem more probable that this was its final threat of terror. It was making as if to follow them, so that they could never be free of it. But they left, as we have said, and were troubled by it no more.

The subsequent fate of the house is described in the notes that accompany the diary. For some time the mill stood empty; and then it became a tenement, and was lived in by several families. A visit to it is described, in these changed circumstances. That terrible attic floor had become the abode of a whole family. But none of the occupants had any complaints to voice. Nothing at all mysterious ever happened. It was sad, we are told, to see the degradation of the house into a slum tenement. The garden wall had disappeared. The jargonelle pear trees that used to blossom up to the third storey were mere ghosts with blackened stumps, the large old thorn tree of red blossom that flowered so luxuriously had been cut down, and the old beds of iris and auricula removed. Nothing hardly was left and—of the real interest of that house—nothing whatever remained. This account of it was given when the son, Mr. Edmund Procter, revisited his home as lately as 1890. Long, long ago, it has been pulled down and utterly demolished, and it may be thought doubtful, even, whether any local tradition still survives of the strange stories that had once, nearly a hundred years ago, made this house famous in its neighbourhood.[1]

---

[1] William Howitt, in *Visits to Remarkable Places*, gives the following description of Willington Mill. 'Between the railway running from Newcastle-on-Tyne to North Shields and the river Tyne, there lie

EXAMINATION

It would seem impossible that this whole diary is a fabrication of lies. We have to admit, then, that something very peculiar was abroad in the house. Exaggeration on the part of the women and children, and of the servants in the house, is only natural, but there remains the basis of peculiar and unaccountable happenings. The two things, though, which put the haunting of Willington Mill into a category by itself are the long continuance of the phenomena, and the absence of any agent. There were, apparently, three periods of intensive activity, the early months of 1835 until December 1840—then five months comparative respite until May 1841—after which the hauntings continued, if anything, worse than before—and then a final period, during 1846 and 1847, leading up to the almost compulsory desertion of their home by the Procter family, a period for which, unfortunately, the diary was lost, so that its details are not known. As to the other

in a hollow, some few cottages, a parsonage, and a mill and a miller's house. These constitute the hamlet of Willington. Just above these the railway is carried across the valley on lofty arches, and from it you look down on the mill and cottages, lying at a considerable depth below. The mill is a large steam flour mill, like a factory, and the miller's house stands near it but not adjoining it. None of the cottages which lie between these premises and the railway, either, are in contact with them. The house stands on a sort of little promontory, round which runs the channel of a watercourse, which appears to fill and empty with the tides. On one side of the mill and house, slopes away upwards a field, to a considerable distance, where it is terminated by other enclosures; on the other stands a considerable extent of ballast-hill, i.e. one of the numerous hills on the banks of the Tyne, made by the deposit of ballast from the vessels trading thither. At a distance, the top of the mill seems about level with the country around it. The place lies about half-way between Newcastle and North Shields. . . . The house is not an old house, as will appear; it was built about the year 1800. It has no particularly spectral look about it. . . . Yet looking down from the railway, and seeing it and the mill lying in a deep hole, one might imagine various strange noises likely to be heard in such a place in the night, from vessels on the river, from winds sweeping and howling down the gully in which it stands, from engines in the neighbourhood connected with coal mines, one of which, I could not tell where, was making, at the time I was there, a wild sighing noise as I stood on the hill above.' This account was written in 1846–7, while the haunted mill was still tenanted by Mr. Procter and his family.

We learn from William Howitt's book that one of the ghosts of Willington Mill, that of a man, was well known to the neighbours as 'Old Jeffrey'. This is in the direct descent from Epworth Rectory—down to Cashen's Gap!

point, the absence of any agent or medium, this is, perhaps, the most peculiar feature of all. In every other known case of a Poltergeist, without exception, there is, always and invariably, a child, or some young person, who, it becomes obvious, is the instrument of the phenomena. Upon this occasion there is no one upon whom this charge can be laid. As to any possible cause, there is only a memorandum in the diary, which breaks off dramatically and was never continued, a literary device, it may be added, of which telling use was made by Maturin, one of the great masters of the macabre, in his *Melmoth the Wanderer*, where the old manuscript that deals with the ghost breaks off, in just this manner. The memorandum reads 'An infirm old woman, the mother-in-law of R. Oxon, the builder of the premises, lived and died in the house, and after her death the haunting was attributed'——[1] And there is that other peculiar entry, at the start of the diary in 1835, when the hauntings had but just begun: 'Those who deem all intrusion from the world of spirits impossible in the present constitution of things will feel assured that a natural solution of the difficulty will still be obtained on further investigation; while those who believe that ... there still remain some well-attested instances in which good or evil spirits have manifested their presence by sensible token will probably deem it possible that this may be referred to the latter class—especially when they learn that several circumstances tending to corroborate such a view are withheld from this narrative.' And the son, Mr. Edmund Procter, adds, significantly, to this, 'Whether the "several circumstances withheld" are disclosed in the written narrative which follows I am unable to say.'

The visual phantoms at Willington Mill are the least interesting part of the story. There is, indeed, nothing at all remarkable about them, if we except the two animal phantasms, the monkey seen by the children, that is to say, and the large white cat, bigger than a real cat and with a long snout, seen by Mrs. Hargrave, one of Mrs. Procter's sisters. In the *Journal of*

[1] The Rev. Montague Summers, an authority whom it is unwise to contradict, states in his *Geography of Witchcraft*, that Willington Mill was built upon the 'site of a cottage which had once been the home of a notorious witch'. I have, unfortunately, been unable to discover any additional information about this.

EXAMINATION

the Society for Psychical Research from which we quote, there is Mrs. Hargrave's deposition, made to Professor Sidgwick, the Editor of the *Journal*, under the date January 3rd, 1884, more than forty years, that is to say, after this apparition was seen. It appeared to go through the closed garden door, or through the wall into the engine house, where Mr. Procter, being in the mill yard, saw it go into the engine house, and disappear as if it had gone into the fire. This was in the daytime. The cat was also seen by her in one of the bedrooms, going through a closed door. It can, therefore, have been only an apparition and have had no substance.

There seems no reason to doubt that this particular haunting, that of the large white cat, was akin to an imp, or animal familiar, many dozens of examples of which occur in the old trials of witches. For instance, Matthew Hopkins, the notorious witch-finder of Essex, in the case of Elizabeth Clarke, at the Chelmsford Assizes, in 1645, caused her to be 'watched'. He went, with Master Stearn, by the justices' direction, to the woman's room, on March 24th, when she offered to call one of her white imps and play with it in her lap; but they would not allow it. She had been kept from sleep for two or three nights before this, and it was on the fourth night that this offer was made, there being, then, ten persons in the room. She confessed to having had carnal connection with the Devil for six or seven years, who appeared to her three or four times a week, in the shape of a proper gentleman with a laced band, and would say 'Besse, I must lie with you,' which he would do for half a night together. Within a quarter of an hour after she told them this, there appeared an imp like a white dog with sandy spots, very fat and plump, with very short legs, which forthwith vanished away. This was Jarmara. Then came another imp, Vinegar Tom, like a greyhound with long legs; and a black imp, like a polecat; Holt, like a white kitling; Sack-and-Sugar, like a black rabbit; and Newes, like a polecat. Then she 'confessed several other witches, from whom she had her imps, and named to divers women where their marks were, the number of their marks, and imps, and imps' names, as Elemanzer, Pyewacket, Peck in the Crown, Grizzel Greediguts, etc. She further confessed that she had one imp for

EXAMINATION

which she would fight up to her knees in blood before she would lose it.' There is no question, it should here be added, but that the self-confessed witches kept little animals, toads, newts or ferrets, which they fed with a drop of blood from their fingers, and which, having tasted of blood would return every day for more. Ordinary pet animals, cats or dogs, may have existed in some such horrid bond with their masters; but Jarmara, Vinegar Tom, Sack-and-Sugar, what are we to make of these? Against another witch, Ursley Kemp, of St. Osyth, in 1582, her son, a little boy of eight years old, bore witness that she had four spirits; Tyffin, like a white lamb; Tyttey, like a little grey cat; Pygine, like a black toad; and Jacke, like a black cat.[1] All these, in fact, are completely credible. The son

[1] The names of these familiars may have their particular significance. According to a note, 119, by the Rev. Montague Summers, on page 194 of *The Geography of Witchcraft*, London (Kegan Paul), 1927, 'Tyffey was also known as Tyssey. Tyssey and Jack were males and could inflict death, being more powerful than Tyffine and Pygine, who were females, and only destroyed goods and cattle, or punished with lighter ailments. In 1646 a Huntingdon witch, Elizabeth Werd of Great Catworth, gave a sister witch, Frances Moore, a white cat, a familiar, named Tissy.'

We append, in this footnote, a curious story taken from John Wesley's *Journal*, Vol. III, p. 149, under date October 1, 1763. It is an instance of what Wesley considered to be diabolic possession, or witchcraft, but which would, in our own day, be classed as hysterical obsession. The reader will compare it in his mind with the confessions of witches and with certain instances of Poltergeist hauntings. The *Journal* reads: 'I now received a very strange account from a man of sense as well as integrity.

'I asked M. S. many questions before she would give me any answer. At length, after much persuasion, she said, "On old Michaelmas day was three year, I was sitting by myself at my father's with a Bible before me, and one whom I took to be my uncle came into the room and sat down by me. He talked to me some time, till, not liking his discourse, I looked more carefully at him; he was dressed like my uncle, but I observed one of his feet was just like that of an ox. Then I was much frighted, and he began torturing me sadly, and told me he would torture men ten times more if I would not swear to kill my father, which at last I did. He said he would come again on that day four years, between half-past two and three o'clock.

' "I have several times since strove to write this down, but when I did, the use of my hand was taken from me; I strove to speak it, but whenever I did, my speech was taken from me; and I am afraid I shall be tormented a deal more for what I have spoken now."

'Presently she fell into such a fit as was dreadful to look upon: one

EXAMINATION

alleged that he had seen his mother give them beer to drink, and of a white loaf or cake to eat, and that, in the night, the spirits would come 'and sucke blood of her upon her armes and other places of her body'. And the mother, Ursley Kemp, confessed that all this was true.

The animal apparition of Willington Mill is of the type, therefore, of Jarmara, of Vinegar Tom, of Sack-and-Sugar; for the four spirits of Ursley Kemp can have been nothing more than a white lamb, a grey cat, a black toad, and a black cat, however sinister may have been their servitude to the witch who was their mistress. Vinegar Tom and his satellites, we are told by Matthew Hopkins, came into the room through a hole in the wall and disappeared, presumably in the same way. This unlikely entrance and exit of a whole troupe of improbable animals was accomplished in the presence of ten witnesses, which puts a severe strain, it might be thought, upon the veracity of the evidence. And yet there is always the possibility that there may have been something.

would have thought she would be torn to pieces. Several persons could scarce hold her; till, after a time, she sank down as dead.

'From that Michaelmas Day she was continually tormented with the thought of killing her father, as likewise of killing herself, which she often attempted, but was, as often, hindered. Once she attempted to cut her own throat; once to throw herself into Richmond's Pond; several times to strangle herself, which, once or twice, was with much difficulty prevented.

'Her brother, fearing lest she should at last succeed in her attempt and finding her fits come more frequently, got a strait-waistcoat made for her, such as they use at Bedlam. It was made of strong ticking, with two straps on the shoulders to fasten her down to the bed, one across her breast, another across her middle, and another across her knees; one likewise was buckled on each leg, and fastened to the side of her bed. The arms of the waistcoat drew over her fingers and fastened like a purse. In a few minutes after she was thus secured, her brother coming to the bed found she was gone. After some time he found she was up the chimney, so high up that he could scarce touch her feet. When Mary Loftus called her she came down, having her hands as fast as ever.

'The night after I fastened her arms to her body with new straps over and above the rest. She looked at me and laughed, then gave her hands a slight turn and all the fastenings were off.

'In the morning Mr. Spark came. On our telling him this he said, "But I will take upon me to fasten her so that she shall not get loose." Accordingly he sent for some girth-web, with which he fastened her arms to her sides, first above her elbows, round her body, then below

EXAMINATION

In the case of Ursley Kemp, the details are so circumstantial as to be readily acceptable in evidence. There is the statement of this witch that, 'she went unto Mother Bennet's house for a mess of milk, the which she had promised her. But at her coming this Examinate saith that she knocked at her door, and nobody made her any answer, whereupon she went to her chamber window and looked in thereat, saying "Ho, ho, Mother Bennet, are you at home?" And casting her eyes aside, she saw a spirit lift up a cloth lying over a pot, looking much like a ferret.' Another witness, at the Essex trials, stated that, 'about the fourteenth or fifteenth day of January last she went to the house of William Hunt to see how his wife did, and she being from home she called at her chamber window and looked in, and then espied a spirit to look out of a potcharde from under a cloth, the nose thereof being brown like a ferret'. But this same Mother Bennet, of the preceding incident, admitted to having familiars. 'Many times did they drink of her milk bowl. And when, and as often as they did drink the milk, this

her elbows, then he put it round each wrist, and braced them down to each side of the bedstead. After this she was quiet a night and a day, then all this was off like the rest.

'After this we did not tie her down any more, only watched over her night and day. I asked the physician that attended her whether it was a natural disorder? He said, "Partly natural, partly diabolical." We then judged there was no remedy but prayer.... About half an hour after ten, ten of us came together, as we had agreed the day before.... I then fastened her down to the bed on both sides, and set two on each side to hold her if need be. We began laying her case before the Lord and claiming His promise on her behalf. Immediately Satan raged vehemently. He caused her to roar in an uncommon manner, then to shriek, so that it went through our heads, then to bark like a dog. Then her face was distorted to an amazing degree, her mouth being drawn from ear to ear, and her eyes turning opposite ways, and starting as if they would start out of her head. Presently her throat was so convulsed, that she appeared to be quite strangled; then the convulsions were in her bowels, and her body swelled as if ready to burst. At other times she was stiff from head to foot as an iron bar, being at the same time wholly deprived of her sense and motion, not even breathing at all. Soon after her body was so writhed, one would have thought all her bones must be dislocated.'

In the end, according to the *Journal*: 'She mightily rejoiced in the God of her salvation. It was a glorious sight. Her fierce countenance was changed, and she looked innocent as a child.' But we are told no more of this strange history. And it is probable that the cure did not last for long.

EXAMINATION

Examinate saith they went into the earthern pot, and lay in the wool.' Another Essex Witch, Mother Waterhouse, 'kept her cat a great while in wool in a pot'.

Vinegar Tom, Jarmara, Sack-and-Sugar, are more difficult to explain. For, at the outset, there is no suggestion that the haunting of Willington Mill is a case of witchcraft. If the contemporary case of the talking mongoose tallies most exactly with the old animal familiars of the witches, there is, as well, the little animal of Epworth Rectory. Both Cashen's Gap (the home of the mongoose) and Epworth Rectory are clear and simple cases of the Poltergeist. In both cases the medium is plainly established with a suspicion, in either story, that mother as well as daughter was knowingly or unknowingly involved in it. In Cashen's Gap there is, as well, a certainty, almost, that ventriloquism was practised, again, it is likely, in a trance-like state that precludes deliberate fraud. The argument that ventriloquism is so difficult to learn, and that a doll or puppet has to be used in order to direct the hearer's attention to where the voice is supposed to come from, is disposed of by the very existence of the supposed talking mongoose, which was, in effect, the marionette of the haunted action. In addition to which the farmhouse was panelled to such fortuitous result that its whole area is described by witnesses as being like a sounding board or a speaking tube.

But the animal phantasm of Willington Mill does not play so important a part in the haunting. It is no more than incidental to the whole story. Are we to believe that it was created, so to speak, in the imagination of Mr. Procter, and conveyed by him before the eyes of his sister-in-law, Mrs. Hargraves? Or that the reverse process brought it from Mrs. Hargraves, through the closed garden door, or through the wall, into the engine house, where it was seen by Mr. Procter to 'disappear as if it had gone into the fire'? For it is certain that this apparition can have had no real existence; while we must believe, as well, that it was definitely seen, and that this is no lying deposition. The attitude of Mrs. Hargraves, in her evidence given forty years afterwards, and of the whole diary of Mr. Procter, as it reflects upon his personal character, is that both saw the thing, but could not explain it. In the words of his son, Mr. Edmund

EXAMINATION

Procter, when describing the phantasm of the monkey seen by himself, as a small boy: 'I am merely recording facts as simply as I can; readers may smile or mock as seemeth good unto them—I cannot alter what has taken place to suit either them or anyone else.' They undoubtedly saw it; and, just as surely, it was not there. It must be classed as an hallucination. At the time, of course, at which this mysterious apparition was seen the hauntings had already been in force for several years, and it is to be imagined that the nerves of everyone in the family were beginning to suffer. This is, though, not enough to account for this thing, which, for once, was not heard but seen. It is probable that it occurred during the latter years of the haunting, between 1841, when the diary abruptly ceases, and 1847. It is the more to be regretted, therefore, that the rest of the diary was never found, for there is no account of the animal phantasm in Mr. Procter's own words, but only in the testimony given, nearly half a century later, by his sister-in-law. As to what this apparition may have been, who can tell? For such a thing is like a shape poured into a vacuum of fear.

The most curious point in all the haunting of Willington Mill is the absence of any one person who can have been the medium. In every other case, a child or a young person is conscious or unconscious go-between, is purveyor, as it were, of the supernatural effects. Here, there is no person to be discovered to whom the blame can be attached. There is only this one thing to be taken into consideration, that any person of the Quaker sect was, probably, familiar with the life of Wesley, and had, therefore, read of the haunting of Epworth Rectory. This slight fact might seem to incriminate, to however small a degree, Mr. Joseph Procter himself. The appendix to this volume of the *Journal of the Society for Psychical Research* contains the correspondence between Mr. Joseph Procter and a young doctor, Mr. Edward Drury. This is taken from the *Local Historian's Table Book*, by M. A. Richardson, published in London, in 1843. Mr. Edward Drury is writing to ask leave to sit up in the house in the absence of the family—and, in the end, permission being granted, it may be added that he was rewarded with a silly and conventional experience, such as befalls those who do such things. Mr. Edward Drury writes: 'I beg leave to tell you that I have read attentively Wesley's account of such things, but with, I must confess, no great belief; but an account of this report coming from one of your sect, which I admire for candour and simplicity, my curiosity is excited to a high pitch—which I would fain satisfy.' The date of this letter is June 17th, 1840. By 1840, in other words, at the very height of these disturbances, Mr. Joseph Procter is proved as being conversant with the story of what the Wesley family had undergone in similar circumstances. The fact that Mr. Procter, in answering, 'thinks it best to inform him that particular disturbances are far from frequent at present, being only occasional and quite uncertain, and therefore the satisfaction of E. D.'s curiosity must be considered as problematical', looks like a rather shame-faced or half-hearted disavowal on the part of the owner of the haunted house. An educated Quaker, though, would certainly know the details of Wesley's life, for, in the son's words, his father's 'ordinary reading was fairly extensive, the *Quarterly* and *Edinburgh* being sandwiched with George Fox's *Journal* and the old *Examiner*, and Ebenezer Eliot taken alternately with some French author or the *British Friend*'. There is, then, nothing particularly remarkable in the fact that Mr. Joseph Procter knew the details of Epworth Rectory. It would be, in any case, to a Dissenter, the classical instance of similar occurrences.

The diary, on the other hand, is essentially a document meant only for his own, or his family's information in after years. It bears no trace whatever of any leanings towards the sensational. This is not the record of someone who is trying to become famous through such odd and peculiar occurrences. Neither was Willington Mill in such a lonely situation that the hauntings can be reckoned as solitary entertainment of its occupants. The Newcastle and North Shields Railway, opened in 1840, ran about a quarter of a mile from the house, which is described as being 'near a large steam corn mill in full view of the Willington viaduct'. It is presumed as certain, in view of all this evidence, that there was something exceptionally curious and unaccountable at work upon these premises.

For this is one of three or four great instances, during the last

EXAMINATION

three centuries, of something genuinely rare and inexplicable. It is, as we have said, more difficult to explain than the mystery of Epworth Rectory, or the haunting of Cashen's Gap. There is only the Narrative of the Drummer of Tedworth, which is as remarkable. Once in a century, and perhaps not more often, it is reasonable to expect supernatural events upon this scale of magnitude and reality. The circumstances have to be deeply and entirely propitious, as much so as at the birth of a Mozart, a Liszt, a Paganini.

There are, though, certain curious and inexplicable similarities to be found in all the cases that have been under discussion. The 'signal', as they called it at Epworth Rectory, the 'signal of its beginning to play', 'like the strong winding up of a jack' 'resembling the loud creaking of a saw', 'or rather that of a windmill, when the body of it is turned about, in order to shift the sails to the wind'; 'like a carpenter planing deals': such are some of the descriptions of its sound. This is to be compared with, at Willington Mill: 'a noise similar to the winding up of a clock, apparently on the stairs where the clock stands, which continued for the space of ten minutes.' At Cashen's Gap there is the voice of the mongoose, always high and shrill, and fitting exactly to the description of a ventriloquist at work.[1] At Epworth Rectory there was 'never heard any articulate voice, and only, once or twice, two or three feeble squeaks, a little louder than the chirping of a bird'. At Willington Mill, Mr. Procter, 'another night heard two very peculiar sounds as of whistling or whizzing', sounds which, as we have seen, he could imitate in after years. Upon another night 'he had heard several prolonged and peculiar whistles, which were, also, heard by the nurse in another room; they seemed to come from the landing'. On yet another occasion Jon. D. Carr, the brother of Mrs. Procter, 'also heard a peculiar whistle, which he imitated so as exactly to resemble what J. P.' (Mr. Procter) 'heard some time before'. The mongoose of Cashen's Gap was, also, in the habit of whistling. One evening Captain Macdonald, the observer sent down to interview it by Mr.

---

[1] This theory of ventriloquism at Cashen's Gap should be compared with the Saragossa ghost of 1934. The culprit in this case was the sixteen-year-old maid, Maria Pascuela.

EXAMINATION

Harry Price, of the Society for Psychical Research, took out his watch and timed it whistling for twenty-two seconds. And how does this compare, for instance, with the 'whisling and whisting' of the spirit of Ringcroft!

But there is a parallel which is more extraordinary still. The spirit of Ringcroft cried out 'Kick cuck'; the mongoose of Cashen's Gap greeted Mr. Northwood with a cry of 'Charlie, Charlie, chuck, chuck, chuck'; the Poltergeist of Willington Mill called in the children's bedroom, 'Chuck, chuck', and then made a noise like a child sucking. The immaterial form créated by this evil spirit, for it is impossible to credit it with a benign purpose, is of childish propensity, or like an old and puking woman. It babbles, as though in the struggles of life or death. It is dying, or but just born, an embryonic phantasm which is only upon the borderlands, upon one frontier or the other, of human life. None can pity it, or feel sorrow for it. There is an obscene or drivelling sense to it, and nothing more than that. It is in all things unholy, unhallowed, and not human. Who can doubt that it is the projection, not of the brain, but of the obscene senses, of the deep, hidden underworld which is at the back of every mind. This universality of the 'chuck, chucking' cries of Ringcroft, of Cashen's Gap, of Willington Mill, is paralleled to a certain extent, also, at Epworth Rectory, where, 'My man who lay in the garret, heard some one come slaring through the garret to his chamber . . . at other times walking up and down stairs, when all the house were in bed, and gobbling like a turkeycock.' And we get this significant description of the subsidence of the noises, when the knocking was about to die down: 'At its going off, it was like the rubbing of a beast against a wall.' This, so to speak, was how the engine of the hauntings at Epworth Rectory ran down. It began with that well-known signal of its beginning to play; and ended like the rubbing of a horse or cow against a wall, a sound which is known to all persons who have ever lived in the country. Surely, and certainly, its secret is in this.

Now it is to be noticed that, in all things, these hauntings are conformable to the mentality of those who may be thought to be responsible for them. The only visual phantasms at Willington Mill that are of interest are the large white cat and

EXAMINATION

the monkey. A figure of a woman in a grey mantle coming through a wall, the feet of the figure appearing to be about three feet from the floor, as seen by Mrs Hargraves; or the similar apparition seen by Mr. Drury, who sat up for it and was then rewarded for his temerity, these are the ordinary hallucinations seen by frightened, half-sleeping persons. No particular reliance should be placed upon their evidence, and the 'ghosts', in any case, are conventional and of no importance. All they argue is a condition of nervous receptivity on the part of the victim. At this point it must almost be agreed that Mr. Procter, who also saw the large white cat, larger than a real cat and with a long snout, may have had some neutral or nervous kink that predisposed him to accept such suggestions from his sister-in-law. She suggested the white cat; and he agreed that he had seen it 'going into the engine house and disappearing as if it had gone into the fire'. Such would be this explanation; but it is disproved by every entry, almost, in his diary. We have to consider that Mr. Procter, no less than his sister-in-law, did see something.

The cries of 'Chuck, chuck'; the 'turkey gobbling'; the 'prolonged and peculiar sounds as of whistling or whizzing'; the noise of 'winding up, as of a strong jack', or 'a clock', 'the loud creaking of a saw', 'the planing of deal boards', all these sounds, which are common to all four cases, must have a common or mutual significance. It is impossible not to see, in these, the very workings of the machinery. They are the tricks, or stock-in-trade, of the Poltergeist, together with the throwing of small stones or pebbles, of handfuls of coins, or of pieces of crockery, deceits which, in other cases, are traced down to the child who is medium, and who, in all probability, is detected in the act of hurling these objects. For, being in possession of certain remarkable powers, there is not a Poltergeist who will not improve upon the position by cheating, and by childish imposture. It is for this that they are, in the end, discredited; and, once that has happened, their genuine feats are forgotten and all is explained away upon the basis of charlatanism. There is, though, no doubt whatever that they have the power to move about and dislodge objects, and in most of the instances in which this has been described the

EXAMINATION

trajectory covered by these missiles has this peculiar feature to it, that the flight is never straight, the objects always whirl and zigzag in the air, as though the control upon them did not cease until their flight is finished. They are not picked up and thrown by some invisible hand; they are in the power of some force that moves them. In the haunting of Willington Mill these customary phenomena of the Poltergeist are not present; but this is because, as we have already pointed out, this is no ordinary case of a Poltergeist. The medium is missing. There is no-one upon whom to fasten the guilt.

The opinion of Mr. Procter upon this matter seems to be fairly clear. Those words of his, which break off so suddenly: 'An infirm old woman, the mother-in-law of R. Oxon, the builder of the premises, lived and died in the house, and after her death the haunting was attributed . . .'; this half-finished sentence must hold his definition of the cause of so much trouble. Or else we have to believe that the whole story is lies from beginning to end. If Mr. Procter, a typical Quaker of his generation, had this one curious kink of liking to be frightened, and of arousing an infectious fear in others during a space of twelve years, and for all the most impressionable years of his families' childhood, then, indeed, we have an explanation of the entire episode. But such an idea is dispelled by the unpleasant and profitless notoriety which is all he can have gained by it. No-one who reads his diary in its bare simplicity, and in the plain statement of so many mysterious happenings narrated without exaggeration or hysteria, could for a moment entertain this easy explanation of the hauntings. There must, and there can only have been, something peculiar and inexplicable in Willington Mill. If Mr. Procter lied, then the Wesley family were liars; and that it would be difficult to believe. But the Epworth Rectory case is universally accepted as being the work of a Poltergeist; a manifestation of the subconscious which is an established, if insufficiently studied, truth in that world of new discoveries. And, if that is the case, then a like amount of indulgence can be asked for on behalf of Willington Mill.

If Mr. Procter was not, himself, the cause of these disturbances their origin must be looked for in a mood, or legacy, from the past which found itself perpetuated, perhaps, to its own displeasure, in the ideal circumstances of this household. For a congenial atmosphere is an essential, or the miracles cannot work. Everything, in persons and in environment, must be in complete harmony. There must be no teetotaller at this festival of wine. And the doubters can be the most tender and alluring strings in all this music. That animal phantasm, to which we have so often referred in the course of this narrative, is most easily explained, of course, by hypnotic suggestion. But who was the hypnotist? Are we to suppose that Mr. Procter summoned it up, out of the depths of his own imagination, saw it himself, and handed on the vision to his sister-in-law? If so, then it is the same with those peculiar whistling sounds. They were also heard by the nurse in another room. Had they some natural explanation? Did they not exist at all, but in the infection of one imagination to another? Was it, perhaps, Mr. Procter himself, since he was so adept at imitating their sounds? But, then, they were heard, another day, and imitated, also, by Jon. D. Carr, the brother-in-law of Mr. Procter. We must conclude, I think, that their sound was indisputably heard; and that Mr. Procter was as much the victim of this trick, or imposture, as the children's nurse, or as his brother-in-law.

Now the phenomena, it will have been noticed, are exactly such as would occur to the mind of a child, or of an ignorant old woman. There is that night, in particular, upon which Jane Carr, Mrs. Procter's sister, 'had been poorly, and was awake about 4.30 a.m. as well as her companion, when they heard footsteps descending from the upper storey which passed their door and went down into the kitchen; they thought it was the cook and wondered at her being so early. They then heard the sound of the kitchen door opening and then of the kitchen window being thrown up and the shutters opened with more than usual noise.' This, if it could have such an explanation, is clearly the spite of someone who has suffered much from being made to get up at early hours in the morning. It is not suggested that any of these things really happened; they appeared to happen, and must have been hallucinations, or hypnotic effects, produced by the power that was at large in the house. The noise like the winding up of the clock upon the landing, this, again, is a joke, or freak, belonging to the same order of the imagination. The sound like the throwing down of a clothes horse upon the floor; the dragging of boxes or pieces of wood upon the ceiling above; the shifting of chairs, the clashing down of box lids; the thumping, as of a fist; these are playthings of the household gods, or devils, being so much a part of the household economy of every human dwelling that they could be true of a house in China or Tibet, or of anywhere, all over the world. These are household hauntings at the instigation, it might be thought, of an old infirm woman, whose evil fancies were running riot within the house. In the theory of such things being a possibility, once, it may be, among many hundreds of millions of opportunities, it is to be considered that its tricks would be, of necessity, limited in their range and in their application. A person, we might say, could imitate a jew's harp or a banjo, while sitting at the piano; but he must not be expected therefore to conjure up a vision of the Mona Lisa upon the wall, or to recreate the scene between Julius Caesar and Brutus. The possibilities of his tricks are limited to what it is possible for him to accomplish. In the same way, with a Poltergeist, the throwing of handfuls of stones or pebbles, the knocking and thumping, the moving of pieces of crockery, and so forth, are the ordinary curriculum beyond which it can only advance upon rare occasions and in exceptional circumstances. Hypnotism, or mesmerism, are not suggested in the case of a Poltergeist. But, at Willington Mill, where there was, apparently, no living agent or medium within the house, something in that nature must be accepted as possible, unless, once more, we are to categorize everything that has to do with this story as lies, and nothing but lies. What motive was there, after all, to induce such a fabrication of untruth? Their lives must have been made nearly unendurable by this perpetual state of emergency, this lying awake listening for sounds, this readiness for anything peculiar and frightening to happen.

Being, now, sufficiently primed with what customary disturbance, or peculiarities to expect, we come to the earliest, as it is, probably, the most famous of our classical instances of

EXAMINATION

the Poltergeist. This is the Drummer of Tedworth, or the case of Mr. Mompesson. We have reprinted it, entire, from Relation I, the enlarged narrative, in *Saducismus Triumphatus: or, full and plain evidence concerning Witches and Apparitions*, by Joseph Glanvil, late Chaplain in ordinary to His Majesty, (Charles II) and Fellow of the Royal Society (the second edition), London, 1682. This narrative has the advantage that it is written in the splendid and supple English of the reign of Charles II. But, before we resume its story, we would draw the reader's attention to the poem, 'The Drum', printed as foreword or introduction to this whole book, for we believe that this could not be bettered as an interpretation of our subject in all its different manifestations. This is the Poltergeist, and all that it conveys of the supernormal or supernatural, expressed, or even immortalized in a work of art. The author of this poem has herself put forward an explanation of some of its meanings and the manner of its effects in her notes on her own poetry which preface her *Selected Poems* (London, Duckworth & Co., 1936), and we take the liberty of adding to them some views of our own in extension of her principles. In an examination into the detail of this sinister poem, we can prepare our minds for the narrative that is to follow. For the sake of convenience her poem is here reprinted in full, in order to save the reader the trouble of turning back the page to where it appears in the place of honour at the beginning of this book.

THE DRUM

(The Narrative of the Demon of Tedworth)

In his tall senatorial,
Black and manorial,
House where decoy-duck
Dust doth clack—
Clatter and quack
To a shadow black—
Said the musty Justice Mompesson
'What is that dark stark beating drum
That we hear rolling like the sea?'
'It is a beggar with a pass

EXAMINATION

Signed by you.' 'I signed not one.'
They took the ragged drum that we
Once heard rolling like the sea;
In the house of the Justice it must lie
And usher in Eternity.

. . . . .

Is it black night?
Black as Hecate howls a star
Wolfishly, and whined
The wind from very far.

In the pomp of the Mompesson house is one
Candle that lolls like the midnight sun,
Or the coral comb of a cock; . . . it rocks . . .
Only the goatish snow's locks
Watch the candles lit by fright
One by one through the black night.

Through the kitchen there runs a hare—
Whinnying, whines like grass, the air;
It passes; now is standing there
A lovely lady . . . see her eyes—
Black angels in a heavenly place,
Her shady locks and her dangerous grace.

'I thought I saw the wicked old witch in
The richest gallipot in the kitchen!'
A lolloping galloping candle confesses.
'Outside in the passage are wildernesses
Of darkness rustling like witches' dresses.'
Out go the candles one by one
Hearing the rolling of a Drum!

What is the march we hear groan
As the hoofèd sound of a drum marched on
With a pang like darkness, with a clang
Blacker than an orang-outang?
'Heliogabalus is alone,—
Only his bones to play upon!'

EXAMINATION

The mocking money in the pockets
Then turned black ... now caws
The fire ... outside, one scratched the door
As with iron claws,—

Scratching under the children's bed
And up the trembling stairs ... 'Long dead'
Moaned the water black as crape.
Over the snow the wintry moon
Limp as henbane, or herb paris,
Spotted the bare trees; and soon

Whinnying, neighed the maned blue wind
Turning the burning milk to snow,
Whining it shied down the corridor—
Over the floor I heard it go
Where the drum rolls up the stairs, nor tarries.

The author of this poem states in her notes that it belongs 'neither to the world of "Façade", nor to that of "Bucolic Comedies", but to a night-world which lies between!' Readers who know her poems will understand this careful distinction. But she continues—and we choose those parts of her explanation which are most apt to our own purpose—'black', 'duck', 'clack', 'clatter' and 'quack', with their hard consonants and dead vowels, are dry as dust, and the deadness of dust is conveyed thus. 'By "decoy-duck dust", she writes, 'I mean very thick dry dust. A duck's quacking is, to me, one of the driest of sounds, and it has a peculiar deadness.' Such is her interpretation of 'decoy-duck dust doth clack', a phrase which may be said to have become famous. 'In the lines,' she continues:

'Clatter and quack
To a shadow black,

"Clatter", coming, as it does, immediately after "clack" has an odd sound, like that of a challenge thrown down in an empty place by one who, having offered it, then shrinks away in fear. It is a fact that the second syllable of "clatter", instead

EXAMINATION

of casting a shadow, shrinks away into itself and dies.' 'In the lines:

> *Said the musty Justice Mompesson*
> *What is that dark stark beating drum?*

the thick assonances of "musty Justice", the rhymes "dark stark" placed so closely together, produce a menacing echo.... In the lines:

> *Black as Hecate howls a star*
> *Wolfishly, and whined*
> *The wind from very fear*

the small-vowelled, quick three-syllabled word "Hecate" makes the line rock up and down. In the next line "wolfishly" *pretends* to balance "Hecate", but in reality does nothing of the kind.'... 'The "is" dimming from "whined" down to "wind" are meant to give the impression of a faint breeze.'... 'In the line:

> *Or the coral comb of a cock; it rocks*

the sharp "c's" seem pin-points of light, which leap into a sudden flare with the word "comb". Later on, when we come to the lines:

> *Through the kitchen there runs a hare,*
> *Whinnying, whines like grass the air*

the rhythm is given by the assonances "kitchen" and "whinnying", rising to the high "i" of "whines", and by the balance of the two-syllabled, three-syllabled, and one-syllabled words; and the image was brought to my mind by the fact that thin grass trembling in the wind seems to resemble in its movement a high whining or whinnying sound, whilst the dampness and coldness of the air on certain winter days resembles the dampness and coldness of grass.'

'In:

> *A lolloping galloping candle confesses*

"lolloping" is a queer reversed dissonance of "gallipot"—"galloping" is an almost equally crazy assonance; they convey the impression of candle flames, blown now backwards, now sideways, ... and the lines following:

EXAMINATION

*Outside in the passage are wildernesses
Of darkness rustling like witches' dresses*

give the softness of the flame that is speaking; then, much later, we come to the line:

The mocking money in the pockets

where the faint variations in the castanet—thin, elfish, sound, seem like pin-points of candlelight, blown by the cold air.'

Such a discussion in technical terms, and in the poet's own words, will bring us so much nearer an understanding of the apparent difficulties of this poem. In effect, it is the seventeenth century in every tale of ghost or Poltergeist, and all the trials of the witches, expressed or recreated into a work of art. In the space of some fifty to sixty lines the whole subject is given, with nothing omitted and much, even, added, including those images that form the peculiar genius of the poem. The invention of:

*Black as Hecate howled a star
Wolfishly, and whined
The wind from very far*

is but one of the many extraordinary flights of imagination made apposite by this particular atmosphere. The lines beginning:

Through the kitchen there runs a hare—

are of so general a truth in regard to all these stories that they describe, as well, the haunting of Epworth Rectory. We cannot but remember those words: 'After 9, Robert Brown—the servant—sitting alone by the fire in the back kitchen something came out of the copper hole like a rabbit, but less, and turned round five times, very swiftly. Its ears lay flat upon its neck, and its little scut stood straight up.'

*The mocking money in the pockets
Then turned black ... now caws
The fire ... outside, one scratched the door
As with iron claws—*

is remarkable for the reason that everything in these four

EXAMINATION

lines comes from the actual narrative, except the invention of: 'now caws the fire . . .', which is an inspired image that exactly fits the context.

> . . . *'Long dead'*
> *Moaned the water black as crape,*

is yet another conception coming straight from that night-world which it describes. The last five lines:

> *Whinnying, whined the maned blue wind*
> *Turning the burning milk to snow,*
> *Whining it shied down the corridor—*
> *Over the floor I heard it go*
> *Where the drum rolls up the stairs, nor tarries*

change the wind, in metamorphosis, into a rough, young animal, but 'blue maned' and, therefore, of magical beauty. It describes its noises in the corridor:

> *Outside in the passage are wildernesses*
> *Of darkness rustling like witches' dresses,*

and the dying away of the haunted drumming, ending uncertain, as though it might begin once more. It is to be remarked about *The Drum* that certain of its features are not strictly accurate to the narrative. Mr. Mompesson, for instance, does not seem to have been a magistrate. He may have been a Justice of the Peace, but would not, then, be Mr. Justice Mompesson. Again, the hare that ran through the kitchen did not become:

> *A lovely lady . . . see her eyes—*
> *Black angels in a heavenly place,*
> *Her shady locks and her dangerous grace.*

But such inventions are so close to the idiom of the piece that they have become part of it, and may even be warranted by the actual circumstances. 'The idle drummer', 'who had been a soldier under Cromwel' (*sic*), can be easily excused this confusion of titles. Other episodes in the poem, for the images assume the importance and reality of factual happenings, are so close in their implication to the story that they may be said to

118

EXAMINATION

be, surely, under the control of that influence. Except that the extreme subtlety and force of this creative intelligence has dragged over the narrative into her own domain or territory. Once the poem has been read, the Drummer of Tedworth and his haunted drum are in her custody, or have been made free of the world of her imagination.

In our commentary upon the actual story we must draw attention, too, to the words and phrases used, for these, as in the haunting of Epworth Rectory, could scarcely be improved upon. 'My man heard someone come slaring through the garret to his chamber, rattling by his side as if against his shoes, though he had none there, at other times walking up and down stairs, when all the house were in bed, and gobbling like a turkeycock.' In the Drummer of Tedworth we read, soon after Mr. Mompesson had taken away the 'idle fellow's drum', and it had been brought into his house, that: 'the sign of it just before it came was, they still heard an hurling in the air over the House, and at its going off, the beating of a Drum like that at the breaking up of a Guard' . . . 'Mrs. Mompesson, being brought to bed, there was but little noise the night she was in Travail, nor any for three weeks after, till she had recovered strength. But after this civil cessation, it returned in a ruder manner than before, and followed and vexed the younger children, beating their Bedsteds with such violence that all present expected when they would fall in pieces. . . . For an hour together it would beat, *Round-heads and Cuckolds, the Tat-too*, and several other points of War, as well as any drummer. After this they should hear a scratching under the children's bed, as if by something that had Iron Tallons. . . .' 'That morning it left a sulphurous smell behind it which was very offensive. . . .' 'At the same time a Bedstaff was thrown at the Minister, which hit him on the Leg, but so favourably that a Lock of Wool could not have fallen more softly, and it was observed, that it stopt just where it lighted, without rolling or moving from the place.'

All, indeed, is proceeding in this story according to the accepted pattern of these things. So often in tales of Poltergeists, observers are hit softly by flying objects. The missiles even appear to travel more slowly than could normally be the case. They have, moreover, a curving flight, not moving in straight lines, and when picked up in the hand are often too hot to be held, and have to be dropped. But we continue with the tapping of the Drum. 'It was observed that it would exactly answer in Drumming any thing that was beaten or called for.' An exact parallel, in fact, to the happenings, sixty years later, at Epworth Rectory. And, as the narrative goes on, the Poltergeist becomes both more supernatural and more human. 'After this it desisted from the ruder noises, and employed itself in little Apish and less troublesome tricks....' 'The night after Christmas Day it threw the old Gentlewoman's cloaths about the Room, and hid her Bible in the Ashes. In such silly tricks it was frequent.' Here, though, is a characteristic instance of its knocking. 'During the time of the knocking, when many were present, a Gentleman of the Company said, Satan, if the Drummer set thee to work, give three knocks and no more, which it did very distinctly and stopt. Then the Gentleman knockt, to see if it would answer him, as it was wont, but it did not. For further trial, he bid it for confirmation, if it were the Drummer, to give five knocks and no more that night, which it did, and left the House quiet all the night after. This was done in the presence of Sir Thomas Chamberlaine of Oxfordshire, and divers others.'

The Demon is now in full tide of activity. 'On Saturday morning, a hour before day, Jan. 10, a Drum was heard beat upon the outsides of Mr. Mompesson's Chamber, from whence it went to the other end of the House, where some Gentlemen strangers lay, playing at their door and without, four or five several Tunes, and so went off into the air.' ... And then a typically bucolic, or apish trick: 'The next night, a Smith in the village lying with John the Man, they heard a noise in the room, as if one had been shoeing of an Horse, and somewhat came, as if it were with a pair of Pincers, snipping at the Smith's nose most part of the night.' At this time, too, it performed some extraordinary tricks in the stables. 'Mr. Mompesson, coming one morning into his stable, found his horse on the ground, having one of his hinder legs in his mouth, and so fastened there that it was difficult for several men with a leaver to get it out.'

EXAMINATION

Later, comes a little episode reminiscent of the haunting of Cashen's Gap. 'One morning Mr. Mompesson rising early to go a journey, heard a great noise below, where the children lay, and running down with a Pistol in his hand, he heard a voice, crying A witch, A witch, as they had also heard it once before. Upon his entrance all was quiet.' Mr. Mompesson, at this time, can not have been enjoying any rest or peace of mind. It was 'at him', or 'after him', the whole time, night and day. 'Having one night played some little tricks at Mr. Mompesson's Beds feet, it went into another Bed, where one of his daughters lay.... The night after it came panting like a dog out of breath.... And company coming up, the room was presently filled with a bloomy noisome smell, and was very hot though without fire, in a very sharp and severe winter. It continued in the Bed panting and scratching an hour and a half, and then went into the next Chamber, where it knockt a little, and seemed to rattle a Chain; this it did for two or three nights together.... After this the old Gentlewoman's Bible was found in the Ashes, the Paper side being downwards. Mr. Mompesson took it up, and observed that it lay open at the third Chapter of St. Mark, where there is mention of the unclean spirits falling down before our Saviour, and of his giving power to the Twelve to cast out Devils, and of the Scribes opinion, that he cast them out through Beelzebub.'[1] This, also, is paralleled in the haunting of Cashen's Gap, where the mongoose, to whom we feel tempted in the spirit of Mr. Glanvil, the narrator, to give the honour of a capital letter before its name, would give out chapter and verse or direct where certain things would be found written in a book or newspaper.

At this point in the story, the narrator himself arrived at Mr. Mompessons' house. 'At this time it used to haunt the Children, and that as soon as they were laid. They went to Bed that night I was there, about Eight of the clock, when a Maid-servant coming down from them, told us it was come. Mr. Mompesson and I, and a Gentleman that came with me, went up. I heard a strange scratching as I went up the Stairs,

[1] Compare this with the tableau scene in the house of Dr. Eliakim Phelps.

and when we came into the Room, I perceived it was just behind the bolster of the Children's Bed, and seemed to be against the Tick. It was as loud a scratching as one with long Nails could make upon a bolster . . . I had been told that it would imitate noises, and made trial by scratching several times upon the Sheet, as 5, and 7, and 10, which it followed and still stopt at my number. . . . After it had scratched half an hour or more, it went into the midst of the Bed under the children, and there seemed to pant like a dog out of breath very loudly. . . . The motion caused by this panting was so strong, that it shook the Room and Windows very sensibly. . . . During the panting I chanced to see as it had been something (which I thought was a Rat or Mouse) moving in a Linnen Bag, that hung up against another Bed that was in the room. I stept and caught it by the upper end with one Hand, with which I held it, and drew it through the other, but found nothing at all in it. There was nobody near to shake the bag, or if there had, no one could have made such a motion, which seemed to be from within, as if a Living Creature had moved in it.' This incident, again, comes straight, as it were, from Cashen's Gap.[1] Had it happened there, the visitor would have been told that it was indeed 'Jeff', the talking mongoose, whom he had caught a sight of in the 'Linnen Bag'. No-one who went to that lonely farmhouse had ever more than this fleeting sight of the little animal, to whom so many curious actions were ascribed by those whom the mongoose always referred to as 'his family'.

As to the Drummer, who plays so malevolent but evasive a part in this story, we are told the following. 'The Drummer was tryed at the Assizes at Salisbury upon this occasion. He was committed first to Gloucester Gaol for stealing, and a Wiltshire man coming to see him, he askt what news in Wiltshire. The visitant said, he knew of none. No, saith the Drummer! Do not you hear of the Drumming at a Gentleman's House at Tedworth? That I do enough, said the other. I, quoth the Drummer, I have plagued him (or to that purpose) and he shall never be quiet, till he hath made me satisfaction for taking away my Drum. Upon information of this, the

[1] Or from Stratford, Connecticut, the home of Dr. Eliakim Phelps.

EXAMINATION

fellow was tryed for a Witch at Sarum, and all the main circumstances I have related were sworn at the Assizes by the Minister of the Parish, and divers others of the most intelligent and substantial Inhabitants, who had been eye and ear witnesses of them, time after time, for divers years together.

'The fellow was condemned to Transportation, and accordingly sent away; but I know not how ('tis said by raising storms and affrighting the Seamen) he made a shift to come back again. And 'tis observable that, during all the time of his restraint and absence the house was quiet, but as soon as ever he came back at liberty, the disturbance returned.

'He had been a soldier under Cromwel [sic], and used to talk much of Gallant Books he had of an odd fellow, who was counted a Wizzard.'

It does not appear that search has ever been made for more details in the records of Old Sarum, which, presumably, must still exist. The story, then, rests mostly upon the narrative of Mr. Joseph Glanvil, as here reprinted.

The name of the 'idle drummer' was William Drury. He had been tried for stealing in 1662, was sentenced to transportation, and had escaped from a boat, or barge, in April 1663. It sounds, therefore, as if this escape took place in England, while he was being conveyed to the port of embarkation for Trinidad, or Barbados. In prison he heard of these disturbances and, having a grudge against Mr. Mompesson, accused himself of being their author. He then came back to his village, Uscut, in Wiltshire, where Mr. Mompesson had him arrested for witchcraft; the Grand Jury found a true bill against him, but he was acquitted by the Petty Jury, and this is the last we hear of him.[1] The disturbances at Tedworth began in April 1661, and finished two years later, in April

[1] There is some variance in the details. According to other accounts, William Drury of Uscut, a tailor, was taken for stealing pigs in March, 1663. He escaped from a barge, on 11 April, within a mile of Newnham, near Awre, while the bargemen were sleeping. He reached Malmesbury, on Monday, 13 April. He then went to Uscut and bought a drum from Mr. Farler, who had before supplied him, and beat it at Uscut. This would seem to have been an act of effrontery upon his part. The following day he was seized by Mr. Mompesson on a charge of witchcraft, was acquitted of this, but transported to Virginia for stealing pigs. No more is heard of him.

1663. So great was the commotion caused by them that King Charles sent down Lord Falmouth to report to him upon them. The Queen, at the same time, sent Lord Chesterfield for this purpose, but no important phenomena were witnessed by the courtiers, and they went back to London in a sceptical mood. There is, however, such a weight of irrefutable evidence that it is certain that most curious phenomena were taking place, though, in spite of its *prima facie* probability, it is not by any means certain that it was the Drummer who caused these things to happen. We would say it was, more probably, the elder or both of 'the two little modest girls in the bed, between seven and eleven years old as I guess', who, having been told this story of the confiscation of the drum by their father built up their chain of psychical disturbances around this core of fact.

The other Relations in *Saducismus Triumphatus* are, unfortunately, of much less interest. They are twenty-eight in number, with a few more added in a Continuation. It is, however, irresistible to mention, at least, the case of the witchcraft of Elizabeth Style, of Stoke Trister in the County of Somerset, for here again the language used by Glanvil is of high dramatic value to his narrative.[1] It is the third of Glanvil's Relations. 'Her confession was free and unforced, without any torturing or watching, drawn from her by a gentle examination, meeting with the convictions of a guilty conscience. . . . She confesseth further, That the Devil useth to suck her in the Poll, about four a Clock in the Morning, in the form of a fly like a Millar, concerning which, let us bear Testimony.

'Nicholas Lambert Examined again Jan. 26. 1664, before Rob. Hunt Esqre.; concerning what happened after Style's confession, testifyeth That Eliz. Style having been examined before the Justice, made her Confession, and Committed to the officer, the Justice required this examinant, William Thick and William Read of Bayford, to watch her, which they did; and this Informant sitting near Style by the Fire, and reading in the Practice of Piety about Three of the Clock in the Morning,

[1] This case, also, has been made the subject of a poem by the hand that wrote *The Drum*.

there came from her head a glittering bright fly, about an inch in length, which pitched at first in the chimney, and then vanished. In less than a quarter of an hour after, there appeared two flies more of a less size and another colour which seemed to strike at the examinant's hand, in which he held his book, but missed it, the one going over, the other under at the same time. He looking stedfastly then on Style, perceived her countenance to change, and to become very black and gastly, the Fire also at the same time changing its colour; whereupon the Examinant, Thick and Read conceiving that her Familiar was then about her, looked to her Poll, and seeing her Hair shake very strangely, took it up, and then a Fly like a great Millar flew out from the place, and pitched on the Tableboard, and then vanished away. Upon this the Examinant, and the other two persons looking again in Style's Poll, found it very red and like raw beef. The Examinant askt her what it was that went out of her Poll, she said that it was a Butterfly, and askt them why they had not caught it. Lambert said, they could not. I think so too, answered she. A little while after, the Informant and the others looking again into her Poll, found the place to be of its former colour. The Examinant demanding again what the Fly was, she confessed it was her Familiar, and that she felt it tickle in her Poll, and that was the usual time when her Familiar came to her.'

This particular witch, Elizabeth Style, had the good fortune to die in prison before worse befell her. In Glanvil's words: 'But she prevented Execution by dying in Gaol, a little before the expiring of the term her confederate Daemon had set for her enjoyment of Diabolical pleasures in this life.' And the book carries on for two hundred pages, and more, with accounts of various extraordinary cases of hauntings and witchcrafts. The very next case, Relation IV, gives the examination and confession of Alice Duke, alias Manning, the Witch of Wincanton in Somerset, in 1644. 'She saith that after their meetings, they all make very low obeysances to the Devil who appears in black Clothes and a little Band. He bids them welcome at their coming . . . to a green place near Marnhull, as she was then told . . . or in Lie Common . . . and brings Wine, Beer, Cakes, Meat, or the like. He sits at the

EXAMINATION

higher end and usually Ann Bishop sits next to him, (who was there in a green Apron, or French wastcoat and a red Petticoat). They eat, drink, dance, and have Musick. At their parting they use to say, *Merry meet merry part*, and that before they are carried to their meetings, their Foreheads are anointed with greenish oyl that they have from the spirit which smells raw. They for the most part are carried in the Air.[1] As they pass, they say, *Thout, tout a tout, tout, throughout and about.* Passing back they say, *Rentum Tormentum*, and another word which she doth not remember.' But we must trespass no further into the pages of *Saducismus Triumphatus*, for its Relations are concerned mainly with cases of Witchcraft, though these are near, necessarily, in some of their detail, to the tricks of the Poltergeist.

The fourth of our classical cases of the Poltergeist has some points of similarity with the haunting of Willington Mill. As a narrative, or assessing it for its dramatic value, it has these advantages that the history of the persons concerned is romantic and that the mere untangling of their relationships in books of extinct peerage is a pursuit that calls for ingenuity, and for the detective sense strongly developed. Also some parts of the story are told in the words of one of the most famous of our sea captains, Earl St. Vincent, a character of known veracity, to whose word full confidence should be attached. The house in which the hauntings took place was

---

[1] This refers, of course, to the celebrated 'flying ointment' with which the witches rubbed themselves before going to the Sabbath. Several recipes for this ointment have been preserved and doctors, to whom these have been submitted, have agreed that certain substances would give the sensation of flying. cf. Miss Margaret Murray, *The Witch Cult in Northern Europe*, 1926, pp. 93-4.

Professor A. J. Clark has reported on three of these recipes and shows that aconite and belladonna are among the ingredients; aconite produces irregular action of the heart and belladonna causes delirium. 'Irregular action of the heart in a person falling asleep produces the well-known sensation of suddenly falling through space; and it seems quite possible that the combination of a delirifacient, like belladonna, with a drug producing irregular action of the heart, like aconite, might produce the sensation of flying.' 'It seems therefore,' Miss Margaret Murray concludes, 'that it was immaterial whether the [broom]stick or the rider were anointed; sooner or later the sensation of flying would be felt and the rider would be convinced that she had flown through the air.'

EXAMINATION

Hinton Ampner, in Hampshire. We are allowed to reprint the narrative from the *Journal of the Society for Psychical Research* for April 1893.[1] It took the form of an old pamphlet, communicated to the Society by the Marquess of Bute, who added his criticisms and his notes as to the persons concerned. They are mentioned by him under fictitious initials, with only a clue, here and there, by which to discover their identities. The circumstances in the case were that Mrs. Ricketts, the sister of Lord St. Vincent, in the absence of her husband in Jamaica, took a lease of the house for the sake of her three children. It is unnecessary for us to impede this part of our remarks with suggestions as to the identity of the persons mentioned, and we reserve that information for the actual narrative, where it will be found in footnotes. We, therefore, in this place, only resume the important points, drawing attention to salient or characteristic details in the story.

In the first place we must note the noises of explosions that were heard, 'sometimes as loud as the bursting of cannon'. Compare with this the hauntings at Tackley, in Oxfordshire (*A Disturbed House and its Relief*, by Ada M. Sharpe, 1905), where tremendous explosive sounds were heard in the house, 'like bombs', and in another case on record, the 'loud explosive sounds' which 'shook the house', reported in the home of Mlle. d'Ourches, sister of Comte d'Ourches, at Poitiers (cf. *Report on Spiritualism of the Committee of the London Dialectical Society*).[2] Later, in a letter from her steward, Robert Camis to Mrs. Ricketts, we read: 'I have heard no noise myself, but on Saturday about eleven a clock my Mother went home to make her bed, and left sister Martha in the chicking att work with her needle. She heard a noise like a roleing clap of thunder; it did not surprise her because she thought it was thunder, for it gered the windows. . . . The noise appeared to be towards the yallow room. Itt seemed to roll along, which made her think itt was thunder.' Mrs. Ricketts

[1] The original letters were, also, edited and published by Mrs. Henley Jervis, granddaughter of Mrs. Ricketts, in *The Gentlemen's Magazine* for November and December 1872.
[2] There were explosions like bombs, and continual ringing of bells, at Owatonna, Minnesota, in 1880, in the house of Mr. Dimant, cf. *Religio-Philosophical Journal* for December 25th of that year.

says: 'In the beginning of the year 1771, I was frequently sensible of a hollow murmuring that seemed to possess the whole house; it was independent of wind, being equally heard on the calmest nights, and it was a sound I had never been accustomed to hear.... I stood in the middle of the room, pondering with much astonishment, when suddenly the door that opens into the little recess leading to the yellow apartment sounded as if played to and fro by a person standing behind it. This was more than I could bear unmoved.... Half an hour afterwards I heard three distinct knocks, as described before; they seemed below, but I could not then or ever after ascertain the place. The next night I lay in my own room: I now and then heard noises, and frequently the hollow murmur.... On the 7 May this murmur was uncommonly loud. I could not sleep, apprehending it the prelude to some greater noise. I got up and went to the nursery, stayed there till an half past three, and then, being daybreak, I thought I should get some sleep in my own apartment; I returned and lay till ten minutes before four, and then the great hall door directly under me was slapped to with the utmost violence, so as to shake my room perceivably. I jumped out of bed to the window that commands the porch. There was light to distinguish every object, but none to be seen that could account for what I had heard.... From this time I determined to have my woman lie in a little bed in my room. The noises grew more frequent, and she was always sensible of the same sounds, and much in the same direction that they struck me.... After Midsummer the noises became every night more intolerable. They began before I went to bed, and with intermissions were heard till after broad day in the morning. I could frequently distinguish articulate sounds, and usually a shrill female voice would begin, and then two others with deeper and manlike tones seemed to join in the discourse, yet, though this conversation sounded as if close to me, I could never distinguish words. I have often asked Elizabeth Godin [her maid] if she heard any noise and of what sort. She, as often, described the seeming conversation in the manner I have related, and other noises. One night in particular my bed curtains rustled, and sounded as if dragged by a person walking against them. I then asked her if she heard any noise, and of what kind. She spoke of it exactly in the manner I have done. Several times I heard sounds of harmony within the room—no distinct or regular notes, but a vibration of harmonious tones; walking, talking, knocking, opening and slapping of doors were repeated every night.' Lord St. Vincent (her brother) then came to stay with Mrs. Ricketts. 'The morning after he left me to return to Portsmouth,' she continues, 'about three o'clock and daylight, Elizabeth Godin and myself both awake—she had been sitting up in bed looking round her, expecting as she always did to see something terrible, I heard with infinite astonishment the most loud, deep, tremendous noise, which seemed to rush and fall with infinite velocity and force on the lobby floor adjoining to my room. I started up, and called to Godin, "Good God! did you hear that noise?" She made no reply; on repeating the question, she answered with a faltering voice: "She was so frightened she scarce durst speak." Just at that instant we heard a shrill and dreadful shriek, seeming to proceed from under the spot where the rushing noise fell, and repeated three or four times, growing fainter as it seemed to descend, till it sank into earth. Hannah Streeter, who lay in the room with my children, heard the same noises, and was so appalled she lay for two hours almost deprived of sense and motion. Having heard little of the noises preceding, and that little she did not regard, she had rashly expressed a wish to hear more of them, and from that night till she quitted the house there was scarce a night passed that she did not hear the sound as if some person walked towards her door, and pushed against it, as though attempting to force it open.'

When Lord St. Vincent came to stay . . . 'I heard my brother's bell ring with great quickness. I ran to his room, and he asked me if I had heard any noise, "because", said he, "as I was lying wide awake an immense weight seemed to fall through the ceiling to the floor just by that mahogany press, and it is impossible I should be deceived".'

The narrative contains the curious account, too, of when 'Mr. George Ricketts and Mr. Poyntz Ricketts, active young men in the prime of life, were walking to and fro close to the house on the paddock side, when a great noise was heard

EXAMINATION

within it, upon which one of them said: "They are at their tricks again, let us go in and see." ' The house, at that time, was unoccupied and, of course, on entering it, they found nothing disturbed or out of place.

At a later point, Martha H. G. Jervis, the elder granddaughter of Mrs. Ricketts, went to see the old servant, Lucy Camis, at her farm near by. This was fifty years later, under the date July 10, 1818. Lucy Camis had been, the year before this to see Hannah Streeter (the old nurse): 'and asked if she remembered having been disturbed by the noises, particularly one night when the other servants were gone to bed, when, being in the servant's hall, they heard a sound as of the great iron brazier falling through the roof of the pantry (over which there was no room), and that it went "Twirl! twirl! twirl" till it sank into the ground. They were so much terrified that Lucy would not venture up to the garrets, but slept that night in the nursery. They found the brazier, the next morning, in the place where it had been left.'

It may be objected that this case is more of a haunting than of a Poltergeist. There is, for instance, no stone-throwing, and little or no rapping or hammering. The obscene forces were not at play. At the same time, the disturbances, and we are forced to the conclusion that they were genuine, were of so tremendous a nature that some power or volition was certainly at work within the house. If we read on into the narrative, the suggestion of Lord Bute, on the evidence of old Lucy Camis, given fifty years after the events, is to the effect that some dark mystery had taken place in the house, concerned with the birth of an illegitimate child, the mother being the younger sister of Edward Stawell. In leaving this case, we would draw attention again to that tremendous sound, to which there was a parallel in the haunting of Epworth Rectory, for the account of it, read in suitable circumstances, never fails to remind the writer of the directions given by Hector Berlioz, in his *Grande Traité de l'Instrumentation*, for the full use of the 'batterie de cuivres'. That greatest of all masters of orchestration would have used that sound, we cannot doubt, for his *Grande Messe des Morts*, or in his 'Funeral March for the last scene of Hamlet'. But the most alarming feature of these great noises,

EXAMINATION

in many of these cases, is that they are not audible to all. Nothing has fallen, or been moved. It is an auditory hallucination.

This story of Mrs. Ricketts, the fourth of our classical cases of the Poltergeist, we follow with other instances reported at less length, but which are no less curious. Next to it, because there are points of similarity, we put the tale told by Monsieur Camille Flammarion, the famous astronomer, in his *Haunted Houses*. Or, at least, it is reported by him in the words of those to whom it happened, in 1867. The story in question is the haunted castle in Calvados, and our comments upon this case must take note of the following details. This would seem to be, as with the house of Mrs. Ricketts, a case of some mysterious force out of the past. Something sinister and tremendous had once happened in the castle, and its activities would seem to be directed to draw attention to itself, as though it had, definitely, the desire to get into communication with the occupants. Most of all, it will be noted, it haunted the Abbé. The haunting took the form of loud and thunderous knocking; the whole castle reverberated with the sounds. We read of twenty or thirty loud and appalling raps delivered mysteriously, as though with a heavy hammer, or iron bar. 'At 2 a.m. some being rushed up the stairs from the entrance hall to the first floor, along the passage and up to the second floor, with a loud noise of tread which had nothing human about it. Everybody heard it. It was like two legs deprived of their feet and walking on the stumps. Then we heard numerous loud blows on the stairs and on the door of the green room.' For some reason, it would seem to be a mistake in a haunted house to call a room 'the green room'. We have seen how significant a part was played by the green or 'yallow' room at Hinton Ampner.

At another time, the noises in this haunted castle are described, variously, as being like the sound of a heavy stick banged on its point and progressing by that means along the passages and down the stairs, and as though a heavy ball were bounced from step to step, and foot by foot, along the corridors.[1] There was that night, of 10 November, when an appalling thunderstorm broke out, and 'at this moment every-

[1] This sound, as of a ball being bounced, step by step, has been noticed in other Poltergeist disturbances.

EXAMINATION

body heard something like a cry, or a long drawn trumpet call, audible above the storm. It seemed to me to come from outside.' Knowing what we know, it is, too, no surprise to us to read of the Abbé that 'he then heard in a corner of the room a noise as of the winding of a big clock'. The usual tricks were played upon the Abbé. His papers and books were strewn about the room and, upon one occasion, a whole row of books was removed from a shelf and thrown in confusion upon the floor, only excepting a Bible, a hint, perhaps, that the spirit had need of that in order to quiet it, or merely from respect and out of deference. What are we to think of that haunted castle in Calvados! I believe we must agree, all allowances being made for exaggeration, that something very peculiar was on foot, was, in fact, literally on foot and treading noisily about the house, because it could not help it, or because it wanted to draw attention to itself.

This haunting is capped, so to speak, by the stories told by Mrs. Catherine Crowe in her book, *The Night Side of Nature*, from which we reprint Chapter XVI, 'The Poltergeist of the Germans, and Possession'. It begins with a typical instance, the Stockwell Ghost of 1772. The Poltergeist in this case was centred in the person of Ann Robinson, a young maid of twenty. The story is almost exactly similar to the Poltergeists of Worksop and of Wem, both of which are included in this book. 'On Monday, January 6th, 1772, about ten o'clock in the forenoon, as Mrs. Golding was in her parlour, she heard the china and glasses in the back kitchen tumble down and break; her maid came to her and told her the stone plates were falling from the shelf; Mrs. Golding went into the kitchen and saw them broke. Presently after a row of plates from the next shelf fell down likewise, whilst she was there, and nobody near them; this astonished her much, and while she was thinking about it, other things in different places began to tumble about, some of them breaking, attended with violent noises all over the house. . . .' Later, 'about eight o'clock in the evening a fresh scene began; the first thing that happened, was a whole row of pewter dishes, except one, fell from off a shelf to the middle of the floor, rolled about a little while, then settled; and, what is almost beyond belief, as soon as they were quiet, turned up-

EXAMINATION

side down; they were then put on the dresser, and went through the same a second time; next fell a whole row of pewter plates from off the second shelf over the dresser to the ground, and being taken up and put on the dresser one in another, they were thrown down again.' Next, the comic or impish touch: 'Two eggs that were upon one of the pewter shelves; one of them flew off, crossed the kitchen, struck a cat on the head and then broke in pieces. . . . The glasses and china were put down on the floor for fear of undergoing the same fate; they presently began to dance and tumble about, and then broke to pieces . . . a glass tumbler that was put on the floor, jumped about two feet and then broke. Another that stood by it jumped about at the same time, but did not break till some hours after, when it jumped again, and then broke. . . . At all the times of action, Mrs. Golding's servant' (like Emma, the nursemaid, in the case at Wem[1]) 'was walking backwards and forwards, . . . nor could they get her to sit down five minutes together . . . in the midst of the greatest confusion, she was as much composed as at any other time, and with uncommon coolness of temper adviced her mistress not to be alarmed or uneasy, as she said these things could not be helped. . . . A pail of water that stood on the floor boiled like a pot.' (This occurs, too, in the Great Amherst Mystery.[2]) The end of the story is as might be expected. Anna Robinson was discharged and no more disturbances occurred.

Mrs. Crowe, after this, gives us the story of the home of Mr. Williams in the Moscow Road, Bayswater, likewise in 1772. The control, here, was a little Spanish girl, between ten and eleven years of age. Among northern races, we would add, they are generally older than that, for the age of puberty comes later. 'A pewter teapot was seen to hop about as if bewitched, and was actually held down while the tea was being made for Mr. Williams' breakfast, before leaving for his place of business. Candlesticks after a dance on the table, flew off . . . and bonnets and cap boxes, flung about in the oddest manner.' Reviewing rapidly other cases from this chapter in *The Night Side of Nature* we note the well-known story of Angélique Cottin, in 1846. 'Persons who were near her, even without

[1] Compare p. 412.   [2] Compare p. 375.

contact, frequently felt electric shocks. . . . Anything touched by her apron or dress would fly off, although a person held it.' This girl was fourteen years old. A little later we come to the story of the Poltergeist at Rambouillet, in 1846. 'One morning, some travelling merchants, or pedlars, came to the door of a farm house and asked for some bread, which the maid-servant gave them and they went away. Subsequently one of the party returned to ask for more, and was refused. The man, I believe, expressed some resentment and uttered vague threats, but she would not give him anything, and he departed. That night, at supper, the plates began to dance and to roll off the table, without any visible cause, and several other unaccountable phenomena occurred; and the girl going to the door and chancing to place herself just where the pedlar had stood, she was seized with convulsions and an extraordinary rotatory motion.' This resembles, in its beginnings, the Drummer of Tedworth. It is a hysterical power bestowed as a curse. I have, at another page of this present book, suggested that it was the report of the cursings of the Drummer, William Drury, that inspired the two little girls of Mr. Mompesson to become possessed of these invisible faculties and powers.

Mrs. Crowe gives us, also, the amusing story—if not to the person most directly concerned—of Professor Schuppart of Giessen, in Upper Hesse, who was persecuted by having his face incessantly slapped. 'He was persecuted with slaps on the face by day and by night, so that he could get no rest; and when two persons were appointed by the authority to set by his bed to watch him, they got the slaps also.' 'It is very remarkable,' as Mrs. Crowe remarks, 'that the only thing that seemed available as a protection, was a drawn sword brandished over his head by himself, or by others,' which was one of the singularities attending the case of the Drummer of Tedworth. And this brings us with smaller interruptions to Councillor Hahn, a true story, or so we must presume, that is worthy of Hoffmann. It would be a shame to spoil this by complete quotation; so that we content ourselves with all that is necessary to our purpose. 'They resolved to return to the lower room' (having suffered too much from the Poltergeist in the room above), 'and have their beds brought back again; but the

EXAMINATION

people who were sent to fetch them returned, declaring they could not open the door, although it did not appear to be fastened. Then Hahn went himself, and opened it with the greatest ease. The four servants, however, solemnly declared that all their united strengths could make no impression on it.' These effects occurred in the Parc du Mystère at Coimbra, in 1919, mentioned by us at another page (cf. p. 149). There, it was more particularly windows, than doors. This is the same sort of trick, too, that we find where it is a question of noises. They are not heard by all. Some persons do not hear them. Of this there are several instances, and it happened, although Mrs. Ricketts does not stress the point, at Hinton Ampner. A second point of interest in the Hahn narrative is when 'there were lights in the room, and presently all three saw two napkins in the middle of the room, rise slowly up to the ceiling, and having there spread themselves out flutter down again'. We shall read of this same effect, shortly, in the Great Amherst Mystery.

Next in our series of Instances, we have printed the remarks upon Poltergeists contributed to the *Proceedings of the Society for Psychical Research*, by Sir William Barrett, in their volume for 1910. Speaking generally on the phenomena, he observes: 'The movement of objects is usually quite unlike that due to gravitational or other attraction. They slide about, rise in the air, move in eccentric paths, sometimes in a leisurely manner, often turn round in their career, and usually descend quietly without hurting the observers. . . . Stones are thrown, but no one is hurt; I myself have seen a large pebble drop apparently from space in a room where the only culprit could have been myself, and certainly I did not throw it.' And Sir William Barrett follows his remarks by giving an account of two cases of Poltergeists in Ireland, the Derrygonnelly case, and that of Enniscorthy, the former of which was observed by him personally. Both cases are of exceptional interest and value. The first of this pair of Poltergeists occurred at a farm in Enniskillen, which is described as being the most lonely spot imaginable. It stood on a bleak moorland, two miles from an isolated village. The year is 1877, and Sir William Barrett, on information, proceeded to the spot and made a personal investigation. This is, therefore, a most important instance, for nearly always the phenomena have only been observed by ignorant persons, and by the time interest has been aroused they have ceased their play. His account of it is to be found in the *Dublin University Magazine* for December 1877, as well as in these notes contributed by him, more than forty years later, to the *Proceedings of the Society for Psychical Research*. The haunted family in this case were Methodists, who had been thrown into a state of utter alarm by these strange happenings.[1] Sir William Barrett seems from his account to have spent two or three evenings at the farm, and to have taken with him another reliable witness. The centre of the disturbances was Maggie, the twenty year old daughter, and we could have guessed, already, that the phenomena would be likely to begin as soon as Maggie went to bed. Sir William Barrett waited, and before long the knocking had begun. The whole house, as at Cashen's Gap, shook with knocks and rappings. But the horrible feature of this Derrygonnelly case is in the proofs of intelligence exhibited by the Poltergeist. For it would return answers to mental questions. Asking this of it, in silence, Sir William Barret would extend a certain number of fingers of both his hands, in his pockets, and the rappings would answer him back the correct number. This was done so frequently that there could be no question of mere coincidence. He satisfied himself, also, that Maggie could not have produced the knockings. This, indeed, was clearly impossible because they came from every corner of the house. The noises were loudest, though, in the girl's bedroom. At first, and this is again in sign of an intelligence, they would only continue in the darkness. But gradually, little by little, Sir William Barrett was able to bring a lighted candle into the room, and they would go on

[1] We note that the family were Methodists, and wonder whether a life of John Wesley was in the house. If this were so, they would be familiar with the haunting of Epworth Rectory. POSTSCRIPT. On reading, as we go to press, the summary of this case by Andrew Lang, in *Cock Lane and Common Sense*, and the original report on it by Sir William Barrett, in the *Dublin University Magazine*, for December 1877, I find that my surmise is correct. The Methodist family at Derrygonnelly were familiar with the Epworth hauntings from the life of John Wesley. This is important evidence for the continuity of tradition in all these hauntings.

EXAMINATION

knocking, undisturbed. This is a curious point, and does seem to argue that the Poltergeist had animal intelligence. We are given a good description of this weird scene, with the family praying, for they were convinced that it was an evil spirit.

The other Poltergeist, at Enniscorthy, is no less interesting. On this occasion Sir William Barrett came too late upon the scene, though he was able to question the persons concerned, but the first-hand evidence that he quotes is most convincing. The scene was a small, new-built house in Enniscorthy, Co. Wexford, and the time 1910. On this occasion, for a change, the centre was a boy, Randall, eighteen years old, and a Protestant. He had taken lodgings in this house and occupied a small back bedroom with another young man, sharing it, in fact, with two other youths at the time when the disturbances began. They took the form of loud knockings, and of a hauling of the heavy bed in which two of the boys slept across the floor of their room. Soon the rumour of these happenings spread through the town, and a reporter of the local newspaper obtained permission to sit up in their room with another friend. This is the eyewitness whose evidence we are given, and it reads most convincingly. There were, therefore, four persons in the room, the reporter and his friend, Randall and the other boy, and they waited in darkness for the performance to begin. They had not long to wait. Within a few minutes a loud knocking began. The reporter listened, and expressed his opinion that it was a rat. 'You will soon see the rat it is!' Randall's companion answered him. We are told that the knocking, which seemed to centre in the wooden wall quite out of reach of Randall, then became louder and much quicker. After a time it abruptly stopped and then, suddenly, we read of the terrified exclamations made by Randall, culminating with his remark: 'I cannot hold them; they are going, and I am going with them; there is something pushing me from inside: I am going, I am going, I'm gone!' at which moment, lighting a match, the witnesses saw Randall being pulled bodily from his bed and his bedclothes torn from off him. This experience was repeated and, on every occasion, was preceded by that furious knocking, which increased in speed,

EXAMINATION

stopped suddenly, and then the violence would begin. After a few days none of the occupants would stand any more of it and the boy, Randall, left the house and took lodgings elsewhere. This was the end of the phenomena. He was interviewed only a little time afterwards, by Sir William Barrett, who describes him as seeming to be truthful in character and of more than average intelligence. Randall's own testimony, told in his own words, is, therefore, deeply interesting, because it is almost the only intelligible, first-hand evidence that we can find from any person who can be suspected of having been, himself, the home or accomplice of a Poltergeist. He describes the feeling, when his bed was moving, or when the clothes were pulled off his bed, as an irresistible force, and mentions his phrase, 'I am going! I am gone!' as the true description of what he felt.[1] The Enniscorthy case is, in fact, one of the most convincing to read of all the Poltergeist narratives. The setting is so simple, in a back bedroom, in a new-built house, in a little market town. No adventitious aid of loneliness, of weird surroundings, comes to help it.

And this brings us to the Great Amherst mystery of 1879, which we place next in order to that of Enniscorthy because it has points of resemblance, and for the reason that it would be a mistake to end our collection of Instances with a story that sounds so incredible. Nevertheless, it is a mystery, and one which becomes more, and not less, interesting the more that we examine it. The scene is Amherst, in Nova Scotia, a 'beautiful village situated on the famous Bay of Fundy'. 'Great' is only the appellation given to it by Mr. Walter Hubbell, whose account we are forced to read because there is none other, and he aspired, we might say, to become proprietor of the mystery. Hubbell was an American actor and impresario, in modest form, and it is unfortunate that we have only his account of these happenings. He had lived in the world of the music hall and the fair, so that the 'Great' has the meaning of the 'Great Liotard', the 'Great Vance', the 'lions' of the old

---

[1] His remarks, as typifying what he felt, should be compared with the utterances of Esther Cox in the Amherst mystery. Sir William Barrett also interviewed the maidservant in the house. The proprietor, Redmond, he did not see, and this is unfortunate.

music hall. And it is as such, most unfortunately, that he ran this case. Being told of it, and seeing its commercial possibilities, Hubbell hurried to the scene and contrived to install himself in the very house. But we must not precipitate the story. The household, in this little yellow-painted wooden house with bright geraniums in its windows, consisted of Daniel Teed, a shoemaker, his wife, and her two sisters, Jennie and Esther Cox. Jennie was twenty-two years old, and the belle of the village; Esther was nineteen. We are told that she was dark and sullen and of a nervous temperament and we know, immediately, that Esther was the cause of the disturbances.

Their start was after this fashion. The two sisters, one night, heard a rustling in a green pasteboard box filled with patchwork, which was under the bed. Thinking that a mouse had got into it, they placed the box in the middle of the room. Suddenly, to their astonishment, it leaped a foot, and then three feet, into the air. It repeated this peculiar, and premonitory performance, in front of the other members of the family. That night as Esther, who had complained of feeling unwell, lay in her bed, which she shared with her sister Jennie, she started up in great distress, saying, in the bucolic language which is attributed to her by Mr. Hubbell: 'I am swelling up and shall certainly burst, I know I shall.' The phenomena then began the full play of their wayward fancies. She was put back in bed, where it did really appear as though she were swelling up, from head to foot. 'She would fill up and lift the clothes as you would a bladder and then it would suddenly collapse. These spells came in regular order, about every minute.' This was followed up by one or two loud explosions, like claps of thunder, appearing to come from under her bed, and this marked the close of the visitation, for her swellings subsided, she became normal in manner and less hysterical, and was soon fast asleep, as though exhausted by her performance. And so she continued regularly, at intervals of a day or two. Many of the local inhabitants came to watch her, and Doctor Carritte was brought in to soothe her and to give her sedatives. We are now told of yet more extraordinary occurrences. The pillow or bolster which was under her head

EXAMINATION

flew out from its position as though inflated with gas and stood straight up in the air, nor could the exertion of a man's strength restore it to its place.[1] Her sheets flew off her bed and stood up stiffly, of themselves, in the middle of the floor.[2] Any ornament or article in the house was, by now, liable to leave its accustomed place and fly about the room. Soon, there was nothing that was too improbable to happen. Under the eyes of her family, who were sitting at a meal, there appeared writing on the wall: 'Esther Cox, you are mine to kill.' The reader may think that, by now, Esther Cox had gone a little too far; and it is true that the evidence as to this writing on the wall is remarkably scanty. We are not told how it was written; whether it was traced by a hand, with a pencil, or by what means this inscription became visible. Moreover, it is at this moment that Mr. Walter Hubbell appears upon the scene in person. The best of the Great Amherst mystery is over.

As soon as Mr. Hubbell comes to live in the house the scene degenerates almost into farce. Two excessively boring spirits, Bob Nickle and Maggie Fisher, are said to be haunting Esther Cox. And Mr. Hubbell makes the story altogether too fantastic, in default of the really interesting phenomena, which had ceased, as is nearly always the case, a few weeks after they had begun. The most idiotic things begin to happen; and Mr. Hubbell has to spend the whole of one day picking pins out of Esther; though this, it is only fair to add, is no more than the

---

[1] This same phenomenon is reported in the Cideville case, see p. 19 of this present book; and in the story of William Morse of Newberry in New England, in 1679, reported by Increase Mather in his *Remarkable Providences*, which case is summarized on p. 62 of this present volume.

[2] At Cupar, in Scotland, in 1842, clothes hanging on a line shot upwards suddenly; a loud detonation was noted at the same time. Some of the clothes fell to the ground, others vanished, according to a note in *The Times* for July 5th of that year. In Liverpool, on May 11th of the same year, clothes hanging on a line suddenly shot upwards. They moved away slowly. Smoke from chimneys indicated that above ground there was a southward wind, but the clothes moved away northward, cf. *Annals of Electricity*, 6; 499. In 1849, in the home of Robert Gibson of Orlar, in Westmorland, the table cloth was pulled off and blew out like a sail, cf. *The Westmorland Gazette* for that year. This chain of coincidences is pieced together from 'The March of the Poltergeist', by Hereward Carrington, in *Bulletin I* of the International Institute for Psychical Research, Ltd.

EXAMINATION

distortion of a well-known Poltergeist phenomenon.[1] And he obtained the willing consent of Esther to exhibit her talents in public, with, it would seem, but poor results. Immense crowds of people attended her first performances; but nothing whatever happened, and soon the public came no more. Mr. Hubbell, however, wrote his sensational account of the happenings at Amherst, a book which came out in 1888, and, by 1916, was in its tenth edition and had sold fifty-five thousand copies. The phenomena, however, in the better conditions of her own home, continued for some time. But the natural mediumship of Esther Cox had, by this time, degenerated into trickery. She went to live in the house of a neighbour, Mr. Davison, as servant, and not long afterwards his barn was burnt down. This is scarcely surprising, for, while living in the house at Amherst, lighted matches had been seen to fall from the ceiling. This trait of incendiarism, of conscious or unconscious arson, is in the ordinary routine of the Poltergeist and we shall notice another instance of it, shortly, in the case of Wem, in Shropshire. Esther Cox, however, was given in charge by Mr. Davison, and was rewarded with four months in prison. For some time her activities had annoyed sceptical persons, and, already, in the narrative of Mr. Hubbell, one of the leading inhabitants had suggested that a raw-hide whip applied to the bare shoulders of Esther Cox would put a stop to the phenomena for good and all.

In addition to the testimony of Mr. Hubbell there are two other authorities who have to be consulted upon the Amherst mystery. There is, in the first place, Mr. W. F. Prince, who writes his criticisms of the case in Volume XIII of the *Proceedings of the American Society for Psychical Research*. He is writing thirty years after the occurrences and it must be said that it is as easy, after that lapse of time, to criticize too closely, as it is to believe too implicitly, the information that lies before you. He dismisses nearly all the phenomena as being due to trickery. There was the occasion, for instance, when Esther

---

[1] This symptom, which is found in other cases, is nearly related to the cases of pin or nail swallowing, a sort of omnivorous mania of which there is frequent mention in the newspapers. Compare, also, the Aïssaoua and other fanatical or dervish communities in Moslem lands.

EXAMINATION

Cox was living in the house of Mr. Davison, and when he noticed a curry comb following her across the yard. Mr. W. F. Prince has almost too simple an explanation for this. It is, merely, that Esther Cox was pulling it after her by a piece of black thread, and this, he thinks, is proved by the way in which, we are told, the curry comb in following her banged against the corner of a door and came to a dead stop. That does, decidedly, sound suspicious; but it must be realized that, at the time this happened, Esther Cox was in the full decadence of her talent and would almost certainly be resorting to trickery in order to help out her effects. Mr. W. F. Prince makes other strictures of this nature upon the phenomena, but, in the end, he does not deny to Esther Cox that she may have been able to produce some remarkable effects in her prime. And he makes, in the meantime, other valuable criticisms of the case. The phenomena at Amherst had begun shortly after Esther Cox had an unpleasant adventure with an admirer, Bob McNeal, who drove her into the woods and attempted to assault her. This we know from Mr. Hubbell's narrative. It is suggested by Mr. W. F. Prince that the spirit, Bob Nickle, whom Esther said was tormenting her, was nothing else than the transference of Bob McNeal into Bob Nickle. She described the spirit as an old man with white hair; but that is an easy instance of the psychological censor at work. And Maggie Fisher, so to speak, was thrown in by her for company. All this receives close confirmation if we read intently into the narrative of Mr. Hubbell. The attacks came, we are told, at regular intervals of twenty-eight days. This is of obvious significance. And, as to the torments inflicted upon her by the spirit, Bob McNeal: 'Daniel Teed' (her stepbrother) 'explained to me', we read in the narrative, 'the true nature of the torture, but it must be nameless.' It was, in fact, the medieval incubus, or its mid-Victorian variant. And the whole trouble will have had its start in that. Esther Cox had been given a severe nervous shock at a critical time of her youth, and such was its hysterical side play, but no less mysterious for that.

The other authority upon the Amherst mystery is Mr. Hereward Carrington, who writes of it in his interesting book, *Personal Experiences in Spiritualism*. Mr. Carrington had the

EXAMINATION

good fortune and prescience to go to Nova Scotia in 1907 when many of the protagonists were still alive, and to seek out their evidence. Dr. Carritte, who might have given the most valuable testimony of all, was long dead; but Mr. Carrington was able to interview Mrs. Teed, the eldest sister and owner of the haunted house; Mr. Davison, whose barn was burnt down; and even Esther Cox herself. Mrs. Teed seemed willing to speak of the strange experiences of thirty years before and testified to the general truth of the printed narrative, though she said that Mr. Hubbell had exaggerated in order to make it more dramatic and exciting. She showed Mr. Carrington the set of chairs, half a dozen in number, which upon one occasion had been piled up mysteriously, one upon another, the lowest chair of all being, then, as mysteriously withdrawn, so that the whole pile fell clattering to the ground. The chairs had, still, the marks and dents made upon them, when they were seen by Mr. Carrington. She gave him, also, an additional anecdote, not found in the narrative, to the effect that when Esther was lying in bed, with the door open across the passage into Mrs. Teed's room, a heavy chair came across the floor of Esther's room, out through the open door, down to the landing, turning the corner there, and proceeding, thus, slowly and deliberately, to the bottom of the stairs. Mrs. Teed appears to have been convinced of the supernatural origin of the phenomena. Mr. Davison also was seen by Mr. Carrington, and, in a letter written to him, tells the story that we have quoted of the curry comb, and makes the curious remark about Esther: 'I have often watched her to find out how she came downstairs, she seeming to fly.' As climax to his labours, Mr. Carrington set out in order to interview Esther Cox herself. She was long ago married, with a child, but badly married, and living in very dirty surroundings. She was still sullen in manner, as she had been thirty years before, but pretended to know nothing, or to have forgotten all the occurrences of the past. She was unwilling to speak of them. Eventually, her husband said that she would tell Mr. Carrington the whole story for one hundred dollars; but Mr. Carrington, realizing the worthlessness of anything she might say in those circumstances, made his departure and troubled her no more.

EXAMINATION

It would seem, taking it all in all, that the Amherst mystery is, indeed, among the most interesting and convincing of all Poltergeist stories. There remains, even after Mr. Hubbell's narrative, the quaint phrasing of which will amuse, or startle, both the sophisticated and the unsophisticated reader, enough to make us certain that excessively curious forces were at work in the little house in Amherst. The beginning of the disturbances is extremely weird to read of, and if only it had been properly investigated upon scientific lines, and while the forces were still at their strongest, the mystery might well be more mysterious than ever. That Esther Cox cheated at a later stage there can be little doubt, but this is the invariable rule in the great majority of such cases, and, as we have so often had occasion to say in these pages, one, or even several, instances of trickery do not disprove all of the phenomena. The writing on the wall we find to be too much of a strain upon our credibility. And we cannot be impressed when Esther, writing a letter in front of Mr. Hubbell, has a spell of automatic writing and the words appear on the sheet of paper, dictated, we are told, by the spirit, Bob McNeal, 'G—— D— Hubbell's Sole to Hell, and your's!' But, at that stage, as we have said, and largely at Hubbell's instigation, the whole affair had degenerated into farce and its interesting period was over.

A story follows this that is Oriental in setting and, to our taste, must be considered as exceptionally curious. It alarms one in a quiet manner. Nothing whatever really happens, but it is most peculiar. This is the story of Mr. G., of Dordrecht, and its scene is the jungle in Sumatra, in 1903. What is interesting in this story is the hallucinatory nature of the happenings. Mr. G., in the postscript to his own story, notices the slowness of all the movements. His 'boy' would seem to be the pivot of the action; but of this we cannot be certain. Mr. G. says that the 'boy' moved with such slow movements that he wondered if he, himself, were in some form of trance. The 'boy', it will be noticed, was extremely frightened. And there are the odd circumstances that the stones fell so slowly, out of nowhere, and that they felt warm to the touch. This stone-

EXAMINATION

throwing is, of course, typical Poltergeist phenomena, but the particular story is interesting because of that warmth, and for the drugged or hallucinatory atmosphere of this haunting. It is to be related, from its ordinary side, to other instances of stone-throwing, in such different localities as at Upholland, Lancashire, in 1904; Cherbourg, in 1907; La Paz, Bolivia, 1906; near Calcutta, in the same year; in Jamaica at many different times; in Florence, 1909; Java, in 1871; Port of Spain, Trinidad, in 1905; and upon innumerable other occasions. The case of Mr. G. is, however, one of the most convincing, and mysterious, of the lot.[1]

We end our collection of Instances with a pair of Poltergeists, pure and simple. They are most typical of their kind and go well, for this reason, at the end of our Examination. They are the Worksop case, and that of Wem, in Shropshire, both of which are reported in Volume XII of the *Proceedings of the Society for Psychical Research*. Their date is 1883. The first of these, most unfortunately, was never properly investigated at the time of its occurrence. Also, on the surface, there were suspicious features in the case. The owner of the house, a horse dealer, had the reputation, locally, of being a bad character. He was disapproved of by his neighbours. It was suggested that he had caused the disturbances in order to win a bet, though no more is heard of his wager, and damage to the extent of ten pounds was done in his house. One of the more curious features of the Worksop Poltergeist is that the first warning was given before the arrival of Eliza Rose, the young girl in whom the disturbances had their centre.[2] It took the form of a sudden tilting of the kitchen table. A few days later Eliza Rose arrived, and the phenomena began. Objects, and we have read elsewhere of this, made an abortive jump from the floor, perhaps to the height of a foot or more; and a few moments later, at a second attempt, levitated themselves

---

[1] This story should be compared with that repeated by Increase Mather as having taken place at Portsmouth, in New England, in 1682 (see p. 64 of this present book). 'They took up nine of the stones and laid them on the table, some of them being as hot as if they came out of the fire.'

[2] It will be noted, in the actual narrative, that Eliza Rose was the child of an imbecile mother.

EXAMINATION

successfully to a greater height. Nothing in the house kept still. All small objects were on the wing. A basin, and this was witnessed by several persons, jumped up and made a rotatory, wobbling flight towards the ceiling, which it touched. The owner of the house seems to have thought the girl was bewitched. We have his exclamation: 'It doesn't matter a damn where that lass goes, there's something smashes.' It is a typical bucolic setting. We read that the entire house, even the bedrooms, were hung with hams and flitches of bacon, and that all was indescribably dirty. The most interesting points in the narrative, as we have seen, are that premonitory signal, given even before the true Poltergeist arrived upon the scene, and the description of the wobbling and slow flight of the china bowl. No sooner had Eliza Rose left the house than the phenomena ceased. They had only lasted for a very few days; and such phenomena, this is the pity of it, can never be repeated. But it would seem certain that, here again, the authentic mystery was at work.

The Wem Poltergeist might be called a fascinating mingling of the false and true. Both genuine phenomena and obvious trickery were at work. The scene is Wem, near Shrewsbury, and the suspected person was the nursemaid, Emma Davies. At the beginning of the manifestations, like Anne Robinson in the Stockwell case, a hundred years before, Emma Davies was completely calm. There is the scene, vouched for upon good evidence, when she stood with arms folded while crockery flew past her out of a cupboard, and generally in a slanting direction. Later on, she becomes hysterical. There is the curious evidence of Miss Maddox, the schoolmistress, who saw her rise from the ground in a chair, and who sat upon the same chair, taking Emma Davies upon her lap, when her boots, so we are told, 'kept on flying off'.[1] While Emma was at

[1] This same phenomenon is to be found in 'The Daemon of Spraiton in Devon', published in *Pandaemonium*, or the *Devil's Cloister Opened*, by Richard Bovet, in 1683. In this instance (the person possessed was Francis Fey, a young servant to Mr. Philip Furze): 'At another time one of his shoe strings was observed (without the assistance of any hand) to come to its own accord out of its shoe and fling itself to the other side of the room; the other was crawling after it, but a maid espying that, with her hand drew it out and it strangely clasp'd, and curl'd about her hand like a living eel or serpent.'

a neighbouring farm, crockery rose off a table into the air. She is then seen by her mistress to be holding a piece of brick in her hand, behind her back, which she throws forward, at the same time crying out in order to draw everyone's attention. The baby's cradle is set on fire. She is found with matches in her hand. The clothes in the cradle smell of paraffin, and much paraffin is used upon the farm. Emma is becoming an incendiarist, like Esther Cox, no doubt because of the dying in her of her original talent. A room catches fire, and a farmer comes running to the house, seeing all the windows lit up, as though with flames. It is noticed that the flames were 'very high and white, and that the articles burnt were very little singed'. It is suspected that she has sprinkled them with paraffin. And the case ends unsatisfactorily, with nothing proved. There has been some trickery, but all of the phenomena cannot be accounted for in this way. We might say that they started in all genuineness and that Emma Davies, finding herself a focus of interest, did all she could to satisfy her audience; but, after a short time, had to produce the phenomena artificially, for the machinery would no longer work in her.

The total of these stories of Poltergeists, if read carefully and taken as a whole, suggest the following remarks. They come in strict pattern from too many different parts of the world for it to be mere coincidence. Every country in Europe, Puritan North America, India, Africa, China, the East and West Indies, Iceland, there is no quarter of the globe that is without them. At the same time, there must be not one, but several causes, to account for the phenomena, where they are genuine. Were we to believe that they are the work of evil spirits, we would have to admit that they are sent to tease more than to injure. The action is, always, that of a wicked fairy in the kitchen, the nursery, the young girl's bedroom, or the haunted attic. It turns the milk, it makes the water boil, it wrecks the china cupboard, raps in the wainscoting, treads upon the stairs, makes pretence to wind the old clock in the corner, rings the bells, writes things in the dust upon the windowpane. In the course of our narratives we have seen it

EXAMINATION

arrange tableaux, ventriloquize, do simple guessing and arithmetic sums, play tunes, write poems, hide the Bible, and play tricks in the stables. This we can say of it, despite so many collected instances, that the Poltergeist is the rarest and most shy of visitors. And, once it has gone, never in any circumstances does it return.

At first glance, there are the two main sorts. There is the haunted house, the castle in Calvados, Willington Mill, Hinton Ampner, the house of Mr. Mompesson; and what could be called the flying visit, the house at Worksop, the carpenter's shop at Swanland, near Hull. The former are set pieces, lasting months, or years; the latter, last only for a week, a day, or only for an hour. They are kitchen scandals, ghosts of the dark cupboard; and science cannot be patient with them. And yet, if the 'luminous woman of Pirano' (Lear-like in sound!) is admitted as true, what of Angélique Cottin, Emma Davies, Anne Robinson, and the rest of them? What, seriously, are we to think of Epworth Rectory, of the Drummer of Tedworth, of Mr. Procter's mill? The great historical instance would seem to be the Drummer of Tedworth. We have seen that this case was known to the Mathers, Cotton and Increase, who wrote of the Poltergeists in New England; that it was known to the Wesley family at Epworth; and that this, in its turn, was familiar to Mr. Procter at Willington Mill, and to the Methodist family at Derrygonnelly. This makes it seem as if these cases were not so isolated as we think.[1] But, in the house at Worksop, one of the most mysterious of all the stories, and at Swanland, there is no such evidence. And why should it be that the foreign cases, that of Councillor Hahn, of Angélique Cottin, for instance, or that of Mme Shchapoff, so closely correspond? There are links of similarity between Mme Shchapoff, in 1870, and the case at Ringcroft in Galloway, in 1695; while Mme Shchapoff was precursor in many ways of Esther Cox in the Great Amherst mystery of 1879. We can only answer that such is the whole repertory, and that the best actors in the company know all the tricks. That is why, in so many different parts of the world, and at varying times, there

[1] It would be interesting to know whether a life of John Wesley was among the books at Cashen's Gap.

are identical phenomena. What is it that they can perform? What are their miracles? The full battery of the hysterical subject is at their command. And this, of course, brings its infection to other persons in the household. Shadow personality comes into play. The tableaux figures in the home of Dr. Phelps are to be accounted for in this way; but, as we have said before, that does not diminish the mystery. The incendiary, Mme Shchapoff, Emma Davies, Esther Cox, and many others, belong to the same category. Such things are to be explained upon purely material grounds.

But there remain other, and deeper, mysteries. The rappings seem never to be, categorically, proved or disproved. And, most important of all, there are the movements of inanimate objects, together with circumstantial accounts of their strange behaviour during flight, descriptions which might apply as much to the witnesses being in a state of hallucination as to the true conduct of chairs or crockery in transit. Circumstantial evidence is to be found concerning the gyrations of the chair in the T. B. Clarke case. It was spun round and round with incredible speed and violence, only to come to an abrupt stop, as though held still again in a grip of steel.[1] In so many other cases the flight of objects seems as though it were controlled until the last moment of their journey. Readers must, already, in the course of these pages, have become familiar with the stories of heavy objects that strike like feathers, or like locks of wool, and with their converse: 'a matchbox was seen to fall to the floor from the mantelpiece, landing with a noise like a bar of iron.'[2] There are other and curious contradictions. Perhaps the best account of these is in a case that we have, so far, omitted to examine, a series of extraordinary events that took place in 1919, in a villa outside Coimbra, in Portugal.[3] The

[1] See *Proceedings of the American Society for Psychical Research*, Vol. VII.
[2] See p. 48 of this present work: the case of Dr. Eliakim Phelps.
[3] They are described in *Le Parc du Mystére*, by Homen Christo and Madame Rachilde, Paris, 1923. M. Christo was a student of Coimbra University, newly married, with a child, who took the villa in question just outside the town of Coimbra. Madame Rachilde, a sceptic in these matters, is none other than that last, or belated, member of the Great Romantic Movement, who, from the early 'eighties until a year or two ago, has published one or more books, every year,

EXAMINATION

whole story, into which there is, unfortunately, not space to enter here, reads like an infectious condition of hallucination. You open a window, or door, and a moment later it is shut again. You close the shutters and, as soon as you blow out the candle, you see the shutters opening and letting in the moonlight. There is a loud and tremendous noise just outside, in the garden, and, running out, you find the police in the lane leading to the house, who have heard nothing. You walk out into the lane; the police go inside; again there is the noise and, again, the policemen hear nothing. But, before long, everyone is in tune with the disturbances. It is a world of contradiction. Or, indeed, you are having an experience of a world, where time and common sense and truth are different, or have lost their meaning. It is a mistake to say that such a house was haunted. A force more interesting than that was reigning there. Was this really the case? Or did it exist only in their minds? If the latter, then what we need for our information are their reactions to it. The same power held its dominion, for an afternoon, in the carpenter's shop at Swanland, in the house at Worksop, at Enniscorthy, Derrygonnelly, with Dr. Eliakim Phelps, and in the house of Mr. Mompesson. Was it the Kingdom of Cockayne; or any other name we like to give it?

What is the explanation? We do not know. And no-one knows, though, of course, there is a reason. It is not more mysterious than freak lightning. As I write this, that power

in the vein of Mrs. Radcliffe, Petrus Borel, Maturin, an interesting figure in herself because of her friendship with Verlaine, with Arthur Rimbaud, even with Marinetti. An account of her books can be read in *The Romantic Agony*, by Mario Praz, London, 1932. Her collaboration in *Le Parc du Mystére* cannot but have helped the story, which, in any case, is remarkable enough in itself. Many of the noises in this villa appear to have been auditory hallucinations. The phenomena only took place in the darkness, and consisted chiefly of a 'cat and mouse game' played by the Poltergeist with the window shutters. If securely barred they would open immediately the candle was put out, letting in the moonlight. And, if you went to the window, they would resist with full force, or suddenly fly back and be slammed before your face. The wife of M. Christo, going upstairs, felt as though some force were pulling upon her legs. Eventually, terrible shriekings were heard (as in the T. B. Clarke case) and M. Christo and his family left the house. So did the police, who would seem to have been equally alarmed. No explanation of these extraordinary disturbances was ever forthcoming.

EXAMINATION

might remove my shoes and put them on the mantelpiece; place the books from my shelves in a neat pile upon the floor, leaving open *Saducismus Triumphatus* at a certain page; and remove the pen from my hand with such force that it scores a bull's eye in the face of Signor Mussolini, who looks at me from *The Times* upon another table. Were that to happen to me, I should be alarmed; but not superstitiously frightened.

But the moment comes to take leave of these mysteries; to bid them farewell and introduce them in person, in their original, before the reader. He may try, if he can, to find a reason for them. And once more, in imagination, we walk by the dark walls of Malking Tower, wondering, as at Leap Castle in the very middle of Ireland, what secrets we should have to tell from long looking through those sightless windows, could we only live, summer and winter, with the rooks in the high trees. We would know on what nights the dogs bark. And see the witches, from all the Forest of Pendle, come with their familiars to the conclave. We would know Old Demdike and Old Chattox, both blind, both led along by young maidens who were learning wisdom. We would see the witches of St. Osyth, and that giant woman who is now a skeleton; hear Isobel Gowdie talk of the magic Elfhame; hear them dance *Tinkletum Tankletum* among the graves of Forfar; and *Thout, tout a tout, tout, throughout and about* upon the way to the Sabbath at Wincanton, with *Rentum Tormentum* as they are passing back.

And the subtler mysteries begin their play, worked, most of them, by maidens. There is magic, and much of terror in the air. It is the kitchen world, enchanted. These are old days and ancient stories, even in this year. It is the tale of Cinderella and her ugly sisters. The fairy Carabosse drives up in her coach, drawn by rats and mice, and the rappings and the breakings and the flying crocks and pots begin. The bedroom of Cinderella creaks and rattles with the fairy prince. He is coming to lie beside her. There is an aching longing; and the life of the household drudge has become an empty void. Or two or three young men, together, have this spiritual disturbance. Or the little boy, who plays with soot and coal, goes out and hangs himself, and is found in time. The young girl, who

EXAMINATION

has no doll, imagines one, and it becomes her pet, her familiar, her magic lover, who talks to her, and raps in the panelling, and will do everything but show himself.

We see the iron trees and the ballast hills, and hear the wild sighings of the engines (ghosts, themselves, for they are the engines of the 'thirties) at the haunted mill, looking down from the viaduct; we find Nancy Wesley kneeling on the stairs and blowing a horn in the haunted rectory; hear a sound as of the great iron brazier falling 'Twirl! twirl! twirl! till it sinks into the ground'; and, in the dining-room, disturb someone who is dressing and preparing eleven figures for the tableaux. The matchbox slides towards the bed; a heavy footfall comes down the stairs, but it is like a ball that bounces, step by step; bits of wood are moving in a straight line, striking a door noiselessly as a feather, and again as though borne along on gently heaving waves. What, by all the powers of good and evil, are these sights and sounds! No one can tell. It is still, and may ever, be a mystery. So listen to the Poltergeist, himself, who was once, and for a time, the Cauld Lad O' Hilton:

> *Wae's me, wae's me,*
> *The acorn's not yet*
> *Fallen from the tree*
> *That's to grow the wood,*
> *That's to make the cradle,*
> *That's to rock the bairn,*
> *That's to grow a man,*
> *That's to lay me.*[1]

[1] This poem, which is well known among English folk ballads, has the following story attached to it: 'This fairy or goblin was seldom seen, but his gambols were heard nightly in the hall of the great house. He overturned everything in the kitchen after the servants had gone to bed, and was, in short, one of the most mischievous sprites you could imagine. One night, however, the kitchen happened to be left in great confusion, and the goblin, who did everything by contraries, set it completely to rights; and the next morning it was in perfect apple-pie order. We may be quite sure that, after this occurrence, the kitchen was not again made orderly by the servants.

'Notwithstanding, however, the service thus nightly rendered by the Cauld Lad, the servants did not like it. They preferred to do their own work, without preternatural agency, and accordingly resolved to do their best to drive him from their haunts. The goblin soon

EXAMINATION

understood what was going on, and he was heard in the dead of night to warble the following lines in a melancholy strain:

> *Wae's me! wae's me!*
> *The acorn's not yet*
> *Fallen from the tree,*
> *That's to grow the wood*
> *That's to make the cradle,*
> *That's to rock the bairn,*
> *That's to grow to a man,*
> *That's to lay me.*

'He was, however, deceived in this prediction; for one night being colder than usual, he complained in moving verse of his condition. Accordingly, on the following evening, a cloak and hood were placed for him near the fire. The servants had unconsciously accomplished their deliverance, for present gifts to fairies, and they for ever disappear. On the next morning, the following lines were found inscribed on the wall:

> *I've taken your cloak, I've taken your hood;*
> *The Cauld Lad of Hilton will do no more good!*

'A great variety of stories in which fairies are frightened away by presents, are still to be heard in the rural districts of England. Another narrative, by Mr. Longstaffe, relates that on one occasion a woman found her washing and ironing regularly performed for her every night by the fairies. In gratitude to the "good people", she placed green mantles for their acceptance, and the next night the fairies departed, exclaiming—

> *Now the pixies' work is done!*
> *We take our clothes, and off we run.*

'Mrs. Bray tells a similar story of a Devonshire pixy, who helped an old woman to spin. One evening she spied the fairy jumping out of her door, and observed that it was very raggedly dressed; so the next day she thought to win the services of the elf further by placing some smart new clothes, as big as those made for a doll, by the side of her wheel. The pixy came, put on the clothes, and clapping his hands with delight, vanished, saying these lines:

> *Pixy fine, pixy gay,*
> *Pixy now will run away.*

'Fairies always talk in rhyme. Mr. Allies mentions a Worcestershire fairy legend which says that, upon one occasion, a pixy came to a ploughman in a field, and exclaimed:

> *Oh, lend a hammer and a nail,*
> *Which we want to mend our pail.*

—From *Nursery Rhymes and Nursery Tales of England*, collected by James Orchard Halliwell.

CHOSEN INSTANCES

1. THE HAUNTING OF EPWORTH RECTORY *page* 157
2. THE HAUNTING OF WILLINGTON MILL 189
   from the Diary of Mr. Joseph Procter, reprinted by permission of the Society for Psychical Research
3. THE DRUMMER OF TEDWORTH 214
   from Saducismus Triumphatus, by the Rev. Joseph Glanvil
4. THE HAUNTING AT HINTON AMPNER 230
   from the Journal of Mrs. Ricketts, reprinted by permission of the Society for Psychical Research
5. HAUNTED HOUSES 268
   reprinted from the book of that name by M. Camille Flammarion, by permission of Messrs. Ernest Benn, Ltd.
6. THE POLTERGEIST OF THE GERMANS 288
   from 'The Night Side of Nature', by Mrs. Catherine Crowe, London, 1834
7. THE ENNISCORTHY, DERRYGONNELLY AND OTHER POLTERGEIST CASES 328
   reported by Sir William Barrett, reprinted by permission of the Society for Psychical Research
8. THE GREAT AMHERST MYSTERY 359
   by Walter Hubbell, New York, Brentano's, 1885
9. THE CASE OF MR. G—— IN SUMATRA 380
   reprinted by permission of the Society for Psychical Research
10. THE WORKSOP AND WEM POLTERGEISTS 387
    a report by Frank Podmore, reprinted by permission of the Society for Psychical Research

1. THE HAUNTING OF EPWORTH RECTORY

THE RECORDS OF SAMUEL WESLEY

Collected and described by John Wesley, in his own words, and in letters from his family

---

Letters concerning some Supernatural Disturbances at my father's house at Epworth in Lincolnshire—John Wesley

---

LETTER I—TO MR. SAMUEL WESLEY FROM HIS MOTHER

January 12, 1716-17[1]

DEAR SAM,

This evening we were agreeably surprised with your pacquet, which brought the welcome news of your being alive, after we had been in the greatest panic imaginable, almost a month, thinking either you was dead, or one of your brothers by some misfortune been killed.

The reason of our fears is as follows. On the first of December our maid heard, at the door of the dining-room, several dismal groans, like a person in extremes, at the point of death. We gave little heed to her relation, and endeavoured to laugh her out of her fears. Some nights (two or three) after, several of the family heard a strange knocking in divers places, usually three or four knocks at a time, and then stayed a little. This continued every night for a fortnight; sometimes it was in the

[1] There is conflicting evidence as to the dates of these disturbances. Some authorities state that they only took place during the two months of November and December 1719. Equally confusing are the number of children in the Wesley household, and their names.

garret, but most commonly in the nursery, or green chamber.[1] We all heard it but your father, and I was not willing he should be informed of it, lest he should fancy it was against his own death, which, indeed, we all apprehended. But when it began to be troublesome, both day and night, that few or none of the family durst be alone, I resolved to tell him of it, being minded he should speak to it. At first he would not believe but somebody did it to alarm us; but the night after, as soon as he was in bed, it knocked loudly nine times, just by his bedside. He rose, and went to see if he could find out what it was, but could see nothing. Afterwards he heard it as the rest.

One night it made such a noise in the room over our heads, as if several people were walking, then run up and down stairs, and was so outrageous that we thought the children would be frighted, so your father and I rose and went down in the dark to light a candle. Just as we came to the bottom of the broad stairs, having hold of each other, on my side there seemed as if somebody had emptied a bag of money at my feet; and on his, as if all the bottles under the stairs (which were many) had been dashed in a thousand pieces. We passed through the hall into the kitchen, and got the candle and went to see the children, whom we found asleep.

The next night your father would get Mr. Hoole to lie at our house, and we all sat together till one or two o'clock in the morning, and heard the knocking as usual. Sometimes it would make a noise like the winding up of a jack, at other times, as that night Mr. Hoole was with us, like a carpenter planing deals, but most commonly it knocked thrice and stopped, and then thrice again, and so many hours together. We persuaded your father to speak and try if any voice would be heard. One night about six o'clock he went into the nursery in the dark, and at first heard several deep groans, then knocking. He adjured it to speak if it had power and tell him why it troubled his house, but no voice was heard, but it knocked thrice aloud. Then he questioned if it were Sammy, and bid it, if it were and could not speak, knock again, but it knocked no more that night, which made us hope it was not against your death.

Thus it continued till the 26th of December, when it loudly

[1] The green chamber again.

EPWORTH RECTORY

knocked (as your father used to do at the gate) in the nursery and departed. We have various conjectures what this may mean. For my own part, I fear nothing now you are safe at London hitherto, and I hope God will still preserve you. Though sometimes I am inclined to think my brother is dead. Let me know your thoughts on it.

S. W.

LETTER II—TO MY FATHER

January 30, Saturday

HONOURED SIR,

My mother tells me a very strange story of disturbances in your house. I wish I could have some more particulars from you. I would thank Mr. Hoole if he would favour me with a letter concerning it. Not that I want to be confirmed myself in the belief of it, but for any other person's satisfaction. My mother sent to me to know my thoughts of it, and I cannot think at all of any interpretation. Wit, I fancy, might find many, but wisdom none.

Your dutiful and loving son,

S. WESLEY

LETTER III—FROM MR. S. WESLEY TO HIS MOTHER

Dean's Yard, Westminster,
January 19, 1716–17, Saturday

DEAR MOTHER,

Those who are so wise as not to believe any supernatural occurrences, though ever so well attested, could find a hundred questions to ask about those strange noises you wrote me an account of: but for my part, I know not what question to put, which, if answered, would confirm me more in the belief of what you tell me. Two or three I have heard from others. Was there never a new maid, or man, in the house that might play tricks? Was there nobody above in the garrets when the walking was there? Did all the family hear it together when they were in one room, or at one time? Did it seem to be at all in the same place, at the same time? Could not cats, or rats, or dogs be the sprights? Was the whole family asleep when my father and you went downstairs? Such doubts as these being replied to, though they could not, as God himself assures us, convince them who believe not Moses and the prophets, yet would strengthen such as do believe. As to my particular opinion concerning the events foreboded by these noises, I cannot, I must confess, form any. I think since it was not permitted to speak, all guesses must be in vain. The end of spirits' actions is yet more hidden than that of men, and even this latter puzzles the most subtle politicians. That we may be struck so as to prepare seriously for any ill may, it is possible, be one design of Providence. It is surely our duty and wisdom to do so.

Dear mother, I beg your blessing on your dutiful and affectionate son,

S. WESLEY

I expect a particular account from every one.

LETTER IV—FROM MRS. WESLEY TO HER SON SAMUEL

January 26 or 27, 1716–17

DEAR SAM,

Though I am not one of those that will believe nothing supernatural, but am rather inclined to think there would be frequent intercourse between good spirits and us did not our deep lapse into sensuality prevent it, yet I was a great while ere I could credit anything of what the children and servants reported concerning the noises they heard in several parts of our house. Nay, after I had heard them myself, I was willing to persuade myself and them that it was only rats or weasels that disturbed us; and having been formerly troubled with rats, which were frightened away by sounding a horn, I caused a horn to be procured, and made them blow it all over the house. But from that night they began to blow the noises were more loud and distinct, both day and night, than before, and that night we rose and went down I was entirely convinced that it was beyond the power of any human creature to make such strange and various noises.

As to your questions, I will answer them particularly, but withal, I desire my answers may satisfy none but yourself, for I would not have the matter imparted to any. We had both man and maid now last Martinmas, yet I do not believe either of them occasioned the disturbance, both for the reason above mentioned and because they were more affrighted than anybody else. Besides, we have often heard the noises when they were in the room by us; and the maid particularly was in such a panic, that she was almost incapable of all business, nor durst ever go from one room to another, or stay by herself a minute after it began to be dark.

The man, Robert Brown, whom you well know, was most visited by it lying in the garret, and has been often frighted down barefoot and almost naked, not daring to stay alone to put on his clothes, nor do I think if he had power he would be guilty of such villainy. When the walking was heard in the garret Robert was in bed in the next room, in a sleep so sound, that he hever heard your father and me walk up and down, though we walked not softly, I am sure. All the family has heard it together, in the same room, at the same time, particularly at family prayers. It always seemed to all present in the same place at the same time, though often before any could say it was here, it would remove to another place.

All the family, as well as Robin, were asleep when your father and I went downstairs, nor did they wake in the nursery when we held the candle close by them, only we observed that Hetty trembled exceedingly in her sleep, as she always did before the noise awaked her. It commonly was nearer her than the rest, which she took notice of, and was much frightened, because she thought it had a particular spite at her: I could multiply particular instances, but I forbear. I believe your father will write to you about it shortly. Whatever may be the design of Providence in permitting these things, I cannot say. *Secret things belong to God*; but I entirely agree with you, that it is our wisdom and duty to prepare seriously for all events.

S. WESLEY

LETTER V—FROM MISS SUSANNAH WESLEY TO HER BROTHER SAMUEL

DEAR BROTHER,

About the first of December a most terrible and astonishing noise was heard by a maid-servant as at the dining-room door, which caused the upstarting of her hair, and made her ears prick forth at an unusual rate. She said it was like the groans of one expiring. These so frightened her, that for a great while she durst not go out of one room into another, after it began to be dark, without company. But, to lay aside jesting, which should not be done in serious matters, I assure you that from the first to the last of a lunar month the groans, squeaks, tinglings, and knockings were frightful enough.

Though it is needless for me to send you any account of what we all heard, my father himself having a larger account of the matter than I am able to give, which he designs to send you, yet, in compliance with your desire, I will tell you as briefly as I can what I heard of it. The first night I ever heard it my sister Nancy and I were set in the dining-room. We heard something rush on the outside of the doors that opened into the garden, then three loud knocks, immediately after other three, and in half a minute the same number over our heads. We enquired whether anybody had been in the garden, or in the room above us, but there was nobody. Soon after my sister Molly and I were up after all the family were abed, except my sister Nancy, about some business. We heard three bouncing bumps under our feet, which soon made us throw away our work and tumble into bed. Afterwards the tingling of the latch and warming-pan, and so it took its leave that night.

Soon after the above mentioned we heard a noise as if a great piece of sounding metal was thrown down on the outside of our chamber. We, lying in the quietest part of the house, heard less than the rest for a pretty while, but the latter end of the night Mr. Hoole sat up on I lay in the nursery, where it was very violent. I then heard frequent knocks over and under the room where I lay, and at the children's bed head, which was made of boards. It seemed to rap against it very hard and loud, so that the bed shook under them. I heard something walk by my bedside, like a man in a long nightgown. The knocks were so loud, that Mr. Hoole came out of their chamber to us. It still continued. My father spoke, but nothing answered. It ended that night with my father's particular knock very fierce.

It is now pretty quiet, only at our repeating the prayers for the king and prince, when it usually begins, especially when my father says, 'Our most gracious Sovereign Lord,' etc. This my father is angry at, and designs to say *three* instead of *two* for the royal family. We all heard the same noise, and at the same time, and as coming from the same place. To conclude this, it now makes its personal appearance; but of this more hereafter. Do not say one word of this to our folks, nor give the least hint.

I am, your sincere friend and affectionate sister,
SUSANNAH WESLEY

LETTER VI—MR. S. WESLEY IN ANSWER

DEAR SISTER SUKY,

Your telling me the spirit has made its personal appearances without saying how, or to whom, or when, or how long, has excited my curiosity very much. I long mightily for a farther account of every circumstance by your next letter. Do not keep me any longer in the dark. Why need you write the less because my father is to send me the whole story. Has the disturbance continued since the 28th of December? I understand my father did not hear it at all but a fortnight after the rest. What did he say remarkable to any of you when he did hear it? As to the devil being an enemy to King George, were I the king myself I should rather Old Nick should be my enemy than my friend. I do not like the noise of the nightgown sweeping along the ground, nor its knocking like my father. Write when you receive this, though nobody else should, to your loving brother.

LETTER VII—MR. S. WESLEY TO HIS MOTHER

February 12

DEAR MOTHER,

You say you could multiply particular instances of the spirit's noises, but I want to know whether nothing was ever seen by any. For though it is hard to conceive, nay, morally impossible, that the hearing of so many people could be deceived, yet the truth will be still more manifest and undeniable if it is grounded on the testimony of two senses. Has it never at all disturbed you since the 28th of December? Did no circumstance give no light into the design of the whole?

Your obedient and loving son,
S. WESLEY

Have you dug in the place where the money seemed poured at your feet?

LETTER VIII—MR. S. WESLEY TO HIS FATHER

February 12

HONOURED SIR,

I have not yet received any answer to the letter I wrote some time ago, and my mother in her last seems to say that as yet I know but a very small part of the whole story of strange noises in our house. I shall be exceeding glad to have the entire account from you. Whatever may be the main design of such wonders, I cannot think they were ever meant to be kept secret. If they bode anything remarkable to our family, I am sure I am a party concerned.

Your dutiful son,
S. WESLEY

LETTER IX—FROM MR. S. WESLEY TO HIS SISTER EMILY

DEAR SISTER EMILY,

I wish you would let me have a letter from you about the spirit, as indeed from every one of my sisters. I cannot think any of you very superstitious, unless you are much changed since I saw you. My sister Hetty, I find, was more particularly troubled. Let me know all. Did anything appear to her?

I am your affectionate brother,
S. WESLEY

LETTER X—FROM OLD MR. WESLEY TO HIS SON SAMUEL

DEAR SAM,

As for the noises, etc., in our family, I thank God we are now all quiet. There were some surprising circumstances in that affair. Your mother has not written you a third part of it. When

EPWORTH RECTORY

I see you here, you shall see the whole account which I wrote down. It would make a glorious penny book for Jack Dunton, but while I live, I am not ambitious for anything of that nature. I think that's all, but blessings, from your loving father,

SAM WESLEY

The following letter I received at the same time, though it has no date:

LETTER XI—FROM MISS EMILY WESLEY TO
HER BROTHER SAMUEL

DEAR BROTHER,

I thank you for your last, and shall give you what satisfaction is in my power concerning what has happened in our family. I am so far from being superstitious that I was too much inclined to infidelity, so that I heartily rejoice at having such an opportunity of convincing myself past doubt or scruple of the existence of some beings besides those we see. A whole month was sufficient to convince anybody of the reality of the thing, and to try all ways of discovering any trick, had it been possible for any such to have been used. I shall only tell you what I myself heard, and leave the rest to others.

My sisters in the paper chamber had heard noises and told me of them, but I did not much believe, till one night, about a week after the first groans were heard, which was the beginning, just after the clock had struck ten I went downstairs to lock the doors, which I always do. Scarce had I got up the best stairs when I heard the noise, like a person throwing down a vast coal in the middle of the fore kitchen, and all the splinters seemed to fly about from it. I was not much frighted, but went to my sister Suky, and we together went all over the low rooms, but there was nothing out of order.

Our dog was fast asleep, and our only cat in the other end of the house. No sooner was I got upstairs, and undressing for bed, but I heard a noise among many bottles that stand under the best stairs, just like the throwing of a great stone among them, which had broke them all to pieces. This made me hasten to bed; but my sister Hetty, who sits always to wait on my father going to bed, was still sitting on the lowest step on the garret stairs, the door being shut at her back, when soon after there came down the stairs behind her something like a man, in a loose nightgown trailing after him, which made her fly rather than run to me in the nursery.

All this time we never told our father of it, but soon after we did. He smiled and gave no answer, but was more careful than usual, from that time, to see us in bed, imagining it to be some of us young women, that sat up late and made a noise. His incredulity, and especially his imputing it to us, or our lovers, made me, I own, desirous of its continuance till he was convinced. As for my mother, she firmly believed it to be rats, and sent for a horn to blow them away. I laughed to think how wisely they were employed, who were striving half a day to fright away Jeffery, for that name I gave it, with a horn.

But whatever it was, I perceived it could be made angry. For from that time it was so outrageous, there was no quiet for us after ten at night. I heard frequently, between ten and eleven, something like the quick winding up of a jack in the corner of the room by my bed's head, just like the running of the wheels and the creaking of the iron-work. This was the common signal of its coming. Then it would knock on the floor three times, then at my sister's bed head, in the same room, almost always three together, and then stay. The sound was hollow and loud, so as none of us could ever imitate.

It would answer to my mother if she stamped on the floor and bid it. It would knock when I was putting the children to bed, just under me where I sat. One time little Kesy, pretending to scare Patty as I was undressing them, stamped with her foot on the floor, and immediately it answered with three knocks, just in the same place. It was more loud and fierce if anyone said it was rats or anything natural.

I could tell you abundance more of it, but the rest will write, and therefore it would be needless. I was not much frighted at first, and very little at last; but it was never near me, except two or three times, and never followed me, as it did my sister Hetty. I have been with her when it has knocked under her, and when she has removed has followed and still kept just under her feet, which was enough to terrify a stouter person.

If you would know my opinion of the reason of this, I shall

briefly tell you. I believe it to be witchcraft, for these reasons. About a year since there was a disturbance at a town near us that was undoubtedly witches, and if so near, why may they not reach us? Then my father had for several Sundays before its coming preached warmly against those that are called cunning men, which our people are given to; and it had a particular spite at my father.

Besides something was thrice seen. The first time by me that was discernible. The same creature was sat by the dining-room fire one evening; when our man went into the room, it run by him, through the hall under the stairs. He followed with a candle and searched, but it was departed. The last time he saw it in the kitchen like a white rabbit, which seems likely to be some witch; and I do so really believe it to be one, that I would venture to fire a pistol at it if I saw it long enough. It has been heard by me and others since December. I have filled up all my room, and have only time to tell you I am your loving sister,

EMILIA WESLEY

LETTER XII—MISS SUSANNAH WESLEY TO HER BROTHER SAMUEL

DEAR BROTHER WESLEY,

I should farther satisfy you concerning the disturbances, but it is needless, because my sisters Emilia and Hetty write so particularly about it. One thing I believe you do not know—that is, last Sunday, to my father's no small amazement, his trencher danced upon the table a pretty while, without anybody's stirring the table. When lo! an adventurous wretch took it up, and spoiled the sport, for it remained still ever after. How glad should I be to talk with you about it. Send me some news, for we are secluded from the sight, or hearing, of any versal thing except Jeffery.

SUSANNAH WESLEY

A PASSAGE IN A LETTER FROM MY MOTHER TO ME, DATED MARCH 27TH, 1717

I cannot imagine how you should be so curious about our unwelcome guest. For my part I am quite tired with hearing

EPWORTH RECTORY

or speaking of it; but if you come among us, you will find enough to satisfy all your scruples, and perhaps may hear or see it yourself.

S. WESLEY

A PASSAGE IN A LETTER FROM MY SISTER EMILY TO MR. M. BORRY, DATED APRIL 1

Tell my brother the spright was with us last night, and heard by many of our family, especially by our maid and myself. She sat up with drink, and it came just at one o'clock and opened the dining-room door. After some time it shut again. She saw as well as heard it both shut and open; then it began to knock as usual. But I dare write no longer, lest I should hear it.

EMILIA WESLEY

MY FATHER'S JOURNAL, OR DIARY, TRANSCRIBED BY MY BROTHER JACK, AUGUST 27, 1726, AND FROM HIM BY ME, FEBRUARY 7, 1730-1

An Account of Noises and Disturbances in my House at Epworth, Lincolnshire, in December and January 1716

From the 1st of December, my children and servants heard many strange noises, groans, knockings, etc., in every story and most of the rooms of my house, but I hearing nothing of it myself—they would not tell me for some time, because, according to the vulgar opinion, if it boded any ill to me I could not hear it. When it increased, and the family could not easily conceal it, they told me of it.

My daughters, Susannah and Ann, were below stairs in the dining-room, and heard first at the doors, then over their heads, and the night after a knocking under their feet, though nobody was in the chambers or below them. The like they and my servants heard in both the kitchens, at the door against the partition, and over them. The maid-servant heard groans as of a dying man. My daughter Emilia coming downstairs to draw up the clock and lock the doors at ten o'clock at night, as usual, heard under the staircase a sound among some bottles there, as if they had been all dashed to pieces; but when she looked, all was safe.

Something, like the steps of a man, was heard going up and downstairs at all hours of the night, and vast rumblings below stairs and in the garrets. My man, who lay in the garret, heard someone come slaring through the garret to his chamber, rattling by his side as if against his shoes, though he had none there; at other times walking up and downstairs, when all the house were in bed, and gobbling like a turkey-cock. Noises were heard in the nursery and all the other chambers; knocking first at the feet of the bed and behind it; and a sound like that of dancing in a matted chamber, next the nursery, when the door was locked and nobody in it.

My wife would have persuaded them it was rats within doors, and some unlucky people knocking without; till at last we heard several loud knocks in our own chamber, on my side of the bed; but till, I think, the 21st at night I heard nothing of it. That night I was waked a little before one by nine distinct very loud knocks, which seemed to be in the next room to ours, with a sort of pause at every third stroke. I thought it might be somebody without the house, and having got a stout mastiff, hoped he would soon rid me of it.

The next night I heard six knocks, but not so loud as the former. I know not whether it was in the morning after Sunday, the 23rd, when about seven my daughter Emily called her mother into the nursery, and told her she might now hear the noises there. She went in, and heard it at the bedsteads, and then under the beds, then at the head of it. She knocked, and it answered her. She looked under the bed, and thought something ran from thence, but could not well tell of what shape, but thought it most like a badger.

The next night but one we were awaked about one by the

noises, which were so violent it was in vain to think of sleep while they continued. I rose, but my wife would rise with me. We went into every chamber and downstairs; and generally as we went into one room, we heard it in that behind us, though all the family had been in bed several hours. When we were going downstairs, and at the bottom of them, we heard, as Emily had done before, a clashing among the bottles, as if they had been broke all to pieces, and another sound distinct from it, as if a piece of money had been thrown before us. The same, three of my daughters heard at another time.

We went through the hall into the kitchen, when our mastiff came whining to us, as he did always after the first night of its coming; for then he barked violently at it, but was silent afterwards, and seemed more afraid than any of the children. We still heard it rattle and thunder in every room above or behind us, locked as well as open, except my study, where as yet it never came. After two we went to bed, and were pretty quiet the rest of the night.

Wednesday night, December 26, after or a little before ten, my daughter Emilia heard the signal of its beginning to play, with which she was perfectly acquainted; it was like the strong winding up of a jack. She called us, and I went into the nursery where it used to be most violent. The rest of the children were asleep. It began with knocking in the kitchen underneath, then seemed to be at the bed's feet, then under the bed, and last at the head of it. I went downstairs, and knocked with my stick against the joists of the kitchen. It answered me as often and as loud as I knocked; but then I knocked, as I usually do, at my door, 1—23456—7, but this puzzled it, and it did not answer, or not in the same method, though the children heard it do the same twice or thrice after.

I went upstairs and found it still knocking hard, though with some respite, sometimes under the bed, sometimes at the bed's head. I observed my children that they were frightened in their sleep, and trembled very much till it waked them. I stayed there alone, bid them go to sleep, and sat at the bed's head by them, when the noise began again. I asked what it was, and why it disturbed innocent children, and did not come to me in my study if it had anything to say to me. Soon after it gave one knock on the outside of the house. All the rest were within, and knocked off for that night.

I went out of doors, sometimes alone, at others with company, and walked round the house, but could see or hear nothing. Several nights the latch of our lodging chamber would be lifted up very often when all were in bed. One night, when the noise was great in the kitchen, and on a deal partition, and the door in the yard, the latch whereof was often lifted up, my daughter Emilia went and held it fast on the inside, but it was still lifted up, and the door pushed violently against her, though nothing was to be seen on the outside.

When we were at prayers and came to the prayer for King George and the prince it would make a great noise over our heads constantly, whence some of the family called it a Jacobite. I have been thrice pushed by an invisible power, once against the corner of my desk in the study, a second time against the door of the matted chamber, a third time against the right side of the frame of my study door as I was going in.

I followed the noise into almost every room in the house, both by day and by night, with lights and without, and have sat alone for some time, and when I heard a noise, spoke to it to tell me what it was, but never heard any articulate voice, and only once or twice two or three feeble squeaks, a little louder than the chirping of a bird, but not like the noise of rats, which I have often heard.

I had designed on Friday, December the 28th, to make a visit to a friend, Mr. Downs, at Normandy, and stay some days with him, but the noises were so boisterous on Thursday night that I did not care to leave my family. So I went to Mr. Hoole of Haxey, and desired his company on Friday night. He came, and it began after ten, a little later than ordinary. The younger children were gone to bed, the rest of the family and Mr. Hoole were together in the matted chamber. I sent the servants down to fetch in some fuel, went with them, and staid in the kitchen till they came in. When they were gone I heard loud noises against the doors and partition, and at length the usual signal, though somewhat after the time. I had never heard it before, but knew it by the description my daughter had given me. It was much like the turning of a windmill when the wind changes. When the servants returned I went up to the company, who had heard the other noises below, but not the signal. We heard all the knockings as usual from one chamber to another, but at its going off, like the rubbing of a beast against the wall, but from that time till January the 24th we were quiet.

Having received a letter from Samuel the day before relating to it, I read what I had written of it to my family, and this day at morning prayer the family heard the usual knocks at the prayer for the king. At night they were more distinct, both in the prayer for the king and that for the prince, and one very loud knock at the *amen* was heard by my wife and most of my children at the inside of my bed. I heard nothing myself. After nine, Robert Brown, sitting alone by the fire in the back kitchen, saw something come out of the copper-hole like a rabbit, but less, and turned round five times very swiftly. Its ears lay flat upon its neck, and its little scut stood straight up. He ran after it with the tongs in his hands, but when he could find nothing he was frighted, and went to the maid in the parlour.

On Friday, the 25th, having prayers at church, I shortened as usual those in the family at morning, omitting the confession, absolution, and prayers for the king and prince. I observed when this is done there is no knocking. I therefore used them one morning for a trial; at the name of King George it began to knock, and did the same when I prayed for the prince. Two knocks I heard, but took no notice after prayers, till after all who were in the room, ten persons besides me, spoke of it, and said they heard it. No noise at all at the rest of the prayers.

Sunday, January 27.—Two soft strokes at the morning prayers for King George above stairs.

ADDENDA TO AND FROM MY FATHER'S DIARY

Friday, December 21.—Knocking I heard first, I think, this night; to which disturbances, I hope, God will in His good time put an end.

Sunday, December 23.—Not much disturbed with the noises that are now grown customary to me.

EPWORTH RECTORY

Wednesday, December 26.—Sat up to hear noises. Strange! spoke to it, knocked off.

Friday 28.—The noises very boisterous and disturbing this night.

Saturday 29.—Not frighted with the continued disturbances of my family.

Tuesday, January 1, 1717.—My family have had no disturbance since I went.

MEMORANDUM OF JACK'S

The first time my mother ever heard any unusual noise at Epworth was long before the disturbance of Old Jeffery. My brother, lately come from London, had one evening a sharp quarrel with my sister Suky, at which time my mother happened to be above in her own chamber, the door and windows rung and jarred very loud, and presently several distinct strokes, three by three, were struck. From that night it never failed to give notice in much the same manner against any signal misfortune or illness of any belonging to the family.

SUMMARY OF THE PHENOMENA

Of the general circumstances which follow, most, if not all, the Family were frequent Witnesses

1. Presently after any noise was heard the wind commonly rose, and whistled very loud round the house, and increased with it.

2. The signal was given, which my father likens to the turning round of a windmill when the wind changes; Mr. Hoole (Rector of Haxey) to the planing of deal boards; my sister, to the swift winding up of a jack. It commonly began at the corner of the top of the nursery.

3. Before it came into any room the latches were frequently lifted up, the windows clattered, and whatever iron or brass was about the chamber rung and jarred exceedingly.

4. When it was in any room, let them make what noise they would, as they sometimes did on purpose, its dead, hollow note would be closely heard above them all.

5. It constantly knocked while the prayers for the king and prince were repeating, and was plainly heard by all in the room but my father, and sometimes by him, as were also the thundering knocks at the *amen*.

6. The sound very often seemed in the air in the middle of a room, nor could they ever make any such themselves by any contrivance.

7. Though it seemed to rattle down the pewter, to clap the doors, draw the curtains, kick the man's shoes up and down, etc., yet it never moved anything except the latches, otherwise than making it tremble; unless once, when it threw open the nursery door.

8. The mastiff, though he barked violently at it the first day he came, yet whenever it came after that, nay, sometimes before the family perceived it, he ran whining, or quite silent, to shelter himself behind some of the company.

9. It never came by day till my mother ordered the horn to be blown.

10. After that time scarce any one would go from one room into another but the latch of the room they went to was lifted up before they touched it.

11. It never came once into my father's study till he talked to it sharply, called it *deaf and dumb devil*, and bid it cease to disturb the innocent children, and come to him in his study if it had anything to say to him.

12. From the time of my mother desiring it not to disturb her from five to six, it was never heard in her chamber from five till she came downstairs, nor at any other time when she was employed in devotion.

13. Whether our clock went right or wrong, it always came as near as could be guessed when by the night it wanted a quarter of ten.

EPWORTH RECTORY

STATEMENTS SUPPLIED TO JOHN WESLEY

MRS. SAMUEL WESLEY'S STATEMENT TO HER SON JOHN

August 27, 1726

About ten days after Nanny Marshall had heard unusual groans at the dining-room door, Emily came and told me that the servants and children had been several times frighted with strange groans and knockings about the house. I answered that the rats John Maw had frighted from his house by blowing a horn there were come into ours, and ordered that one should be sent for. Molly was much displeased at it, and said, if it was anything supernatural, it certainly would be very angry and more troublesome. However, the horn was blown in the garrets; and the effect was, that whereas before the noises were always in the night, from this time they were heard at all hours, day and night.

Soon after, about seven in the morning, Emily came and desired me to go into the nursery, where I should be convinced they were not startled at nothing. On my coming thither I heard a knocking at the feet, and quickly after at the head of the bed. I desired if it was a spirit it would answer me, and knocking several times with my foot on the ground with several pauses, it repeated under the sole of my feet exactly the same number of strokes, with the very same intervals. Kezzy, then six or seven years old, said, let it answer me too if it can, and stamping, the same sounds were returned that she made, many times, successively.

Upon my looking under the bed something ran out pretty much like a badger and seemed to run directly underneath Emily's petticoats, who sat opposite to me on the other side. I went out, and one or two nights afterwards, when we were just got to bed, I heard nine strokes, three by three, on the other side of the bed, as if one had struck violently on a chest with a large stick. Mr. Wesley leapt up, called Hetty, who alone was up in the house, and searched every room in the house, but to no purpose. It continued from this time to knock and groan frequently at all hours, day and night; only I earnestly desired it might not disturb me between five and six in the evening, and there never was any noise in my room after during that time.

At other times I have often heard it over my mantel tree, and once, coming up after dinner, a cradle seemed to be strongly rocked in my chamber. When I went in the sound seemed to be in the nursery. When I was in the nursery it seemed to be in my chamber again. One night Mr. W. and I were waked by some one running down the garret stairs, then down the broad stairs, then up the narrow ones, then up the garret stairs, then down again, and so the same round. The rooms trembled as it passed along, and the doors shook exceedingly, so that the clattering of the latches was very loud.

Mr. W. proposing to rise, I rose with him, and went down the broad stairs, hand in hand, to light a candle. Near the foot of them a large pot of money seemed to be poured out at my waist, and to run jingling down my nightgown to my feet. Presently after we heard the noise as of a vast stone thrown among several dozen of bottles which lay under the stairs, but upon our looking no hurt was done. In the hall the mastiff met us, crying, and striving to get between us. We returned up into the nursery, where the noise was very great. The children were all asleep, but panting, trembling, and sweating extremely.

Shortly after, on Mr. Wesley's invitation, Mr Hoole staid a night with us. As we were all sitting round the fire in the matted chamber, he asked whether that gentle knocking was *it*. I told him yes, and it continued the sound, which was much lower than usual. This was observable whilst we were talking loud in the same room; the noise, seemingly lower than any of our voices, was distinctly heard above them all. These were the most remarkable passages I remember, except such as were common to all the family.

MISS EMILY WESLEY'S ACCOUNT TO HER BROTHER JOHN

About a fortnight after the time when, as I was told, the noises were heard, I went from my mother's room, who had just gone to bed, to the best chamber to fetch my sister Suky's candle. When I was there the windows and doors began to jar and ring exceedingly, and presently after I heard a sound in the kitchen, as if a vast stone coal had been thrown down and mashed to pieces. I went down thither with my candle, and found nothing more than usual; but as I was going by the screen, something began knocking on the other side, just even with my head. When I looked on the inside, the knocking was on the outside of it; but as soon as I could get round, it was at the inside again. I followed it to and fro several times, till at last, finding it to no purpose, and turning about to go away, before I was out of the room the latch of the back kitchen door was lifted up many times. I opened the door and looked out, but could see nobody. I tried to shut the door, but it was thrust against me, and I could feel the latch, which I held in my hand, moving upwards at the same time. I looked out again, but finding it was labour lost, clapped the door to and locked it. Immediately the latch was moved strongly up and down, but I left it, and went up the worst stairs, from whence I heard as if a great stone had been thrown among the bottles, which lay under the best stairs. However, I went to bed.

From this time I heard it every night for two or three weeks. It continued a month in its full majesty night and day. Then it intermitted a fortnight or more, and when it began again it knocked only on nights, and grew less and less troublesome, till at last it went quite away. Towards the latter end it used to knock on the outside of the house, and seemed farther and farther off, till it ceased to be heard at all.

MOLLY WESLEY'S ACCOUNT TO HER BROTHER JOHN

August 27

I have always thought it was in November, the rest of our family think it was the 1st of December 1716, when Nanny Marshall, who had a bowl of butter in her hand, ran to me and two or three more of my sisters in the dining-room, and told us she had heard several groans in the hall as of a dying man. We thought it was Mr. Turpine, who had the stone, and used sometimes to come and see us. About a fortnight after, when my sister Suky and I were going to bed, she told us how she was frightened in the dining-room the day before by a noise, first at the folding-door, and then overhead. I was reading at the table, and had scarce told her I believed nothing of it, when several knocks were given just under my feet. We both made haste into bed, and just as we laid down the warming-pan by the bedside jarred and rung, as did the latch of the door, which was lifted slowly up and down; presently a great chain seemed to fall on the outside of the door (we were in the best chamber), the door latch hinges, the warming-pan, and windows jarred, and the house shook from top to bottom.

A few days after, between five and six in the evening, I was by myself in the dining-room. The door seemed to open, though it was still shut, and somebody walked in, a nightgown trailing upon the ground (nothing appearing), and seemed to go leisurely round me. I started up and ran upstairs to my mother's chamber, and told the story to her and my sister Emily. A few nights after my father ordered me to light him to his study. Just as he had unlocked it the latch was lifted up for him. The same (after we blew the horn) was often done to me, as well by day as by night. Of many other things all the family as well as me were witnesses.

My father went into the nursery from the matted chamber, where we were, by himself in the dark. It knocked very loud on the press bed head. He adjured it to tell him why it came, but it seemed to take no notice; at which he was very angry, spoke sharply, called it *deaf and dumb devil*, and repeated his adjuration. My sisters were terribly afraid it would speak. When he had done, it knocked his knock on the bed's head so exceedingly violently, as if it would break it to shivers, and from that time we heard nothing till near a month after.

SUSANNAH WESLEY'S ACCOUNT TO HER BROTHER JOHN

I believed nothing of it till about a fortnight after the first noises, then one night I sat up on purpose to hear it. While I was working in the best chamber, and earnestly desiring to hear it, a knocking began just under my feet. As I knew the room below me was locked I was frighted, and leaped into bed with all my clothes on. I afterwards heard, as it were, a great chain fall, and after some time the usual noises at all hours of the day and night. One night, hearing it was most violent in the nursery, I resolved to lie there. Late at night several strong knocks were given on the two lowest steps of the garret stairs, which were close to the nursery door. The latch of the door then jarred, and seemed to be swiftly moved to and fro, and presently began knocking about a yard within the room on the floor. It then came gradually to sister Hetty's bed, who trembled strongly in her sleep. It beat very loud three strokes at a time on the bed's head. My father came and adjured it to speak, but it knocked on for some time, and then removed to the room over, where it knocked my father's knock on the ground, as if it would beat the house down. I had no mind to stay longer, but got up and went to sister Em and my mother, who were in her room, from whence he heard the noises again from the nursery. I proposed playing a game of cards, but we had scarce begun when a knocking began under our feet. We left off playing, and it removed back again into the nursery, where it continued till towards morning.

NANCY WESLEY'S ACCOUNT TO HER BROTHER JOHN, AS RECORDED BY SAMUEL WESLEY

September 10

The first noise my sister Nancy heard was in the best chamber with my sister Molly and my sister Suky; soon after my father had ordered her to blow a horn in the garrets, where it was knocking violently. She was terribly afraid, being obliged to go in the dark, and kneeling down on the stairs desired that, as she acted not to please herself, it might have no power over her. As soon as she came into the room the noise ceased, nor did it begin again till near ten; but then, and for a good while, it made much greater and more frequent noises than it had done before. When she afterwards came into the chamber in the day time it commonly walked after her from room to room. It followed her from one side of the bed to the other and back again, as often as she went back, and whatever she did which made any sort of noise, the same thing seemed just to be done behind her.

EPWORTH RECTORY

When five or six were set in the nursery together a cradle would seem to be strongly rocked in the room over, though no cradle had ever been there. One night she was sitting on the press bed playing at cards with some of my sisters, when my sisters Molly, Hetty, Patty, and Kezzy were in the room, and Robert Brown. The bed on which my sister Nancy sat was lifted up with her on it. She leaped down and said, 'Surely Old Jeffery would not run away with her.' However, they persuaded her to sit down again, which she had scarce done when it was again lifted up several times successively a considerable height, upon which she left her seat and would not be prevailed upon to sit there any more.

Whenever they began to mention Mr. S. it presently began to knock, and continued to do so till they changed the discourse. All the time my sister Suky was writing her last letter to him it made a very great noise all round the room, and the night after she set out for London it knocked till morning with scarce any intermission.

Mr. Hoole read prayers once, but it knocked as usual at the prayers for the king and prince. The knockings at these prayers were only towards the beginning of the disturbance, for a week or thereabouts.

THE REV. MR. HOOLE'S[1] ACCOUNT

September 16

As soon as I came to Hepworth, Mr. Wesley telling me he sent for me to conjure, I knew not what he meant, till some of your sisters told me what had happened, and that I was sent for to sit up. I expected every hour to hear something extraordinary, but to no purpose. At supper too, and at prayers, all was silent, contrary to custom; but soon after one of the maids, who went up to sheet a bed, brought down the alarm that Jeffery was come above stairs. We all went up, and as we were standing round the fire in the east chamber something began knocking just on the other side of the wall, on the chimneypiece, as with a key. Presently the knocking was under our feet. Mr. Wesley and I went down, he with a great deal of hope, and

[1] Vicar of Haxey.

EPWORTH RECTORY

I with fear. As soon as we were in the kitchen the sound was above us, in the room we had left. We returned up the narrow stairs, and heard, at the broad stairs head, some one slaring with their feet (all the family being now in bed beside us) and then trailing, as it were, and rustling with a silk nightgown. Quickly it was in the nursery, at the bed's head, knocking as it had done at first, three by three. Mr. Wesley spoke to it and said he believed it was the devil, and soon after it knocked at the window, and changed its sound into one like the planing of boards. From thence it went on the outward south side of the house, sounding fainter and fainter, till it was heard no more.

I was at no other time than this during the noises at Epworth, and do not now remember any more circumstances than these.

[NOTE BY JOHN WESLEY]

Epworth, September 1

My sister Kezzy says she remembers nothing else, but that it knocked my father's knock, ready to beat the house down in the nursery one night.

ROBIN BROWN'S ACCOUNT TO JOHN WESLEY, AS RECORDED BY SAMUEL WESLEY

The first time Robin Brown, my father's man, heard it, was when he was fetching down some corn from the garrets. Something knocked on a door just by him, which made him run away downstairs. From that time it used frequently to visit him in bed, walking up the garret stairs, and in the garrets, like a man in jack-boots, with a nightgown trailing after him, then lifting up his latch and making it jar, and making presently a noise in his room like the gobbling of a turkey-cock, then stumbling over his boots or shoes by the bedside. He was resolved once to be too hard for it, and so took a large mastiff we had just got to bed with him, and left his shoes and boots below stairs; but he might as well have spared his labour, for it was exactly the same thing whether any were there or no. The same sound was heard as if there had been forty pairs. The dog indeed was no great comfort to him, for as soon as the latch began to jar he crept into bed, made such a howling and barking together, in spite of all the man could do, that he alarmed most of the family.

Soon after, being grinding corn in the garrets, and happening to stop a little, the handle of the mill was turned round with great swiftness. He said nothing vexed him but that the mill was empty. If corn had been in it, Old Jeffery might have ground his heart out for him; he would never have disturbed him.

One night, being ill, he was leaning his head upon the back kitchen chimney (the jam he called it) with the tongs in his hands, when from behind the oven's top, which lay by the fire, something came out like a white rabbit. It turned round before him several times, and then ran to the same place again. He was frighted, started up, and ran with the tongs into the parlour (dining-room).

Epworth, August 31

Betty Massy one day came to me in the parlour and asked me if I had heard Old Jeffery, for she said she thought there was no such thing. When we had talked a little about it, I knocked three times with a reel I had in my hand against the dining-room ceiling, and the same were presently repeated. She desired me to knock so again, which I did, but they were answered with three more so violently as shook the house, though no one was in the chamber over us. She prayed me to knock no more for fear it should come in to us.

Epworth, August 31, 1726

John and Kitty Maw, who lived over against us, listened several nights in the time of the disturbance, but could never hear anything.

EPWORTH RECTORY

NARRATIVE DRAWN UP BY JOHN WESLEY, AND PUBLISHED BY HIM IN 'THE ARMINIAN MAGAZINE'

When I was very young I heard several letters read, wrote to my elder brother by my father, giving an account of strange disturbances which were in his house at Epworth, in Lincolnshire.

When I went down thither, in the year 1720, I carefully enquired into the particulars. I spoke to each of the persons who were then in the house, and took down what each could testify of his or her knowledge. The sum of which was this:

On December 2, 1716, while Robert Brown, my father's servant, was sitting with one of the maids a little before ten at night in the dining-room, which opened into the garden, they both heard knocking at the door. Robert rose and opened it, but could see nobody. Quickly it knocked again and groaned. 'It is Mr. Turpine,' said Robert. 'He has the stone, and uses to groan so.' We opened the door again twice or thrice, the knocking being twice or thrice repeated. But still seeing nothing, and being a little startled, they rose and went to bed. When Robert came to the top of the garret stairs he saw a hand-mill, which was at a little distance, whirled about very swiftly. When he related all this he said, 'Nought vexed me but that it was empty. I thought if it had been full of malt he might have ground out his heart for me.' When he was in bed he heard, as it were, the gobbling of a turkey-cock close to the bedside; and soon after the sound of one stumbling over his shoes and boots, but there were none there; he had left them below. The next day he and the maid related these things to the other maid, who laughed heartily and said, 'What a couple of fools are you! I defy anything to fright me.' After churning in the evening she put the butter in the tray, and had no sooner carried it into the dairy than she heard a knocking on the shelf where several puncheons of milk stood, first above the shelf and then below; she took the candle and searched both above and below; but being able to find nothing, threw down butter, tray, and all, and ran away for life. The next evening between five and six o'clock, my sister, Molly, then about twenty years of age, sitting in the dining-room reading, heard as it were the door that led into the hall open and a person walking in, that seemed to have on a silk nightgown, rustling and trailing along. It seemed to walk round her, then to the door, then round again; but she could see nothing. She thought 'It signifies nothing to run away; for whatever it is, it can run faster than me.' Presently a knocking began under the table. She took the candle and looked, but could find nothing. Then the iron casement began to clatter and the lid of a warming-pan. Next the latch of the door moved up and down without ceasing. She started up, leaped into her bed without undressing, pulled the bed-clothes over her head, and never ventured to look up till next morning. A night or two after, my sister Hetty, a year younger than my sister Molly, was waiting as usual, between nine and ten, to take away my father's candle, when she heard someone coming down the garret stairs, walking slowly by her, then going down the best stairs, then up the back stairs, and up the garret stairs. And at every step it seemed the house shook from top to bottom. Just then my father knocked. She went in, took his candle, and got to bed as fast as possible. She told this to my eldest sister in the morning, who told her, 'You know, I believe none of these things. Pray let me take away the candle to-night and I will find out the trick.' She accordingly took my sister Hetty's place, and had no sooner taken away the candle than she heard a noise below. She hastened downstairs to the hall where the noise was. But it was then in the kitchen. She ran into the kitchen, where it was drumming on the inside of the screen. When she went round it was drumming on the outside, and so always on the side opposite to her. Then she heard a knocking at the back kitchen door. She ran to it, unlocked it softly, and when the knocking was repeated, suddenly opened it; but nothing was to be seen. As soon as she had shut it the knocking began again; she opened it again, but could see nothing; when she went to shut the door it was violently thrust against her; she let it fly open, but nothing appeared. She went again to shut it, and it was again thrust against her; but she set her knee and her shoulder to the door, forced it to, and turned the key. Then the knocking began again; but she let it go on, and went up to bed. However, from that time she was thoroughly convinced that there was no imposture in the affair.

The next morning my sister, telling my mother what had happened, she said, 'If I hear anything myself, I shall know how to judge.' Soon after she begged her to come into the nursery. She did, and heard in the corner of the room, as it were, the violent rocking of a cradle, but no cradle had been there for some years. She was convinced it was preternatural, and earnestly prayed it might not disturb her in her own chamber at the hours of retirement; and it never did. She now thought it was proper to tell my father. But he was extremely angry, and said, 'Suky, I am ashamed of you; these boys and girls frighten one another, but you are a woman of sense and should know better. Let me hear of it no more.' At six in the evening he had family prayers as usual. When he began the prayer for the king, a knocking began all round the room, and a thundering knock attended the 'Amen'. The same was heard from this time every morning and evening while the prayer for the king was repeated. As both my father and mother are now at rest and incapable of being pained thereby, I think it my duty to furnish the serious reader with a key to this circumstance.

The year before King William died my father observed my mother did not say 'Amen' to the prayer for the king. She said she could not, for she did not believe the Prince of Orange was king. He vowed he would never cohabit with her till she did. He then took his horse and rode away, nor did she hear anything of him for a twelvemonth. He then came back and lived with her as before. But I fear his vow was not forgotten before God.

Being informed that Mr. Hoole, the vicar of Haxey (an eminently pious and sensible man), could give me some further information, I walked over to him. He said, 'Robert Brown came over to me and told me your father desired my company. When I came he gave me an account of all that had happened,

EPWORTH RECTORY

particularly the knocking during family prayer. But that evening (to my great satisfaction) we had no knocking at all. But between nine and ten a servant came in and said, "Old Ferries is coming" (that was the name of one that died in the house), "for I hear the signal." This they informed us was heard every night about a quarter before ten. It was toward the top of the house on the outside, at the north-east corner, resembling the loud creaking of a saw, or rather that of a windmill when the body of it is turned about in order to shift the sails to the wind. We then heard a knocking over our heads, and Mr. Wesley, catching up a candle, said, "Come, sir, you shall now hear for yourself." We went upstairs, he with much hope, and I (to say the truth) with much fear. When we came into the nursery it was knocking in the next room; when we were there it was knocking in the nursery. And there it continued to knock, though we came in, particularly at the head of the bed (which was of wood) in which Miss Hetty and two of her younger sisters lay. Mr. Wesley, observing that they were much affected, though asleep, sweating and trembling exceedingly, was very angry, and, pulling out a pistol, was going to fire at the place from whence the sound came. But I catched him by the arm and said, "Sir, you are convinced this is something preternatural. If so, you cannot hurt it, but you give it power to hurt you." He then went close to the place and said sternly, "Thou deaf and dumb devil, why dost thou frighten these children that cannot answer for themselves? Come to me to my study that am a man!" Instantly it knocked his knock (the particular knock which he always used at the gate) as if it would shiver the board in pieces, and we heard nothing more that night.' Till this time my father had never heard the least disturbance in his study. But the next evening, as he attempted to go out into this study (of which none had any key but himself), when he opened the door it was thrust back with such violence as had like to have thrown him down. However, he thrust the door open and went in. Presently there was knocking, first on one side, then on the other, and after a time in the next room, wherein my sister Nancy was. He went into that room, and (the noise continuing) adjured it to speak; but in vain. He then said, 'These spirits love darkness; put out the candle, and perhaps it will speak.' She did so, and he repeated his adjuration; but still there was only knocking, and no articulate sound. Upon this he said, 'Nancy, two Christians are an overmatch for the devil. Go all of you downstairs; it may be when I am alone he will have courage to speak.' When she was gone a thought came in and he said, 'If thou are the spirit of my son Samuel, I pray, knock three knocks and no more.' Immediately all was silence, and there was no more knocking at all that night. I asked my sister Nancy (then about fifteen years old) whether she was not afraid when my father used that adjuration? She answered she was sadly afraid it would speak when she put out the candle; but she was not at all afraid in the daytime, when it walked after her, as she swept the chambers, as it constantly did, and seemed to sweep after her. Only she thought it might have done it for her, and saved her the trouble. By this time all my sisters were so accustomed to these noises that they gave them little disturbance. A gentle tapping at their bed head usually began between nine and ten at night. They then commonly said to each other, 'Jeffery is coming, it is time to go to sleep.' And if they heard a noise in the day and said to my youngest sister, 'Hark, Kezzy, Jeffery is knocking above,' she would run upstairs, and pursue it from room to room, saying she desired no better diversion.

A few nights after, my father and mother were just gone to bed, and the candle was not taken away, when they heard three blows and a second, and a third three, as it were with a large oaken staff, struck upon a chest which stood by the bedside. My father immediately arose, put on his nightgown, and hearing great noises below, took the candle and went down; my mother walked by his side. As they went down the broad stairs they heard as if a vessel full of silver was poured upon my mother's breast and ran jingling down to her feet. Quickly after there was a sound, as if a large iron ball was thrown among many bottles under the stairs; but nothing was hurt. Soon after, our large mastiff dog came and ran to shelter himself between them. While the disturbances continued he used to bark and leap, and snap on one side and the other, and that frequently before any person in the room heard any noise at all. But after two or three days he used to tremble and creep

EPWORTH RECTORY

away before the noise began. And by this the family knew it was at hand, nor did the observation ever fail. A little before my father and mother came into the hall it seemed as if a very large coal was violently thrown upon the floor and dashed all to pieces, but nothing was seen. My father then cried out, 'Suky, do you not hear? All the pewter is thrown about the kitchen.' But when they looked all the pewter was in its place. Then there was a loud knocking at the back door. My father opened it, but saw nothing. It was then at the front door. He opened that, but it was still lost labour. After opening first the one and then the other several times he turned and went up to bed. But the noises were so violent all over the house that he could not sleep till four in the morning.

Several gentlemen and clergymen now earnestly advised my father to quit the house. But he constantly answered, 'No, let the devil flee from me; I will never flee from the devil.' But he wrote to my eldest brother at London to come down. He was preparing to do so when another letter came, informing him that the disturbances were over, after they had continued (the latter part of the time day and night) from the 2nd of December to the end of January.

2. THE HAUNTING OF WILLINGTON MILL

Reprinted from No. XCV, Vol. V, December 1892, of the 'Journal of the Society for Psychical Research'

MR. JOSEPH PROCTER'S DIARY

The 'Haunted House at Willington' has been a familiar theme on Tyneside for half a century, and the general public have been made acquainted with it in William Howitt's *Visits to Remarkable Places*, Catherine Crowe's *Night Side of Nature*, *The Local Historian's Table Book*, Stead's *Ghost Stories*, and other publications. I was myself born in this 'haunted house', and have vivid recollections of many singular occurrences. As my parents, however, ceased to reside there when I was but a child of seven, any evidence of my own can be but of trifling value. On my father's death in 1875, a diary that he had kept almost from the outset of the disturbances, and during many years of their occurrence, was found among his papers. The publication of this diary has been delayed for two reasons: first, my mother's objection to their publicity during her lifetime: secondly, because the manuscript breaks off suddenly, and I have long hoped, but in vain, to find the continuation and conclusion. To such readers as were not personally acquainted with the writer of this diary I may briefly state that he was a member of the Society of Friends, belonging to a family which had been attached members of that body from its very foundation. During many years he was an 'overseer' or 'elder', and was frequently appointed to offices of trust in church matters. Like many other Quakers, he took an active interest in the

Peace Society, the Anti-Slavery Society, and other philanthropic organizations. He was also among the earliest teetotallers in the north of England.

His reading was fairly extensive, the *Quarterly* and *Edinburgh* being sandwiched with *George Fox's Journal* and the old *Examiner*, and Ebenezer Elliot taken alternately with some French author or the *British Friend*. I mention these details solely to place outsiders in a position to judge of the character and the reliability of the writer of the diary, and will only add my own testimony that a man with a more delicate sense of what it means to speak the truth I have yet to meet.

It only remains to add that throughout the narrative 'J.P.' stands for my father himself, and 'E.P.' for my mother, and that the paragraphs between brackets are my own additions. The earliest statement I can find is the following, in his own handwriting:

'Particulars relating to some unaccountable noises heard in the house of J. and E. Procter, Willington Mill, which began about three months prior to the present time, viz., 1 mo. 28th, 1835, still continuing, and for which no adequate natural cause has hitherto been discovered.

'About six weeks ago the nursemaid first told her mistress of the state of dread and alarm she was kept in, in consequence of noises she had heard for about two months, occurring more particularly nearly every evening when left alone to watch the child [my eldest brother, then about two years old] to sleep in the nursery, a room on the second floor; she declared she distinctly heard a dull heavy tread on the boarded floor of the unoccupied room above, commonly pacing backwards and forwards, and, on coming over the window, giving the floor such a shake as to cause the window of the nursery to rattle violently in its frame. This disturbance generally lasted ten minutes at a time, and though she did not heed it at first, yet she was now persuaded it was supernatural, and "it quite overset her". The latter was indeed evident from the agitation she manifested.

'The kitchen girl said that the nursemaid had called her upstairs sometimes when frightened in this manner, and that she had found her trembling much and very pale. On examining her further in reference to this improbable tale, she did not vary in her statement, but on searching the rooms above and finding nothing to cause such results, but little credit was attached to the story.

'Before many days had elapsed, however, every member of the family had witnessed precisely what the girl described, and from that time to the present, nearly every day, and sometimes several times in the day, the same has been heard by one or more of the inmates, varying unimportantly in the nature of the sound. A few particular instances may here be selected, in which imagination or fear could have no influence.

'On sixth day, 1st month 23rd, 1835, my wife had in the forenoon requested one of the servants to sweep out the disturbed room in the course of the day, and being herself in the nursery [the room below] after dinner, heard a noise in the room like a person stirring about, which she took for granted was the maid cleaning out the chamber, when, to her surprise, she afterwards found that neither of the girls had been upstairs at all. The next day one of the maids, being in the nursery, supposed, from the noise she heard, that the other was lighting a fire in the room above, as had been desired, which proved a similar mistake to that on the preceding day. It may be remarked that the nursemaid first mentioned had left, and another engaged, from whom the affair was carefully concealed. A day or two after her arrival the noise was observed by her fellow servant whilst they were together in the nursery, but she apparently did not observe it herself, from her companion talking and using the rocking-chair. Later, however, the same evening it began suddenly when she was present, and she, somewhat alarmed, inquired who or what was in the room above.

'On First day, the 25th, being kept at home by indisposition, my wife was in the nursery about eleven o'clock in the forenoon, and heard on the floor above, about the centre of the room, a step as of a man with a strong shoe or boot going towards the window and returning. The same day, when we were at dinner, the maid, being with the child in the nursery, heard the same heavy tread for about five minutes; she came into the sitting-room to satisfy herself that her master was there, thinking it must have been he who was upstairs. The following day the dull sound was resumed, and up to this day the boots have not done duty again. It may be noted that frequently the room has been examined immediately after the occurrence of the noise; it has been sat in, in one instance slept in all night, and in every case nothing has been elicited. Several of our friends who have waited to hear the invisible disturber have all, with one exception, been disappointed.

'My brother, John Richardson Procter,[1] remained in the room below some time after the usual period of operation, fruitlessly, but within ten minutes of his departure the nurse was so terrified by the loudness of its onset that she ran downstairs with the child half asleep in her arms. My cousin, Mary Unthank, stayed two nights and was much in the room without being gratified. All the persons who have heard, and six have been so far privileged, are confident that the noise is within the room on the third floor, as the precise part of the floor above on which the impression is made is clearly distinguishable through the ceiling below, and the weight apparently laid on, shaking violently the window in the room below, when no other window in the house is affected, and during a dead calm, is of itself a proof of this.

'It seems impossible there can be any trick in the case; there is a garret above, and the roof is inaccessible from without; the house stands alone, and during most of the time the window was built up with lath and plaster, whilst the only other communication with the outside, by the chimney, was closed by a fireboard which was so covered over with soot as to prove that not a pebble or a mouse had passed. The room is devoid of furniture, and for some time the door was nailed up. Not a rat has been seen in the house for years, nor at any time anything heard like a scratch or squeak, or running between the floor and ceiling; nor, it is conceived, could a hundred rats so shake the floor by their weight as to cause the window below to rattle as it does.

'The noise has been heard at every hour of the day, though oftenest in the evening, rarely in the night; has no connection with weather nor with the going of the mill; [the mill was

---

[1] A portrait and biographical notice of this brother will be found in *Quaker Records*, by Mrs. A. O. Boyce.

WILLINGTON MILL

contiguous, but there was a road between it and the house] in short, it is difficult to imagine a natural cause having a shadow of pretension to belief.

'Those who deem all intrusion from the world of spirits impossible in the present constitution of things will feel assured that a natural solution of the difficulty will still be obtained on further investigation; whilst those who believe with the poet "that millions of spiritual creatures walk the earth unseen", and that, even in modern times, amidst a thousand creations of fancy, fear, fraud, or superstition, there still remain some well-attested instances in which good or evil spirits have manifested their presence by sensible tokens, will probably deem it possible that this may be referred to the latter class—especially when they learn that several circumstances tending to corroborate such a view are withheld from this narrative.

[Whether the 'several circumstances withheld' are disclosed in the written narratives which follow I am unable to say. I find the following consecutive:]

'Additional particulars relating to unaccountable noises, &c., heard at Willington Mill, containing the most remarkable from first month 25th, to the present time, second month 18th, 1835.

'On the First day night, the 31st of first month, soon after retiring to bed, before going to sleep, my wife and I both heard ten or twelve obtuse deadened beats as of a mallet on a block of wood, apparently within two feet of the bed curtain, on one side by the crib in which the child was laid. The next night, before undressing, I had hushed the child asleep in his crib, and while leaning over it with one hand laid upon it and listening to some indistinct sounds overhead, which had just ceased, I heard a tap on the cradle leg as with a piece of steel, and distinctly felt the vibration of the wood in my hand from the blow. This might be a sudden crack, not unfrequent when wood is drying in, but it sounded like a knock on the outside. Since this time the walking in the empty room has not been heard oftener than twice or thrice, of which this afternoon was the last time.

'On the same evening I heard that Thomas Mann, the foreman of the mill—a man of strict integrity and veracity, who

WILLINGTON MILL

has been two years in Unthank and Procter's employ—had heard something remarkable, and on questioning him elicited the following statement. It may be premised that U. and P. have a wooden cistern on iron wheels to bring water for their horses, which stands in the mill yard. When in motion, drawn by a horse to be filled, it makes a very peculiar noise which may be heard a considerable distance, especially when the wheels want greasing, and by any person accustomed to it the noise of its going could not be mistaken for that of any other vehicle. The mill was going all night, and T. M.'s place was to attend the engine till 2 a.m. Going out to fill the barrow with coals about one o'clock, he heard this machine, as he thought, going along the yard, which did not at the moment strike him as out of the usual course; but remembering the hour, the apprehension that it was being stolen flashed on his mind; it was creaking excessively, from want of oil as might be supposed, and was then drawing near the yard gates, towards which he pursued after it, when, to his astonishment, he found it had never stirred from its place near where he at first was, and looking round everywhere all was still and not a creature to be found. He afterwards searched round the premises with a lantern but descried nothing. He was much puzzled, but it was not till the next day that he felt himself compelled to attribute the phenomenon to a supernatural cause.

'More than once I have, on coming through the garden at night, heard a sound like someone stepping down the gravel walk and have not been able to discover anyone. This step on the gravel has been heard by one or two others, but nothing seen.

'On First day, 2 mo., 15th [1835], my wife and I were informed by our cousin Unthanks that they understood that the house, and that room in particular in which the noises now occurred, was said to be haunted before they entered it in 1806, but that nothing that they knew of had been heard during their occupancy of 25 years.

[On the same page as the above, and in my father's handwriting, is the following memorandum below the above recital; there is a line drawn through them, however, whether by myself I am unable to say, and the sentence is apparently unfinished:]

'An infirm old woman, the mother-in-law of R. Oxon, the

WILLINGTON MILL

builder of the premises, lived and died in the house, and after her death the haunting was attributed——

[I have heard my father speak of this circumstance, but the evidence appeared to be of a slight and hearsay character.

I find the following occurrence described on a separate sheet of paper, but believe, although it is not dated, that this is the correct sequence of the manuscript. I have myself heard all the particulars from the lips of all the parties concerned, which completely agreed with this account in my father's handwriting.]

'For about two months previously there had rarely been 24 hours without indications by noises, &c., not in any other way accountable, of the presence of the ghostly visitant, to some or all of the inmates. A few days previously a respectable neighbour had seen a transparent white female figure in a window in the second storey of the house. On the 13th of last month (November), early in the evening, two of the children in the house, one aged about 8, the other under two years, both saw, unknown to each other, an object which could not be real, and which went into the room where the apparition was afterwards seen, and disappeared there. A near connection of the family on a visit [my mother's sister], but for whom, for obvious reasons, a lodging was obtained at the house of Thomas Mann (the foreman of the flour mill adjoining and much respected by his employers), went out as usual to sleep about 9.30 p.m. Soon after going to her bedroom T. M.'s wife went out of the house for some coals, and was struck with a figure in the window previously referred to [nothing being between the two houses but a kitchen garden and a road]; she called her husband, who saw the same figure passing backwards and forwards and then standing still in the window. It was very luminous and likewise transparent, and had the appearance of a priest in a white surplice. T. M. then called out the relative of the family and his own daughter. When they came the head was nearly gone and the brightness somewhat abated, but it was fully ten minutes before it quite disappeared by fading gradually downwards. Both when standing and moving it was about 3 feet from the floor of the room. T. M. went down close under the window, and also went to inform the inmates of the

WILLINGTON MILL

circumstance, but finding they had locked-up for the night did not accomplish it. It was a dark night, without a moon, and there was not a ray of light, nor any person anywhere near the house. The window blind was close down, and the figure seemed to come through both it and the glass, as had the brightness been all inside of the glass the framing of the window would have intervened, which was not visible. In walking the figure seemed to enter the wall on each side. The occupier of the house [my father] slept in that room, and must have gone in shortly after the disappearance of the apparition.

[My aunt, the 'near connection' referred to above, Mrs. Christiana Wright, of Mansfield, who is still living, has read the manuscript of this incident this year (1892). She has corrected it in two or three unimportant details, but otherwise confirms it as strictly according to her own observation.

The following account of my father's has no year stated, but it appears to be about this time. J. C. is my mother's sister, Jane Carr, of Carlisle.]

'On the 16th of 12th mo., a little before twelve o'clock at night, J. C. and her bedfellow were disturbed by a noise similar to the winding up of a clock, apparently on the stairs where the clock stands, which continued for the space of ten minutes. When that ceased footsteps were heard in the room above, which is unoccupied, for perhaps a quarter of an hour; whilst this was going on the bed was felt to shake, and J. C. distinctly heard the sound like a sack falling on the floor above. On the 3rd of 1st month, about 12 o'clock at night, J. C. being quite awake, was disturbed by a noise similar to a person knocking quickly and strongly five times on a piece of board in the room; when that ceased she distinctly heard the sound of a footstep close by the side of her bed. About the beginning of the year J. P. was awoke by a sound like a bullet lodged in the floor above or in the wall of his bedroom, and looked at his watch to ascertain the time; he found next morning that his wife in the next room was awoke by the same sound.

'About the 21st inst. E. P. and nurse Pollard both felt themselves raised up and let down three times. [My mother has described this experience to me; she said the bed was lifted up as if a man were underneath pushing it up with his back. She did not speak to nurse Pollard, nor the nurse to her, each thinking the other was asleep; this not being disclosed until breakfast time.] On the 15th, about 8 p.m., J. P., jun., who had been in bed about half an hour, called on someone to come to him and begged for a light; he said that something under the crib raised him up very quickly many times, and wished to know what it could be. On the 11th of 1st mo., whilst the servants were at dinner, E. P. was lying on the sofa in her lodging-room when she felt the floor to vibrate as from a heavy foot in an adjoining room; in the writing-room underneath J. C. at the same time heard the sound of a person walking backwards and forwards in the room above. Soon after this E. P. heard the sound of a closet door in the room above shutting three times, after which footsteps came into the middle of the room and then all was silent. E. P. feels assured there was nobody upstairs at the time. On the 17th, at 7 p.m., the two elder children and two nursemaids were in the nursery when a loud clattering or jingling was heard in the room; it sounded from the closet; the girls were very much terrified, as was also Jane P., who is four years and a half old. Little Joseph, perceiving his sister affrighted, endeavoured to calm her by saying, "Never mind, Jane; God will take care of thee." Some weeks before this little Joseph said in the morning to his aunt, Jane Carr, who was sleeping with him, that he was a long time in getting to sleep the night before from some people walking very fast in the room above; he wondered who it could be. This was an unoccupied room. One night, whilst sleeping in a crib in his parents' room, he awoke his father to say that somebody had stepped close to his bed. One night about this time J. P. heard, early in the morning, a noise as of wood moving from the middle to one side of the boarded floor of the empty room above; after which he heard a loud beating in the mill yard. Another night he heard two very peculiar sounds as of whistling or whizzing. [I have sometimes heard my father imitate this peculiar and horrid sound.] About 11 o'clock on the night of the 23rd, J. C. and her little bedfellow heard a succession of thumps or blows in the empty room above which continued for the space of ten minutes. A little after one o'clock the same night J. P. was awakened by a single beat or blow in the room above, after which one of the chairs in his own room seemed shifted.

'On the night of the 26th J. P. heard the sound of footsteps in the attic, and afterwards as of setting things down in the room above, from about 11.30 p.m. to 2 a.m. A little after eleven he had heard several prolonged and peculiar whistles which were also heard by the nurse in another room; they seemed to come from the landing; she had described it without knowing that J. P. had heard it. Joseph was shaken in his crib early the same night.

'On the 27th no one slept in the third storey; about eleven o'clock Jane C. and the nursemaid heard in the room above the sound of some person with strong shoes sometimes walking, sometimes running backwards and forwards, moving chairs and clashing down box lids and sometimes thumping as with a fist. These sounds also moved on to the stair-head. About midnight J. C. felt the bed raised up under one side as if to turn her over, giving two lifts. Nurse Pollard in another room on the same floor heard a noise which aroused her as she was going to sleep; something then pressed against the night part of the curtain and came down on to her arm, which was weighed down with the same force; in great terror she called out, "Lord, have mercy upon me!" Nothing further occurred to her that night, nor was the maid who slept with her aroused.

'2nd month, 3rd. On nearly every day or night since the last entry more or less has been heard that could be referred to no other than the same cause; amongst them the following may be noted: Joseph and Henry have been several times disturbed in their cribs during the evening; once they heard a loud shriek which seemed to come from near the foot of the bed. On going up Joseph was found trembling and perspiring from the fright. One evening J. P. heard a very peculiar moan or cry in the same room; also J. and E. P. and Jane C. heard footsteps and noises which ceased on running upstairs to prevent the children being frightened. Another time Joseph said his bed moved backwards and forwards; also a voice by the foot of the bed said, "Chuck" twice, and then made a noise like a child sucking. He describes other voices; he is very inquisitive as to the origin of these noises, and says he never heard or felt anything like it whilst we lived at Shields.

'It may be proper to mention that neither he nor any of the children have any idea of anything supernatural. Jane sleeps in another room; she told her mother that she felt the bed go up and down, and other things of that kind, not having heard of her brother Joseph, or any of us, having felt anything of the same kind.

'About the 30th J. and E. P. heard loud thumps in the room above, also footsteps in the night, when they knew no one was upstairs, as the cook was at that time sleeping for company with the nurses on the second floor. A day or two later, about six in the evening, whilst the servants were at tea in the kitchen, E. P. and J. C., whilst in the nursery on the second floor, heard what seemed to be heavy pieces of wood jarring on the floor above.

'2nd mo., 1st. About 11 p.m. some little time after all had gone to bed, the sound of chairs, &c., being moved about on the kitchen floor was heard.

'2nd mo., 4th. Jane C. had been poorly, and was awake about 4.30 a.m., as well as her companion, when they heard footsteps descending from the upper storey which passed their door and went down into the kitchen; they thought it was the cook and wondered at her being so early. They then heard the sound of the kitchen door opening and then of the kitchen window being thrown up and the shutters opened with more than usual noise. About seven o'clock they were surprised by the cook calling at their room for a light; having been up early to do washing the previous morning she had this time overslept herself. She had clearly not yet been downstairs.

'On the afternoon of the same day Jon. D. Carr [my mother's brother of Carlisle] came to the house and stayed all night, sleeping alone on the second storey. Soon after going to bed he heard noises in the room above, as of a piece of wood or a balance rapidly striking each end on the floor; afterwards many beats as with a mallet, some very loud; also like a person stamping in a passion. He also heard a peculiar whistle, which he imitated so as exactly to resemble what J. P. heard some time before; he further heard a noise on the stairs and landing,

WILLINGTON MILL

and for some time felt his bed to vibrate very much; he put his hand down to the stock and felt it shaking. This suddenly ceased. He was quite awake and collected, indeed did not sleep till two o'clock, though unusually disposed to it. He said in the morning he would not live in the house for any money.

'The account he gave to Jonathan Carr [his father] induced the latter to come over from Carlisle next morning to see if he could assist with his advice under such disagreeable and dangerous disturbances.

[I can find no other allusion to my grandfather's visit among my father's papers.]

'On 2nd mo., 5th, between 11 and 12 at night, Jane C. heard a thump on the landing near the bedroom door, upon which she awoke her companion, Mary Young. [This was the cook whom my aunt had to sleep with her, not daring to sleep alone in such a house; she was a most respectable and intelligent woman whom I well remember; she was eight years in my mother's service when she married the principal tradesman in the village.] Mary Young heard the slot in the door apparently slide back, the handle to turn and the door to open. A rushlight was burning on the dressing-table, but the bed was an old four-poster, and the curtains being drawn, nothing could be seen. A step then went to the rushlight, and appeared by the sound to snuff it and then lay down the snuffers. In the act of snuffing the light was transiently obscured, as when that act is customarily performed. Jane C. then felt it raise up the clothes over her twice; then they both heard something rustle the curtains as it went round the bed; on getting to Mary Young's side she distinctly saw a dark shadow on the curtain. On getting to the bed-board where Jane C. lay a loud thump as with a fist was heard on it; something was then felt to press on the counterpane on M. Young's side of the bed, the bed curtain being pushed in but nothing more seen. Whatever the visitor might be was then heard to go out, seeming to leave the door open. In the morning they found the door still bolted as it was left when they went to bed. In this occurrence Jane C. heard and felt everything described, but having her head under the bedclothes could not see the shadow as her companion did. [I have on three or four occasions heard a graphic account of this night of horror both from my aunt Jane Carr in later life, and from Mary Young some years after her marriage. The description they both gave exactly agreed with the above narrative from my father's pen except that one or both of them stated that a few minutes after the dreadful unknown visitor left the room they arose, found the door locked as when they came to bed, and searched the room in every way. This is the only discrepancy I notice. One would naturally expect that my aunt would refuse to stay longer in the house after such an experience, but such was not the case; she was, as I remember her to be, a woman of strong nerve, of very cheerful temper, and not easily disturbed. She died on board the steamer *Prussian Eagle*, in Plymouth Sound, in 1859.]

'On the 7th J. C. heard the noise of a box trailed over the floor above the nursery when she was certain no one was upstairs, the servants being at dinner in the kitchen and the rest of the family in the parlour downstairs.

'On the previous night there had been unaccountable thumpings and bed-shakings but nothing of special note.

'From 2nd mo., 6th to the 20th, nothing particular has been heard; but Jane, about $4\frac{1}{2}$ years old, told her parents that when sleeping with her aunt she one night saw by the washstand at the foot of the bed where the curtains were open, a queer looking head, she thought of an old woman; she saw her hands with two fingers of each hand extended and touching each other; she had something down the sides of her face and passed across the lower part of it. She saw it plainly though it was darkish in the room. She was afraid and put her head under the clothes and by-and-bye fell asleep. On the 17th, about dusk, she described having seen a head on the landing as she was coming downstairs, and appeared to be very much terrified.

'About the 25th, pretty late at night, whilst J. P. was asleep, E. P. felt a heavy pressure which unnerved her very much; it seemed to take her breath away and she felt quite sick after it, but did not tell J. P. of it until the morning. Some night previous E. P. was awoke by feeling a pressure on the face over the eye, of icy coldness; it was suddenly laid on with a good deal of force and as suddenly withdrawn. [I have heard my mother describe this on different occasions 20 or 30 years after it occurred; her face always had a pained expression when she related this experience, which I think was more distressing to her than anything she underwent in the house.]

'3rd mo., 3rd. About 5 a.m. E. P. was awake when several beats were felt on one side of the room, which awoke J. P.; a vibration was felt in the room, the bed shook considerably and the curtain rings rattled. The knocks were repeated on the floor above.

'On the night of the 5th E. P. heard what appeared to be a heavy box turned over twice in the room above where no one was sleeping and the entire household being asleep except herself, and everything still.

[I omit several memoranda about this time as to the children and servants hearing voices and sounds of various descriptions.]

'3rd mo., 13th, 1840. Since the last entry Joseph has heard the sound of a thick stick being broken in his room; of a stepping backwards and forwards; of his name being called, &c. About the same date J. and E. P. heard unaccountable drummings and vibrations; also the sound of someone stirring in the closet.

'On the 21st J. and E. P. heard a handbell rung upstairs; they were quite satisfied at the time that no one was there. On the 28th heavy thumps in the middle of the night, and after breakfast the next morning E. P. heard a handbell rung upstairs when she was quite certain everyone was downstairs. J. and E. P. are sure it is no actual bell in the house that is rung, the tone being altogether different. Joseph has been disturbed nearly every night lately; he says when there is nobody upstairs the voices are loud; he is now afraid of going into his room in the daytime. The words he reports as being uttered, such as "Never mind"—"Come and get", seem to have no particular application. To-night he has heard footsteps twice, and felt a bat on his pillow. At the time two of the servants were at a temperance meeting, the other in the kitchen. [The inference that my brother was simply dreaming, or else shamming, so as to get some one to come beside him, will no doubt readily occur to some minds. I can only say that a more truth-

WILLINGTON MILL

ful boy, or one more transparently honest I do not think ever breathed. He was six years of age at this time, and died eleven years afterwards from an accidental blow on the head at a boarding school.]

'On the 30th Henry (3 years old) was awakened by his brother Joseph ringing the bell at his bedside, saying his bed was shaking, and that he heard someone talking in the room; Henry being asked if he did not think it was Joseph that spoke, said No, and showed where the sound came from; they both heard it again about 10 minutes later on.

'4 mo., 6th. During the last nine days J. and E. P. have often heard something stirring in the night, and knocks in the servants' room above; these they afterwards found the girls had not heard, being very sound sleepers.

'4 mo., 4th.—This evening E. P. plainly heard someone or something stirring and rustling about in a room she knew no one was in, and there and then found that no one was in it.

'6th.—During last night there seemed to be but little quiet in the house till daylight; noises as of a shoe dragged over the boards just outside the door, and as though the servants had got up and were going about; knocks loud, and knocks gentle, indeed all sorts of knocks.'

[It may be well to mention here that the Newcastle and North Shields Railway, which passes about a quarter of a mile from the house, was opened on June 19th, 1840.

A gap occurs in the diary here, but the following letter written by my father to my mother on July 4th, 1840, illustrates a striking incident of which full particulars are given by William Howitt and Mrs. Crowe. The hero, Dr. Drury, a practitioner then well-known in Sunderland, had obtained leave to sit up all night on the stairs with a friend, during the absence of the family except my father and one servant. He had wished to bring a loaded musket and a dog with him; my father objected to firearms, but consented to the dog.]

'*Willington. Seventh day, evening*

'DEAR ELIZABETH, . . . Last night Dr. Drury came with T. Hudson, a shopman of Joseph Ogilvie, chemist, and no dog. After a long chat they sat on the high landing; I went to my own bed; Bell in the Camp room. About one o'clock I heard a most horrid shriek from E. D., slipped on my trousers and went up. He had then swooned, but came to himself again in a state of *extreme nervous excitement*, and accompanied with much coldness and faintness. He had seen the G.; had been struck speechless as it advanced from the closet in the room over the drawing-room to the landing, and then leapt up with an awful shriek and fainted. The other young man had his head laid against the easy-chair and was dozing, and as the G. made no noise in coming up he did not awake till the yell of his friend called him to his help.

'I called up Bell to make on the fires, get coffee, &c., but he continued in a shocking state of tremour for some hours, though not irrational. He had a ghastly look and started at the smallest sound—could not bear to see anything white; he had not been in the least sleepy, and was not at all frightened till the moment when the G. met his gaze. They had both previously heard several noises, but all had been quiet for about a quarter of an hour, and E. D. was thinking of getting his companion to go to bed, not expecting anything more that night. . . . E. D. has got a shock he will not soon cast off. I go to Shields tonight and I question I come back at present.'

[The diary resumes as follows:]

'5 mo., 17th, 1841.—Since the latter end of 12 mo., 1840, we have been entirely free from those very singular disturbances, which had been occurring with some intermissions for about 14 months before; and as we now appear to be threatened with a renewal of them, I here make some memoranda of the circumstances. Our servants for some time have shown no symptoms of timidity, and seemed to have no apprehension of any recurrence of former visitations. E. P. has not been well lately, and has thought she observed something in the demeanour of the servants indicative of fear within a day or two past; on questioning them this afternoon they said the ghost had come back, but they wished to keep it from her if possible, as she was poorly. On the 29th, about 9 p.m., J. P., hearing Joseph call, and going upstairs, heard a rustling, like a female running out of the room, but saw no one and was satisfied no one was

WILLINGTON MILL

there. Joseph said his name had been called several times from near the foot of the bed in a voice like his own. That night J. and E. P. heard a drumming and tapping in different parts of their room; at one moment it seemed to be something heavy falling on the floor of the room above, then on the floor of the room adjoining, where it awoke the youngest child, and then to pounce down in the room below on the ground floor. [I have frequently heard my father describe this peculiar case.]

'6 mo., 1st.—The two maids, Davis and E. Mann, report they were unable to sleep before 2 a.m. from constant noises, particularly the apparent treading of bare feet backwards and forwards at the foot of their bed, the noise several times awaking the youngest child; sometimes the tread seemed to pass out on to the landing and run up and down stairs. The nursery door was of course bolted.

'7th day, 11 mo., 13th, 1841.—About 4.30 p.m. Joseph, now eight years old, was in the nursery with his brothers and sisters; he had seated himself on the top of a chest of drawers and was making a pretended speech to them, when he suddenly jumped down, and the nursery door being ajar, J. P., who was in his own bedroom adjoining, heard him exclaim there was a monkey, and that it had pulled his leg by his shoe-strap. J. P. did not himself see the monkey, but coming out of his room saw the children peering under the curtains of the bed in the Blue-room where, they alleged, the animal had disappeared. Joseph afterwards stated that the monkey had given a sharp pull at his shoe-strap, and had tickled his foot; he did not suppose any other but it was a real monkey. Edmund, who is under two years old, was frightened a short time before by what he called a "funny cat", and showed a good deal of timidity the rest of the evening, looking under chairs, &c., lest it should be lurking there, and it is to be noted that he has no fear of a cat.

[Now it so happens that his monkey is the first incident in the lugubrious hauntings, or whatever they may be termed, of which I have any recollection. I suppose it was, or might easily, be the first monkey I had ever seen, which may explain my memory being so impressed that I have not forgotten it. A monkey and, upstairs in the nursery, that is the business. My parents have told me that no monkey was known to be owned in the neighbourhood, and that after diligent inquiry no organ-man or hurdy-gurdy boy, either with or without a monkey, had been seen anywhere about the place or neighbourhood, either on that day or for a length of time. Although I freely admit the evidence of an infant barely two years old is of very small import, yet I may say I have an absolutely distinct recollection of that monkey, and of running to see where it went to as it hopped out of the room and into the adjoining Blue-room. We saw it go under the bed in that room, but it could not be traced or found anywhere afterwards. We hunted and ferretted about that room, and every corner of the house, but no monkey, or any trace of one, was more to be found. I don't know what to make of such a visitation, and have no explanation to offer; but that it was a monkey, that it disappeared under the bed in the Blue-room that Saturday afternoon, and was never seen or heard of again—of this, not merely from my own childish recollection, but from the repeated confirmation of my brothers and sisters in after life, I am perfectly certain. I am merely recording facts as simply as I can; readers may smile or mock as seemeth good unto them—I cannot alter what has taken place to suit either them or anyone else.]

'On the 26th of 10th mo., 1841, about 9 a.m., Joseph and Henry were playing at the foot of the stairs; they both saw a white face looking down upon them over the stair rails leading to the garret. Joseph called for his aunt, Christiana Carr, to come and see it, but just as she was coming he saw it hop away. Henry heard it give a great jump, but Joseph, being very dull of hearing, did not. They both agreed in the description of what they saw.

'On First day evening, 19th of 12th, 1841, about 8 o'clock, E. P. and her sister, Christiana Carr, were in the nursery with the infant, and heard a heavy step coming up the stairs. They at first thought it might be J. P., but recollected that he had put on his slippers, and the step was with heavy shoes; it seemed to pass into the adjoining room in which were some of the children asleep. They soon heard sounds in that room as of something heavy falling, and by-and-bye Henry, about five years old, began to cry as if afraid. The only maid then at home came up to him, when he could not speak for a length of time for sobbing; at last he said something spoke to him, and had also made noises with the chairs.

'About the middle of 11th mo., 1841, Christiana Carr went with Eliz. Mann into a bedroom about 10 p.m. They heard a heavy labouring breathing, first at the far side of the room and then very near them, the floor at the same time shaking with a constant vibration. They hastily retired.

'On the 24th of 11th mo. Joseph, who had gone to bed about 8 o'clock, presently called on his father in some alarm; he said a man had just been in who went to the window, threw up the sash, put it down again and then walked out; he had light or grey hair and no hat on. He was astonished J. P. had not met him. Within a few minutes he called out again; he had heard a step from the door to the closet at the far side of the room where he heard something like a cloak fall. He durst not look up to see who it was. [If any reader exclaim that these are but the dreams and nightmares of children, I will only remind them that I am simply transcribing from my father's diary, written on the dates given by his own hand, and that they must form their own conclusions.

The diary goes on to say that my mother had her own mother staying with her and sleeping with her at this time for about a fortnight.]

'One night, when E. P. was asleep, Jane Carr [her mother] heard a sound like a continued pelting of small substances which at first she took for cinders from the fire; afterwards, as she sat up in bed, with a light burning, and seeing nothing, she heard the sound of somebody going gently about the floor, the dress rustling as it passed from one part of the room to another. On or about the 1st of 11th mo. E. P. awoke at night, heard the sound of an animal leaping down off the easy-chair which stood near the bed; there was no noise of its getting up and running off, but a dead silence.

'7 mo., 14th, 1841.—J. and E. P. heard the spirit in their own room, and in the room overhead, making a noise as of something heavy being hoisted or rolled, or like a barrel set down on its end; also noises in the Camp-room of various and most unaccountable character. Edmund, who is about a year and a half old, roused up with every symptom of being dreadfully frightened; he screamed violently, was a very long time in sleeping again, and frequently awoke in a fright; he became feverish and continued so all the following day, seemed frightened at the sight of his crib and alarmed at any noise he did not understand.

'8 mo., 3rd.—Since the last date there have been few nights during which some branch of the family has not heard our visitor. One night J. P. was awoke and heard something hastily walk, with a step like that of a child of 8 or 10 years, from the foot of the bed towards the side of the room, and come back seemingly towards the door, in a run; then it gave two stamps with one foot; there was a loud rustling as of a frock or nightdress. I need scarcely say the door was locked, and I am quite certain there was no other human being in the room but E. P., who was asleep. The two stamps roused E. P. out of her sleep. About this time Joseph, on two or three occasions, said he had heard voices from underneath his bed and from other parts of the room, and described seeing on one occasion a boy in a drab hat much like his own, the boy much like himself too, walking backwards and forwards between the window and the wardrobe. He was afraid but did not speak.

'Noises as of a band-box falling close at hand, as of someone running upstairs when no one was there, and like the raking of a coal rake, were heard about this time by different members of the family.

'8 mo., 6th.—On the night of the 3rd, just after the previous memorandum was written, about 10.30 p.m., the servants having all retired to bed, J. and E. P. heard a noise like a clothes-horse being thrown down in the kitchen. Soon the noises became louder and appeared as though some persons had burst into the house on the ground floor and were clashing the doors and throwing things down. Eventually J. P. got one of the servants to go downstairs with him, when all was found right, no one there, and apparently nothing moved. The noises now began on the third storey, and the servants were so much alarmed that it was difficult to get them to go to bed at all that night.

'8 mo., 6th to 12th.—My brother-in-law, George Carr, was

with us. He heard steppings and loud rumblings in the middle of the night, and other noises.

[At this point the diary abruptly comes to an end. I know, however, that disturbances of a varied character continued more or less, perhaps less rather than more, for years. One episode during the period has been frequently told to me by my father, and I think no account of it has been published. All his family were in Cumberland and he was sleeping alone, only one servant being in the house. He had retired about 10.30. Owing to the disturbances he and my mother, as well as the domestics, usually burnt a rushlight during the night, a description of candle at that time in common use; but on this occasion he had no light whatever. He had not been two minutes in bed when suddenly, seemingly close to the bedside, there was an awful crash as of a wooden box being wrenched open with a crowbar with terrific force; he started up and cried out with a loud voice, 'Begone! thou wicked spirit!' As if in defiance of this adjuration the fearful crash was almost immediately repeated, and, if possible, louder than before. Cool-headed as my father was, and inured to unwelcome surprises from the unknown, he was painfully agitated by this ostentatious outburst of ill-will or wanton devilry; he arose, struck a light, searched the room, opened his bedroom door, listened on the stairs, looked into other rooms, and explored the house generally, but found everything perfectly quiet. There was no wind, and indeed there seemed no explanation, but one only, of this horrid visitation.

Finding life in the house to be no longer tolerable; fearing also an unhappy effect, if not a permanent injury on the minds of their children should they remain longer in such a plague-ridden dwelling, they finally left it in 1847, and went to reside at Camp Villa, North Shields, social and other reasons also influencing them in taking this step. My parents have both repeatedly told me that during the last night they slept in the old house, the rest of the family having preceded them to the new one, there were continuous noises during the night, boxes being apparently dragged with heavy thuds down the now carpetless stairs, non-human footsteps stumped on the floors, doors were, or seemed to be, clashed and impossible furniture

WILLINGTON MILL

corded at random or dragged hither and thither by inscrutable agency; in short, a pantomimic or spiritualistic repetition of all the noises incident to a household flitting. A miserable night my father and mother had of it, as I have often heard from their own lips; not so much from terror at the unearthly noises, for to these they were habituated, as dread lest this wretched fanfaronade might portend the contemporary flight of the unwelcome visitors to the new abode. Fortunately for the family this dread was not realized. So far as I know, and in this I am confirmed by my elder brother and sisters, the eight years' residence in the new home was absolutely free from all forms of the annoyances and uncomfortable knockings, the stealthy steps and the uncouth mutterings that for ten or eleven years had disturbed the even tenor of a quiet Quaker family in the old house at Willington Mill.

The subsequent history of the house may be briefly told. The foreman and chief clerk in the flour mill, less sensitive perhaps to the disturbances, and with families of maturer years, raised no objection to occupying it after a time, and it was divided into two separate dwellings, and inhabited by them for nearly twenty years. They were occasionally disturbed by unaccountable noises, and Thomas Mann, the foreman, on one or two occasions saw what appeared to be apparitions, but both families were designedly reticent on the subject, and I believe suffered but little throughout their occupancy. About 1867 the mill and house were let for a few months to a firm of millers in an adjoining town whose mill had been burnt down; I have been informed that those then occupying the house were much troubled, one family declining to stay on any terms. Not long afterwards my father sold the entire premises to a firm of guano merchants, and information reached us that two machinists, one of them a German, who were fixing machinery in the mill, spent some restless evenings and unhappy nights in the house in fruitlessly trying to discover the origin of fitful and exasperating disturbances. No effort was made, so far as I know, to test the accuracy of these rumours. On one occasion, whilst the house was unoccupied shortly before its sale, I was one of a party of four or five young men, one of them a doctor, who spent an entire night in the house, upstairs, in the hope of hearing or seeing something, but absolutely without result. Some little time after this I was one of another and larger party, including two ladies, who spent an evening in another upstairs room, accompanied by a 'medium' of repute at that time well-known in Newcastle; no person whatever being in the house besides our own party. The séance was not without incidents, well understood by those acquainted with such proceedings, and which it would be useless at the moment to describe to those who are not, but absolutely futile as to establishing any communication with the alleged spirit or spirits supposed to haunt or to have formerly haunted the premises. My father never made any attempt to open up communication in this way; his experiences were prior to the time when the modern developments of Spiritualism made the lingo of the séance familiar to the public ear, and although he took an earnest interest in the subject, he never attended a séance, and laid stress upon the application of the well-known text about 'seducing spirits and doctrines of demons'. The mill is now only used as a warehouse. The house has been divided into small tenements; I understand the owner, recognizing the doubtful repute of the house, offered the apartments free for a short term. About two years ago I interviewed three or four of the tenants, and was told that no disturbances had been experienced. Although of modest pretensions, it was formerly a comfortable old-fashioned house of ten or twelve rooms, but the untidiness of its present aspect is a painful spectacle to those who remember it at its best; the stables and adjoining out-buildings have been pulled down, the garden wall has disappeared, the jargonelle pear trees that formerly blossomed up to the third storey are represented by the mere ghosts of blackened stumps, the large old thorn tree of red blossom, and the abundance of iris and auricula that were wont to bloom in the garden are as far off as the snows of last winter.

The singular record of the house gives it an interest nevertheless, even in its squalid present and its ungracious decay.

Some may think the whole affair altogether a very paltry story. I admit it is not a very picturesque 'ghost'; but whatever its merit it is at least authentic, and that is a rather important feature in a ghost. The truth has been told without extenuation or reserve, and if the recital points to the conclusion that the spirit or spirits, or whatever you choose to call them, belonged to the residuum of the spirit world, I hope my family may not be held responsible.

I may be permitted finally to briefly indicate some of my own conclusions.

If the gibberings, the preposterous incivilities, and the unwholesome uproar committed in that house for ten unforgettable years by these unhallowed genii may be accepted as an argument tending to establish the continued existence of the individual after death, the seductions of futurity are scarcely increased to

*Exhausted travellers that have undergone
The scorching heats of life's intemperate zone.*

Such questionable intimations of immortality are hardly calculated to soothe us—

*When worn with adverse passions, furious strife,
And the hard passage of tempestuous life.*

Nevertheless, this singular history, taken in connection with others of its class, may to the impartial and philosophic mind hide a lesson of the highest import. M. Renan, in one of the very last of his many charming pages, troubled with doubts as to a future existence, whilst smiling at the superstition of the old-fashioned and orthodox hell, exclaims how glad he would be to be sure even of hell, a hypothesis so preferable to annihilation.

In the same way, may we not justifiably postulate this: that if we can prove the existence of spirits of a low or inferior order, then faith, analogy, and evolution, if not logic and conviction, can claim those of a progressive, a high and superior order? Is it not rational to suppose that the more debased and the most unhappy have the greatest facility in giving tangible proof of their existence, under certain conditions imperfectly understood; whilst the purer and nobler souls find intercourse painful or impossible, but are yet occasionally able to achieve it in those picturesque and beneficent instances where

WILLINGTON MILL

their visitation is recorded, not only in the Old and New Testaments, but scattered all through literature; cases which possibly the many may still deride, but which others cherish as indications of the divine and proofs of immortality? Each must draw his own conclusions; as the prophet of Tréguier says, 'Let us all be free to make our own romance of the infinite'.]

EDMUND PROCTER

Newcastle-on-Tyne, October 1892

3. THE DRUMMER OF TEDWORTH

The enlarged narrative of the Daemon of Tedworth, or of the Disturbances at Mr. Mompesson's House, caused by Witchcraft and the villainy of the Drummer, reprinted from 'Saducismus Triumphatus', by the Rev. Joseph Glanvil, 1682

Mr. John Mompesson of Tedworth, in the County of Wilts, being about the middle of March, in the Year 1661, at a Neighbouring Town called Ludgarshall, and hearing a Drum beat there, he inquired of the Bailiff of the Town, at whose house he then was, what it meant. The Bailiff told him, that they had for some days been troubled with an idle Drummer, who demanded money of the Constable by virtue of a pretended pass, which he thought was counterfeit. Upon this Mr. Mompesson sent for the fellow, and asked him by what authority he went up and down the country in that manner with his Drum. The Drummer answered, he had good authority and produced his pass, with a warrant under the hands of Sir William Cawly, and Colonel Ayliff of Gretenham. Mr. Mompesson, knowing these gentlemen's hands, discovered that the pass and warrant were counterfeit, and thereupon commanded the vagrant to put off his Drum, and charged the constable to carry him before the next Justice of the Peace, to be further examined and punished. The fellow then confessed the cheat, and begged earnestly to have his Drum. Mr. Mompesson told him, that if he understood from Colonel Ayliff, whose Drummer he said he was, that he had been an honest man, he should have it again, but in the meantime he would secure it. So he left the Drum with the Bailiff, and the Drummer in the Constable's hands, who it seems was prevailed on by the Fellow's intreaties to let him go.

THE DRUMMER OF TEDWORTH

About the midst of April following, when Mr. Mompesson was preparing for a journey to London, the Bailiff sent the Drum to his House. When he was returned from that journey, his Wife told him that they had been much affrighted in the night by thieves, and that the house had been like to have been broken up. And he had not been at home above three Nights, when the same noise was heard that had disturbed his family, in his absence. It was a very great knocking at his doors, and the outsides of his house. Hereupon he got up, and went about the house with a brace of pistols in his hands. He opened the door where the great knocking was, and then he heard the noise at another door. He opened that also, and went out round his house, but could discover nothing, only he still heard a strange noise and hollow sound. When he was got back to bed, the noise was a thumping and drumming on the top of his house, which continued a good space, and then by degrees went off into the air.

After this, the noise of thumping and drumming was very frequent, usually five nights together, and then it would intermit three. It was on the outsides of the House, which is most of it of Board. It constantly came as they were going to sleep, whether early or late. After a month's disturbance without, it came into the room where the Drum lay, four or five nights in seven, within half an hour after they were in bed, continuing almost two. The sign of it just before it came, was, they still heard an hurling in the air over the house, and at its going off, the beating of a Drum like that at the breaking up of a guard. It continued in this room for the space of two months, which time Mr. Mompesson himself lay there to observe it. In the fore part of the night it used to be very troublesome, but after two hours all would be quiet.

Mrs. Mompesson being brought to bed, there was but little noise the night she was in travail, nor any for three weeks after, till she had recovered strength. But after this civil cessation, it returned in a ruder manner than before, and followed and vexed the youngest children, beating their bedsteads with that violence, that all present expected when they would fall in pieces. In laying hands on them, one should feel no blows but might perceive them to shake exceedingly. For an hour

THE DRUMMER OF TEDWORTH

together it would beat, Roundheads and Cuckolds, the Tattoo, and several other points of war, as well as any drummer. After this, they should hear a scratching under the children's bed, as if by something that had iron talons. It would lift the children up in their beds, follow them from one room to another, and for a while haunted none particularly but them.

There was a cock-loft in the house which had not been observed to be troubled, thither they removed the children, putting them to bed while it was fair day, where they were no sooner laid, but their troubler was with them as before.

On the fifth of November 1662, it kept a mighty noise and a servant observing two boards in the children's room seeming to move, he bid it give him one of them. Upon which the board came (nothing moving it that he saw) within a yard of him. The man added, 'Nay let me have it in my hand,' upon which it was shoved quite home to him. He thrust it back, and it was driven to him again, and so up and down, to and fro, at least twenty times together, till Mr. Mompesson forbade his servant such familiarities. This was in the daytime, and seen by a whole room full of people. That morning it left a sulphurous smell behind it, which was very offensive. At night the Minister, one Mr. Cragg, and divers of the neighbours came to the house on a visit. The Minister went to prayers with them, kneeling at the children's bedside, where it was then very troublesome and loud. During prayer-time it withdrew into the cock-loft, but returned as soon as prayers were done, and then in sight of the company, the chairs walked about the room of themselves, the children's shoes were hurled over their heads, and every loose thing moved about the chamber. At the same time a bed-staff was thrown at the Minister, which hit him on the leg, but so favourably that a lock of wool could not have fallen more softly, and it was observed, that it stopped just where it lighted, without rolling or moving from the place.

Mr. Mompesson perceiving that it so much persecuted the little children, he lodged them out at a neighbour's house, taking his eldest daughter, who was about ten years of age, into his own chamber, where it had not been a month before. As soon as she was in bed, the disturbance began there again, continuing three weeks Drumming, and making other noises,

THE DRUMMER OF TEDWORTH

and it was observed, that it would exactly answer in Drumming any thing that was beaten or called for. After this, the house where the children were lodged out, happening to be full of strangers, they were taken home, and no disturbance having been known in the parlour, they were lodged there, where also their persecutor found them, but then only pluckt them by the hair and night-clothes without any other disturbance.

It was noted that when the noise was loudest, and came with the most sudden and surprising violence, no dog about the house would move, though the knocking was oft so boisterous and rude, that it hath been heard at a considerable distance in the fields, and awakened the neighbours in the village, none of which live very near this house. The servants sometimes were lift up with their beds, and let them gently down again without hurt, at other times it would lie like a great weight upon their feet.

About the latter end of Dec. 1662, the drummings were less frequent, and they heard a noise like the jingling of money, occasioned, as it was thought, by somewhat Mr. Mompesson's mother had spoken the day before to a neighbour, who talked of fairies leaving money, viz. That she should like it well, if it would leave them some to make amends for their trouble. The night after the speaking of which, there was a great chinking of money over all the house.

After this it desisted from the ruder noises and employed itself in little apish and less troublesome tricks. On Christmas Eve, a little before day, one of the little boys arising out of his bed was hit on a sore place upon his heel, with the latch of the door, the pin that it was fastened with was so small that it was a difficult matter to pick it out. The night after Christmas day, it threw the old gentlewoman's clothes about the room, and hid her Bible in the ashes. In such silly tricks it was frequent.

After this, it was very troublesome to a servant of Mr. Mompesson's, who was a stout fellow, and of sober conversation. This man lay within, during the greatest disturbance, and for several nights something would endeavour to pluck his clothes off the bed, so that he was fain to tug hard to keep them on, and sometimes they would be plucked from him by main force,

THE DRUMMER OF TEDWORTH

and his shoes thrown at his head. And now and then he should find himself forcibly held, as it was bound hand and foot, but he found that whenever he could make use of his sword, and struck with it, the spirit quitted its hold.

A little after these contests, a son of Sir Thomas Bennet, whose workman the Drummer had sometimes been, came to the house, and told Mr. Mompesson some words that he had spoken, which it seems was not well taken. For as soon as they were in bed, the Drum was beat very violently and loudly, the Gentleman arose and called his man to him, who lay with Mr. Mompesson's servant just now spoken of, whose name was John. As soon as Mr. Bennet's man was gone, John heard a rustling noise in his chamber, and something came to his bedside, as if it had been one in silk. The man presently reacheth after his sword, which he found held from him, and 'twas with difficulty and much tugging that he got it into his power, which as soon as he had done, the spectre left him, and it was always observed that it still avoided a sword.

About the beginning of January 1662, they were wont to hear a singing in the chimney before it came down. And one night about this time, lights were seen in the house. One of them came into Mr. Mompesson's chamber which seemed blue and glimmering, and caused great stiffness in the eyes of those that saw it. After the light something was heard coming up the stairs, as if it had been one without shoes. The light was seen also four or five times in the children's chamber; and the maids confidently affirm that the doors were at least ten times opened and shut in their sight, and when they were opened they heard a noise as if half a dozen had entered together. After which some were heard to walk about the room, and one rustled as if it had been in silk. The like Mr. Mompesson himself once heard.

During the time of the knocking, when many were present, a gentleman of the company said, Satan, if the Drummer set thee to work, give three knocks and no more, which it did very distinctly and stopped. Then the gentleman knocked to see if it would answer him as it was wont, but it did not. For further trial, he bid it for confirmation, if it were the Drummer, to give five knocks and no more that night, which it did, and left the

THE DRUMMER OF TEDWORTH

house quiet all the night after. This was done in the presence of Sir Thomas Chamberlain of Oxfordshire, and divers others.

On Saturday morning, an hour before day, Jan. 10, a Drum was heard beat upon the outsides of Mr. Mompesson's chamber, from whence it went to the other end of the house, where some gentlemen strangers lay, playing at their door and without, four or five several tunes, and so went off into the air.

The next night, a smith in the village lying with John the man, they heard a noise in the room, as if one had been shoeing of an horse, and somewhat came, as it were with a pair of pincers, snipping at the smith's nose most part of the night.

One morning, Mr. Mompesson, rising early to go a journey, heard a great noise below, where the children lay, and running down with a pistol in his hand, he heard a voice crying, a Witch, a Witch, as they had also heard it once before. Upon his entrance all was quiet.

Having one night played some little tricks at Mr. Mompesson's bed's feet, it went into another bed, where one of his daughters lay; there it passed from side to side, lifting her up as it passed under. At that time there were three kinds of noises in the bed. They endeavoured to thrust at it with a sword, but it still shifted and carefully avoided the thrust, still getting under the child when they offered at it. The night after it came panting like a dog out of breath. Upon which one took a bedstaff to knock, which was caught out of her hand, and thrown away, and company coming up, the room was presently filled with a bloomy noisome smell, and was very hot, though without fire, in a very sharp and severe winter. It continued in the bed panting and scratching an hour and half, and then went into the next chamber, where it knocked a little and seemed to rattle a chain; thus it did for two or three nights together.

After this, the old Gentlewoman's Bible was found in the ashes, the paper side being downwards. Mr. Mompesson took it up, and observed that it lay open at the third chapter of St. Mark, where there is mention of the unclean spirits falling down before our saviour, and of his giving power to the twelve to cast out devils, and of the scribes' opinion, that he cast them out through Beelzebub. The next night they strewed ashes

THE DRUMMER OF TEDWORTH

over the chamber, to see what impressions it would leave. In the morning they found in one place, the resemblance of a great claw, in another of a lesser, some letters in another, which they could make nothing of, besides many circles and scratches in the ashes.

About this time I went to the house, on purpose to inquire the truth of those passages, of which there was so loud a report. It had ceased from its Drumming and ruder noises before I came thither, but most of the more remarkable circumstances, before related, were confirmed to me there, by several of the neighbours together, who had been present at them. At this time it used to haunt the children, and that as soon as they were laid. They went to bed that night I was there, about eight of the clock, when a maid-servant coming down from them, told us it was come. The neighbours that were there and two ministers who had seen and heard divers times, went away, but Mr. Mompesson and I, and a gentleman that came with me went up. I heard a strange scratching as I went up the stairs, and when we came into the room, I perceived it was just behind the bolster of the children's bed and seemed to be against the tick. It was as loud a scratching as one with long nails could make upon a bolster. There were two little modest girls in the bed, between seven and eleven years old as I guessed. I saw their hands out of the clothes, and they could not contribute to the noise that was behind their heads. They had been used to it, and had still somebody or other in the chamber with them, and therefore seemed not to be much affrighted. I standing at the bed's head, thrust my hand behind the bolster, directing it to the place whence the noise seemed to come. Whereupon the noise ceased there, and was heard in another part of the bed. But when I had taken out my hand it returned, and was heard in the same place as before. I had been told that it would imitate noises, and made trial by scratching several times upon the sheet, as 5, and 7 and 10, which it followed, and still stopped at my number. I searched under and behind the bed, turned up the clothes to the bedcords, grasped the bolster, sounded the wall behind, and made all the search that possibly I could to find if there were any trick, contrivance, or common cause of it; the like did my friend, but we could discover nothing. So that I was then verily persuaded, and am so still, that the noise was made by some demon or spirit. After it had scratched about half an hour or more, it went into the midst of the bed under the children, and there seemed to pant like a dog out of breath very loudly. I put my hand upon the place, and felt the bed bearing up against it, as if something within had thrust it up. I grasped the feathers to feel if any living thing were in it. I looked under and everywhere about, to see if there were any dog or cat, or any such creature in the room, and so we all did, but found nothing. The motion it caused by this panting was so strong that it shook the room and windows very sensibly. It continued thus more than half an hour, while my friend and I stay'd in the room, and as long after, as we were told. During the panting, I chanced to see as it had been something (which I thought was a rat or mouse) moving in a Linen Bag, that hung up against another bed that was in the room. I stepped and caught it by the upper end with one hand, with which I held it, and drew it through the other, but found nothing at all in it. There was no body near to shake the bag, or if there had, no one could have made such a motion, which seemed to be from within, as if a living creature had moved in it. This passage I mention not in the former editions, because it depended upon my single testimony, and might be subject to more evasions than the other I related; but having told it to divers learned and inquisitive men, who thought it not altogether inconsiderable, I have now added it here. It will I know be said by some, that my friend and I were under some affright and so fancied noises and sights that were not. This is the eternal evasion. But if it be possible to know how a man is affected, when in fear, and when unconcerned, I certainly know for mine own part, that during the whole time of my being in the room, and in the house, I was under no more affrightment than I am, while I write this relation. And if I know that I am now awake, and that I see the objects that are before me, I know that I heard and saw the particulars I have told. There is, I am sensible, no great matter for story in them, but there is so much as convinceth me, that there was somewhat extraordinary, and what we usually call preternatural in the business.

THE DRUMMER OF TEDWORTH

There were other passages at my being at Tedworth, which I published not, because they are not such plain and unexceptionable proofs. I shall now briefly mention them, *valeant quantum valere possunt*. My friend and I lay in the chamber, where the first and chief disturbance had been. We slept well all night, but early before day in the morning, I was awakened (and I awakened my bedfellow) by a great knocking just without our chamber door. I asked who was there several times, but the knocking still continued without answer. At last I said, 'In the name of God who is it, and what would you have?' To which a voice answered, 'Nothing with you.' We thinking it had been some servant of the house, went to sleep again. But speaking of it to Mr. Mompesson when we came down, he assured us, that no one of the house lay that way, or had business thereabout, and that his servants were not up till he called them, which was after it was day. Which they confirmed, and protested that the noise was not made by them.

Mr. Mompesson had told us before that it would be gone in the middle of the night, and come again divers times early in the morning about four a clock, and this I suppose was about that time.

Another passage was this, my Man coming up to me in the morning, told me, that one of my horses (that on which I rode) was all in a sweat, and looked as if he had been rid all night. My friend and I went down and found him so. I enquired how he had been used, and was assured that he had been well fed, and ordered as he used to be, and my servant was one that was wont to be very careful about my horses. The horse I had had a good time, and never knew but that he was very sound. But after I had rid him a mile or two, very gently over a plain down from Mr. Mompesson's house, he fell lame, and having made a hard shift to bring me home, died in two or three days, no one being able to imagine what he ailed. This I confess might be accident or some unusual distemper, but all things being put together, it seems very probable that it was somewhat else.

But I go on with Mr. Mompesson's own particulars. There came one morning a light into the children's chamber and a voice crying, a Witch, a Witch, for at least an hundred times together.

THE DRUMMER OF TEDWORTH

Mr. Mompesson at another time (being in the day) seeing some wood move that was in the chimney of a room, where he was, as of itself, discharged a pistol into it, after which they found several drops of blood on the hearth, and in divers places of the stairs.

For two or three nights after the discharge of the pistol, there was a calm in the house, but then it came again, applying itself to a little child newly taken from the nurse. Which it so persecuted, that it would not let the poor infant rest for two nights together, nor suffer a candle in the room, but carry them away lighted up the chimney, or throw them under the bed. It so feared this child by leaping upon it, that for some hours it could not be recovered out of the fright. So that they were forced again to remove the children out of the house. The next night after which, something about midnight came up the stairs, and knocked at Mr. Mompesson's door, but he lying still, it went up another pair of stairs to his man's chamber, to whom it appeared standing at his bed's foot. The exact shape and proportion he could not discover, but he saith he saw a great body with two red and glaring eyes, which for some time were fixed steadily upon him, and at length disappeared.

Another night strangers being present, it purred in the children's bed like a cat, which time also the clothes and children were lift up from the bed, and six men could not keep them down; hereupon they removed the children, intending to have ripped up the bed. But they were no sooner laid in another, but the second bed was more troubled than the first. It continued thus four hours, and so beat the children's legs against the bed-posts, that they were forced to arise, and sit up all night. After this it would empty chamber-pots into their beds, and strew them with ashes, though they were never so carefully watched. It put a long piked iron into Mr. Mompesson's bed, and into his mother's a naked knife upright. It would fill porringers with ashes, throw everything about, and keep a noise all day.

About the beginning of April 1663, a gentleman that lay in the house, had all his money turned black in his pockets; and Mr. Mompesson coming one morning into his stable, found

THE DRUMMER OF TEDWORTH

the horse he was wont to ride, on the ground, having one of his hinder legs in his mouth, and so fastened there, that it was difficult for several men to get it out with a lever. After this, there were some other remarkable things, but my account goes no further. Only Mr. Mompesson writ me word, that afterwards the house was several nights beset with seven or eight in the shape of men, who, as soon as a gun was discharged, would shuffle away together into an arbour.

The Drummer was tryed at the assizes at Salisbury upon this occasion. He was committed first to Gloucester Gaol for stealing and a Wiltshire man coming to see him, he asked what news in Wiltshire. The visitant said, he knew of none. No, saith the Drummer! do not you hear of the Drumming at a gentleman's house at Tedworth? That I do enough, said the other. I, quoth the Drummer, I have plagued him (or to that purpose) and he shall never be quiet, till he hath made me satisfaction for taking away my Drum. Upon information of this, the fellow was tryed for a witch at Sarum, and all the main circumstances I have related, were sworn at the Assizes by the Minister of the Parish, and divers others of the most intelligent and substantial inhabitants, who had been eye and ear witnesses of them, time after time for divers years together.

The fellow was condemned to transportation, and accordingly sent away; but I know not how ('tis said by raising storms, and affrighting the seamen) he made a shift to come back again, and 'tis observable, that during all the time of his restraint and absence the house was quiet, but as soon as ever he came back at liberty, the disturbance returned.

He had been a soldier under Cromwell, and used to talk much of Gallant Books he had of an odd fellow who was counted a wizard. Upon this occasion I shall here add a passage, which I had not from Mr. Mompesson, but yet relates to the main purpose.

The gentleman, who was with me at the house, Mr. Hill, being in company with one Compton of Somersetshire, who practised physick, and pretends to strange matters, related to him this story of Mr. Mompesson's disturbance. The Physician told him, he was sure it was nothing but a

THE DRUMMER OF TEDWORTH

rendezvous of witches, and that for an hundred pounds, he would undertake to rid the house of all disturbance. In pursuit of this discourse, he talked of many high things, and having drawn my friend into another room apart from the rest of the company, said, he would make him sensible he could do something more than ordinary, and asked him who he desired to see. Mr. Hill had no great confidence in his talk, but yet being earnestly pressed to name some one, he said, he desired to see no one so much as his wife, who was then many miles distant from them at her home. Upon this Compton took up a looking-glass that was in the room, and setting it down again, bid my friend look in it; which he did, and there, as he most solemnly and seriously professeth, he saw the exact image of his wife in that habit which she then wore, and working at her needle in such a part of the room (there represented also) in which and about which time she really was, as he found upon enquiry when he came home. The gentleman himself averred this to me, and he is a very sober, intelligent and credible person. Compton had no knowledge of him before, and was an utter stranger to the person of his wife. The same Man we shall meet again in the story of the witchcrafts of Elizabeth Style, whom he discovered to be a witch by foretelling her coming into an house, and going out again without speaking, as is set down in the third Relation. He was by all counted a very odd person.

Thus I have written the sum of Mr. Mompesson's disturbance, which I had partly from his own mouth related before divers, who had been witnesses of all, and confirmed his relation, and partly from his own letters, from which the order and series of things is taken. The same particulars he writ also to Dr. Creed then Doctor of the Chair in Oxford.

Mr. Mompesson is a Gentleman, of whose truth in this account I have not the least ground of suspicion, he being neither vain nor credulous, but a discreet, sagacious and manly person. Now the credit of matters of fact depends much upon the relators, who, if they cannot be deceived themselves, nor supposed any ways interested to impose upon others, ought to be credited. For upon these circumstances, all humane faith is grounded, and matter of fact is not capable of any

THE DRUMMER OF TEDWORTH

proof besides, but that of immediate sensible evidence. Now that he relates be true or no, the scene of all being his own house, himself a witness, and that not of a circumstance or two, but of an hundred, nor for once or twice only, but for the space of some years, during which he was a concerned, and inquisitive observer. So that it cannot with any show of reason be supposed that any of his servants abused him, since in all that time he must needs have detected the deceit. And what interest could any of his family have had (if it had been possible to have managed without discovery) to continue so long, so troublesome, and so injurious an imposture? Nor can it with any whit of more probability be imagined, that his own melancholy deluded him, since (besides that he is no crazy nor imaginative person) that humour could not have been so lasting and pertinacious. Or if it were so in him, can we think he infected his whole family, and those multitudes of neighbours and others, who had so often been witnesses of those passages? Such supposals are wild, and not like to tempt any, but those whose wills are their reasons. So that upon the whole, the principal relator Mr. Mompesson himself knew, whether what he reports was true or not, whether those things acted in his house were contrived cheats, or extraordinary realities. And if so, what interest could he serve in carrying on, or conniving at a juggling design and imposture?

He suffered by it in his name, in his estate, in all his affairs, and in the general peace of his family. The Unbelievers in the matter of spirits and witches took him for an imposter. Many others judged the permission of such an extraordinary evil to be the judgment of God upon him, for some notorious wickedness or impiety. Thus his Name was continually exposed to censure, and his estate suffered, by the concourse of people from all parts to his house, by the diversion it gave him from his affairs, by the discouragement of servants, by reason of which he could hardly get any to live with him. To which if I add the continual hurry that his family was in, the affrights, vexations and tossings up and down of his children, and the watchings and disturbance of his whole house (in all which, himself must needs be the most concerned) I say, if these things are considered, there will be little reason to think he could have any interest to put a cheat upon the world, in which he would most of all have injured and abused himself. Or if he should have designed and managed so incredible, so unprofitable a delusion, 'tis strange that he should have troubled himself so long in such a business only to deceive, and to be talked of. And it is yet more so, that none of those many inquisitive persons that came thither purposely to criticize and examine the truth of those matters, could make any discoveries of the juggling, especially since many came prejudiced against the belief of such things in general, and others resolved beforehand against the belief of this, and all were permitted the utmost freedom of search and enquiry. And after things were weighed and examined, some that were before greatly prejudiced, went away fully convinced. To all which I add, that:

There are divers particulars in the story, in which no abuse or deceit could have been practised, as the motion of Boards and Chairs of themselves, the beating of a Drum in the midst of a room, and in the air, when nothing was to be seen: the great heat in a chamber that had no fire in excessive cold weather, the scratching and panting, the violent beating and shaking of bedsteads, of which there was no perceivable cause or occasion; In these and such like instances, it is not to be conceived how tricks could have been put upon so many, so jealous, and so inquisitive persons as were witnesses of them.

'Tis true, that when the gentlemen the King sent were there, the House was quiet, and nothing seen or heard that night, which was confidently and with triumph urged by many, as a confutation of the story. But 'twas bad logic to conclude in matters of fact from a single Negative and such a one against numerous Affirmatives, and so affirm that a thing was never done, because not at such a particular time, and that nobody ever saw what this man or that did not. By the same way of reasoning, I may infer that there were never any robberies done on Salisbury Plain, Hounslow Heath, or the other noted places, because I have often travelled all those ways, and yet was never robbed; and the Spaniard inferred well that said, 'There was no Sun in England, because he had been six weeks here, and never saw it.' This is the common argument of those

THE DRUMMER OF TEDWORTH

that deny the Being of Apparitions, they have travelled all hours of the night, and never saw any thing worse than themselves (which may well be) and thence they conclude, that all pretended Apparitions are Fancies or Impostures. But why do not such arguers conclude that there was never a Cutpurse in London, because they have lived there many years without being met with by any of those practisers? Certainly he that denies Apparitions upon the confidence of this Negative against the vast heap of positive assurances, is credulous in believing there was never any Highway-man in the world, if he himself was never robb'd. And the trials of Assizes and attestations of those that have (if he will be just) ought to move his assent no more in this case, than in that of Witches and Apparitions, which have the very same evidence.

But as to the quiet of Mr. Mompesson's house when the Courtiers were there, it may be remembered and considered, that the disturbance was not constant, but intermitted sometimes several days, sometimes weeks. So that the intermission at that time might be accidental or perhaps the Demon was not willing to give so public a testimony of those transactions, which possibly might convince those, who he had rather should continue in the unbelief of his existence. But however it were, this circumstance will afford but a very slender interference against the credit of the story, except among those who are willing to take any thing for an Argument against things which they have an interest not to acknowledge.

I have thus related the sum of the story, and noted some circumstances that assure the truth of it. I confess the passages recited are not so dreadful, tragical and amazing, as there are some in story of this kind, yet are they nevertheless probable or true, for their being not so prodigious and astonishing. And they are strange enough to prove themselves effects of some invisible extraordinary agent, and so demonstrate that there are spirits, who sometimes sensibly intermeddle in our affairs. And I think they do it with clearness of evidence. For these things were not done long ago, or at far distance, in an ignorant age, or among a barbarous people, they were not seen by two or three only of the melancholic and superstitious, and reported by those that made them serve the advantage and

THE DRUMMER OF TEDWORTH

interest of a party. They were not the passages of a Day or Night, nor the vanishing glances of an Apparition; but these transactions were near and late, public, frequent, and divers years continuance, witnessed by multitudes of competent and unbiassed attestors, and acted in a searching incredulous age: arguments enough one would think to convince any modest and capable reason.

4. THE HAUNTING OF HINTON AMPNER

The narrative of Mrs. Ricketts, reprinted from the 'Journal of the Society for Psychical Research', Vol. VI, April 1893

Mary Ricketts was the youngest child of Swynfen Jervis, Esq., and Elizabeth Parker, his wife. She was born at Meaford, near Stone, in Staffordshire, in 1737-8. From her early childhood she evinced a love for reading, and an aptitude for mental improvement, which were developed by the wise training of Nicholas Tindal, the learned continuer of Rapin's *History of England*.

Her veracity was proverbial in the family. Her favourite brother and companion was John Jervis, who for his distinguished naval services was created Baron Jervis and Earl St. Vincent. Though his junior by three years, she rapidly outstripped him in book learning, and to her superior acquirements may be traced the unwearied pains which John Jervis took to make up for lost time, when, at the age of eighteen, he devoted his spare hours to study, instead of sharing in the frivolous amusements of West Indian life.

She married in 1757 William Henry Ricketts, of Canaan, in Jamaica, Esq., whose grandfather, William Ricketts, Esq., was a captain in Penn and Venable's army at the conquest of Jamaica. Mrs. Ricketts was called upon to accompany her husband in his visits to the West Indies, or to remain alone in England. The charge of her three infant children determined her to accept the latter alternative in 1769.

During the absence of Mr. Ricketts in Jamaica, his wife continued to inhabit the old Manor House of Hinton Ampner, in Hampshire, and it was there that the following series of strange disturbances occurred, the effect of which was to render her continued occupation of the house an impossibility.

Mrs. Ricketts was a woman of remarkable vigour, both

physical and mental. Her steadfast faith, and sense of the ever abiding presence of God, carried her through many bitter trials, and preserved her intellectual powers unimpaired to the advanced age of ninety-one, when she calmly resigned her spirit into 'the hands of the God who gave it'.

(This pamphlet was edited by the third Marquess of Bute.)

MRS. RICKETTS TO THE REV. MR. NEWBOLT

Hinton Ampner, Wednesday Morning, August, 1771
MY DEAR SIR,
In compliance with my promise to you of yesterday, I would not delay to inform you of the operations of last night. It was settled (contrary to the plan when you left) that John, my brother's man, should accompany Captain Luttrell in the chintz room, and they remain together till my brother was called. Just after twelve they were disturbed with some of the noises I had frequently heard and described, and so plainly heard by my brother that he quitted his bed long before the time agreed on, and joined the other two; the noises frequently proceeding from the garrets, they went up just at break of day, found all the men servants in their proper apartments, who had heard no disturbance whatever. They examined every room. Everything appeared snug and in place, and, contrary to usual custom, the opening and shutting of doors continued (after the other noises ceased) till five o'clock. My brother authorizes me to tell you that neither himself nor Captain Luttrell can account for what they have heard from any natural cause; yet as my brother declares he shall never close his eyes in the house, he and Edward are to watch to-night. At the same time that I derive satisfaction in my reports being fully accredited, I am hurt that the few days and nights he hoped to enjoy repose should be passed in the utmost embarrassment and anxiety.

CAPTAIN JERVIS TO MR. RICKETTS

Portsmouth, August 9th, 1771
The circumstances I am about to relate to you, dear Sir, require more address than I find myself master of; it is easy to undertake but difficult to execute a task of this delicate nature.

HINTON AMPNER

To keep you longer in suspense would be painful. I therefore proceed to tell you that Hinton Ampner House has been disturbed by such strange, unaccountable noises from the 2nd of April to this day, with little or no intermission, that it is very unfit your family should continue any longer in it. The children, happily, have not the least idea of what is doing, but my sister has suffered exceedingly through want of rest, and by keeping this event in her own breast too long.

Happy should I have been to have known it earlier, as I might have got rid of the alarm with the greatest facility, and dedicated myself entirely to her service and support till your return; but engaged as I am with the Duke of Gloucester, there is no retreating without the worst consequences. You will do me the justice to believe I have, during the short space this event has been made known to me, employed every means in my power to investigate it. Captain Luttrell, I, and my man John sat up the night after it was imparted, and I should do great injustice to my sister if I did not acknowledge to have heard what I could not, after the most diligent search and serious reflection, any way account for. Mr. Luttrell had then no doubt of the cause being beyond the reach of human understanding.

My sister having determined on the steps necessary to pursue, of which she will acquaint you, I think her situation ought not to accelerate your return, at least till you are gratified with proving the utility of the laborious alterations you have made. The strength of judgment, fortitude, and perseverance she has shown upon this very trying occasion surpass all example, and as she is harassed, not terrified, by this continual agitation, I have no doubt of her health being established the moment she is removed from the scene of action and impertinent inquiry, or I would risk everything to accompany her to the time of your arrival in England; for which and every other blessing Heaven can bestow you have the constant prayer of

J. JERVIS

[Addition in Mrs. Ricketts' hand]

This letter has just come to hand, and I hope will be in time for Mr. Lewis. Since my brother saw me, I am so extremely recovered both in health and spirits that there is no longer room for apprehension, and to the truth of this Mr. and Mrs. Newbolt, who have been beyond measure kind to me, have set their hand.

J. M. NEWBOLT
S. NEWBOLT

As I wrote you so fully two days ago, I have no particulars to add, save that the dear children have passed the day here, and are very well.—Adieu, my dearest life,

M. R.

Hinton Ampner, August 18th

I omitted to mention there are several people will prove similar disturbances have been known at Hinton Ampner many years past.

To William Henry Ricketts, Esq.,
    Canaan, near Savannah-la-Mar, Jamaica

CAPTAIN JERVIS TO MRS. RICKETTS

Alarm, off Lymington, August 16th, 1771

Our being wind-bound here, gives me an opportunity to repeat my extreme solicitude for the removal of my dearest sister from the inquietude she has so long suffered to the prejudice of her health. The more I consider the incidents, the stronger I see the necessity of a decisive step, and I almost think there will be propriety in your giving up the house, &c., at Christmas. As you have a long quarter's notice to give of this, your own judgment is a better guide than my opinion, but I beg you to resolve never to enter it again, after your London residence. . . . God Almighty bless and preserve Mr. R., you, and your lovely children,

JERVIS

MRS. RICKETTS TO W. HENRY RICKETTS, ESQ.

August 17th, 1771

The captain took his final leave of me last week, and greatly hurt I was to part with him—he has acted so very affectionately to me, and taken that true interest in everything that concerns me, as I never can forget; and most extraordinary is the subject I have to relate. Without the utmost confidence in my veracity—which I believe you have—you could not possibly credit the strange story I must tell. In order to corroborate my relation, the captain means to write to you, and I hope his letter will arrive in time for me to enclose. You may recollect in a letter I wrote about six weeks ago I mentioned there were some things in regard to Hinton Ampner you would not find so agreeable as when you left it, and I added that I could not satisfy your curiosity; nor did I intend it till you came over, had it been possible to have rubbed on till then, but when it was thought absolutely necessary by my brother and all my friends that were consulted that I should quit the place, and that the reason of it was so publicly known that you must hear it from other hands, we concluded it much more proper you should receive the truth from us, than a thousand lies and absurdities from others; and much will you feel for what your poor wife has undergone, though I cannot in writing transmit all the particulars.

On the 2nd of April last I awoke about two in the morning (observe, I lay in the chintz room, having resigned the yellow room to Nurse and Mary) and in a few minutes after I heard the sound of feet in the lobby. I listened a considerable time at the lobby door; the sound drew near; upon this I rang my bell; my maid came, we searched the room, nothing to be found; Robert was called, and went round with as little success. This appeared to me extraordinary, but I should have thought little more of it; had I not, and all the servants in the house, except Sleepy Jack, heard the strangest noises of knocking, opening and shutting of doors, talking, explosions, sometimes as loud as the bursting of cannon.[1]

I kept it to myself, tremendous as it was, except telling Mrs. Newbolt, till four months were almost expired, when, as I was so hurt for want of rest, and thought I could not support it much longer, I took the resolution to tell my brother, who upon that determined to sit up; Captain Luttrell and his own man with him. The noise was heard in the lobby, and in different parts of the house; they went all over it, every door

[1] This by me only once.

shut, every person in his room; they were astonished, and the next morning they both declared that no house was fit to live in where such noises were heard, and no natural cause appeared. You know how much the notion of haunted houses is exploded, and how careful any man would be of asserting it, and in that I think them right; as for myself, I am not afraid or ashamed to pronounce that it must proceed from a supernatural cause; but why, except as Darby imagines—who passed some days with me—there has been a murder committed that remains yet undiscovered, or for some other wise purpose, though not yet manifest? I am at a loss to explain the noises increasing and coming in the daytime. At length I determined quitting the place, and be assured, my dearest life, I did not take this painful step while it was possible to continue there; and I thank God I am as I am; the want of rest created a little fever on my spirits, which the quiet life I have passed with the Newbolts, and Dr. Walsh's prescription, have removed, so that you need not have the least uneasiness about me. Whatever the cause of these disturbances is, I am sure there has always been something of the kind since we have lived here; you must recollect often hearing the doors open and shut below stairs, and your going down sometimes during the night, and finding no person there. The servants have behaved so well, and been so cautious, that the children have heard nothing of it, which was my great dread; they are now at Winchester, which the Bishop desires I will command as my own, and I mean to go there next week, when I shall be able to get some necessaries from Hinton Ampner, and I can stay at Winchester till the cold weather sets in. Sainsbury has behaved in the genteelest manner, and is certain Lady Hillsborough would not wish us to keep the house a moment longer than it would be a convenience. He has wrote to her, and when he receives an answer, will communicate to me; indeed, my dear, we cannot think of living there. Strange and recent [*sic*] as this must appear to you, be assured no means of investigating the truth has been left untried and that it is no trick—though that is the current belief, and that Witerr (?) is concerned—but I know neither he nor any human being could carry it on. I have received the greatest friendship and attention from all my neighbours; the Shipleys have been particularly kind in offering me the house in town till the middle of January, and doing everything to contribute to my peace of mind, and so have the Newbolts. I shall not attempt to fix myself till you come over, as I can have Winchester, I daresay, till that time, but if we should determine on going abroad, it will be very inconvenient to have any besides our own family, and by a letter from the lieutenant (G. Poyntz Ricketts), I forgot to mention that the same noises have been heard by the servants since we quitted the house.

MR. SAINSBURY (LADY HILLSBOROUGH'S AGENT) TO MRS. RICKETTS

September 18th, 1771

MADAM,

At my return home, Sunday, I found a letter from Lady Hillsborough, in consequence of which I am this day going to Hinton Ampner with two of her men to sit up, under the permission you gave me.

Her ladyship desires me to present her best compliments to you, and to inform you that she is very sorry you have been so much disturbed and frightened, and to assure you that she will do everything in her power to find out who have used you so ill, and to beg your leave for me and two more to sit up, and shoot at the place whence any noise proceeds, and if nothing can be discovered by those means, then to advertise a reward of fifty guineas to any person that will discover the contriver of this wicked scheme.—I am, with great respect, madam, your most obedient, humble servant,

JNO. SAINSBURY

ROBERT CAMIS TO MRS. RICKETTS

Sunday Morning

HONOURED MADAM,

Mr. Sainsbury left our house about eleven o'clock, fryday, but he talked with Mother some time before he went of, and asked her a Great many questions Concerning the Noises. She told him Everything as She Could think of, that she had

HINTON AMPNER

heard you and all the Rest of us say, he said he had not much notion of Spirits, but he Could not tell what God would pleas to send to find things out.

Dr. Dunford Gave me the notis to fasen it to the Curch, so I wrote a Coppy of itt and sent itt to you. there is one att Hinton Ampner, one at B——,[1] and one at K——. Dr. Dunford told me Mr. Sainsbury gave itt him. but I do not no what day itt was— ... which is all at present from your Dut. Servant,

ROBERT CAMIS

'THE NOTIS

'WHAREAS some evil disposed person or persons have for severel Months past frequently made divers kinds of noises in the Mantion house occupied by Mrs. RICKETTS, att Hinton Ampner. This is to give notis that if any person or persons will Discover the Auther or Authers thereof to me, such person or persons shall Receive a reward of Fifty Guineas, to be paid on the Conviction of the offenders, or if any person Concerned in making such Noises Will Discover his or her Acomplice or acomplices therein, such person shall be pardoned, and be intitled to the same Reward, to be paid on Conviction of the Offender.

'JNO. SAINSBURY

'*September 20, 1771.*'

ROBERT CAMIS TO MRS. RICKETTS

March ye 8th

HONOURED MADAM,

I hope you have received a letter that was directed to Hinton Ampner. I am very sorry that we cannot find out the reason of the noise, that we might come to Hinton Ampner again, as we have not heard anything since. My mother came one morning last week, and told me she had dreamed three nights after one another that she was upon the great stairs up at the landing-place that leads into the garrots, and was troubled in

---

[1] The initials stand for villages near Hinton Ampner. In the original version every name, of place and person, is represented by an initial followed by a blank. (Note by S.S.)

her dreams, and was rambling about a great way, but att the end she was always there. One of the nights she dremed she was in the road from C——, and found a large pair of stuf shoes laceed with silver very much, and a pair of gloves with a great deal of lace upon itt, and she brought itt to you, and shewed itt to you, and then she carreed it to the top of the great stairs.

So she was there in the greatest part of her dreams. So my mother and I went up and searched every part we coud think of. I pulled up a board in the dark closet in the first garrot where there was a little hole, but found nothing, so we went into the lumber garrot that is over the best bedroom, and lookt every place we could think of, but found nothing.

There was a iron chest lockt that we could not open. I took it up, shook itt, and there was something like iron rattled, and something like a role of paper with itt. So I wrote this to know if you new what was in itt—if the key is lost itt will be very difficult to open itt. My mother gives her duty to you, and hopes you will not be angry for mentioning her dreams to you. My Mother and all of us is very well and joyns with me in duty from your dutifull servant,

ROBERT CAMIS

[Note by Mrs. Ricketts.—The chest was afterwards forced open, and nothing found in it save old accounts of no consequence.]

ROBERT CAMIS TO MRS. RICKETTS

Hinton Ampner, Nov. 24th

HONOURED MADAM,

I have not heard any noises in the house myself, but my mother and sister Martha was in the kitchen on Wednesday last about twelve o'clock, and of a sudden they heard a dismal groaning very loud—one thought it was in the housekeeper's room, and the other thought it was over the meal bin—they ware both surprized very much, and thought they had better go out of doors to see if any body was there, but they found no body, and when they came in again they heard no more of itt. . . .

HINTON AMPNER

ROBERT CAMIS TO MRS. RICKETTS

No Date

I have heard no noise myself, but on Satterday about eleven a clock my mother went home to make her bed, and left sister Martha in the chicking att work with her needle. She heard a noise like a roleing clap of thunder; it did not surprise her because she thought it was thunder, for it gered [jarred?] the windows, but she went to the gardner to no if he herd it thunder, and he said he did not. About twelve o'clock my mother came into the house and said she did not here any thunder. The noise appeared to she to be towards the yallow room. Itt seemed to role along, which made her think itt was thunder.

Hinton Ampner Parsonage, July 7th, 1772

To my dear children I address the following relation, anxious that the truths which I so faithfully have delivered shall be as faithfully transmitted to posterity, to my own in particular. I determined to commit them to writing, which I recommend to their care and attentive consideration, entreating them to bear in mind the peculiar mercy of Providence in preserving them from all affright and terror during the series of wonderful disturbances that surrounded them, wishing them to be assured the veracity of their mother was pure and undoubted, that even in her infancy it was in the family a proverb, and according to the testimony of that excellent person Chancellor Hoadly she was *truth itself*; she writes, not to gratify vanity, but to add weight to her relation.

To the Almighty and Unerring Judgment of Heaven and Earth I dare appeal for the truth, to the best of my memory and comprehension, of what I here relate.

MARY RICKETTS

Hinton Ampner, near Alresford, in Hampshire

The Mansion House and estate of Hinton Ampner, near Alresford, Hampshire, devolved in 1755 to the Right Honourable Henry Bilson Legge in right of his lady, daughter and sole heiress of Lord Stawell, who married the eldest daughter and co-heiress of Sir Hugh Stewkley, Bart., by whose ancestors the estate at Hinton Ampner had been possessed many generations and by this marriage passed to Mr. Legge on the death of the said Sir Hugh.

Mr. Legge (who on the death of his elder brother became Lord Dartmouth)[1] made Hinton Ampner his constant residence. Honoria, the youngest sister of his lady, lived with them during the life of her sister, and so continued with Lord Y. till her death in 1754.[2]

On the evening of April 2nd, 1755, Mr. Legge, sitting alone in the little parlour at Hinton Ampner, was seized with a fit of apoplexy; he articulated one sentence only to be understood, and continued speechless and insensible till the next morning, when he expired.

His lordship's family at the time consisted of the following domestics: Isaac M., house steward and bailiff. Sarah P., housekeeper, who had lived in the family near forty years. Thomas P., coachman, husband to said Sarah, who had lived there upwards of forty years. Elizabeth B., housemaid, an old servant. Jane D., dairymaid. Mary B., cook. Joseph S., butler. Joseph, groom. Richard T., gardener, and so continued by Mr. Ricketts. Mr. Legge had one son, who died at Westminster School, aged sixteen.

Thomas P., his wife, and Elizabeth B. continued to have the care of the house during the lifetime of Mr. Legge,[3] who usually

---

[1] I believe this to be a mistake on the part of the third Marquess of Bute who edited the pamphlet for publication, in 1893. Henry Bilson Legge did not succeed his brother as 2nd Earl of Dartmouth. (Note by S.S.)

[2] A tablet in Hinton Ampner Church records that Honoria Stawell died on November 25th, 1754, in the 67th year of her age.

[3] Henry Bilson Legge, born in 1708, third son of the first Earl of Dartmouth, married Mary Stawell, daughter and heiress of Lord Stawell, who had married the daughter of Sir Hugh Stewkley of Hinton Ampner. She was created Baroness Stawell in her own right. After the death of Henry Bilson Legge, who had been Chancellor of the Exchequer, Mary Stawell married Wills, first Marquess of Downshire. Her younger sister, Honoria, is to be regarded as the villain of this piece. Mary Stawell had one son, Henry, 2nd Lord Stawell, who married Mary, daughter of Viscount Curzon, and died in 1820, when the Barony expired. He left an only daughter, Mary, married to John 2nd Lord Sherborne. She died, leaving several children, in 1864. The estates at Hinton Ampner devolved upon her second son. (Note by S. S.).

came there for one month every year in the shooting season. On his death, in August, 1764, Lady Stawell, so created in her own right, since married to the Earl of Hillsborough, determined to let Hinton Ampner Mansion, and Mr. Ricketts took it in December following. Thomas P. was at that time lying dead in the house. His widow and Elizabeth B. quitted it on our taking possession in January, 1765. We removed thither from town, and had the same domestics that lived with us there and till some time afterwards we had not any house-servant belonging to the neighbourhood. Soon after we were settled at Hinton Ampner I frequently heard noises in the night, as of people shutting, or rather slapping doors with vehemence. Mr. Ricketts went often round the house on supposition there were either housebreakers or irregularity among his servants. In these searches he never could trace any person; the servants were in their proper apartments, and no appearance of disorder. The noises continued to be heard, and I could conceive no other cause than that some of the villagers had false keys to let themselves in and out at pleasure; the only preventive to this evil was changing the locks, which was accordingly done, yet without the effect we had reasonably expected.

About six months after we came thither, Elizabeth Brelsford, nurse to our eldest son, Henry, then about eight months old, was sitting by him when asleep, in the room over the pantry, appropriated for the nursery, and, being a hot summer's evening, the door was open that faces the entrance into the yellow bedchamber, which, with the adjoining dressing-room, was the apartment usually occupied by the lady of the house. She was sitting directly opposite to this door, and plainly saw (as she afterwards related) a gentleman in a drab-coloured suit of clothes go into the yellow room. She was in no way surprised at the time, but on the housemaid, Molly Newman, coming up with her supper, she asked what strange gentleman was come. Upon the other answering there was no one, she related what is already described, and desired her fellow-servant to accompany her to search the room; this they did immediately without any appearance of what she had seen. She was much concerned and disturbed, and she was thoroughly assured she could no ways be deceived, the light being sufficient to distinguish any object clearly. In some time after it was mentioned to me. I treated it as the effect of fear or superstition, to which the lower class of people are so prone, and it was entirely obliterated from my mind till the late astonishing disturbances brought to my recollection this and other previous circumstances.

In the autumn of the same year George T——, son of the gardener of that name, who was then groom, crossing the great hall to go to bed, saw at the other end a man in a drab-coloured coat, whom he concluded to be the butler, who wore such coloured clothes, he being lately come and his livery not made. As he passed immediately upstairs to the room where all the men servants lay, he was in great astonishment to find the butler and other men servants in bed. Thus the person he had seen in the hall remained unaccounted for, like the same person before described by the nurse; and George T——, now living, avers these particulars in the same manner he first related them.

In the month of July, 1767, about seven in the evening, there were sitting in the kitchen, Thomas Wheeler, postilion; Ann Hall, my own woman; Sarah, waiting woman to Mrs. Mary Poyntz; and Dame Lacy; the other servants were out excepting the cook, then employed in washing up her things in the scullery.

The persons in the kitchen heard a woman come downstairs, and along the passage leading towards them, whose clothes rustled as of the stiffest silk; and on their looking that way, the door standing open, a female figure rushed past, and out of the house door, as they conceived. Their view of her was imperfect; but they plainly distinguished a tall figure in dark-coloured clothes. Dame Brown, the cook, instantly coming in, this figure passed close by her, and instantly disappeared. She described the person and drapery as before mentioned, and they all united in astonishment who or what this appearance could be; and their surprise was heightened when a man, coming directly into the yard and into the house the way she went out, on being asked who the woman was he met, declared he had seen no one.

Ann Hall, since married to John Sparks, now living at

Rogate, near Petersfield, will testify to the truth of this relation, as will Dame Brown, now living in Bramdean. The postilion is since dead.

Meanwhile the noises continued to be heard occasionally. Miss Parker's woman, Susan Maidstone, was terrified with the most dismal groans and rustling round her bed. At different times most of the servants were alarmed with noises that could no way be accounted for. In the latter end of the year 1769 Mr. Ricketts went to Jamaica; I continued at Hinton Ampner with my three infant children and eight servants, whose names and connections were as follows: Ann Sparks, late Ann Hall, my own woman, the daughter of very industrious parents. Sarah Horner, nurse, sister to a substantial farmer of that name, and of a family of integrity and property. Hannah Streeter, nursemaid, of reputable parents and virtuous principles. Lucy Webb, housemaid, of honest principles. Dame Brown, cook, quiet and regular. John Sparks, coachman. John Horner, postilion, aged sixteen years, eldest son to the farmer above-mentioned. Lewis Chanson, butler, a Swiss and of strict integrity. Richard T——, gardener, but did not live in the house.

I have been thus particular in the description of those persons of whom my family was composed, to prove the improbability that a set of ignorant country people, excepting the Swiss alone, should league to carry on a diabolical scheme imputed to them so injuriously, and which in truth was far beyond the art and reach of man to compass.

Some time after Mr. Ricketts left me, I—then lying in the bedroom over the kitchen—heard frequently the noise of some one walking in the room within and the rustling as of silk clothes against the door that opened into my room, sometimes so loud and of such continuance as to break my rest. Instant search being often made, we never could discover any appearance of human or brute being.

Repeatedly disturbed in the same manner, I made it my constant practice to search the room and closets within, and to secure the only door that led from that room on the inside in such manner as to be certain no one could gain entrance without passing through my own apartment, which was always made fast by a draw-bolt on the door. Yet this precaution did not preclude the disturbance, which continued with little interruption.

About this time an old man, living in the poor-house at W—— M——, came and desired to speak to me. When admitted, he told me he could not rest in his mind without acquainting me that his wife had often related to him that in her younger days a carpenter whom she had well known, had told her he was once sent for by Sir Hugh Stewkley, and directed by him to take up some boards in the dining-room, known in our time by the name of lobby, and that Sir Hugh had concealed something underneath which he, the carpenter, conceived was treasure, and then he was ordered to put down the boards in the same manner as they lay before. This account I repeated to Mr. Sainsbury, attorney to Lady Hillsborough, that if he thought it were a probability he might have the floor taken up and examined.[1]

In February, 1770, John Sparks and Ann, his wife, quitted my service, and went to live upon their farm at Rogate. In place of John Sparks I hired Robert Camis, one of six sons of Roger and Mary Camis, of the parish of Hinton Ampner, and whose ancestors have been in possession of a little estate there upwards of four hundred years—a family noted for their moral and religious lives. In the room of Ann Sparks I hired Ruth Turpin, but she being disordered in mind continued with me but few months. I then took Elizabeth Godin, of Alresford, sister to an eminent grocer of that place. Lewis Chanson quitted me in August, 1770, and I hired Edward Russel, now living with Mr. Harris, of Alresford, to succeed him.

I mention these changes among my domestics, though in themselves unimportant, to evince the impossibility of a confederacy, for the course of nearly seven years, and with a succession of different persons, so that at the time of my leaving Hinton Ampner I had not one servant that lived with me at my first going thither, nor for some time afterwards.

---

[1] It should be explained that Lady Hillsborough is the same person as Mary, Baroness Stawell. Her second husband was created Earl of Hillsborough in 1772, and Marquess of Downshire in 1789. He died in 1793. (Note by S.S.).

HINTON AMPNER

In the summer of 1770, one night that I was lying in the yellow bedchamber (the same I have mentioned that the person in drab-coloured clothes was seen to enter), I had been in bed half an hour thoroughly awake, and without the least terror or apprehension on my spirits. I plainly heard the footsteps of a man, with plodding step, walking towards the foot of my bed. I thought the danger too near to ring my bell for assistance, but sprang out of bed and in an instant was in the nursery opposite; and with Hannah Streeter and a light I returned to search for what I had heard, but all in vain. There was a light burning in the dressing-room within, as usual, and there was no door or means of escape save at the one that opened to the nursery. This alarm perplexed me more than any preceding, being within my own room, the footsteps as distinct as ever I heard, myself perfectly awake and collected.

I had, nevertheless, resolution to go to bed alone in the same room, and did not form any conclusion as to the cause of this very extraordinary disturbance. For some months afterwards I did not hear any noise that particularly struck my attention, till, in November of the same year, I then being removed to the chintz bedroom over the hall, as a warmer apartment, I once or twice heard sounds of harmony, and one night in particular I heard three distinct and violent knocks as given with a club, or something very ponderous against a door below stairs; it occurred to me that housebreakers must be forcing into some apartment, and I immediately rang my bell. No one hearing the summons and the noise ceasing, I thought no further of it at that time. After this, and in the beginning of the year 1771, I was frequently sensible of a hollow murmuring that seemed to possess the whole house; it was independent of wind, being equally heard on the calmest nights, and it was a sound I had never been accustomed to hear.

On the morning of the 27th of February, when Elizabeth Godin came into my room, I inquired what weather. She replying in a very faint tone, I asked if she were ill. She said she was well, but had never in her life been so terrified as during the preceding night; that she had heard the most dismal groans and fluttering round her bed most part of the night, that she had got up to search the room and up the chimney, and though it was a bright moonlight she could not discover anything. I did not pay much attention to her account, but it occurred to me that should anyone tell her it was the room formerly occupied by Mrs. P., the old housekeeper, she would be afraid to lie there again. Mrs. P. dying a few days before at K——, was brought and interred in Hinton Ampner churchyard the evening of the night this disturbance happened.

That very day five weeks, being the 2nd of April, I waked between one and two o'clock, as I found by my watch, which, with a rushlight, was on a table close to my bedside. I lay thoroughly awake for some time, and then heard one or more persons walking to and fro in the lobby adjoining. I got out of bed and listened at the door for the space of twenty minutes, in which time I distinctly heard the walking with the addition of a loud noise like pushing strongly against a door. Being thus assured my senses were not deceived I determined to ring my bell, to which I had before much reluctance on account of disturbing the nursery maid, who was very ill of a fever.

Elizabeth Godin during her illness lay in the room with my sons, and came immediately on hearing my bell. Thoroughly convinced there were persons in the lobby, before I opened my door, I asked her if she saw no one there. On her replying in the negative, I went out to her, examined the window, which was shut, looked under the couch, the only furniture of concealment there; the chimney board was fastened, and when removed, all was clear behind it. She found the door into the lobby shut, as it was every night. After this examination I stood in the middle of the room, pondering with much astonishment, when suddenly the door that opens into the little recess leading to the yellow apartment sounded as if played to and fro by a person standing behind it. This was more than I could bear unmoved. I ran into the nursery and rang the bell there that goes into the men's apartments. Robert Camis came to the door at the landing place, which door was every night secured, so that no person could get to that floor unless through the windows. Upon opening the door to Robert I told him the reason I had to suppose that someone was intrenched behind the door I before mentioned, and giving him a light and arming him with a billet of wood, myself and Elizabeth

Godin waited the event. Upon opening the door there was not any being whatever, and the yellow apartment was locked, the key, hanging up, and a great bolt drawn across the outside door, as usual when not in use. There was then no further retreat or hiding place. After dismissing Robert and securing the door, I went to bed in my sons' room, and about half an hour afterwards heard three distinct knocks, as described before; they seemed below, but I could not then or ever after ascertain the place. The next night I lay in my own room; I now and then heard noises and frequently the hollow murmur.

On the 7th of May, exactly the day five weeks from the 2nd of April, this murmur was uncommonly loud. I could not sleep, apprehending it the prelude to some greater noise. I got up and went to the nursery, stayed there till half an hour past three, and then, being daybreak, I thought I should get some sleep in my own apartment; I returned and lay till ten minutes before four, and then the great hall door directly under me was slapped to with the utmost violence, so as to shake my room perceivably. I jumped out of bed to the window that commands the porch. There was light to distinguish every object, but none to be seen that could account for what I had heard. Upon examining the door it was found fast locked and bolted as usual.

From this time I determined to have my woman lie in a little bed in my room. The noises grew more frequent, and she was always sensible of the same sounds, and much in the same direction as they struck me. Harassed and perplexed, I was yet very unwilling to divulge my embarrassment. I had taken every method to investigate the cause, and could not discover the least appearance of trick; on the contrary, I became convinced it was beyond the power of any mortal agent to perform, but knowing how exploded such opinions were, I kept them in my own bosom, and hoped my resolution would enable me to support whatever might befall.

After Midsummer the noises became every night more intolerable. They began before I went to bed, and with intermissions were heard till after broad day in the morning. I could frequently distinguish articulate sounds, and usually a shrill female voice would begin, and then two others with deeper and manlike tone seemed to join in the discourse, yet, though this conversation sounded as if close to me, I never could distinguish words.

I have often asked Elizabeth Godin if she heard any noise, and of what sort. She as often described the seeming conversation in the manner I have related, and other noises. One night in particular my bed curtains rustled, and sounded as if dragged by a person walking against them. I then asked her if she heard any noise and of what kind. She spoke of it exactly in the manner I have done. Several times I heard sounds of harmony within the room—no distinct or regular notes, but a vibration of harmonious tones; walking, talking, knocking, opening and slapping of doors were repeated every night. My brother, who had not long before returned from the Mediterranean, had been to stay with me, yet so great was my reluctance to relate anything beyond the bounds of probability that I could not bring myself to disclose my embarrassed situation to the friend and brother who could most essentially serve and comfort me. The noises continuing in the same manner when he was with me, I wished to learn if he heard them, and one morning I carelessly said: 'I was afraid last night the servants would disturb you, and rang my bell to order them to bed.' He replied he had not heard them. The morning after he left me to return to Portsmouth, about three o'clock and daylight, Elizabeth Godin and myself both awake—she had been sitting up in bed looking round her, expecting as she always did to see something terrible—I heard with infinite astonishment the most loud, deep, tremendous noise which seemed to rush and fall with infinite velocity and force on the lobby floor adjoining to my room. I started up, and called to Godin, 'Good God! did you hear that noise?' She made no reply; on repeating the question she answered with a faltering voice, 'She was so frightened she scarce durst speak'. Just as that instant we heard a shrill and dreadful shriek, seeming to proceed from under the spot where the rushing noise fell, and repeated three or four times, growing fainter as it seemed to descend, till it sank into earth. Hannah Streeter, who lay in the room with my children, heard the same noises, and was so appalled she lay for two hours almost deprived of sense and motion.

HINTON AMPNER

Having heard little of the noises preceding and that little she did not regard, she had rashly expressed a wish to hear more of them, and from that night till she quitted the house there was scarce a night passed that she did not hear the sound as if some person walked towards her door, and pushed against it, as though attempting to force it open. This alarm, so more than commonly horrible, determined me to impart the whole series to my brother on his return to Hinton Ampner, expected in a week. The frequency of the noises, harassing to my rest, and getting up often at unreasonable hours, fixed a slow fever and deep cough, my health was much impaired, but my resolution firm. I remained in anxious expectation of my brother, and he being detained a week longer at Portsmouth than he had foreseen, it occurred to me to endeavour, by changing my apartment, to obtain a little rest; I removed to that formerly occupied by Elizabeth Godin; I did not mention my intention till ten at night, when the room was prepared, and I went to bed soon after. I had scarce lain down when the same noises surrounded me that I before related, and I mention the circumstance of changing my room without previous notice, to prove the impossibility of a plan of operations being so suddenly conveyed to another part of the house were they such as human agents could achieve. The week following I was comforted by the arrival of my brother. However desirous to impart the narrative, yet I forbore till the next morning; I wished him to enjoy a night's rest, and therefore contented myself with preparing him to hear on the morrow the most astonishing tale that ever assailed his ears, and that he must summon all his trust of my veracity to meet my relation. He replied it was scarce possible for me to relate any matter he could not believe, little divining the nature of what I had to offer to his faith.

The next morning I began my narrative, to which he attended with mixed surprise and wonder. Just as I had finished, Captain Luttrell, our neighbour at K——, chancing to call, induced my brother to impart the whole to him, who in a very friendly manner offered to unite his endeavours to investigate the cause. It was then agreed he should come late in the evening, and divide the night watch between them, keeping profoundly secret there was any such intention. My brother took the precaution, accompanied by his own servant, John Bolton, to go into every apartment, particularly those on the first and attic storey, examined every place of concealment, and saw each door fastened, save those to chambers occupied by the family; this done, he went to bed in the room over the servants' hall.

Captain Luttrell and my brother's man with arms sat up in the chintz room adjoining, and my brother was to be called on any alarm.

I lay that night in Elizabeth Godin's room, and the children in the nurseries; thus every chamber on that floor was occupied. I bolted and locked the door that opened to that floor from the back stairs, so that there was no entrance unless through the room where Captain Luttrell kept watch.

As soon as I lay down, I heard a rustling as of a person close to the door. I ordered Elizabeth Godin to sit up a while, and if the noise continued, to go and acquaint Mr. Luttrell.

She heard it, and instantly Mr. Luttrell's room door was thrown open, and we heard him speak.

I must now give his account as related to my brother and myself the next morning.

He said he heard the footsteps of a person walking across the lobby, that he instantly threw the door open, and called, 'Who goes there?' That something flitted past him, when my brother directly called out 'Look against my door.' He was awake, and heard what Mr. Luttrell had said, and also the continuance of the same noise till it reached his door. He arose and joined Mr. Luttrell. Both astonished, they heard various other noises, examined everywhere, found the staircase door fast secured as I had left it. I lay so near, and had never closed my eyes, no one could go to that door unheard. My brother and his man proceeded up stairs, and found the servants in their own rooms, and all doors closed as they had seen just before. They sat up together, my brother and Mr. Luttrell, till break of day, when my brother returned to his own chamber. About that time, as I imagined, I heard the chintz room door opened and slammed to with the utmost violence, and immediately that of the hall chamber opened and shut in the same manner.

I mentioned to Godin my surprise that my brother, who was ever attentive not to alarm or disturb the children, should hazard both by such vehement noise. An hour after I heard the house door open and slam in the same way, so as to shake the house. No one person was then up, for as I had never slept, I heard the servants rise and go down about half an hour afterwards. When we were assembled at breakfast, I observed the noise my brother had made with the doors.

Mr. Luttrell replied, 'I assure you Jervis made not the least noise; it was your door and the next I heard opened and slapped in the way you describe.'

My brother did not hear either. He afterwards acknowledged to me that when gone to bed and Mr. Luttrell and I were sitting below, he heard dreadful groans and various noises that he was then and after unable to account for. His servant was at that time with mine below.

Captain Luttrell declared the disturbances of the preceding night were of such a nature that the house was an unfit residence for any human being. My brother, though more guarded in his expressions, concurred in that opinion, and the result of our deliberations was to send an express to Mr. Sainsbury, Lady Hillsborough's steward, to request he would come over immediately on a very particular occasion, with which he would be made acquainted on his arrival.

Unluckily, Mr. Sainsbury was confined with the gout, and sent over his clerk, a youth of fifteen, to whom we judged it useless and improper to divulge the circumstances.

My brother sat up every night of the week he then passed at Hinton Ampner. In the middle of one of these nights, I was surprised with the sound of a gun or pistol let off near me, immediately followed by groans as of a person in agonies, or expiring, that seemed to proceed between my chamber and the next, the nursery. I sent Godin to Nurse Horner, to ask if she had heard any noise; she had not. Upon my inquiry the next morning of my brother, he had [not] heard it, though the report and groans were loud and deep.

Several instances occurred where very loud noises were heard by one or two persons, when those equally near and in the same direction were not sensible of the least impression.

As the watching every night made it necessary for my brother to gain rest in the day, he usually lay down after dinner. During one of these times he was gone to rest, I had sent the children and their attendants out to walk, the dairymaid had gone to milk, the cook in the scullery, my own woman with my brother's man sitting together in the servants' hall; I, reading in the parlour, heard my brother's bell ring with great quickness. I ran to his room, and he asked me if I had heard any noise, 'because', said he, 'as I was lying wide awake an immense weight seemed to fall through the ceiling to the floor just by that mahogany press, and it is impossible I should be deceived'. His man was by this time come up, and said he was sitting underneath the room as I before mentioned, and heard not the least noise. The inquiry and attention my brother devoted to investigate this affair was such as from the reach of his capacity and ardent spirit might be expected; the result was his earnest request that I would quit the place, and when obliged to return to Portsmouth, that I would permit him to send Mr. Nichols, his Lieutenant of Marines, and an old friend of the family, to continue till my removal with me.

One circumstance is of a nature so singularly striking that I cannot omit to relate it. In one of our evening's conversations on this wonderful train of disturbances I mentioned a very extraordinary effect I had frequently observed in a favourite cat that was usually in the parlour with me, and when sitting on table or chair with accustomed unconcern she would suddenly slink down as if struck with the greatest terror, conceal herself under my chair, and put her head close to my feet. In a short space of time she would come forth quite unconcerned. I had not long given him this account before it was verified to him in a striking manner. We neither then, nor I at other times, perceived the least noise that could give alarm to the animal, nor did I ever perceive the like effect before these disturbances, nor afterwards when she was removed with me to another habitation. The servants gave the same account of a spaniel that lived in the house, but to that, as I did not witness, I cannot testify.

There is another copy, and no more to be taken unless either be destroyed.

MARY RICKETTS

HINTON AMPNER

These two narratives are for my grand-daughters Martha and Henrietta Jervis, not to be read until twenty-one or upwards, nor then unless their nerves are firm. The letters, &c., belonging to be carefully preserved.

FIRST NARRATIVE IN MRS. RICKETTS'S HANDWRITING. TO BE READ AT LEISURE

£60 reward was offered on discovery by Marchioness of Downshire, which Mr. Ricketts on his return, increased to £100. The Bishop of Winchester lent me the old Palace at Winchester, to occupy at races or on any public occasion, and thither I removed when it was no longer thought proper I should remain at Hinton Ampner; and when I left, the Bishop of St. Asaph offered me his house in town, where I stayed till I had taken one in Curzon Street.

What determined my removal to Winchester was, after trying to obtain rest by removing to Dame Camis's house, when I returned to the mansion I was soon after assailed by a noise I never before heard, very near me, and the terror I felt not to be described. It then appeared I was no longer to be supported, after my brother was convinced I ought not to delay my removal. I therefore accepted the earnest invitation of my friends Mr. and Mrs. Newbolt, and continued with them till Winchester was prepared for my dear children, where we remained till November, with the exception of three days, with Dr. Gilbert, Canon of S——, and his daughter; and there Lord Radnor—then Lord Folkestone—was very desirous to see the lady that came from the haunted house.

The Bishop of St. Asaph opposed, on the ground that such means were unworthy the Deity to employ, while the good Bishop of Winchester, when I related that Robert Camis had been thrice called at the window in a voice he well remembered, that of the steward of the late Lord Dartmouth,[1] said he should have conjured him by the Father, the Son, and the Holy Ghost; which I told him but believe no such occasion occurred,

---

[1] Henry Bilson Legge. As previously noted, we think that he did not succeed as Earl of Dartmouth. (Note by S.S.)

or courage failed. This steward stole his lord's gold buckles, and was much suspected of other dishonesty; whence, probably arose the idea of concealed treasure. I never heard that any was found.

When Lord Dartmouth was seized with the fit that carried him off, he called to his man, 'Cut a vein, cut a vein!' but no vein was cut. Of the excellent Dame Camis, from whom I had much information of the Stawell and Legge family, Dr. Durnford, minister of B——, who performed duty at Hinton Ampner, also told me that, in the number of years he had officiated, he had never known her miss Divine Service, unless illness of any one of her family or of herself prevented.

When Mr. Ricketts returned from Jamaica, having continued to keep Hinton Ampner on account of our cattle and the manor, Mr. Ricketts took the Parsonage, where we resided for two years, when the purchase of Longwood was made, and we removed thither.

NARRATIVE NO. 2, IN MRS. RICKETTS'S HANDWRITING, AND ATTESTED BY HER SECOND SON, EDWARD JERVIS RICKETTS, AFTERWARDS VISCOUNT ST. VINCENT

After Mrs. Ricketts had quitted Hinton Ampner House, and before possession had been given to Lady Hillsborough, the keys were left with Dame Camis, who came over every fair day to open the windows, she living close by.

Mr. George Ricketts and Mr. Poyntz Ricketts, active young men in the prime of life, were walking to and fro close to the house on the paddock side, when a great noise was heard within it, upon which one of them said, 'They are at their tricks again, let us go in and see.' They lost no time getting through the drawing-room window on the ground floor, and proceeding throughout the house. No living creature was to be found in it, neither was there any appearance of anything that could have been moved so as to occasion the sounds they heard.

(Signed) EDWARD JERVIS RICKETTS

HINTON AMPNER

NARRATIVE NO. 3.—NOTES TAKEN BY OSBORNE
MARKHAM, ESQ., FROM MRS. RICKETTS'S DICTATION

Miss Parker, mentioned in this narrative, was afterwards Lady St. Vincent, who with her sister (afterwards Mrs. Heathcote) was staying in the house during the time their father, Chief Baron Parker, was going the circuit.

It is understood that when Mrs. Ricketts left Hinton Ampner she went to the palace of the Bishop of Winchester, of which his kindness gave her the occasional use, she being an intimate friend and relation to his wife. After Mrs. Ricketts left Hinton Ampner (say within a year) another family (Mr. Lawrence) came to reside there, who stayed about a year and then suddenly quitted it.

After this the house was never occupied. On being pulled down there was found by the workmen under the floor of one of the rooms a small skull, said to be that of a monkey; but the matter was never brought forward by any regular inquiry, or professional opinion resorted to as to the real nature of the skull.

The first appearance of anything being seen or heard was before Mrs. Ricketts took possession of Hinton Ampner, which did not come to her knowledge until some time after the disturbances had been heard in the house. Joseph (the groom) then being one of the servants left in occupation of the house, and being in bed in the garret, the moon shining brightly into the room, and he being clearly awake, saw a man in a drab coat with his hands behind him, in the manner his late master held them, looking steadfastly upon him.

Note by Martha H. G. Jervis.—A number of papers (broadsides, &c.) which had been concealed during the civil wars were found under the floor of the lobby when the house was pulled down, and a small box containing what was said to be the skull of a monkey.

Notes in the handwriting of Martha Honora Georgina Jervis, elder of Mrs. Ricketts's two grand-daughters, to whom the manuscripts were left, and second wife of Osborne Markham, Esq., the writer of the foregoing pages:

HINTON AMPNER

NARRATIVE BY MARTHA H. G. JERVIS

Rosehill, July 10th, 1818

I called on old Lucy Camis at the farm and inquired if she had recently heard of Hannah Streeter. She replied that she lived at the Lower Brook, Winchester, and that she (Lucy) had been to see her last year, and asked if she remembered having been disturbed by the noises at Hinton Ampner, particularly one night when the other servants were gone to bed, when, being in the servants' hall, they heard a sound as of the great iron brazier falling through the roof of the pantry (over which there was no room), and that it went '*Twirl! twirl! twirl!*' till it sank in the ground. They were so much terrified that Lucy would not venture up to the garrets, but slept that night in the nursery. They found the brazier the next morning in the place where it had been left.

When Lord St. Vincent was in the house, and the servants were suspected of making the disturbances, Mrs. Ricketts went one night for something she wanted to the housekeeper's room, which opened into the kitchen, where the domestics were all assembled at supper. She then heard noises, and was near fainting, and called to some one to accompany her up to her brother.

The morning after Mrs. P.'s interment Elizabeth Godin complained to the other servants that she had been dreadfully disturbed the preceding night, and that soon after she was in bed something fell with force against the window, succeeded by a dismal groan.

Lucy said, 'God knows whether these noises were not in consequence of their sins.'

I replied, 'What did you suppose they were guilty of?'

She said, 'God knows whether she had a child and killed it; but I cannot say; it is not for us to suspect them, God knows.'

She spoke of Mrs. Ricketts in the highest terms and with many tears; said she did so much good in the neighbourhood that it was very unlikely any should seek to drive her away, above all, her servants, who loved her and were in perfect harmony with each other.

One night Lucy slept in a small bed in Mrs. Ricketts's

room, Elizabeth Godin being ill. Mrs. Ricketts woke her and asked her if she did not hear music, which she did, and 'the steps of some one moving *stately* to it'. The noises seemed mostly in the lobby and the yellow and adjoining chambers.

Lucy said that when Mr. Lawrence afterwards took possession of the house he forbid the servants from saying a word of the disturbances under penalty of losing their places. She heard that once, as his housemaid was standing in the lobby, a female figure rushed by and disappeared, but of the truth of this she could not vouch.

The foregoing information was given me by Lucy Camis, who was perfectly collected, and I merely made such queries as should lead her on without in any degree prompting her recollection.

MARTHA H. G. JERVIS

NOTES AND REMARKS BY THE THIRD MARQUESS OF BUTE

This case is very interesting, and seems of greater evidential value than many in which it is possible to interrogate the witnesses, because, although the events took place 120 years ago, the witnesses in this instance were very numerous and various as well as simultaneous and consentient, some of them of quite exceptional intelligence, and very great trouble was taken to observe and sift the facts, and to record them at the time in the numerous documents heretofore reprinted.

What small and hypothetical explanation the phenomena will bear must depend in a great measure upon the history of the house, and the following notes have been compiled not only from the printed pamphlet but also from Burke's *Extinct Baronetage*, and his *Extinct Peerage*, and *Extant Peerage*, and Collins's *Peerage*.

The family whose home this house was, was an ancient one, but was originally of M., in S—hire. The first who lived at Hinton Ampner appears to have been *Sir Thomas Stewkley*, knight, described in the Heraldic Visitation of 1623 (Berry's *County Genealogist—Hants*) as 'Sir Thomas [Stewkley] of M——, and now of Hinton Ampner, 1623'. It seems not improbable that he built the house, which is described in the pamphlet as 'the old manor-house'. It is a pity that there is no description, plan, or drawing of the house. It seems to have been small, as all the servants except the housekeeper or lady's maid, and the nurse, slept in the attics, and Mrs. Ricketts remarks that when two people were staying there every room on the bedroom floor was occupied. On the ground floor there was a drawing-room, probably also the little parlour (unless these were the same) where Lord Dartmouth was taken ill, and, it is to be presumed, a dining-room. There was also a large hall, seemingly used as a servants' hall. There were two staircases, a principal and a back stair, and from the foot of one of these a passage ran past the kitchen to an outer door, perhaps the main house door. Off the kitchen was a housekeeper's room, and near it a scullery. There was also a pantry, over which there was no room. On the bedroom floor there was a principal bedroom, the yellow one, which had a dressing-room opening near the back stair. The yellow bedroom itself opened into a recess, and this into a lobby, a place with one window and a fireplace, which Mrs. Ricketts says had been used as a dining-room. Opposite the door of the yellow room was that of the nursery; over the hall was another bedroom, called the chintz room, and another room. On this floor also there was at least one other room, usually occupied by the housekeeper or lady's maid. At the top of the principal staircase was a landing from which was a way to go up to the attics.

Sir Thomas married Elizabeth, daughter and co-heir of John G. of W——, B——shire, son and heir of Sir John G. of the same, and had at least three sons, Hugh, Thomas, and John. He was probably an old man in 1623, as his sister Joan had married George L., of D——, S——shire, who was High Sheriff of that county in 1593. He seems to have died soon after the visitation, as his eldest son, *Sir Hugh X.*, was created a baronet in 1627. He is said to have married Sarah, daughter and co-heir of Ambrose D., of L., W——shire, and to have died about 1642.

Sir Hugh Stewkley, son of the preceding, and second baronet is the Sir Hugh Stewkley mentioned in the pamphlet as having concealed some papers under the floor of the dining-room, called by the Ricketts the lobby. These papers are stated to have been found when the house was pulled down, and to have been 'broadsides, &c., which had been concealed during the civil wars'. They were probably compromising under the Republican Government, but, after the Restoration, were either forgotten by Sir Hugh or regarded with indifference. Under this floor also was found a small box containing a little skull, which 'was said to be that of a monkey; but the matter was never brought forward by any regular inquiry or professional opinion resorted to as to the real nature of the skull'. It is not stated whether the box containing this curious object was found along with the papers, or under another part of the floor. It is impossible to conceive any motive to induce either Sir Hugh or anybody else who possessed a monkey's skull as a zoological curiosity—the only reason why they could have had it at all—to bury it in a box underneath a floor. It is not stated whether the skull fitted closely into the box, or whether there might have been room for anything else. A further remark will be made on this skull at the end of this paper.

This Sir Hugh Stewkley married twice. His first wife was Catherine, daughter and heir of Sir John T., of L——, H—— shire, only baronet of that name, as created in 1660, and who died without male issue in 1672. His second wife was Mary, daughter of John Y. It is not stated which of these ladies was the mother of Mary Stewkley, afterwards Mrs. Stawell. Sir Hugh can scarcely have been less than 80 years of age when he died in 1719, and as he left no male issue, the baronetcy became extinct. He seems to have left several daughters, but I have only the names of Mary, the eldest, and Honoria, the youngest.

Mary Stawell was married on May 10th, 1719 (the same year as her father's death, but doubtless before that event), to Edward Stawell, third son of Ralph Stawell, first Lord Stawell of S——, S——shire, Mrs. Stawell had issue a son S., who died, at Westminster School, aged 16, and a daughter, Mary. She herself died in July, 1740.

Edward Stawell, her widower, continued to live constantly at Hinton Ampner, and with him continued to reside her sister Honoria, as she had already been used to do in her sister's lifetime. Collins usually gives very full biographical notices,

HINTON AMPNER

but this case is a curious exception, as he gives nothing but alliances and a very few dates. That of Edward Stawell's birth is not mentioned, but as his father died on August 5th, 1689, he cannot have been under 50 years of age at the death of his wife in 1740. His daughter Mary married, September 3rd, 1750, the Right Hon. Henry Bilson Legge, fourth son of William Legge, first Earl of Dartmouth. On the death of the second of his elder brothers, January 23rd, 1742, he succeeded to the peerage of Y.[1] According to Collins he died at A——, B——shire (which is there called his seat, but which appears more probably to have been that of his niece Charlotte, daughter of his brother the third Lord Dartmouth, in right of her mother, whose property it was), on April 13th, 1755, and was buried at Hinton Ampner; but according to the pamphlet, which appears more likely to be correct, he died suddenly, at Hinton Ampner, on the morning of April 3rd, from an apoplectic fit with which he had been seized on the preceding evening.

Mary Stawell, his only daughter and surviving child, was presumably born not later than 1730, and was married, as already stated, on September 3rd, 1750, to Mr. Legge. Mr. Legge was a politician of eminence, and though for a short time Envoy Extraordinary at Berlin, seems to have returned to England in 1749. Mrs. Legge seems entirely to have abandoned Hinton Ampner, which remained in the charge of a few servants, Mr. Legge only coming there usually for one month in the shooting season, presumably September or October. Mr. and Mrs. Legge seem to have had only one child, Henry, 2nd Lord Stawell, born February 22nd, 1757. On May 20th, 1760, Mrs. Legge was created Lady Stawell in her own right, with remainder to her male issue by Mr. Legge. In 1762 Mr. Legge was turned out of office (to use his own expression) and retired into private life. He died August 21st, 1764. After this his widow proceeded to try and let Hinton Ampner, and the phenomena mentioned in the pamphlet, which had, however, commenced very soon, as appears, after her father Lord Dartmouth's death, took place. On October 11th, 1768, she became

---

[1] We have already stated that we do not believe this to have been the case. (Note by S.S.)

the second wife of Wills Hillsborough, then Earl of Hillsborough, but created in 1789 (after her death) Marquess of Downshire. By him she had no issue. She was, as is recorded, fully cognizant of the phenomena and even made a sort of apparent attempt to have them investigated, with a view to show that they were caused by trickery. It seems also probable that it was by her orders that the house was pulled down. She died July 29th, 1780.

Her son, Henry, succeeded her as second Lord Stawell of the new creation. He had married, in 1779, the year preceding her death, Mary Curzon, daughter of Assheton Curzon, first Viscount Curzon, by whom (who died in 1804) he had a daughter Mary, married, August 11th, 1803, to John Dutton, second Lord Sherborne. Lord Stawell died without male issue in 1820, and the peerage thereupon expired. Lady Sherborne died October 21st, 1864. The property of Hinton Ampner was apparently settled upon her second son and descended to his heirs.

It would be interesting to know whether any abnormal phenomena are now or are recorded to have ever been observed on or about the site of the old house, whether occupied by the new house or not.

The following is a chronological arrangement of the facts, as far as they relate to the phenomena or to the persons who were or may have been connected with them.

1715. In or previous to this year Thomas P., coachman to Lord Stawell, entered the service of the family, since he had been more than forty years with them when Lord Stawell died in 1755, and he can hardly have been under 15 years of age at the time. Some time after this Sarah P., his wife, entered the service of the family, since she had been nearly forty years with them in 1755, and a similar assumption may be made as to her age.

1719. May 10th. Marriage of Mary Stewkley to Edward Stawell.

Same year. Death of her father, Sir Hugh Stewkley, aged about 80.

1740. July. Death of Mrs. Stawell. Her sister Honoria goes on living with Mr. Stawell.

1742. January 23rd. Mr. Stawell becomes Lord Stawell.

1750. September 3rd. Marriage of his daughter, Mary Stawell, to Mr. Legge.

1754. [November 25th.] Death of Honoria Stawell, aged [66].

1755. April 2nd. Lord Stawell seized with a fit, and dies the next morning, aged at least 65. It is remarkable that his cries to be bled were not complied with, as though those about him wished him to die.

After this all the servants were dismissed, except the P.'s and Elizabeth B., and Richard T., the gardener, who lived out of the house. The house is only occupied by Mr. Legge for a month in the autumn, a time as to which we are not informed that any phenomena were ever observed, at least till the middle of November, which is rather past the shooting season. The phenomena were in fact specially observable about 2nd April (Lord Stawell's anniversary), February, after Mrs. P.'s death, July, and at least in 1771, the beginning of August. It would appear from the Cheltenham case that such things have a tendency to recur at anniversaries; we do not know the day of the death of Isaac M., nor the date of any crime, if crime there were. It may however be remarked that July was the month of the death of Mrs. Stawell (Mary Stewkley), a woman who may have been deeply wronged by the rivalry of a younger sister.

Before, however, the dismissal of the other servants, and therefore very soon after Lord Stawell's death, the first phenomenon occurred. The groom Joseph saw in his room, by bright moonlight, a man in a drab coat, whom he evidently took to be 'his old master', i.e. Lord Stawell. It does not appear to have been very distinct, since the mark of identity he specified was the way in which the hands were held; not much importance for such a purpose can generally be assigned to such a thing, since automatic tricks, such as movements of the hands, are particularly affected by heredity; but in this case none of Lord Stawell's ancestors had ever inhabited the house.

Among the dismissed servants was Isaac M., house steward. He is spoken of as dishonest. If such dishonesty were, as indicated, notorious, his impunity appears strange, and looks as if he had some hold over Lord Stawell. The time of his death is not mentioned, but it must have been before or not long after February, 1770, as his voice was heard and recognized by Robert Camis, who entered Mrs. Ricketts's service at that time, and does not appear to have lived in the house long after she left in August, 1771. Camis's latest information is in November of that year. Henceforward disturbances similar to those suffered by the Ricketts took place in the house.

1760. May 20th. Mrs. Stawell was created Lady Stawell in her own right.

1764. August 21st. Mr. Stawell died. His widow, Lady Stawell, then tried to let the house.

Same year. December. Thomas P. died, aged about 70, and was lying dead in the house when it was taken by the Ricketts family.

1765. January. The Ricketts family entered into occupation, with an entirely new set of servants, all strangers from London, and Mrs. P. and Elizabeth B. left. Noises as of slamming doors were continually heard, though no door was ever found open, and a new set of locks was fixed to them but without any result. Same year. July. The gentleman in drab, apparently the same seen by the groom Joseph about ten years before, and believed by him to be Lord Stawell, was seen towards evening. Same year. Autumn. The same figure was seen in the great hall, at night, by the groom George Turner.

1767. July. A woman dressed in dark clothes which rustled as though of very stiff silk, was seen.

Occasional noises were afterwards heard, including groans and rustling.

1768. Lady Stawell (Mary Stawell, Mrs. Legge) married Lord Hillsborough.

1769. End of the year. Mr. Ricketts went to Jamaica.

Mrs. Ricketts afterwards heard footsteps and the rustling of silk.

1770. February. The servants John and Anne Sparks left, and Robert Camis and Elizabeth Godin came. Same year. Summer. Mrs. Ricketts hears heavy men's footsteps in her room. Same year. August. Lewis Chanson the Swiss left and Edward Russel came. Same year. November. Mrs. Ricketts changed her room, and in the new one heard music, once three heavy knocks, and afterwards, and in

1771, the beginning of the year, a frequent sound like the murmuring wind throughout the house. Same year, February 26th, Mrs. P., who had died a few days before, probably aged between 60 and 70, was buried at Hinton Ampner, and that night Elizabeth Godin, sleeping in the room which the deceased had formerly occupied, heard much groaning and fluttering.

Same year. April 2nd. (Sixteenth anniversary of Lord Stawell's fatal seizure.) A variety of sounds, concluding with three heavy knocks, as before (two separate accounts). After this the noises continued.

Same year. May 7th. Great accession of the disturbances henceforward. Same year, after Midsummer, the disturbances became much worse. A woman and two men now often heard talking.

Mr. Jervis (afterwards Lord St. Vincent) came to stay with his sister. The day after he left, the peculiar crash was heard, followed by piercing shrieks, dying away as though sinking into the earth. The nurse, Hannah Streeter, expresses a wish to hear more, and thenceforth is troubled every night. Mr. Jervis returns, and with Captain Luttrell, and his own servant, sits up night after night, &c., hearing the divers sounds, &c.

Mr. Jervis left before August 9th, and his sister and family very soon after. Mrs. Ricketts seems to have once returned, first to the Camis's house, and then to the manor-house, but there heard a sound she had never heard before, which caused her indescribable terror, and which she does not describe. Same year. September. Lady Hillsborough sent her agent, Mr. Sainsbury, to sit up in the house. Whether he did so or not is not stated, and he can hardly have done so more than one night.

A reward of £50, then £60, and finally £100 was offered for detection, but with no result.

1772. Some time within a year the house was let to a family named Lawrence, who endeavoured by threatening the servants, to stifle their statements. An apparition of a woman was said to have appeared once.

1773. In a year the Lawrences left suddenly.
The house was never again inhabited and was pulled down.

In the phenomena themselves there is not much that is very remarkable. They consist mainly of percussive and explosive sounds, and bear generally a very great resemblance to those which Fr. Hayden, S.J., heard at Ballechin, which he detailed to Mr. Huggins and myself, and of which I wrote an account to Mr. Myers. It will be observed that the intelligences seemed desirous to attract attention, as the phenomena became much more marked when watched for by Mr. Jervis, &c., and were very fully bestowed upon Hannah Streeter, when she had expressed a wish to hear them. They also became very marked after the death of Mrs. P., as though the spirits were disturbed by hers having joined them.

There seems to be little doubt, both from the dates, &c., and from the groom Joseph's recognition, that the figure in drab was that of Lord Stawell.

Isaac M., the dishonest house-steward, was also recognized by his voice by Robert Camis.

Some of the phenomena which occurred in Mrs. P.'s room and elsewhere on the night of her funeral, and subsequently, may be attributed to her, but a phantom of another woman had been seen and heard for years before her death. This phantom appeared to be dressed in rich silk, and moved more quickly than a very old woman would naturally do. All the indications seem to point to Honoria Stawell, Lord Stawell's sister-in-law, who had pre-deceased him, perhaps by only a few months.

Lucy Camis, who certainly knew a great many more facts than we do, suggested that certain persons were suffering for their sins, and said that God knew whether 'she' had a child and killed it. No one is mentioned to whom the pronoun 'she' can refer except Honoria Stawell, and the imputation is that she had unlawful relations with her brother-in-law, Lord Stawell, and that a crime was committed in which the old housekeeper, Mrs. P., and the dishonest steward, Isaac M., were accomplices.

It seems to be suggested that the skull which was found in a small box under the floor of the lobby when the house was pulled down, was the head of the child, and it is extremely suspicious that it was said to be a monkey's (it being absolutely inexplicable that a monkey's skull should be buried in a small box under the floor of a room), but that no inquiry was ever made, or the object shown to a medical man.

It is consonant with this suspicion that the phenomena took place chiefly in and about the yellow room, where the crime may have been committed, and the lobby, under the floor of which the head was found, where an unhappy creature sank shrieking earthwards.

In a letter to Mr. Myers, Lord Bute adds:

November 26th, 1892

I think that you will observe that Mrs. Ricketts says in one place that she conversed much with Dame Camis, and that the latter gave her much information as to the Legges and Stawells; and, in another place that she (Mrs. Ricketts) could only account for the phenomena upon the hypothesis of an undiscovered murder. My impression is that Dame Camis gave to Mrs. Ricketts and Mrs. Ricketts believed, the explanation which I have indicated, but that she felt her mouth shut by being practically unable to bring a terrible accusation against the memories of the father and aunt of the then still living Lady Hillsborough, who, as she warmly acknowledges, had always treated her with the utmost courtesy and consideration. This delicacy (which is only what one would expect from Mrs. Ricketts) also accounts for the reticence used about the narrative, only two copies being made.

The theory suggested by Lord Bute as to the cause of the 'haunting' seems to me incompletely established for the following reasons:

(1) The persons who were being discussed in the conversation between Lucy Camis and Miss Jervis were the old housekeeper, Mrs. P., and Elizabeth Godin. There is no positive evidence that their remarks referred to a third person, Honoria Stawell.

(2) The evidence that a crime was committed consists in the discovery of a small skull, said to be that of a monkey, but which may have been a child's, and the fact that Honoria

Stawell lived in Lord Stawell's house during the lifetime of her sister and also after her death, at which time she was 52 years of age. The fact of the 'haunting' does not add to this evidence.

(3) The 'haunting' does not appear to have been definitely connected with any anniversary since it went on almost continuously from April 2nd to the middle of August in one year, also in January, February, 'summer', July, 'autumn', November and December of other years. April 3rd was, according to one authority, the date of Lord Stawell's death, while the seizure which ended in his death was said to have taken place on April 2nd, but Collins's *Peerage* gives the date of death as April 13th, and it does not seem that the phenomena were more pronounced on April 2nd than on many other days.

(4) The only evidence for connecting the apparitions that were seen with the former inmates of the house is that, in one case out of the four, the apparition was said to have some resemblance to Lord Stawell.

EDITOR OF *The Journal of*
The Society for Psychical Research

With regard to the Hinton Ampner case it should be stated that, owing to present circumstances, I have not had the facilities I would have wished of identifying the persons concerned. Thus, I have been unable to find out for certain whether Mr. Bilson Legge did, or did not, become Earl of Dartmouth. The books of reference available to me are silent upon this point. Whether he did, or did not, succeed his brother is, however, of no great moment and does not affect the narrative. The old peerages are full of contradictions and, perhaps, we should assume that I am wrong and that the Marquess of Bute was right. The identification of the character in this story is quite a pursuit in itself and may recommend itself to persons with more time and a more precise interest in these genealogical questions. (Note by S. S.)

5. STRANGE PHENOMENA IN A CALVADOS CASTLE

*From 'Haunted Houses' by Camille Flammarion,
T. Fisher Unwin, London, 1924*

Here, as I have just said, we penetrate to the heart of our subject. The following account of the strange phenomena observed in 1875 in a Norman castle was drawn up by M. J. Morice, doctor of laws, on the report of the owner and witnesses, and was published in the *Annales des Sciences Psychiques* of 1893. 'The honesty and intelligence of the owner of this castle', so writes my learned friend Dr. Dariex, the editor of the *Annales*, 'cannot be questioned by anyone. He is an energetic and intelligent man. He himself noted down every day all the extraordinary facts which he and the inhabitants of the castle witnessed, just as they occurred. These persons attested in turn the reality of the facts. But the owner has asked the narrator to see that *no names are printed.*' (We may regret this restriction.) Here follows the account, abridged where possible for the observations were numerous, and last a long time:[1]

About the year 1835 there existed in that parish an old castle belonging to the B. family.

The place was in such a state of decay that a restoration was considered out of the question. It was replaced by another, built 150 yards to the north of the old castle.

M. de X. inherited it in 1867, and took up his residence there.

In the month of October of that year there was a series of extraordinary incidents, nocturnal noises and blows, which,

[1] See *Annales des Sciences Psychiques*, 1893, p. 65.

THE HAUNTED CASTLE IN CALVADOS

after ceasing for some years, says M. de X. in his diary of 1875, commenced afresh at that time.

The Château du T. had always passed for a scene of fantastic phenomena, and the haunt of more or less evil ghosts. The X. family knew nothing of these noises when it took possession.

Here are some extracts from the diary in question. These detailed relations are very long, but of intense interest. They form, indeed, a documentary procès-verbal.

'This is October, 1875 [writes the owner]. I propose to note down and record every day what happened during the night before. I must point out that when the noises occurred while the ground was covered with snow, there was no trace of footsteps round the castle. I drew threads across all openings, secretly. They were never found broken.

'At present our household consists of the following: M. and Mme de X. and their son; the Abbé Y., tutor to the son; Émile, coachman; Auguste, gardener; Amélina, housemaid; Célina, cook. All the domestics sleep in the house and are entirely trustworthy.

'*Wednesday, October 13, 1875.*—The Abbé Y. having told us that his armchair changed its place, my wife and I accompanied him to his room, and we minutely observed the place of every object. We attached gummed paper to the foot of the armchair, and so fixed it to the floor. We left him then, asking him to call me should anything extraordinary happen. At a quarter to ten the Abbé heard on the wall of his room a series of slight raps, which, however, were loud enough to be also heard by Amélina, who slept in the opposite room. He then heard in a corner of the room as of the winding of a big clock. Then a candlestick on his mantelpiece was moved with a grating noise, and finally he heard and thought he saw his armchair move. As he durst not get up, he rang the bell, and I went up. On entering the room I found the armchair had moved over a yard and was turned towards the fireplace. An extinguisher placed on the base of the candlestick was put on the candle; the other candlestick had been moved into a position where it overhung the mantelpiece by about an inch. A statuette placed against the mirror had been advanced 8 inches.

THE HAUNTED CASTLE IN CALVADOS

I retired after twenty minutes. We heard two violent blows from the Abbé's direction, who rang the bell, and assured me that the blows had been struck on the door of his wardrobe, at the foot of his bed.'

There is a promising beginning. But let us continue the diary:

'*Thursday, October 14.*—Violent blows are heard. We arm ourselves, and go over the castle, but discover nothing.

'*Friday, October 15.*—About 10 p.m. the Abbé and Amélina clearly heard steps imitating my wife's and mine, as well as our conversation. It sounded to them as if we were going along the passage into our room. Amélina maintains that she recognized both our voices. Then she heard the opening of my wife's door, but was not frightened because she thought it was ourselves. We were asleep and heard nothing. But at a quarter past eleven everybody was awakened by a series of very loud blows in the green room. Auguste and I made a general tour of inspection, and while in the drawing-room we heard blows near the linen-press. We went there, but found nothing, and came down. Madame and Amélina heard a piece of furniture being dragged on the floor above, where nobody was. It then seemed to fall heavily.

'*Saturday, October 16.*—Everybody is awakened by a series of heavy blows, about half an hour after midnight. An armed tour of inspection yields no result.

'*Monday, October 18.*—The number of witnesses is increased. The curate of the parish has kindly come to sleep in the castle since Saturday. He has heard the noises quite clearly, and will continue to pass the nights here. He will therefore be a witness of anything else which may be heard. To-night Marcel de X. will arrive. He will sleep on the second floor, and leave his door open so as to estimate the nature and direction of the noises. Auguste sleeps in the passage near his door. About eleven o'clock everybody was awakened by the noise of a large and heavy ball descending from the second floor to the first, and jumping from step to step. After half a minute there was a very loud single blow, and then nine or ten muffled ones.

'*Tuesday, October 19.*—The parish priest of M. has come at our request to sleep here. He clearly heard a heavy tread

THE HAUNTED CASTLE IN CALVADOS

slowly descending the stairs, and then, as the night before, half a minute afterwards, a single heavy blow from about the middle of the staircase which leads down to the ground floor. He has no doubt this is supernatural. Marcel returns home with the same conviction.'

Why supernatural? Do we know all the forces of nature? But let us continue this fantastic story:

'The sounds ceased completely until Saturday, October 30, when everybody was awakened by a series of loud blows.

'*Sunday, October 31.*—A very disturbed night. It sounded as if someone went up the stairs with superhuman speed from the ground floor, stamping his feet. Arrived on the landing, he gave five heavy blows, so strong that objects suspended on the wall rattled in their places. Then it seemed as if a heavy anvil or a big log had been thrown on to the wall, so as to shake the house. Nobody could say whence came these blows. Everybody got up and assembled in the passage of the first floor. We made a minute inspection but found nothing. We went to bed, but more noises obliged us to get up again. We could only go to rest about three o'clock.

'*Wednesday, November 3.*—At 10.20 p.m. everybody was awakened by resounding steps, which quickly ascended the stairs. A series of blows shook the walls. We immediately got up. Shortly afterwards we heard the noise of a heavy elastic body rolling down the stairs from the second to the first floor, and bouncing from step to step. Arriving at the landing, it continued on its course along the passage and stopping at the balusters. Then came two loud thumps, followed by a formidable blow as with a carpenter's mallet swung at arm's length upon the door of the green room. Then a series of tripping and repeated raps sounding like the steps of animals.

'*Thursday, November 4.*—When we were going to bed Auguste asked me to come and hear a long series of taps he heard on the second floor, where he sleeps now. When I got there I heard nothing. I minutely inspected the granary and the red room, leaving the door of the latter open. Auguste and Armand, Amélina's brother, were with me, and we carried a light. At the end of three minutes, five very distinct blows were heard in the red room, which nobody could enter without

THE HAUNTED CASTLE IN CALVADOS

being seen or heard, nor, I must add, without coming within range of my revolver, which never leaves me, as everybody knows. Hardly had I gone downstairs when five more blows were heard, distinctly by Auguste, and feebly by me, as I was on the floor below.

'*Friday, November 5.*—At 2 a.m. some being rushed at top speed up the stairs from the entrance hall to the first floor, along the passage, and up to the second floor, with a loud noise of tread which had nothing human about it. Everybody heard it. It was like two legs deprived of their feet and walking on the stumps. Then we heard numerous loud blows on the stairs and the door of the green room.

'*Wednesday, November 10.*—At 1 a.m. there was a rushing gallop in the hall and on the stairs. A big blow was heard on the landing, followed by another violent one on the door of the green room. This took two minutes. A storm of wind, thunder, and lightning came and made the night hideous. At 1.20 the door of the green room was unlatched. Then there were two loud knocks on the door, three inside the room, three more on the door, and finally a prolonged rapping on the second floor, forty raps at least. This lasted $2\frac{1}{2}$ minutes. At that moment everybody heard something like a cry, or a long-drawn trumpet call, audible above the storm. It seemed to me to come from outside. A little while afterwards everybody heard a long shriek, and then another, as of a woman outside calling for help. At 1.45 we suddenly heard three or four loud cries in the hall, and then on the staircase. We all got up and went round inspecting carefully. At 3.20 there was a galloping in the passage. We heard two fainter cries, but these were in the house.

'*Friday, November 12.*—Several blows were heard, then shrill and loud cries as if there were several people. More plaintive cries in the hall. At 11.45 these stifled cries seemed to come from the cellar, then other louder ones on the staircase. At midnight everybody got up, for cries were heard in the cellar, then inside the green room, and finally sobs and cries of a woman in horrible suffering.

'*Saturday, November 13.*—Not only are we troubled by night, but even to-day in the daytime: at 3 p.m. blows in the dining room; inspection without result. At 3.15, noises in the green room: we go there and find an easy-chair moved and placed against the door so as to prevent its opening. We put it back. At 3.40, steps in Madame's room, and easy-chair was moved. We paid a second visit to the green room, and found the easy-chair placed against the door again. Madame and Amélina went with the Abbé to his room, and before their eyes the window of the cabinet, which was closed, opened. The wind was southerly and that window was to the north. In Madame's room an easy-chair changed place again. In the Abbé's room, the window, which was closed, was opened again.

'*Saturday, November 13, at night.*—Galloping as on preceding nights. Thirteen raps on the landing, eight violent ones on the door of the green room. The door opens and is banged violently. At 12.15 a.m., two loud cries on the landing. It is no longer the cry of a weeping woman, but shrill, furious, despairing cries, the cries "of demons or the damned". For another hour violent blows are heard.

'*Sunday, November 14.*—The Abbé's windows, though well closed, were opened during Mass. He had locked his door and taken the key with him. Nobody could get into his room. During Vespers another of his windows opened.

'*Tuesday, November 23.*—About two o'clock I was awakened from my profound sleep by knocks in the passage and other noises in my room, but the sudden and painful awakening did not allow me time to find out their true nature. Next morning the Abbé told us he had heard at the same hour, similar noises coming from the same direction. My wife, on getting up, found a general upset on her dressing-table.

'*Sunday, December 19.*—During Vespers Émile, who stayed in the house, heard the shovels and fire tongs in the kitchen fall on the floor. On returning from Vespers, Mme de X. heard walking up and down. It was the noise of heavy steps in the Abbé's room, where there was nobody.

'*Monday, December 20.*—At a quarter past twelve Mme de X. found on entering her room two chairs placed upside down on two armchairs. I went into the other rooms. In the blue room I found a chair placed on the side table.

'*Friday, December 24.*—At midday, when all the domestic servants were at table, we found, in the Abbé's room, the bed turned on its side and the table pushed under it. In the evening, at six o'clock, we opened the door of the same room, which was locked, and found the table placed on the middle of the bed.

'*Saturday, December 25.*—At noon, when all the servants were at table, knocks were heard in the Abbé's room, though his door was locked. We inspected it and found an armchair placed on Maurice's desk. On returning from Vespers we found in the Abbé's room the couch upside down, the alarum on the glass case of the clock, and a chair on the table. In the evening, at 9 p.m., we heard the broom moving about the passage of the second floor. On going up we found that it had changed its place.

'*Sunday, December 26.*—Coming home from High Mass, we went with the Abbé up to his locked room. The cushions of the couch had disappeared. We found them placed on end, one beside the other, on the outer window-sill of his toilet cabinet. Before I put in a second window I had stopped up this window by a piece of wood securely nailed to the inner frame. That piece of wood had been torn out without the trace of any tool and placed beside the cushions. The window was closed again.

'*1 p.m.:* Twice we heard knocks in the house. Mme de X. went on a round and found the Abbé's room open, though he had locked it. A few minutes afterwards the drawing-room couch moved forward in two noisy rushes. Further noises upstairs, and another inspection. The Abbé's door, which had been locked, had opened.

'*5 p.m.:* After vespers we found a candlestick on the top of the Abbé's lamp, and the water-bottle placed on the base of the glass, which had been reversed. In his cabinet two shoes had been disposed fanwise on the window and others on the plate by the nightlight.

'*Sunday, December 26 to Monday, December 27.*—In the evening, at nine o'clock, I went with Auguste to stay in the linen-room, leaving the door open. We heard a series of knocks like those of a stick walking and knocking on the floor of the passage facing us. We had lighted a light. Shortly afterwards Amélina heard steps descending to the kitchen, and the noise of pieces of wood being broken, though none were in the kitchen. Nobody was visible.

'*Monday, December 27.*—In the afternoon we all went to V——. The cook, who remained alone with a daily help, told us that all was quiet. We went into the Abbé's room, which had been locked, and found all his books, at least a hundred, strewn over the floor. Only three volumes remained up, each on its shelf. These were books of the Holy Scriptures. Devotional books had also been thrown on the floor from the mantelpiece, and the broom had been placed over them.'

This account is very lengthy, of course, but it is evidently very varied. I abridge it as much as is possible while preserving its intrinsic value. Here is the sequel:

'*Night of Tuesday, December 28, to Wednesday, December 29.*—Three loud muffled blows on the second floor, followed immediately by numerous knocks along the second-floor passage. Then three series of three knocks each delivered sharply on the Abbé's door, then two isolated knocks followed by the noise of ironware. Two more sets of three knocks, sharp and impatient, and finally a big blow on the door of the green room. Total duration, three minutes.

'*Wednesday, December 29.*—One of my music books is placed inside the piano. Mme de X., hearing a noise in the Abbé's room, goes up there, followed by the latter. She heard a movement in the room, and put out her right hand to open the latch of the door. Before she could touch it she saw the key turn quickly in the lock and detach itself, hitting her left hand. The Abbé witnessed this. The blow was so strong that the place was sensitive and visible two days afterwards. In the evening we found in the blue room a coverlet thrown into the middle of the room and a night-table taken into the cabinet and resting on a pillow. The ewer had changed places with a crystal bottle.

'*Night of Wednesday, December 29, to Thursday, December 30.*—At 12.30 a.m. we were suddenly awakened by four thunderous blows on the door of Mme de X.'s room. To acquire some idea of their violence, one must imagine a wall collapsing, or a horse or four cannon-balls thrown against a door. It would be no exaggeration. The noise suddenly changed over to the other end of the passage and a violent blow was heard on the door of the green room. Several loud muffled knocks were heard upstairs, which shook the house. They moved about, growing in loudness.

'*12.40 a.m.:* Two noises of ironware at the end of the passage. A loud knock on the door of the green room.

'*12.50 a.m.:* A prolonged walking with great strides on the second floor. A witness counted thirty-two paces. Forty blows on the Abbé's door, five on the green room, ten on the flooring, two on the door, and five muffled blows which made the walls and furniture tremble on every floor. Total duration, four minutes.

'*Thursday, December 30.*—After lunch, when all the servants were at table, we found in the Abbé's room a footstool placed on my son's desk and covered with an antimacassar. At 2 p.m. I went up with the Abbé to his room, and we found the armchair on the table. On its seat the antimacassar was spread out, and a lamp was placed on the antimacassar. A cross and some blest medals, which had been attached to the door, had disappeared.

'*Night of Thursday, December 30.*—At 12.40 a.m. three blows were struck slowly on the door of the green room; eight muffled blows upstairs, shaking the house. Three noisy blows on the first-floor landing. Many steps were heard along the whole second-floor passage, sometimes quick, sometimes slow. These steps were quite unlike human steps. No animal could walk like that; it was more like a stick jumping on one of its ends.

'*6 a.m.:* More raps on the second floor, witnessed by the parish priest of Saint P——, who slept here. Some things happened in his room. He heard something like the noise of an animal with boards under its feet, coming to the room adjoining his own, climbing on to the side table, crossing over to his pillow, entering his bed and stopping at the level of his left elbow. The priest had a light and was wide awake, but saw nothing. At 6 a.m., having gone into the green room, he heard something like the noise of rubbed straw, first on the couch, then in the window corner, on the curtain rod, and finally on the bed. The priest said there was no straw or anything like it in the room. Martial, our farm-manager, slept with us that night. He was followed by noises heard under his feet in the gardener's presence.

'*New Year's Eve, 1876.*—At 12.40 we were all awakened by a series of terrible blows on the door of the green room. After these came others inside the room, and then a single blow, followed by quick running along passages and stairs. Nine strong blows inside the green room. Prolonged rappings in the second-floor passage, and finally four muffled blows. Total duration, seven minutes.

'*Night of Saturday, January 1, to Sunday, January 2.*—At 1.5 a.m. loud blows were struck on the door of the green room, and we all awoke. A stampede along the passage of the first floor and then of the second floor. Afterwards we heard thirteen irregular knocks in pairs, inside the green room. Then various steps coming from above. A violent blow fell on the door of the green room, and three more inside. Eight muffled blows seemed to come from the second floor. The taper beside me shook at each blow.

'*6.30 a.m.:* Several blows in the passage resembling those of the night. It is notable that for the last three mornings those who come downstairs from their rooms are followed step by step down to the ground floor by raps which stop and start with them. The parish curate has been followed in this way, but saw nothing.

'*Monday, January 3.*—In the evening I was alone in the drawing-room about 5.15 p.m. I had a light and heard six well-marked raps on the small table standing two yards away from me. I turned round but saw nothing.

'*Night of Monday, January 3, to Tuesday, January 4.*—At 3 a.m. a dozen blows were struck in pairs on the door of Mme de X.'s room. The nearest window shook at every blow. There was a light in the room. We were wide awake and quite cool, but saw nothing. Five minutes afterwards we heard a stampede, something like a stick jumping on one of its ends, in the first-floor and then in the second-floor passage; then some dull and feeble knocks. Dr. L., who has slept here, heard the noise of the running in the passage, but nothing else. The parish priest of La B—— slept in the red room, and heard during the greater part of the night a series of feeble but very extraordinary noises in his passage. He did not venture to go to bed. He is convinced that this can only be supernatural.

'*Wednesday, January 5.*—The Rev. Fr. H. L., a Premonstrant Canon, has been sent here by the Bishop to judge the facts and help us. About 5 p.m., a few moments before his arrival, Mme de X. heard in the drawing-room with her son the sound of the door shaken violently and saw the handle turn quickly. Maurice was frightened, and Mme de X. begun to sing loudly to prevent him hearing it.

'*Presence of the Rev. Fr. H. L.*—From the moment the Rev. Father arrived a sudden and absolute calm set in. Nothing happened either by day or by night. On January 15 he made a religious ceremony. From that day we heard some isolated and unusual noises in the night, but always from places too far away from Fr. H. L. for him to hear. He left us on Monday, the 17th, and his departure was immediately followed by a new set of phenomena as intense and serious as those which preceded his coming.

'*Night of January 17 to 18.*—At 11 p.m. there was a noise as of a body falling in the first-floor passage, followed by that of a rolling ball giving a violent blow on the door of the green room. Prolonged stampede on the second floor, followed by twenty dull knocks in the same place and eighteen inside the green room. At 11.35 p.m. there were five great blows on the door of the green room, and fifteen dull ones on the second-floor staircase, two kicks on the landing, and ten dull knocks on the second-floor staircase, making everything round us shake.

'*Night of January 19 to 20.*—At 11.15 p.m. we were wakened by a stampede upstairs, followed by fifteen violent blows on the door of the green room and fifty-five more inside. Shortly afterwards five blows as with a carpenter's mallet on the first-floor stairs. Prolonged stampede. Five dull blows, drumming inside the green room, three blows on the door of the room, twenty-seven on the window of my room, the last two of which made the windows of Mme de X. shake. Duration, ten minutes.

'At 1.45 a.m. eleven blows in my room.'

THE HAUNTED CASTLE IN CALVADOS

M. de X., having left for a few days on a visit to his brother, requested his wife to take notes in his absence. Here are these notes:

'*Night of January 20 to 21.*—1.8 a.m.: Five ordinary raps, followed by nineteen blows in the passage; two on the door of the linen-room, followed by six more; nine on the door of the green room, and eleven on the second floor, followed by a number of rhythmic raps on the second floor. Duration, seven minutes. Twelve dull knocks on the second floor, and eight raps seeming to pass from door to door.

'*1.25 a.m.:* Everybody hears four loud cries like bellowings, outside but at the level of the window, then something like strokes with a wand on the stairs. Shortly afterwards ten stronger blows, followed by drumming on the second floor.

'*1.30 a.m.:* Two heavy blows on the second floor, shaking mirrors and other objects in the rooms.

'*2.5 a.m.:* Numerous raps on the stairs, one on the door of the linen-room, several on the door of the green room, one of them a resounding one; five strong dull blows on the second floor, which shake all the furniture. Five feebler blows on the stairs, four on the second floor. Bellowing in the north, outside the house at the level of the first-floor windows.

'*5.45 a.m.:* A blow sounds in the passage. Running is heard, then the door of the green room opens and shuts violently. It is locked and the handle is torn off. Finally a sort of ball seems to roll along the same passage and to deliver a blow near the top of the stairs. The same night Mme de X. heard a voluminous body falling heavily from her table to the ground. She looked, but could see nothing.

'*Night of January 21 to 22.*—At 3 a.m. we are awakened by fifteen knocks on the second floor.

'*Night of January 22 to 23.*—At 3 a.m. we are awakened by a set of twenty dull blows on the second floor.'

The following notes are by M. de X.:

'*Night of January 23 to 24.*—At 9 p.m. a stampede was heard in our passage followed by a series of feebler raps. The night was calm. This morning at 6 a.m. and then at 7 a.m. we heard a series of raps also in our passage. To-day I leave for P——. My wife will note what takes place in my absence.

THE HAUNTED CASTLE IN CALVADOS

'*January 25.*—At 4.30 p.m. much noise upstairs. Madame goes up with Amélina and finds the beds of Auguste and Émile turned over, and, strangely enough, in an absolutely identical manner. After observing this disorder, Madame goes to the red room; the door resists, being obstructed by a heavy armchair. She puts it back and continues her inspection. As she goes to my study a frame placed inside against the door falls against her legs, and she finds everything in disorder—prints thrown on the ground, the armchair upside down and heaped with papers, maps, etc.

'*5.10 p.m.:* The Abbé was reading his breviary. Although for three days there had been beautiful weather, a mass of water fell through the chimney on to the fire, extinguishing it and scattering the ashes. The Abbé was blinded and had his face covered with ashes.

'*Night of January 25 to 26.*—At 12.20 a.m. two blows in the hall. At 1 a.m. twelve blows, followed by long drumming, then thirty rapid blows of a peculiar character, or, rather, a shaking of the whole house. Beds all over the house shaken. Afterwards nine blows in succession, five on the door of the green room, then a long stampede. The total duration was only five minutes. A minute afterwards the entire house was shaken from top to bottom. Then there were ten terrible blows on the door of the green room, a dozen cries outside, three bellowings, then furious shouts. A very loud drumming in the hall, apparently in rhythm. Fifty blows quite close to my room. Several knocks at the door of my son Maurice.

'*1.30 a.m.:* The house was shaken twenty times, seven blows on the door of the green room, followed by blows so rapid that they could not be counted; two on the door of the green room, twelve near Maurice's room, thirteen which made everything tremble, then in succession five, ten, and eighteen blows, shaking walls and furniture. There was hardly time to note them down. Nine terrible blows on the door of the green room, a drumming interspersed with loud blows, seven which shake everything, one very resounding, then a series of ten blows in pairs. At this moment a sound was heard like a bull roaring, then other inhuman furious cries in the passage near my wife's room, who got up and rang to waken all the servants. When everybody was up and assembled in the Abbé's room, we heard two bellowings and a shout.

'At 4.20 everybody went back to bed. Mme de X. heard a rather loud blow on the organ in her room, two yards from her bed. It was followed by three more blows whose direction she could not make out. The noises were heard clearly on the farm.

'*Night of January 26 to 27.*—Two further witnesses: the parish priest of Saint M—— came to pass the night, and Mlle de L. came for several days.

'At 12.15 a.m. everybody was awakened by a very violent noise such as would be caused by a board falling on the floor of the first-floor passage. It was followed by a cry. At 12.45, a stampede and heavy blows. After a short pause they began again and seemed accompanied by the shifting of heavy boxes. Maurice's door was shaken. Finally there were four blows on the door of the green room.

'*Night of January 28 to 29.*—At 11.15 p.m., a piercing cry on the stairs, raucous and sharp. Seven blows in the green room; six very loud ones on the door of the room.

'At 11.45, nineteen very dull blows on one of the doors in the passage.

'At 12.55 a.m. we heard something like the voice of a man in the first-floor passage. It seemed to cry twice Ha! Ha! Immediately there were ten resounding blows, shaking everything all round. One blow on the door of the green room. Then the sound of coughing in the first-floor passage. We rose quickly, saw nothing, and found at my wife's door a large earthenware plate broken into ten pieces.

'We have had a Novena of Masses said at Lourdes. The Reverend Father has made the exorcisms and everything has stopped.'

I must admit that every worldly reader who has never heard of the phenomena of haunting might attribute the preceding descriptions to the brains of lunatics or persons under hallucination. Yet these facts are true. The idea of the supernatural is evidently dominant in this family and their surroundings. We have to appreciate these things in a purely scientific manner. Out of the numerous attestations collected by Dr. Dariex

THE HAUNTED CASTLE IN CALVADOS

I shall quote some documents as complementary declarations, which will replace details suppressed in the preceding descriptions to avoid undue prolixity.

A LETTER FROM THE ABBÉ D., LATE TUTOR OF THE SON OF MADAME DE X., AND NOW PARISH PRIEST IN NORMANDY, TO M. MORICE

I have been a witness of all the things which happened at the Castle of T—— from October 12, 1875, to January 30, 1876. I can testify that the things related in the preceding MS. cannot be the work of a man. All these noises were not only heard by one person but by a large number of witnesses, and the blows were so loud that they could be heard at a distance of 500 yards. I shall not give a new account of the facts, because you know them. Occurrences of this nature also took place in the older castle. During all these troubles M. de X. took every imaginable precaution. How could a man have got into my room and changed the places of all the objects without my seeing him? How could he have got on the chimney-piece and poured water on my fire so as to cover me with ashes? And this in the daytime, and at a time of drought? My pupil was a witness of the occurrence, and I can still see him running. How was it that M. de X.'s dog, a well-trained animal, showed no astonishment amidst the greatest noises? How explain the opening of a well-closed window before our eyes? The cries we heard were not the cries of human beings. Often the walls of the castle were so much shaken that I was afraid of the ceiling falling on my head. Where could we find a man who could do all that? I, for one, can only think of the Devil.

M——,
January 12, 1893

LETTER FROM M. MORICE TO M. DARIEX

DEAR DOCTOR,

M. de X. as we see by the last sentence of his MS., attributed the cessation of the phenomena to the ceremony of exorcism and to the prayers he had said after the ceremony. When he

THE HAUNTED CASTLE IN CALVADOS

wrote it—*i.e.*, on January 29—M. de X. certainly had some reason; but circumstances soon disillusioned him.

By itself, the ceremony of exorcism yielded no result at all. It was performed on January 14 or 15, and we know by the account given by M. de X. himself what happened from that date until January 29. We must admit that after the prayers prescribed by the exorcizing priest peace seemed to return at the end of January. But at the end of August and especially in September the castle of T—— again became the scene of events as strange as those which we know already.

I have applied to one of the witnesses who spent the whole year 1876 at the castle of T—— as tutor to M. de X.'s son, and this is his answer:

Letters from the Abbé M. to M. G. Morice

B——,
January 20, 1893

'SIR,

'After the exorcisms a great calm set in. One almost incredible thing took place, which gave us much hope for the future. Here it is: You have seen from the diary that medals of St. Bénoit, indulgence crosses, and Lourdes medals had been placed on all the doors. These medals and crosses amounted to a good-sized package. You have also seen that on the following night a tremendous noise occurred and that next day medals and crosses had disappeared so that nothing could be found, though they and the doors were very numerous. Now the exorcisms had ceased and were succeeded by several days of peace. You may imagine how agreeable these days were. But two or three days afterwards Madame was writing some lines on her knees by a little desk when suddenly an immense packet of medals and crosses fell in front of her on the desk. It might have been about 10.30 a.m. Whence came these medals? They were all the medals placed on the doors except those of Lourdes.

'The good priest of T——, to whom the story was told, and who, like myself, knew the sincerity and honesty of the castle people and wished to keep them in his parish, said to them: "Have courage; the Devil surrenders his arms; everything is finished I may assure you. You will be left in peace." But to me the good man said: "I am still afraid, much afraid, because Lourdes has not come back."

'Towards the end of August the small noises came back more frequently and clearly. One night several persons, including myself, heard quick and fairly loud knocks in the linen-room. They were just like those produced the previous year when the phenomena commenced.

'One Saturday night before the third Sunday in September a great noise occurred in the drawing-room and continued for a part of the night. In the morning, M. de X., who had the key of the drawing-room in his pocket, went down in some anxiety. He opened the door and found the couch and armchairs moved far from their places. All was arranged as for a council meeting, horseshoe-fashion, with the couch in the centre.

'Well, the Devil had held council and was about to begin again. M. de X. opened his harmonium and played for a long time. As he closed the instrument, some of the airs he had been playing were repeated in the opposite corner of the drawing-room for a considerable time.

'Some days afterwards M. de X. was away for three days. During that time Madame kept a lamp and two candles alight in her room. As she was particularly afraid of ghosts, she bolted the door of her toilet cabinet and said to herself, "Now I shall only have the entrance door to keep in view." At midnight we all heard a terrible blow, which awakened us, and Madame heard something like the noise of a package of linen which had fallen into her room. At that moment the lamp and candle went out and Madame heard the click of the bolt being withdrawn. And *it had been drawn*.

'The next day Madame heard a note of a small organ in her room sound for some time. The next day after that I heard about 2.30 p.m. the same organ playing several airs. Madame and a lady friend were away. I expected M. de X. back, but he only came in at 6 p.m. I told him what had happened, and he said: "I have the key of the organ in my pocket." It was true, *and the organ had been locked*.

'Another time, in my own room, a cupboard heavily laden with books and linen *rose* 20 inches from the ground and

THE HAUNTED CASTLE IN CALVADOS

remained up for some time. My young pupil pointed it out to me. I pressed on the cupboard, but it did not yield. It resumed its place of itself afterwards. It may have been 3 o'clock in the afternoon.

'One evening the windows of my room opened several times. There was no wind.

(Sg.) X
(*Parish Priest of B——*)'

There is only one thing to be added, viz., that the writers of the above letters are priests whose perfect good faith cannot be doubted for a moment.

(Sg.) G. Morice

Here, to clinch the matter, is an extract from a letter of Mme Le N. de V. to Dr. Dariex:

'The Castle came into the possession of M. de X., I believe, by inheritance. The former owner is said to have died in final impenitence, and was supposed to revisit her castle.

'When the first noises occurred, M. de X. thought he had to do with living people wishing to frighten him sufficiently to make him abandon the castle, which would in such circumstances have been sold for a song with its surrounding land. He therefore instituted a close examination and sounded the walls and cellars to find the forgotten passages by which one could enter. In spite of the most careful vigilance no origin of these noises could be found, and they increased in spite of all precautions.

'He bought two formidable watch dogs, which were released every night, but to no purpose.

'One day the animals started barking in the direction of one of the thickets of the garden with such persistence that M. de X. thought the miscreants had hidden themselves there. He armed himself and his servants, surrounded the thicket and released the dogs. They rushed in with fury, but hardly had they got in when their barks changed into plaintive whines, like those of dogs being chastised. They ran away with their tails between their legs and could not be prevailed upon to go back. The men then went in and searched in every direction, but found absolutely nothing.

THE HAUNTED CASTLE IN CALVADOS

'The Abbé's room was always the place where the greatest devilries took place. He never went out without double-locking it and putting the key in his pocket. It made no difference. His window, carefully closed, was found open. His furniture had been moved and upset. The window was screwed up. It was opened all the same, and the screws were found on the floor. One day, as the Abbé descended, he heard in his room a noise so loud that he immediately went up again. His library was upset and his books thrown to the other end of the room, not pell-mell as out of a piece of furniture which fell, but in regular files, just as they had been on the shelves.

'The state of fear became so great that the Abbé and his pupil went to stay with the parish priest.

'Another thing: A friend or cousin, an officer, wanted to spend a night in the particularly haunted room where nobody slept as a rule. He had his revolver and was determined to shoot at anyone who would disturb his sleep. He kept a light burning. He was awakened by the *frou-frou* of a silken robe. He felt that that coverlet over his feet was drawn away. He addressed the nocturnal visitor without eliciting a reply and lighted his candle, which went out again at once. Three times he lighted it, and three times it went out. And still the *frou-frou* and the interference with the coverlet continued. He decided to shoot at the point indicated by the displacement of the bedclothes as the probable position of the intruder and thought to hit that being point blank. He fired without any result. Yet the balls had not been withdrawn from the cartridges, for they were found in the wall next morning.'

Here is another supplementary letter:

LETTER FROM FR. J., PARISH PRIEST, TO M. MORICE

MONSIEUR LE DOCTEUR,

I can testify that I heard the strange noises reported in the diary of M. de X. I have read that diary and find it perfectly accurate.

I have no doubt concerning the nature of the occurrences at the castle of T——. To me they are *diabolically supernatural*. You might consult Rev. Fr. H., who is acting as parish priest of M——. He passed a fortnight or three weeks at the castle. He had been sent by the Bishop to make the (secret) exorcisms if he judged it appropriate.

(Sg.) J. A.
Parish Priest of S—— D——

The letter of the Reverend Father has also been published. But, indeed, any further documents would be superfluous. The reality of these amazing phenomena is beyond doubt.

As a consequence of this intolerable state of things, the despairing owner sold the castle, and went to live elsewhere.

Dr. Dariex terminates this important account of the incomprehensible occurrences in the following lines:

'I have recently had a visit from Prince H., who will try, with M. Morice, to extend, if possible, this enquiry already so rich in documents and testimony from witnesses of undoubted honesty and credibility.

'The castle of T—— is by far the most remarkable case of haunting we have come across which rests upon such rigorous documents and testimony.

'We can cast no doubt upon these numerous observations. They are very remarkable in many ways, and the good faith of those who report the phenomena is undoubted.

(Sg.) XAVIER DARIEX'

This whole story is most extraordinary, no doubt. But its authenticity is as certain as that of the German war of 1914–1918, which, with its terrible crimes, was still more mad and stupid. It is one of the best-established cases within our knowledge, and on that account it is here given with its principal details, and not summarized. I shall not stop to consider the matter of the 'diabolically supernatural'. That discussion must be reserved. Let us continue our investigations without any preconceived ideas. Explanatory researches can only come logically when we have all the observations before us.

Yet it seems to me that we cannot but feel authorized to conclude from all this that *there are invisible beings*.

6. THE POLTERGEIST OF THE GERMANS

*Reprinted from 'The Night-Side of Nature', by
Mrs. Catherine Crowe, 1849*

With regard to some so-called *hauntings*, there seems reason to believe that the invisible guest was formerly a dweller upon earth, in the flesh, who is prevented by some circumstance which we are not qualified to explain, from pursuing the destiny of the human race, by entering freely into the next state prepared for him. He is like an unfortunate caterpillar that cannot entirely free itself from the integuments of its reptile life which chain it to the earth, whilst its fluttering wings vainly seek to bear it into the region to which it now belongs. But there is another kind of *haunting*, which is still more mysterious and strange, though by no means infrequent, and which, from the odd, sportive, mischievous nature of the disturbances created, one can scarcely reconcile to our notions of what we understand by the term *ghost*. For in those cases where the unseen visitant appears to be the spirit of a person deceased, we see evidences of grief, remorse and dissatisfaction, together with, in many instances, a disposition to repeat the acts of life, or at least to stimulate a repetition of them: but they are seldom sportive or mischievous, nor, except where an injunction is disobeyed, or a request refused, are there generally any evidences of anger or malignity. But in the other cases alluded to, the annoyances appear rather like the tricks of a mischievous imp. I refer to what the Germans call the *Poltergeist*, or racketing spectre, for the phenomenon is known in all countries, and has been known in all ages.

THE POLTERGEIST OF THE GERMANS

Since hearing the phenomenon of the electric girl, which attracted so much attention and occasioned so much controversy in Paris lately, and other similar cases, which have since reached me, I feel doubtful whether some of these strange circumstances may not have been connected with electricity in one form or another. The famous story of what is familiarly called the Stockwell Ghost, for example, might possibly be brought under this category. I have heard some people assert that the mystery of this affair was subsequently explained away, and the whole found to be a trick. But that is a mistake. Some years ago I was acquainted with persons whose parents were living on the spot at the time, who knew all the details, and to them it remained just as great a mystery as ever. Not the smallest light had ever been thrown upon it. People are so glad to get rid of troublesome mysteries of this description, that they are always ready to say, 'The trick has been found out!' and those who pride themselves on not believing idle stories, are to the last degree credulous when 'the idle story' flatters their scepticism.

The circumstances of the so-called Stockwell Ghost, which I extract from a report published at the time, are as follows:

The pamphlet was entitled:

'An Authentic Candid and Circumstantial Narrative, of the astonishing Transactions at Stockwell, in the County of Surrey, on Monday and Tuesday, the 6th and 7th days of January, 1772, containing a Series of the most surprising and unaccountable Events that ever happened, which continued from first to last, upwards of Twenty Hours, and at different places.

'Published with the consent and approbation of the family and other parties concerned, to authenticate which, the original copy is signed by them.

'Before we enter upon a description of the most extraordinary transactions that perhaps ever happened, we shall begin with an account of the parties who were principally concerned, and, in justice to them, give their characters, by which means the impartial world may see what credit is due to the following narrative.

'The events indeed are of so strange and singular a nature, that we cannot be at all surprised the public should be doubtful of the truth of them, more especially as there have been too many impositions of this sort; but, let us consider, here are no sinister ends to be answered, no contributions to be wished for, nor would be accepted, as the parties are in reputable situations and good circumstances, particularly Mrs. Golding, who is a lady of an independent fortune. Richard Fowler and his wife might be looked upon as an exception to this assertion; but as their loss was trivial, they must be left out of the question, except so far as they appear corroborating evidences.

'Mr. Pain's maid lost nothing.

'How or by what means these transactions were brought about has never transpired; we have only to rest our confidence on the veracity of the parties, whose descriptions have been most strictly attended to, without the least deviation: nothing here offered is either exaggerated or diminished; the whole stated in the clearest manner just as they occurred: as such only we lay them before the candid and impartial public.

'Mrs. Golding, an elderly lady at Stockwell, in Surrey, at whose house the transactions began, was born in the same parish (Lambeth), has lived in it ever since, and has always been well known and respected as a gentlewoman of unblemished honour and character. Mrs. Pain, a niece of Mrs. Golding, has been married several years to Mr. Pain, a farmer, at Brixton Causeway, a little above Mr. Angel's, has several children, and is well known and respected in the parish. Mary Martin, Mr. Pain's servant, an elderly woman, has lived two years with them, and four years with Mrs. Golding, where she came from. Richard Fowler lives almost opposite to Mr. Pain, at the Brick Pound, an honest, industrious and sober man. And Sarah Fowler, wife to the above, is an industrious and sober woman.

'These are the subscribing evidences that we must rest the truth of the facts upon; yet there are numbers of other persons who were eye-witnesses of many of the transactions during the time they happened, all of whom must acknowledge the truth of them.

'Another person who bore a principal part in these scenes was Ann Robinson, Mrs. Golding's maid, a young woman, about twenty years old, who had lived with her but one week

THE POLTERGEIST OF THE GERMANS

and three days. So much for the *historiæ personae*; and now for the narrative.

'On Monday, January 6th, 1772, about ten o'clock in the forenoon, as Mrs. Golding was in her parlour, she heard the china and glasses in the back kitchen tumble down and break; her maid came to her and told her the stone plates were falling from the shelf; Mrs. Golding went into the kitchen and saw them broke. Presently after a row of plates from the next shelf fell down likewise, whilst she was there, and nobody near them; this astonished her much, and while she was thinking about it, other things in different places began to tumble about, some of them breaking, attended with violent noises all over the house; a clock tumbled down and the case broke; a lantern that hung on the stair-case was thrown down, and the glass broke to pieces; an earthen pan of salted beef broke to pieces, and the beef fell about; all this increased her surprise, and brought several persons about her, among whom was Mr. Rowlidge, a carpenter, who gave it as his opinion that the foundation was giving way, and that the house was tumbling down, occasioned by the too great weight of an additional room erected above; so ready are we to discover natural causes for everything! But no such thing happened, as the reader will find, for whatever was the cause, that cause ceased almost as soon as Mrs. Golding and her maid left any place, and followed them wherever they went. Mrs. Golding ran into Mr. Gresham's house, a gentleman living next door to her, where she fainted.

'In the interim, Mr. Rowlidge and other persons were removing Mrs. Golding's effects from her house, for fear of the consequences he had prognosticated. At this time all was quiet; Mrs. Golding's maid remaining in her house, was gone up stairs, and when called upon several times to come down, for fear of the dangerous situation she was thought to be in, she answered very coolly, and after some time came down as deliberately, without any seeming fearful apprehensions.

'Mrs. Pain was sent for from Brixton Causeway, and desired to come directly, as her aunt was supposed to be dead: this was the message to her. When Mrs. Pain came, Mrs. Golding was come to herself, but very faint.

THE POLTERGEIST OF THE GERMANS

'Among the persons who were present was Mr. Gardner, a surgeon, of Clapham; whom Mrs. Pain desired to bleed her aunt, which he did; Mrs. Pain asked him if the blood should be thrown away; he desired it might not, as he would examine it when cold. These minute particulars would not be taken notice of, but as a chain to what follows. For the next circumstance is of a more astonishing nature than anything that had preceded it; the blood that was just congealed, sprang out of the basin upon the floor, and presently after the basin broke to pieces: this china basin was the only thing broken belonging to Mr. Gresham: a bottle of rum that stood by it broke at the same time.

'Amongst the things that were removed to Mr. Gresham's was a tray full of china, etc., a japan bread basket, some mahogany waiters, with some bottles of liquors, jars of pickles, etc., and a pier glass, which was taken down by Mr. Saville (a neighbour of Mrs. Goldings); he gave it to one Robert Hames, who laid it on the grass-plot at Mr. Gresham's: but before he could put it out of his hands, some parts of the frame on each side flew off; it rained at that time. Mrs. Golding desired it might be brought into the parlour, where it was put under a sideboard, and a dressing-glass along with it; it had not been there long before the glasses and china which stood on the side-board began to tumble about and fall down, and broke both the glasses to pieces. Mr. Saville and others being asked to drink a glass of wine or rum, both the bottles broke in pieces before they were uncorked.

'Mrs. Golding's surprise and fear increasing, she did not know what to do, or where to go; wherever she and her maid were, these strange destructive circumstances followed her, and how to help or free herself from them, was not in her power or any other person's present: her mind was one confused chaos, lost to herself and everything about her, drove from her own home, and afraid there would be none other to receive her: at last she left Mr. Gresham's, and went to Mr. Mayling's, a gentleman at the next door; here she stayed about three-quarters of an hour, during which time nothing happened. Her maid stayed at Mr. Gresham's to put up what few things remained unbroken of her mistress's, in a back apart-

THE POLTERGEIST OF THE GERMANS

ment, when a jar of pickles that stood upon a table turned upside down, then a jar of raspberry jam broke to pieces, next two mahogany waiters and a quadrille-box likewise broke to pieces.

'Mrs. Pain, not choosing her aunt should stay too long at Mr. Mayling's, for fear of being troublesome, persuaded her to go to her house at Rush Common, next Brixton Causeway, where she would endeavour to make her as happy as she could, hoping by this time all was over, as nothing had happened at that gentleman's house, while she was there. This was about two o'clock in the afternoon.

'Mr. and Miss Gresham were at Mr. Pain's house when Mrs. Pain, Mrs. Golding and her maid went there. It being about dinner time, they all dined together; in the interim, Mrs. Golding's servant was sent to her house to see how things remained. When she returned, she told them nothing had happened since they left it. Some time after, Mr. Gresham and Miss Gresham went home, everything remaining quiet at Mr. Pain's; but about eight o'clock in the evening a fresh scene began; the first thing that happened, was a whole row of pewter dishes, except one, fell from off a shelf to the middle of the floor, rolled about a little while, then settled; and, what is almost beyond belief, as soon as they were quiet, turned upside down; they were then put on the dresser, and went through the same a second time; next fell a whole row of pewter plates from off the second shelf over the dresser to the ground, and being taken up and put on the dresser one in another, they were thrown down again.

'The next thing was two eggs that were upon one of the pewter shelves; one of them flew off, crossed the kitchen, struck a cat on the head, and then broke in pieces.

'Next, Mary Martin, Mrs. Pain's servant, went to stir the kitchen fire; she got to the right-hand side of it, being a large chimney, as is usual in farm houses; a pestle and mortar, that stood nearer the left-hand end of the chimney shelf, jumped about six feet on the floor. Then went candlesticks and other brasses, scarce anything remaining in its place. After this, the glasses and china were put down on the floor for fear of undergoing the same fate; they presently began to dance and tumble

THE POLTERGEIST OF THE GERMANS

about, and then broke to pieces. A teapot, that was among them, flew to Mrs. Golding's maid's foot, and struck it.

'A glass tumbler that was put on the floor, jumped about two feet and then broke. Another that stood by it jumped about at the same time, but did not break till some hours after, when it jumped again, and then broke. A china bowl that stood in the parlour jumped from the floor to behind a table that stood there. This was most astonishing, as the distance from where it stood was between seven and eight feet, but was not broke. It was put back by Richard Fowler to its place, where it remained some time, and then flew to pieces.

'The next thing that followed was a mustard pot, that jumped out of a closet and was broken. A single cup that stood upon the table (almost the only thing remaining) jumped up, flew across the kitchen, ringing like a bell, and then was dashed to pieces against the dresser. A candlestick that stood on the chimney-shelf flew across the kitchen to the parlour door, at about fifteen feet distance. A tea-kettle, under the dresser, was thrown out about two feet; another kettle that stood at one end of the range, was thrown against the iron that is fixed to prevent children falling into the fire. A tumbler with rum-and-water in it that stood upon a waiter upon a table in the parlour, jumped about ten feet, and was broken. The table then fell down, and along with it a silver tankard belonging to Mrs. Golding, the waiter, in which stood the tumbler, and a candlestick. A case bottle then flew to pieces.

'The next circumstance was a ham that hung in one side of the kitchen chimney; it raised itself from the hook and fell down to the ground. Some time after, another ham that hung on the other side of the chimney, likewise underwent the same fate. Then a flitch of bacon, which hung up in the same chimney, fell down.

'All the family were eye-witnesses to these circumstances, as well as other persons, some of whom were so alarmed and shocked, that they could not bear to stay, and were happy in getting away, though the unhappy family were left in the midst of their distresses. Most of the genteel families around were continually sending to inquire after them, and whether all was over or not. Is it not surprising that some among them had not the inclination and resolution to try to unravel this most intricate affair, at a time when it would have been in their power to have done so? there certainly was sufficient time for so doing, as the whole, from first to last, continued upwards of twenty hours.

'At all the times of action, Mrs. Golding's servant was walking backwards and forwards, either in the kitchen or parlour, or wherever some of the family happened to be. Nor could they get her to sit down five minutes together, except at one time for about half an hour towards the morning, when the family were at prayers in the parlour; then all was quiet; but in the midst of the greatest confusion, she was as much composed as at any other time, and with uncommon coolness of temper advised her mistress not to be alarmed or uneasy, as she said these things could not be helped. Thus she argued, as if they were common occurrences which must happen in every family.

'This advice surprised and startled her mistress almost as much as the circumstances that occasioned it. For how can we suppose that a girl of about twenty years old (an age when female timidity is too often assisted by superstition) could remain in the midst of such calamitous circumstances (except they proceed from causes best known to herself) and not be struck with the same terror as every other person was who was present? These reflections led Mr. Pain, and at the end of the transactions, likewise Mrs. Golding, to think that she was not altogether so unconcerned as she appeared to be. But hitherto, the whole remains mysterious and unravelled.

'About ten o'clock at night, they sent over the way to Richard Fowler, to desire he would come and stay with them. He came, and continued till one in the morning, and was so terrified that he could remain no longer.

'As Mrs. Golding could not be persuaded to go to bed, Mrs. Pain at that time (one o'clock) made an excuse to go up stairs to her youngest child, under pretence of getting it to sleep, but she really acknowledges it was through fear, as she declares she could not sit up to see such strange things going on, as everything, one after another, was broken, till there was not above two or three cups and saucers remaining out of a considerable quantity of china, etc., which was destroyed to the amount of some pounds.

'About five o'clock on Tuesday morning, Mrs. Golding went up to her niece, and desired her to get up, as the noises and destruction were so great, she could continue in the house no longer. At this time all the tables, chairs, drawers, etc., were tumbling about. When Mrs. Pain came down, it was amazing beyond all description. Their only security then was to quit the house, for fear of the same catastrophe as had been expected the morning before, at Mrs. Golding's; in consequence of this resolution, Mrs. Golding and her maid went over the way to Richard Fowler's. When Mrs. Golding's maid had seen her safe to Richard Fowler's, she came back to Mrs. Pain, to help her to dress the children in the barn, where she had carried them for fear of the house falling. At this time all was quiet; they then went to Fowler's, and then began the same scene as had happened at the other places. It must be remarked, all was quiet here as well as elsewhere, till the maid returned.

'When they got to Mr. Fowler's, he began to light a fire in his back room. When done, he put the candle and candlestick upon a table in the fore room. This apartment Mrs. Golding and her maid had passed through. Another candlestick with a tin lamp in it, that stood by it, were both dashed together, and fell to the ground. A lantern with which Mrs. Golding was lighted across the road, sprang from a hook to the ground, and a quantity of oil spilled on the floor. The last thing was the basket of coals tumbled over; the coals rolling about the room; the maid then desired Richard Fowler not to let her mistress remain there, as she said, wherever she was the same things would follow. In consequence of this advice, and fearing greater losses to himself, he desired she would quit his house; but first begged her to consider within herself, for her own and the public's sake, whether or not she had not been guilty of some atrocious crime, for which Providence was determined to pursue her on this side of the grave, for he could not help thinking she was the object that was to be made an example to posterity, by the all-seeing eye of Providence, for crimes which but too often none but that Providence can penetrate, and by such means as these bring to light.

'Thus was the poor gentlewoman's measure of affliction complete, not only to have undergone all which has been related, but to have added to it, the character of a bad and wicked woman, when till this time she was esteemed as a most deserving person. In candour to Fowler, he could not be blamed; what could he do? what would any man have done that was so circumstanced? Mrs. Golding soon satisfied him; she told him she would not stay in his house, or any other person's, as her conscience was quite clear, and she could as well wait the will of Providence in her own house as in any other place whatever: upon which she and her maid went home. Mr. Pain went with them. After they had got to Mrs. Golding's, the last time, the same transactions once more began upon the remains that were left.

'A nine-gallon cask of beer, that was in the cellar, the door being open, and no person near it, turned upside down. A pail of water that stood on the floor, boiled like a pot. A box of candles fell from a shelf in the kitchen to the floor; they rolled out, but none were broken; and a round mahogany table upset in the parlour.

'Mr. Pain then desired Mrs. Golding to send her maid for his wife to come to them; when she was gone, all was quiet; upon her return she was immediately discharged, and no disturbances have happened since; this was between six and seven o'clock on Tuesday morning.

'At Mrs. Golding's were broken the quantity of three pailsful of glass, china, etc. At Mrs. Pain's they filled two pails.

'Thus ends the narrative: a true, circumstantial, and faithful account of which we have laid before the public; and have endeavoured, as much as possible, throughout the whole, to state only facts, without presuming to obtrude any opinion on them. If we have in part hinted anything that may appear unfavourable to the girl, it is not from a determination to charge her with the cause, right or wrong, but only from a strict adherence to truth, most sincerely wishing this extraordinary affair may be unravelled.

'The above narrative is absolutely and strictly true, in

THE POLTERGEIST OF THE GERMANS

witness whereof we have set our hands this eleventh day of January, 1772.

(Sgd.) MARY GOLDING
JOHN PAIN
MARY PAIN
RICHARD FOWLER
SARAH FOWLER
MARY MARTIN

'The original copy of this narrative, signed as above, with the parties' own hands, was put into the hands of Mr. Marks, bookseller, in St. Martin's Lane, to satisfy persons who choose to inspect the same.'

Such phenomena as this of the Stockwell Ghost are by no means uncommon; and I am acquainted with many more instances than I can allude to here. One occurred very lately in the neighbourhood of London, as I learnt from the following newspaper paragraph. I subsequently heard that the little girl had been sent away, but whether the phenomena then ceased, or whether she carried the disturbance with her, I have not been able to ascertain, nor does it appear certain that she had anything to do with it.

'A MISCHIEVOUS AND MYSTERIOUS GHOST.—(From a Correspondent.)—The whole of the neighbourhood of Black Lion-lane, Bayswater, is ringing with the extraordinary occurrences that have recently happened in the house of a Mr. Williams, in the Moscow Road, and which bear a strong resemblance to the celebrated Stockwell ghost affair of 1772. The house is inhabited by Mr. and Mrs. Williams; a grown-up son and daughter, and a little girl between ten and eleven years of age. On the first day, the family, who are remarkable for their piety, were startled all at once by a mysterious movement among the things in the sitting-rooms and kitchen, and other parts of the house. At one time, without any visible agency, one of the jugs came off the hook over the dresser, and was broken; then followed another; and next day another. A china teapot, with the tea just made in it, and placed on the mantelpiece, whisked off on the floor, and was smashed. A pewter one, which had been substituted immediately after, did the same, and when

THE POLTERGEIST OF THE GERMANS

put on the table, was seen to hop about as if bewitched, and was actually held down while the tea was made for Mr. Williams's breakfast, before leaving for his place of business. When for a time all had been quiet, off came from its place on the wall a picture in a heavy gilt frame, and fell to the floor without being broken. All was now amazement and terror, for the old people are very superstitious, and ascribing it to a supernatural agency, the other pictures were removed, and stowed away on the floor. But the spirit of locomotion was not to be arrested. Jugs and plates continued at intervals to quit their posts, and skip off their hooks and shelves into the middle of the room, as though they were inspired by the magic flute; and at supper, when the little girl's mug was filled with beer, the mug slided off the table on to the floor. Three times it was replenished and replaced, and three times it moved off again. It would be tedious to relate the fantastic tricks which have been played by household articles of every kind. An Egyptian vase jumped off the table suddenly when no soul was near, and was smashed to pieces. The tea-kettle popped off the fire into the grate as Mr. Williams had filled the teapot, which fell off the chimney-piece. Candlesticks, after a dance on the table, flew off, and ornaments from the shelves, and bonnets and cap-boxes flung about in the oddest manner. A looking-glass hopped off a dressing-table followed by combs and brushes and several bottles, and a great pincushion has been remarkably conspicuous for its incessant jigs from one part to another. The little girl, who is a Spaniard, and under the care of Mr. and Mrs. Williams, is supposed by their friends to be the cause of it all, however extraordinary it may seem in one of her age; but up to the present time it continues a mystery, and the *modus operandi* is invisible.'—*Morning Post*.

To imagine that these extraordinary effects were produced by the voluntary agency of the child, furnishes one of those remarkable instances of the credulity of the sceptical, to which I have referred. But when we read a true statement of the effects involuntarily exhibited by Angélique Cottin, we begin to see that it is just possible the other strange phenomena may be produced by a similar agency.

The French Academy of Sciences had determined, as they

had formerly done by Mesmerism, that the thing should not be true, and Monsieur Arago was non-suited; but although it is extremely possible that either the phenomenon had run its course and arrived at a natural termination, or that the removal of the girl to Paris had extinguished it, there appears no doubt that it had previously existed.

Angélique Cottin was a native of La Perrière, aged fourteen, when on the 15th January, 1846, at eight o'clock in the evening, whilst weaving silk gloves at an oaken frame, in company with other girls, the frame began to jerk and they could not by any efforts keep it steady. It seemed as if it were alive, and becoming alarmed, they called in the neighbours, who would not believe them; but desired them to sit down and go on with their work. Being timid, they went one by one, and the frame remained still, till Angélique approached, when it recommenced its movements, whilst she was also attracted by the frame: thinking she was bewitched or possessed, her parents took her to the Presbytery that the spirit might be exorcized. The curate, however, being a sensible man, refused to do it: but set himself, on the contrary, to observe the phenomenon; and being perfectly satisfied of the fact, he bade them take her to a physician.

Meanwhile, the intensity of the influence, whatever it was, augmented; not only articles made of oak, but all sorts of things were acted upon by it and reacted upon her, whilst persons who were near her, even without contact, frequently felt electric shocks. The effects, which were diminished when she was on a carpet or even a waxed cloth, were most remarkable when she was on the bare earth. They sometimes entirely ceased for two or three days, and then recommenced. Metals were not affected. Anything touched by her apron or dress would fly off, although a person held it; and Monsieur Hebert, whilst seated on a heavy tub or trough, was raised up with it. In short, the only place she could repose on was a stone covered with cork; they also kept her still by isolating her. When she was fatigued the effects diminished. A needle suspended horizontally, oscillated rapidly with the motion of her arm without contact, or remained fixed, whilst deviating from the magnetic direction. Great numbers of enlightened medical and scientific men witnessed these phenomena, and investigated them with every precaution to prevent imposition. She was often hurt by the violent involuntary movements she was thrown into, and was evidently afflicted by chorea.

Unfortunately, her parents, poor and ignorant, insisted, much against the advice of the doctors, on exhibiting her for money; and, under these circumstances, she was brought to Paris; and nothing is more probable, than, that after the phenomena had really ceased, the girl may have been induced to simulate what had originally been genuine; the thing avowedly ceased altogether on the evening of the 10th April, and there has been no return of it.

In 1831, a young girl, also aged fourteen, who lived as under nursery-maid, in a French family, exhibited the same phenomena; and when the case of Angélique Cottin was made public, her master published hers. He says that things of such an extraordinary nature occurred as he dare not repeat, since none but an eye-witness could believe them. The thing lasted for three years, and there was ample time for observation.

In the year 1686 a man, at Brussels, called Breekmans was similarly affected. A commission was appointed by the magistrates to investigate his condition; and, being pronounced a sorcerer, he would have been burnt, had he not luckily made his escape.

Many somnambulic persons are capable of giving an electric shock; and I have met with one person, not somnambulic, who informs me that he has frequently been able to do it by an effort of the will.

Dr. Ennemsoer relates the case of a Mademoiselle Emmerich, sister to the professor of theology at Strasburg, who also possessed this power. This young lady, who appears to have been a person of very rare merit and endowments, was afflicted with a long and singular malady, originating in a fright, in the course of which she exhibited many very curious phenomena, having fallen into a state of natural somnambulism, accompanied by a high degree of lucidity. Her body became so surcharged with electricity that it was necessary to her relief to discharge it; and she sometimes imparted a complete battery of shocks to her brother and her physician, or whoever was near, and that, frequently, when they did not touch her. Professor Emmerich mentions also, that she sent him a smart shock, one day, when he was several rooms off. He started up, and rushed into her chamber, where she was in bed, and as soon as she saw him she said, laughing, 'Ah, you felt it, did you?' Mademoiselle Emmerich's illness terminated in death.

Catugno, a surgeon, relates that having touched with his scalpel the intercostal nerve of a mouse that had bitten his leg, he received an electric shock; and where the torpedo abounds, the fishermen, in pouring water over the fish they have caught, for the purpose of washing them, know if one is amongst them by the shock they sustain.

A very extraordinary circumstance, which we may possibly attribute to some such influence as the above, occurred at Rambouillet, in November, 1846. The particulars are furnished by a gentleman residing on the spot at the time, and were published by the Baron Dupotet, who, however, attempts no explanation of the mystery.

One morning, some travelling merchants, or pedlars, came to the door of a farm house, belonging to a man named Bottel, and asked for some bread, which the maid servant gave them and they went away. Subsequently one of the party returned to ask for more, and was refused. The man I believe expressed some resentment, and uttered vague threats, but she would not give him anything, and he departed. That night at supper the plates began to dance and to roll off the table, without any visible cause, and several other unaccountable phenomena occurred; and the girl going to the door and chancing to place herself just where the pedlar had stood, she was seized with convulsions and an extraordinary rotatory motion. The carter who was standing by, laughed at her, and out of bravado, placed himself on the same spot, when he felt almost suffocated, and was so unable to command his movements, that he was overturned into a large pool that was in front of the house.

Upon this, they rushed to the curé of the parish for assistance, but he had scarcely said a prayer or two, before he was attacked in the same manner, though in his own house; and his furniture beginning to oscillate and crack as if it were bewitched, the poor people were frightened out of their wits.

THE POLTERGEIST OF THE GERMANS

By and by the phenomena intermitted, and they hoped all was over; but presently it began again; and this occurred more than once before it subsided wholly.

On the 8th December, 1836, at Stuttgart, Carl Fischer, a baker's boy, aged seventeen, of steady habits and good character, was fixed with a basket on his shoulders in some unaccountable way in front of his master's house. He foresaw the thing was to happen when he went out very early, with his bread in the morning; earnestly wished that the day was over, and told his companion that if he could only cross the threshold, on his return, he should escape it. It was about six when he did return; and his master hearing a fearful noise, which he could not describe, 'as if proceeding from a multitude of beings,' looked out of the window, where he saw Carl violently struggling and fighting with his apron, though his feet were immovably fixed to one spot. A hissing sound proceeded from his mouth and nose, and a voice which was neither his nor that of any person present, was heard to cry, 'Stand fast, Carl!' The master says, that he could not have believed such a thing; and he was so alarmed that he did not venture into the street, where numerous persons were assembled. The boy said he must remain there till eleven o'clock: and the police kept guard over him till that time, as the physician said he must not be interfered with, and the people sought to push him from the spot. When the time had expired, he was carried to the hospital, where he seemed exceedingly exhausted, and fell into a profound sleep.

I meet with numerous extraordinary records of a preternatural ringing of all the bells in a house; sometimes occurring periodically for a considerable time; and continuing after precautions have been taken which precluded the possibility of trick or deception, the wires being cut, and vigilant eyes watching them; and yet they rung on by day or night, just the same.

It is certainly very difficult to conceive, but at the same time it is not impossible that such strange phenomena as that of the Stockwell Ghost and many similar ones, may be the manifestations of some extraordinary electrical influence; but there are other cases of poltergeists, which it is impossible to attribute to the same cause, since they are accompanied by evident manifestations of will and intelligence. Such was the instance related in Southey's *Life of Wesley*, which occurred in the year 1716, beginning with a groaning, and subsequently proceeding to all manner of noises, lifting of latches, clattering of windows, knockings of a most mysterious kind, etc., etc. The family were not generally frightened, but the young children, when asleep, showed symptoms of great terror. This annoyance lasted, I think, two or three months, and then ceased. As in most of these cases, the dog was extremely frightened, and hid himself when the visitation commenced.

In the year 1838, a circumstance of the same kind occurred in Paris, in the Rue St. Honoré, and not very long ago, there was one in Caithness, in which most unaccountable circumstances transpired. Amongst the rest, stones were flung, which never hit people, but fell at their feet, in rooms perfectly closed on all sides. A gentleman who witnessed these extraordinary phenomena, related the whole story to an advocate of my acquaintance; who assured me, that however impossible he found it to credit such things, he should certainly place entire reliance on that gentleman's word in any other case.

Then there is the famous story of the Drummer of Tedworth;[1] and the persecution of Professor Schuppart, at Giessen, in Upper Hesse, which continued with occasional intermission for six years. This affair began with a violent knocking at the door one night; next day stones were sent whizzing through closed rooms in all directions; so that although no one was struck, the windows were all broken; and no sooner were new panes put in, than they were broken again. He was persecuted with slaps on the face by day and by night, so that he could get no rest; and when two persons were appointed by the authorities to sit by his bed to watch him, they got the slaps also. When he was reading at his desk, his lamp would suddenly rise up and remove to the other end of

[1] There was also a remarkable case of this sort at Mr. Chave's, in Devonshire, in the year 1810, where affidavits were made before the magistrates attesting the facts, and large rewards offered for discovery; but in vain. The phenomena continued several months, and the spiritual agent was frequently seen in the form of some strange animal.

THE POLTERGEIST OF THE GERMANS

the room—not as if thrown, but evidently carried: his books were torn to pieces and flung at his feet, and when he was lecturing, this mischievous sprite would tear out the leaf he was reading; and it is very remarkable that the only thing that seemed available, as a protection, was a drawn sword brandished over his head by himself, or others, which was one of the singularities attending the case of the Drummer of Tedworth. Schuppart narrated all these circumstances in his public lectures, and nobody ever disputed the facts.

A remarkable case of this sort occurred in the year 1670, at Keppoch, near Glasgow; there also stones were thrown which hit nobody; but the annoyance only continued eight days; and there are several more to be found recorded in works of that period. The disturbance that happened in the house of Gilbert Campbell, at Glenluce, excited considerable notice. Here, as elsewhere, stones were thrown; but, as in most similar instance I meet with, no human being was damaged; the licence of these spirits or goblins, or whatever they be, seeming generally to extend no further than worrying and tormenting their victims. In this case, however, the spirit spoke to them, though he was never seen. The annoyance commenced in November of the year 1654, I think, and continued till April, when there was some intermission till July, when it recommenced. The loss of the family from the things destroyed was ruining; for their household goods and chattels were rendered useless, their food was polluted and spoiled, and their very clothes cut to pieces whilst on their backs by invisible hands; and it was in vain that all the ministers about the country assembled to exorcize this troublesome spirit, for whoever was there, the thing continued exactly the same.

At length, poor Campbell applied to the Synod of Presbyters for advice; a meeting was convened in October, 1655, and a solemn day of humiliation was imposed through the whole bounds of the Presbytery, for the sake of the afflicted family. Whether it was owing to this or not, there ensued an alleviation from that time to April; and from April till August they were entirely free, and hoped all was over; but then it began again worse than ever, and they were dreadfully tormented through the autumn; after which the disturbance ceased, and although the family lived in the house many years afterwards, nothing of the sort ever happened again.

There was another famous case, which occurred at a place called Ring-Croft, in Kirkcudbright, in the year 1695. The afflicted family bore the name of Mackie. In this instance, the stones did sometimes hit them, and they were beaten as if by staves; they, as well as strangers who came to the house, were lifted off the ground by their clothes, their bed coverings were taken off their beds; things were visibly carried about the house by invisible hands; several people were hurt, even to the effusion of blood, by stones and blows; there were fire-balls seen about the house, which was several times actually ignited: people, both of the family and others, felt themselves grasped as if by a hand; then there was groaning, crying, whistling, and a voice that frequently spoke to them; crowds of people went to the house, but the thing continued just the same whether there were many or few, and sometimes the whole building shook as if it were coming down.

A day of humiliation was appointed in this case also, but without the least effect. The disturbance commenced in February, and ended on the 1st of May. Numberless people witnessed the phenomena, and the account of it is attested by fourteen ministers and gentlemen.

The same sort of thing occurred in the year 1659, in a place inhabited by an Evangelical bishop, called Schlotterbeck. It began in the same manner by throwing of stones and other things, many of which came through the roof; insomuch that they believed at first that some animal was concealed there. However, nothing could be found, and the invisible guest soon proceeded to other annoyances similar to those above-mentioned; and though they could not see him, his footsteps were for ever heard about the house. At length, wearied out, the bishop applied to the Government for aid, and they sent him a company of soldiers to guard the house by day and night, out of which he and his family retired. But the goblin cared no more for the soldiers than it had done for the city watch; the thing continued without intermission, whoever was there, till it ceased of its own accord. There was a house at Aix-la-Chapelle that was for several years quite uninhabitable from a similar cause.

THE POLTERGEIST OF THE GERMANS

I could mention many other cases, and, as I have said before, they occur in all countries; but these will suffice as specimens of the class. It is in vain for people who were not on the spot to laugh, and assert that these were the mischievous tricks of servants, or others, when those who were there, and who had such a deep interest in unravelling the mystery, and such abundance of time and opportunity for doing it, could find no solution whatever. In many of the above cases the cattle were unloosed, the horses were turned out of their stables, and uniformly all the animals in the way exhibited great terror, sweating and trembling whilst the visitation continued.

Since we cannot but believe that man forms but one class in an immense range of existences, do not these strange occurrences suggest the idea, that occasionally some individual out of this gamut of beings comes into rapport with us, or crosses our path like a comet, and that, whilst certain conditions last, it can hover about us, and play these puckish, mischievous tricks, till the charm is broken, and then it re-enters its own sphere, and we are cognizant of it no more!

But one of the most extraordinary examples of this kind of annoyance, is that which occurred in the year 1806, in the castle of Prince Hohenlohe, in Silesia. The account is given at length by Councillor Hahn, of Ingelfingen, who witnessed the circumstances; and, in consequence of the various remarks that have been since made on the subject, in different publications, he has repeatedly reasserted the facts in letters which have been printed and laid before the public. I cannot, therefore, see what right we have to disbelieve a man of honour and character, as he is said to be, merely because the circumstances he narrates are unaccountable, more especially as the story, strange as it is, by no means stands alone in the annals of demonology. The following details were written down at the time the events occurred, and they were communicated by Councillor Hahn to Dr. Kerner in the year 1828.

'After the campaign of the Prussians against the French in the year 1806, the reigning Prince of Hohenlohe gave orders to Councillor Hahn, who was in his service, to proceed to Slawensick, and there to wait his return. His Serene Highness advanced from Leignitz towards his principality, and Hahn also commenced his journey towards Upper Silesia on the 19th November. At the same period, Charles Kern, of Kuntzlau, who had fallen into the hands of the French, being released on parole, and arriving at Leignitz, in an infirm condition, he was allowed to spend some time with Hahn, whilst awaiting his exchange.

'Hahn and Kern had been friends in their youth, and their destinies having brought them both at this time into the Prussian States, they were lodged together in the same apartment of the castle, which was one on the first floor, forming an angle at the back of the building, one side looking towards the north, and the other to the east. On the right of the door of this room was a glass door, which led into a chamber divided from those which followed by a wainscot partition. The door in this wainscot, which communicated to those adjoining rooms, was entirely closed up, because in them all sorts of household utensils were kept. Neither in this chamber, nor in the sitting-room which preceded it, was there any opening whatever which could furnish the means of communication from without; nor was there anybody in the castle besides the two friends, except the Prince's two coachmen and Hahn's servant. The whole party were fearless people; and as for Hahn and Kern they believed in nothing less than ghosts or witches, nor had any previous experience induced them to turn their thoughts in that direction. Hahn, during his collegiate life had been much given to philosophy—had listened to Fichte, and earnestly studied the writings of Kant. The result of his reflections was a pure materialism; and he looked upon created man, not as an aim, but merely as a means to a yet undeveloped end. These opinions he has since changed, like many others, who think very differently in their fortieth year to what they did in their twentieth. The particulars here given are necessary in order to obtain credence for the following extraordinary narrative, and to establish the fact that the phenomena were not merely accepted by ignorant superstition, but coolly and courageously investigated by enlightened minds. During the first days of their residence in the castle, the two friends, living together in solitude, amused their long evenings by the works of Schiller, of whom they were both great admirers; and

THE POLTERGEIST OF THE GERMANS

Hahn usually read aloud. Three days had thus passed quietly away, when, as they were sitting at the table, which stood in the middle of the room, about nine o'clock in the evening, their reading was interrupted by a small shower of lime, which fell around them. They looked at the ceiling, concluding it must have come thence, but could perceive no abraded parts, and whilst they were yet seeking to ascertain whence the lime had proceeded, there suddenly fell several larger pieces, which were quite cold, and appeared as if they had belonged to the external wall. At length, concluding the lime must have fallen from some part of the wall, and giving further inquiry, they went to bed, and slept quietly till the morning, when, on awaking, they were somewhat surprised at the quantity which strewed the floor, more especially as they could still discover no part of the walls or ceiling from which it could have fallen. But they thought no more of the matter till evening, when, instead of the lime falling as before, it was thrown, and several pieces struck Hahn. At the same time, they heard heavy blows, sometimes below, and sometimes over their heads, like the sound of distant guns; still attributing these sounds to natural causes, they went to bed as usual, but the uproar prevented their sleeping, and each accused the other of occasioning it by kicking with his feet against the footboard of his bed, till, finding that the noise continued when they both got out and stood together in the middle of the room, they were satisfied that this was not the case. On the following evening, a third noise was added, which resembled the faint and distant beating of a drum. Upon this, they requested the governess of the castle to send them the key of the apartments above and below, which was brought them by her son; and, whilst he and Kern went to make their investigations, Hahn remained in their own room. Above, they found an empty room; below, a kitchen. They knocked, but the noise they made was very different to that which Hahn continued all the while to hear around him. When they returned, Hahn said jestingly, 'The place is haunted!' On this night, when they went to bed with a light burning, they heard what seemed like a person walking about the room with slippers on, and a stick, with which he struck the floor as he moved step by step. Hahn continued to jest, and Kern to laugh, at the oddness of these circumstances for some time, when they both as usual fell asleep, neither in the slightest degree disturbed by these events, nor inclined to attribute them to any supernatural cause. But on the following evening the affair became more inexplicable; various articles in the room were thrown about; knives, forks, brushes, caps, slippers, padlocks, funnel, snuffers, soap—everything in short that was moveable; whilst lights darted from corner to corner, and everything was in confusion; at the same time the lime fell, and the blows continued. Upon this, the two friends called up the servants, Knittel, the castle watch and whoever else was at hand, to be witnesses of these mysterious operations. In the morning all was quiet, and generally continued so till about an hour after midnight. One evening, Kern going into the above-mentioned chamber to fetch something, and hearing such an uproar that it almost drove him backwards to the door, Hahn caught up the light, and both rushed into the room, where they found a large piece of wood lying close to the wainscot. But supposing this to be the cause of the noise, who had set it in motion? For Kern was sure the door was shut, even whilst the noise was making; neither had there been any wood in the room. Frequently, before their eyes, the knives and snuffers rose from the table, and fell, after some minutes, to the ground; and Hahn's large shears were once lifted in this manner, between him and one of the Prince's cooks, and, falling to the ground, stuck into the floor. As some nights, however, passed quite quietly, Hahn was determined not to leave the rooms; but when, for three weeks, the disturbance was so constant that they could get no rest, they resolved on removing their beds into the large room above, in hopes of once more enjoying a little quiet sleep. Their hopes were vain—the thumping continued as before; and not only so, but articles flew about the room, which they were quite sure they had left below. 'They may fling as they will,' cried Hahn, 'sleep I must'; whilst Kern began to undress, pondering on these matters as he walked up and down the room. Suddenly Hahn saw him stand, as if transfixed, before the looking-glass, on which he had accidentally cast his eyes. He had so stood for some minutes, when he was seized with a violent trembling, and turned from the mirror with his face as white as death. Hahn, fancying the cold of the uninhabited room had seized him, hastened to throw a cloak over him; when Kern, who was naturally very courageous, recovered himself, and related, though with trembling lips, that, as he had accidentally looked in the glass, he had seen a white female figure looking out of it; she was in front of his own image, which he distinctly saw behind her. At first he could not believe his eyes; he thought it must be fancy, and for that reason he had stood so long; but when he saw that the eyes of the figure moved, and looked into his, a shudder had seized him, and he had turned away. Hahn upon this advanced with firm steps to the front of the mirror, and called upon the apparition to show itself to him; but he saw nothing, although he remained a quarter of an hour before the glass, and frequently repeated his exhortation. Kern then further related that the features of the apparition were very old, but not gloomy or morose; the expression indeed was rather that of indifference; but the face was very pale, and the head was wrapped in a cloth which left only the features visible.

'By this time it was four o'clock in the morning—sleep was banished from their eyes—and they resolved to return to the lower room, and have their beds brought back again; but the people who were sent to fetch them returned, declaring they could not open the door, although it did not appear to be fastened. They were sent back again; but a second and a third time they returned with the same answer. Then Hahn went himself, and opened it with the greatest ease. The four servants, however, solemnly declared that all their united strengths could make no impression on it.

'In this way a month had elapsed: the strange events at the castle had got spread abroad; and amongst others who desired to convince themselves of the fact were two Bavarian officers of dragoons, namely, Captain Cornet and Lieutenant Magerle, of the regiment of Minuci. Magerle offering to remain in the room alone, the others left him, but scarcely had they passed into the next apartment, when they heard Magerle storming like a man in a passion, and cutting away at the tables and chairs with his sabre, whereupon the Captain thought it advisable to return, in order to rescue the furniture from his rage. They found the door shut, but he opened it on their summons and related, in great excitement, that as soon as they had quitted the room, some cursed thing had begun to fling lime, and other matters, at him; and, having examined every part of the room without being able to discover the agent of the mischief, he had fallen into a rage and cut madly about him.

'The party now passed the rest of the evening together in the room, and the two Bavarians closely watched Hahn and Kern, in order to satisfy themselves that the mystery was no trick of theirs. All at once, as they were quietly sitting at the table, the snuffers rose into the air, and fell again to the ground behind Magerle; and a leaden ball flew at Hahn, and hit him upon the breast, and presently afterwards they heard a noise at the glass door, as if somebody had struck his fist through it, together with a sound of falling glass. On investigation they found the door entire, but a broken drinking-glass on the floor. By this time the Bavarians were convinced, and they retired from the room to seek repose in one more peaceful.

'Amongst other strange circumstances, the following, which occurred to Hahn, is remarkable. One evening about eight o'clock, being about to shave himself, the implements for the purpose, which were lying on a pyramidal stand in a corner of the room, flew at him, one after the other—the soap-box, the razor, the brush and the soap—and fell at his feet, although he was standing several paces from the pyramid. He and Kern, who was sitting at the table, laughed, for they were now so accustomed to these events, that they only made them subjects of diversion. In the meantime, Hahn poured some water, which had been standing on the stove, in a basin, observing as he dipped his finger into it, that it was of a nice heat for shaving. He seated himself before the table, and stropped his razor; but when he attempted to prepare the lather, the water had clean vanished out of the basin. Another time, Hahn was awakened by goblins throwing at him a squeezed-up piece of sheet-lead, in which tobacco had been wrapped, and when he stooped to pick it up, the self-same piece was flung at him again. When this was repeated a third time, Hahn flung a heavy stick at his invisible assailant.

'Dorfel, the book-keeper, was frequently a witness to these

strange events. He once laid his cap on the table by the stove, when, being about to depart, he sought for it, it had vanished. Four of five times he examined the table in vain; presently afterwards he saw it lying exactly where he had placed it when he came in. On the same table, Knittel having once placed his cap, and drawn himself a seat, suddenly—although there was nobody near the table—he saw it flying through the room to his feet, where it fell.

'Hahn now determined to find out the secret himself; and for this purpose seated himself with two lights before him, in a position where he could see the whole of the room, and all the windows and doors it contained; but the same things occurred even when Kern was out, the servants in the stables, and nobody in the castle but himself; and the snuffers were as usual flung about, although the closest observation could not detect by whom.

'The forest-master, Radzensky, spent a night in the room; but although the two friends slept, he could get no rest. He was bombarded without intermission; and in the morning, his bed was found full of all manner of household articles.

'One evening, in spite of all the drumming and flinging, Hahn was determined to sleep; but a heavy blow on the wall, close to his bed soon waked him from his slumbers. A second time he went to sleep, and was awaked by a sensation, as if some person had dipped his finger in water, and was sprinkling his face with it. He pretended to sleep again, whilst he watched Kern and Knittel, who were sitting at the table, the sensation of sprinkling returned; but he could find no water on his face.

'About this time, Hahn had occasion to make a journey as far as Breslau; and when he returned he heard the strangest story of all. In order not to be alone in this mysterious chamber, Kern had engaged Hahn's servant, a man of about forty years of age, and of entire singleness of character, to stay with him. One night as Kern lay in his bed, and this man was standing near the glass door in conversation with him, to his utter amazement he beheld a jug of beer, which stood on a table, in a room, at some distance from him, slowly lifted to a height of about three feet, and the contents poured into a glass, that was standing there also, until the latter was half full. The jug was then gently replaced, and the glass lifted and emptied, as by someone drinking: whilst John, the servant, exclaimed, in terrified surprise, "Lord Jesus! it swallows!" The glass was quietly replaced, and not a drop of beer was to be found on the floor. Hahn was about to require an oath of John, in corfirmation of this fact; but forbore, seeing how ready the man was to take one, and satisfied of the truth of the relation.

'One night, Knetsch, an inspector of the works, passed the night with the two friends, and in spite of the unintermitting flinging they all three went to bed. There were lights in the room, and presently all three saw two napkins, in the middle of the room, rise slowly up to the ceiling, and having there spread themselves out flutter down again. The china bowl of a pipe, belonging to Kern, flew about and was broken. Knives and forks were flung; and at last one of the latter fell on Hahn's head, though fortunately with the handle downwards; and having now endured this annoyance for two months, it was unanimously resolved to abandon this mysterious chamber for this night at all events. John and Kern took up one of the beds and carried it into the opposite room, but they were no sooner gone than a pitcher for holding chalybeate water flew to the feet of the two who remained behind, although no door was open, and a brass candlestick was flung to the ground. In the opposite room the night passed quietly, although some sounds still issued from the forsaken chamber. After this, there was a cessation to these strange proceedings, and nothing more remarkable occurred, with the exception of the following circumstance. Some weeks after the above-mentioned removal, as Hahn was returning home, and crossing the bridge that leads to the castle gate, he heard the foot of a dog behind him. He looked round, and called repeatedly on the name of a greyhound that was much attached to him, thinking it might be she, but although he still heard the foot, even when he ascended the stairs, as he could see nothing, he concluded it was an illusion. Scarcely, however, had he set foot within the room, than Kern advanced and took the door out of his hand, at the same time calling the dog by name; adding, however, immediately that he thought he had seen the dog, but that he had no sooner called her than she disappeared. Hahn then inquired if he had really seen the dog. "Certainly I did," replied Kern; "she was close behind you—half within the door—and that was the reason I took it out of your hand, lest, not observing her, you should have shut it suddenly and crushed her. It was a white dog and I took it for Flora." Search was immediately made for the dog, but she was found locked up in the stable, and had not been out of it the whole day. It is certainly remarkable—even supposing Hahn to have been deceived with respect to the footsteps—that Kern should have seen a white dog behind him before he had heard a word on the subject from his friend, especially as there was no such animal in the neighbourhood; besides, it was not yet dark, and Kern was very sharp-sighted.

'Hahn remained in the castle for half-a-year after this, without experiencing anything extraordinary; and even persons who had possession of these mysterious chambers were not subjected to any annoyance.

'The riddle, however, in spite of all the perquisitions and investigations that were set on foot remained unsolved—no explanation of these strange events could be found; and even supposing any motive could exist, there was nobody in the neighbourhood clever enough to have carried on such a system of persecution, which lasted so long that the inhabitants of the chamber became almost indifferent to it.

'In conclusion, it is only necessary to add that Councillor Hahn wrote down this account for his own satisfaction, with the strictest regard to truth. His words are:

' "I have described these events exactly as I heard and saw them; from beginning to end I observed them with the most entire self-possession. I had no fear, nor the slightest tendency to it; yet the whole thing remains to me perfectly inexplicable. Written the 19th November, 1808.

' "AUGUSTUS HAHN, *Councillor*"

'Doubtless many natural explanations of these phenomena will be suggested, by those who consider themselves above the weakness of crediting stories of this description. Some say that Kern was a dexterous juggler, who contrived to throw dust in the eyes of his friend Hahn; whilst others affirm that both

Hahn and Kern were intoxicated every evening. I did not fail to communicate these objections to Hahn, and here insert his answer.

' "After the events alluded to, I resided with Kern for a quarter of a year in another part of the Castle of Slawensick (which has been since struck by lightning and burnt), without finding a solution of the mystery, or experiencing a repetition of the annoyance, which discontinued from the moment we quitted those particular apartments. Those persons must suppose me very weak, who can imagine it possible, that with only one companion, I could have been the subject of his sport for two months without detecting him. As for Kern himself, he was, from the first, very anxious to leave the rooms; but as I was unwilling to resign the hope of discovering some natural cause for these phenomena, I persisted in remaining; and the thing that at last induced me to yield to his wishes was his vexation at the loss of his china pipe, which had been thrown against the wall and broken. Besides, jugglery requires a juggler, and I was frequently quite alone when these things occurred. It is equally absurd to accuse us of intoxication. The wine there was too dear for us to drink at all, and we confined ourselves wholly to weak beer. All the circumstances that happened are not set down in the narration; but my recollection of the whole is as vivid as if it had occurred yesterday. We had also many witnesses, some of whom have been mentioned. Councillor Klenk also visited me at a later period, with every desire to investigate the mystery; and when one morning he had mounted on a table for the purpose of doing so, and was knocking at the ceiling with a stick, a powder horn fell upon him, which he had just before left on the table in another room. At that time Kern had been for some time absent. I neglected no possible means that could have led to a discovery of the secret; and at least as many people have blamed me, for my unwillingness to believe in a supernatural cause, as the reverse. Fear is not my failing, as all who are acquainted with me know; and to avoid the possibility of error, I frequently asked others what they saw when I was myself present; and their answers always coincided with what I saw myself. From 1809 till 1811 I lived in Jacobswald, very near the Castle where the Prince

THE POLTERGEIST OF THE GERMANS

himself was residing. I am aware that some singular circumstances occurred whilst he was there; but as I did not witness them myself, I cannot speak of them more particularly.

' "I am still as unable as ever to account for those events, and I am content to submit to the hasty remarks of the world, knowing that I have only related the truth, and what many persons now alive witnessed, as well as myself.

' "Councillor Hahn
' "*Ingelfingen, 24th August, 1829.*[1]" '

The only key to this mystery ever discovered was, that after the destruction of the castle by lightning, when the ruins were removed, there was found the skeleton of a man without a coffin. His skull had been split, and a sword lay by his side.

Now, I am very well aware how absurd and impossible these events will appear to many people, and that they will have recourse to any explanation rather than admit them for facts. Yet, so late as the year 1835, a suit was brought before the Sheriff of Edinburgh, in which Captain Molesworth was defendant, and the landlord of the house he inhabited (which was at Trinity, about a couple of miles from Edinburgh) was plaintiff, founded upon circumstances not so varied, certainly, but quite as inexplicable. The suit lasted two years, and I have been favoured with the particulars of the case by Mr. M. L. the advocate employed by the plaintiff, who spent many hours in examining the numerous witnesses, several of whom were officers of the army, and gentlemen of undoubted honour and capacity for observation.

Captain Molesworth took the house of a Mr. Webster, who resided in the adjoining one, in May or June, 1835; and when he had been in it about two months, he began to complain of sundry extraordinary noises, which, finding it impossible to account for, he took it into his head, strangely enough, were made by Mr. Webster. The latter naturally represented that it was not probable he should desire to damage the reputation of his own house, or drive his tenant out of it, and retorted the accusation. Still, as these noises and knockings continued, Captain M., not only lifted the boards in the room most

---

[1] Translated from the original German.—C.C.

infected, but actually made holes in the wall which divided his residence from Mr. W's, for the purpose of detecting the delinquent—of course without success. Do what they would, the thing went on just the same; footsteps of invisible feet, knockings and scratchings, and rustlings, first on one side, and then on the other, were heard daily and nightly. Sometimes this unseen agent seemed to be knocking to a certain tune, and if a question were addressed to it which could be answered numerically, as, 'How many people there are in this room?' for example, it would answer by so many knocks. The beds, too, were occasionally heaved up, as if somebody were underneath, and where the knockings were, the wall trembled visibly, but, search as they would, no one could be found. Captain Molesworth had had two daughters, one of whom, named Matilda, had lately died; the other, a girl between twelve and thirteen, called Jane, was sickly, and generally kept her bed; and, as it was observed that, wherever she was, these noises most frequently prevailed, Mr. Webster, who did not like the *mala fama* that was attaching itself to his house, declared that she made them, whilst the people in the neighbourhood believed that it was the ghost of Matilda, warning her sister that she was soon to follow. Sheriff's officers, masons, justices of peace, and the officers of the regiment quartered at Leith, who were friends of Captain M., all came to his aid, in hopes of detecting or frightening away his tormentor, but in vain. Sometimes it was said to be a trick of somebody outside the house, and then they formed a cordon round it; and next, as the poor sick girl was suspected, they tied her up in a bag, but it was all to no purpose.

At length, ill and wearied out by the annoyances and the anxieties attending the affair, Captain M. quitted the house, and Mr. W. brought an action against him for the damages committed, by lifting the boards, breaking the walls, and firing at the wainscot, as well as for the injury done to his house by saying it was haunted, which prevented other tenants taking it.

The poor young lady died, hastened out of the world, it is said, by the severe measures used whilst she was under suspicion; and the persons that have since inhabited the house have experienced no repetition of the annoyance.

THE POLTERGEIST OF THE GERMANS

The manner in which these strange persecutions attach themselves to certain persons and places seems somewhat analogous to another class of cases, which bear a great similarity to what was formerly called *possession*; and I must here observe, that many German physicians maintain, that to this day instances of genuine possession occur, and there are several works published in their language on the subject; and for this malady they consider magnetism the only remedy, all others being worse than useless. Indeed, they look upon *possession* itself as a demono-magnetic state, in which the patient is in rapport with mischievous or evil spirits; as in the Agatho (or good) magnetic state, which is the opposite pole, he is in rapport with good ones; and they particularly warn their readers against confounding this infliction with cases of epilepsy or mania. They assert, that although instances are comparatively rare, both sexes and all ages are equally subject to this misfortune; and that it is quite an error to suppose, either, that it has ceased since the Resurrection of Christ, or that the expression used in the Scriptures 'possessed by a devil', meant merely insanity or convulsions. This disease, which is not contagious, was well-known to the Greeks; and in later times Hofman has recorded several well-established instances. Amongst the distinguishing symptoms, they reckon the patient's speaking in a voice that is not his own, frightful convulsions and motions of the body, which arise suddenly, without any previous indisposition—blasphemous and obscene talk, a knowledge of what is secret, and of the future—a vomiting of extraordinary things, such as hair, stones, pins, needles, etc., etc. I need scarcely observe that this opinion is not universal in Germany; still it obtains amongst many who have had considerable opportunities for observation.

Dr. Bardili had a case in the year 1830, which he considered decidedly to be one of possession. The patient was a peasant woman, aged thirty-four, who never had any sickness whatever; and the whole of whose bodily functions continued perfectly regular whilst she exhibited the following strange phenomena. I must observe that she was happily married, had three children, was not a fanatic, and bore an excellent character for regularity and industry, when, without any warning or perceptible cause, she was seized with the most extraordinary convulsions, whilst a strange voice proceeded from her, which assumed to be that of an unblessed spirit, who had formerly inhabited a human form. Whilst these fits were on her, she entirely lost her own individuality, and became this person; on returning to herself, her understanding and character were as entire as before. The blasphemy and cursing and barking and screeching, were dreadful. She was wounded and injured severely by the violent falls and blows she gave herself; and when she had an intermission, she could do nothing but weep over what they told her had passed, and the state in which she saw herself. She was moreover reduced to a skeleton; for when she wanted to eat, the spoon was turned round in her hand, and she often fasted for days together. This affliction lasted for three years; all remedies failed, and the only alleviation she obtained was by the continued and earnest prayers of those about her and her own; for although this demon did not like prayers, and violently opposed her kneeling down, even forcing her to outrageous fits of laughter, still they had a power over him. It is remarkable that pregnancy, confinement, and the nursing her child, made not the least difference in this woman's condition. All went on regularly, but the demon kept his post. At length, being magnetized, the patient fell into a partially somnambulic state, in which another voice was heard to proceed from her, being that of her protecting spirit, which encouraged her to patience and hope, and promised that the evil guest would be obliged to vacate his quarters. She often now fell into a magnetic state without the aid of a magnetizer. At the end of three years she was entirely relieved, and as well as ever.

In the case of Rosina Wildin, aged ten years, which occurred at Pleidelsheim, in 1834, the demon used to announce himself by crying out 'Here I am again!' Whereupon the weak exhausted child, who had been lying like one dead, would rage and storm in a voice like a man's, perform the most extraordinary movements and feats of violence and strength, till he would cry out, 'Now I must be off again!' This spirit spoke generally in the plural number, for he said, she had another beside himself, a dumb devil, who plagued her most. 'He it is that twirls her round and round, distorts her features, turns her eyes, locks her teeth, etc. What he bids me, I must do!' This child was at length cured by magnetism.

Barbara Rieger, of Steinbach, aged ten, in 1834, was possessed by two spirits, who spoke in two distinctly different male voices and dialects; one said he had formerly been a mason, the other gave himself out for a deceased provisor; the latter of whom was much the worst of the two. When they spoke, the child closed her eyes, and when she opened them again, she knew nothing of what they had said. The mason confessed to have been a great sinner, but the provisor was proud and hardened, and would confess nothing. They often commanded food, and made her eat it, which when she recovered her individuality, she felt nothing of, but was very hungry. The mason was very fond of brandy, and drank a great deal; and if not brought when he ordered it, his raging and storming was dreadful. In her own individuality, the child had the greatest aversion to this liquor. They treated her for worms and other disorders, without the least effect; till at length, by magnetism, the mason was cast out. The provisor was more tenacious, but, finally, they got rid of him, too, and the girl remained quite well.

In 1835, a respectable citizen, whose full name is not given, was brought to Dr. Kerner. He was aged thirty-seven, and till the last seven years had been unexceptionable in conduct and character. An unaccountable change had, however, come over him in his thirtieth year, which made his family very unhappy; and at length one day, a strange voice suddenly spoke out of him, saying, that he was the late magistrate, S., and that he had been in him for six years. When this spirit was driven out, by magnetism, the man fell to the earth, and was almost torn to pieces by the violence of the struggle; he then lay for a space as if dead, and arose quite well and free.

In another case, a young woman, at Gruppenbach was quite in her senses, and heard the voice of her demon (who was also a deceased person) speak out of her, without having any power to suppress it.

In short, instances of this description seem by no means rare; and if such a phenomenon as possession ever did exist,

THE POLTERGEIST OF THE GERMANS

I do not see what right we have to assert that it exists no longer, since, in fact, we know nothing about it; only, that being determined to admit nothing so contrary to the ideas of the present day, we set out by deciding that the thing is impossible.

Since these cases occur in other countries, no doubt they must do so in this; and, indeed, I have met with one instance much more remarkable in its details than any of those abovementioned, which occurred at Bishopwearmouth, near Sunderland, in the year 1840; and as the particulars in this case have been published and attested by two physicians and two surgeons, not to mention the evidence of numerous other persons, I think we are bound to accept the facts, whatever interpretation we may choose to put upon them.

The patient, named Mary Jobson, was between twelve and thirteen years of age; her parents, respectable people in humble life, and herself an attendant on a Sunday school. She became ill in November, 1839, and was soon afterwards seized with terrific fits, which continued, at intervals, for eleven weeks. It was during this period that the family first observed a strange knocking, which they could not account for. It was sometimes in one place, and sometimes in another; and even about the bed when the girl lay in a quiet sleep, with her hands folded outside the clothes. They next heard a strange voice, which told them circumstances they did not know, but which they afterwards found to be correct. Then there was a noise like the clashing of arms, and such a rumbling that the tenant below thought the house was coming down; footsteps where nobody was to be seen, water falling on the floor, no one knew whence, locked doors opened, and above all sounds of ineffably sweet music. The doctors and the father were suspicious, and every precaution was taken, but no solution of the mystery could be found. This spirit, however, was a good one, and it preached to them, and gave them a great deal of good advice. Many persons went to witness this strange phenomenon, and some were desired to go by the voice, when in their own homes. Thus Elizabeth Gauntlett, whilst attending to some domestic affairs at home, was startled by hearing a voice say, 'Be thou faithful, and thou shalt see the works of thy God, and shalt

THE POLTERGEIST OF THE GERMANS

hear with thine ears!' She cried out, 'My God! what can this be!' and presently she saw a large white cloud near her. On the same evening, the voice said to her, 'Mary Jobson, one of your scholars, is sick; go and see her; and it will be good for you.' This person did not know where the child lived; but having inquired the address, she went: and at the door she heard the same voice bid her go up. On entering the room, she heard another voice, soft and beautiful, which bade her be faithful, and said, 'I am the Virgin Mary.' This voice promised her a sign at home; and accordingly that night, whilst reading the Bible, she heard it say, 'Jemima, be not afraid; it is I: if you keep my commandments, it shall be well with you.' When she repeated her visit, the same things occurred, and she heard the most exquisite music.

The same sort of phenomena were witnessed by everybody who went—the immoral were rebuked, the good encouraged. Some were bidden instantly depart, and were forced to go. The voices of several deceased persons of the family were also heard, and made revelations.

Once the voice said, 'Look up, and you shall see the sun, and moon on the ceiling!' and immediately there appeared a beautiful representation of these planets in lively colours, viz., green, yellow and orange. Moreover, these figures were permanent; but the father, who was a long time sceptical, insisted on whitewashing them over; however, they still remained visible.

Amongst other things, the voice said that though the child appeared to suffer, that she did not; that she did not know where her body was, and that her own spirit had left it and another had entered; and that her body was made a speaking-trumpet. The voice told the family and visitors many things of their distant friends, which proved true.

The girl twice saw a divine form standing by her bedside who spoke to her, and Joseph Ragg, one of the persons who had been invited by the voice to go, saw a beautiful and heavenly figure come to his bedside, about eleven o'clock at night, on the 17th January. It was in male attire, surrounded by a radiance; it came a second time on the same night. On each occasion it opened his curtains and looked at him benignantly, remaining about a quarter of an hour. When it went away, the curtains fell back in their former position. One day, whilst in the sick child's room, Margaret Watson saw a lamb, which passed through the door and entered a place where the father, John Jobson, was; but he did not see it.

One of the most remarkable features in this case is the beautiful music which was heard by all parties, as well as the family, including the unbelieving father, and, indeed, it seems to have been, in a great degree, this that converted him at last. This music was heard repeatedly during a space of sixteen weeks; sometimes it was like an organ, but more beautiful; at others, there was singing of holy songs, in parts, and the words distinctly heard. The sudden appearance of water in the room, too, was most unaccountable; for they felt it and it was really water. When the voice desired that water should be sprinkled, it immediately appeared as if sprinkled. At another time a sign being promised to the sceptical father, water would suddenly appear on the floor; this happened 'not once, but twenty times'.

During the whole course of this affair the voices told them that there was a miracle to be wrought on this child; and accordingly, on the 22nd of June, when she was as ill as ever, and they were only praying for her death, at five o'clock the voice ordered that her clothes should be laid out, and that everybody should leave the room, except the infant, which was two years and a half old. They obeyed; and having been outside the door a quarter of an hour, the voice cried, 'Come in!' and when they entered they saw the girl completely dressed and quite well, sitting in a chair with the infant on her knee, and she had not an hour's illness from that time till the report was published, which was on the 30th of January, 1841.

Now, it is very easy to laugh at all this, and assert that these things never happened, because they are absurd and impossible; but whilst honest, well-meaning, and intelligent people, who were on the spot, assert that they did, I confess I find myself constrained to believe them, however much I find in the case which is discrepant with my notions. It was not an affair of a day or an hour; there was ample time for observation, for the phenomena continued from the 9th of February

THE POLTERGEIST OF THE GERMANS

to the 22nd of June; and the determined unbelief of the father, with regard to the possibility of spiritual appearances, insomuch that he ultimately expressed great regret for the harshness he had used—is a tolerable security against imposition. Moreover, they pertinaciously refused to receive any money or assistance whatever, and were more likely to suffer in public opinion than otherwise by the avowal of these circumstances.

Dr. Reid Clanny, who publishes the report, with the attestations of the witnesses, is a physician of many years' experience, and is also, I believe, the original inventor of the safety lamp; and he declares his entire conviction of the facts, assuring his readers that 'many persons holding high rank in the Established Church, ministers of other denominations, as well as many lay-members of society, highly respected for learning and piety, are equally satisfied'. When he first saw the child lying on her back, apparently insensible, with her eyes suffused with florid blood, he felt assured that she had a disease of the brain; and he was not in the least disposed to believe in the mysterious part of the affair, till subsequent investigation compelled him to do so; and that his belief is of a very decided character we may feel assured, when he is content to submit to all the obloquy he must incur by avowing it.[1]

He adds, that since the girl has been quite well, both her family and that of Joseph Ragg have frequently heard the same heavenly music as they did during her illness; and a Mr. Torbock, a surgeon, who expresses himself satisfied of the truth of the above particulars, also mentions another case, in which he as well as a dying person he was attending, heard divine music just before the dissolution.

Of this last phenomenon, namely, sounds as of heavenly music being heard when a death is occurring, I have met with numerous instances.

From investigation of the above case, Dr. Clanny has arrived at the conviction that the spiritual world do occasionally identify themselves with our affairs, and Dr. Drury asserts, that besides this instance he has met with another circumstance which has left him firmly convinced that we live in a world of

---

[1] Dr. Clanny informs me that Mary Jobson is now a very well educated and extremely respectable young woman.

THE POLTERGEIST OF THE GERMANS

spirits, and that he has been in the presence of an unearthly being, who had 'passed that bourne from which, it is said, no traveller returns'.[1]

But the most extraordinary case I have yet met with is the following; because it is one which cannot by any possibility be attributed to disease or illusion. It is furnished to me from the most undoubted authority, and I give it as I received it, with the omission of the names. I have indeed in this instance thought it right to change the initial, and substitute G. for the right one, the particulars being of a nature which demand delicacy, as regards the parties concerned:

'Mrs. S. C. Hall, in early life, was intimately acquainted with a family named G., one of whom, Richard G., a young officer in the army, was subject to a harassing visitation of a kind that is usually regarded as supernatural. Mrs. H. once proposed to pay a visit to her particular friend, Catherine G., but was told that it would not be convenient exactly at that time, as Richard was on the point of coming home. She thought the inconveniences consisted in the want of a bedroom and spoke of sleeping with Miss G., and found that the objection really lay in the fact of Richard being 'haunted', which rendered it impossible for anybody else to be comfortable in the same house with him. A few weeks after Richard's return, Mrs. H. heard of Mrs. G.'s being extremely ill; and found, on going to call, that it was owing to nothing but the distress the old lady suffered in consequence of the strange circumstance connected with her son. It appeared that Richard wherever he was, at home, in camp, in lodgings, abroad, or in his own country, was liable to be visited in his bedroom at night by certain extraordinary noises. Any light he kept in the room was sure to be put out. Something went beating about the walls and his bed, making a great noise, and often sniffing close to his face, but never becoming visible. If a cage-bird was in his room, it was certain to be found dead in the morning. If he kept a dog in the apartment, it would make away from him as soon as released, and never come near him again. His brother, even his mother, had slept in the room; but the visitation took place as usual. According to Miss G.'s report, she and

[1] Alluding, I conclude, to the affair at Willington.

other members of the family would listen at the bedroom door after Richard had gone to sleep, and would hear the noises commence, and they would then hear him sit up and express his vexation by a few military execrations. The young man, at length, was obliged by this pest to quit the army, and go upon half-pay. Under its influence he became a sort of Cain; for wherever he lived, the annoyance was so great that he was quickly obliged to remove. Mrs. H. heard of him being ultimately gone to settle in Ireland, where, however, according to the report of a brother whom she met about four years ago, the visitation which afflicted him in his early years, was in no degree abated.'

This cannot be called a case of possession, but seems to be one of rapport, which attaches this invisible tormentor to his victim.

7. POLTERGEISTS IN IRELAND AND ELSEWHERE

Report on the Enniscorthy, Derrygonnelly and other Poltergeist Cases, by Sir William Barrett, F.R.S., reprinted from Vol. XXV of the Proceedings of the Society for Psychical Research

The term 'Poltergeist' is translated Hobgoblin in our German dictionaries, but that is not the equivalent, nor have we any English equivalent to the German word. It is derived from *polter*, a rumbling noise, or *poltern*, to make a row, to rattle; a *polterer* is a boisterous fellow, a *poltergeist* therefore a boisterous ghost. It is a convenient term to describe those apparently meaningless noises, disturbances and movements of objects, for which we can discover no assignable cause.

The phenomena are especially sporadic, breaking out suddenly and unexpectedly, and disappearing as suddenly after a few days, or weeks, or months of annoyance to those concerned. They differ from hauntings, inasmuch as they appear to be attached to an individual, usually a young person, more than to a place, or rather to *a person in a particular place*. Moreover, ghostly forms (except, if we may trust one or two witnesses, a hand and arm) are not seen. They appear to have some intelligence behind them, for they frequently respond to requests made for a given number of raps; the intelligence is therefore in some way related to our intelligence, and moreover is occasionally in telepathic rapport with our minds. For in one case, which I submitted to a long and searching enquiry, I found that when I mentally asked for a given number of raps, no word being spoken, the response was given promptly and correctly, and this four times in succession, a

THE ENNISCORTHY CASE

different number being silently asked for in each case. There are other characteristics which bring the subject of poltergeists into close connection with the physical phenomena of spiritualism. The movement of objects is usually quite unlike that due to gravitational or other attraction. They slide about, rise in the air, move in eccentric paths, sometimes in a leisurely manner, often turn round in their career, and usually descend quietly without hurting the observers. At other times an immense weight is lifted, often in daylight, no one being near, crockery is thrown about and broken, bedclothes are dragged off, the occupants sometimes lifted gently to the ground, and the bedstead tilted up or dragged about the room. The phenomena occur both in broad daylight and at night. Sometimes bells are continuously rung, even if all the bell wires are removed. Stones are frequently thrown, but no one is hurt; I myself have seen a large pebble drop apparently from space in a room where the only culprit could have been myself, and certainly I did not throw it. Loud scratchings on bedclothes, walls and furniture are a frequent characteristic; sometimes a sound like whispering or panting is heard, and footsteps are often heard without any visible cause. More frequently than otherwise the disturbances are associated with the presence of children or young people, and cease when they are taken from the place where the disturbance originated, only to be renewed on their return, and then abruptly the annoyance ends.

If upon the cessation of the disturbances, investigators appear on the scene and ask for something to occur in their presence, and are sufficiently persistent and incredulous, they may possibly see a clumsy attempt to reproduce some of the phenomena, and will thereupon catch the culprit child in the act. Then we hear the customary 'I told you so', and forthwith the clever investigator will not fail to let the world know of his acumen, and how credulous and stupid everybody is but himself. I will return later on to the psychological cause of this not infrequent simulation of mysterious phenomena, especially by children.

The point to which I am anxious to draw attention is the essentially temporary and fugitive nature of the phenomena, and that if we are fortunate enough to hear of them at once, and are able to visit the place whilst the disturbances are going on, the presence of the most skilful and incredulous observer will not affect the result—and under such circumstances I challenge the scornful to produce a single adverse witness. In fact, to any one who has made a serious and prolonged study of the subject of poltergeists, it is simply waste of time to reply to the arguments of those who assert that fraud and hallucination are adequate explanations of the whole phenomena.

THE ENNISCORTHY CASE

The first case I will relate has recently occurred at Enniscorthy, a town in Co. Wexford. My attention was drawn to the matter through a letter from the representative of a local newspaper, Mr. Murphy. After some correspondence, and in answer to my request, Mr. Murphy kindly drew up the accompanying admirable report:

STATEMENT BY MR. N. J. MURPHY

The strange manifestations which took place at Enniscorthy last July, 1910, may perhaps interest some students of Psychology, and more particularly the members of the Dublin Section of the Society for Psychical Research.

At the outset let me say that I am a journalist by profession and in pursuit of 'copy' for the paper I represent, *The Enniscorthy Guardian*, I was brought into touch with those concerned in the manifestations, and introduced to the room where these manifestations occurred.

The 'haunted' house was one in which a labouring man named Nicholas Redmond and his wife resided in Court Street, Enniscorthy. Redmond's earnings were supplemented by his wife keeping boarders. On the ground floor of the house are two rooms—a shop and a kitchen. Both are lofty and spacious, and the latter is situated under the room in which the manifestations occurred. The upstairs portion of the premises consists of three bedrooms. The floors of these bedrooms are of wood, and are all intact, the house being a comparatively new one.

THE ENNISCORTHY CASE

Two of the bedrooms look out on the street, and the third, in which the occurrences took place, is situate at the back of these. All three are entered from the same landing and are on the same level. Redmond and his wife slept in the front room immediately adjoining the room in which the occurrences described below took place. The rear bedroom was occupied by two young men who were boarders. They had separate beds. Their names are John Randall, a native of Killurin, in this county, and George Sinnott, of Ballyhogue, in this county. Both these men are carpenters by trade. I can bear personal testimony to the occurrences which I am about to describe. I accepted nothing on hearsay evidence, and I place my experiences before your Society exactly as the circumstances occurred to me. Many of the details have already been published in the daily papers, and are quite true, much of what appeared having been written by myself.

Hearing strange rumours about the house, I proceeded to make enquiries. The owner of the house replied to my questions that the rumours I had heard of the house were quite true, and in response to my application for permission to remain all night in the 'haunted' room, he replied: 'I will make you as comfortable as I can, and you can remain as long as you want to, and bring a friend with you, too, because you will feel more comfortable.' My next move was to procure a volunteer to accompany me, who was found in the person of Mr. Owen Devereux, of the 'Devereux' Cycle Works, Enniscorthy. Together we went to the house on the night of the 29th July, 1910, and immediately proceeded to make a tour of inspection. Sinnott, Randall and the owner of the house having gone out of the room for a few moments, we made a close inspection of the apartment. The beds were pulled out from the walls and examined, the clothing being searched; the flooring was minutely inspected, and the walls and fireplace examined. Everything was found quite normal. Sinnott's bed was placed with the head at the window. The window faced the door as one entered the room. Randall's bed was placed at the opposite end of the room at right angles to Sinnott's, and with the foot to the door. The two boys prepared to retire, Mrs. Redmond having placed two chairs in their bedroom for the use of the narrator and his companion. The occupants of the room having been comfortably disposed of—each in his own bed and chair respectively—the light was extinguished. This was about 11.20 p.m.

The night was a clear, starlight night. No blind obstructed the view from outside, and one could see the outlines of the beds and their occupants clearly. At about 11.30 a tapping was heard close at the foot of Randall's bed. My companion remarked that it appeared to be like the noise of a rat eating at timber. Sinnott replied, 'You'll soon see the rat it is.' The tapping went on slowly at first, say at about the rate of fifty taps to the minute. Then the speed gradually increased to about 100 or 120 per minute, the noise growing louder. This continued for about five minutes, when it stopped suddenly. Randall then spoke. He said: 'The clothes are slipping off my bed: look at them sliding off. Good God! they are going off me.' Mr. Devereux immediately struck a match which he had ready in his hand. The bedclothes had partly left the boy's bed, having gone diagonally towards the foot, going out at the left corner, and not alone did they seem to be drawn off the bed, but they appeared to be actually going back under the bed much in the same position one would expect bedclothes to be if a strong breeze were blowing through the room at the time. But then everything was perfectly calm.

Mr. Devereux lighted the candle and a thorough search was made under the bed for strings or wires, but nothing could be found. Randall, who stated that this sort of thing had occurred to him on previous nights, appeared very much frightened. I adjusted the clothing again properly on the bed and Randall lay down. The candle was again extinguished. After about ten minutes the rapping recommenced. First slowly, as before. It again increased in speed and volume, and after about the same interval of time it again stopped. When the clothes were going in under the bed on the first occasion, Sinnott sat up in bed and said: 'Oh God! look at the clothes going in under the bed.' He also appeared very nervous. The rapping having stopped on the second occasion, Randall's voice again broke the silence. 'They are going again,' he cried; 'the clothes are leaving me again.' I said, 'Hold them and do not let them go:

you only imagine they are going.' He said: 'I cannot hold them; they are going, and I am going with them; there is something pushing me from inside: I am going, I am going, I'm gone.' My companion struck a light just in time to see Randall slide from the bed, the sheet under him, and the sheets, blankets and coverlet over him. He lay on his back on the floor. The movement of his coming out of bed was gentle and regular. There did not appear to be any jerking motion. Whilst he lay on the floor, Randall's face was bathed in perspiration, which rolled off him in great drops. He was much agitated and trembled in every limb. His terribly frightened condition, especially the beads of perspiration on his face, precludes any supposition that he was privy to any human agency being employed to effect the manifestations. Sinnott again sat up in bed, and appeared terrified also. Mr. Redmond, hearing the commotion, came into the room at this time. Randall said: 'Oh, isn't this dreadful? I can't stand it; I can't stay any longer here.' We took him from the floor and persuaded him to re-enter the bed again. He did so, and we adjusted the bedclothes.

It was now about midnight. The owner of the house returned to his own room, and we remained watching until about 1.45, and during that time nothing further occurred. Redmond returned then to see how we were getting on, and took a seat by my side in Randall's bedroom. The three of us having sat there for about five minutes, the rapping again commenced, this time in a different part of the room. Instead of being near the foot of Randall's bed as heretofore, I located it about the middle of the room at a place about equally distant from each bed. It went on for about fifteen minutes, and then ceased. It was at this time fairly bright, the dawn having appeared in the eastern sky. Randall was not interfered with any further that night, and we remained watching till close on three o'clock, and nothing further having occurred we left the house.

On the following night I remained in that room from eleven o'clock till long past midnight. Neither Randall nor Sinnott were there, having gone home to the country for the usual week-end. I heard or saw nothing unusual.

Randall could not reach that part of the floor from which the rapping came on any occasion without attracting my attention

THE ENNISCORTHY CASE

and that of my comrade. I give up the attempt to explain away the strange manifestations. I hope some member of the Society may be able to do so.

NICHOLAS J. MURPHY

1 George Street, Enniscorthy,
August 4th, 1910

I have read the foregoing, and I corroborate the statements therein.

OWEN DEVEREUX

August 4th, 1910

In reply to my enquiry whether any further disturbances had since occurred, and that in any case I should wish to make a personal investigation of the matter, I received the following letter from Mr. Murphy:

Enniscorthy, November 11, 1910

DEAR SIR,

In reply to yours, I beg to say that the house in which the phenomena occurred is now vacant. The tenant, Mr. Redmond, and his wife, left Enniscorthy about the middle of August. Randall left the house on the Monday evening after the occurrence described took place. Nothing unusual was ever seen or heard in the house until Randall went to lodge there. However, I should be very glad to see you in Enniscorthy. Randall and Sinnott are in the town, and you can question them. Mr. Devereux and myself are always at your service, and we have no objection to our names and addresses being published.

Yours faithfully,

N. J. MURPHY

I was not able to visit Enniscorthy until a few weeks later, when I spent a day examining the witnesses and the house where the disturbances occurred. The following notes written at the time give the result of my enquiry:

On Tuesday, December 6th, 1910, I visited Enniscorthy, and saw and closely questioned the eye-witnesses mentioned in Mr. Murphy's paper, with the exception of Sinnott and Redmond, who were away. I also saw the servant who slept in a small room adjoining the one in which the disturbances

THE ENNISCORTHY CASE

occurred. She scouted the idea of the boys playing tricks, and added an important fact, viz. that the large iron bed in which Sinnott slept along with another lodger had lost one of its castors; nevertheless, it was dragged across the room with the two young men in it, leaving a mark along the floor where the iron leg had scraped along. The bed, she told me, was so heavy that, even with no one in it, she had to get assistance when moving it. She was terribly scared by the disturbances, and left the place as soon as she could. I begged her to write down what she had observed, and Mr. Murphy sent me her statement, which follows.

I then visited the house where the disturbances took place. It was empty and unfurnished, and in the hands of the painters. The descriptions given by Mr. Murphy and by Randall are quite correct.

I had a long interview with Randall and he impressed me very favourably; an intelligent, straightforward youth about eighteen years old. He undertook to write down a detailed account of what had occurred during the time he lodged with Redmond. This he did, and his statement is annexed. Randall is a Protestant, and I saw the rector of his parish, who knew the young man well and testified to his good character and trustworthiness. His letter to me is given later on.

I saw Mr. Devereux, the companion whom Mr. Murphy took with him. He owns a cycle shop in Enniscorthy, and is a skilled mechanic, an excellent witness. He corroborated Mr. Murphy's statement, and said he went to the house feeling sure he would be able to discover that one or other of the lads was playing a practical joke. But he was unable to unravel the mystery. He said that what occurred in his presence could not possibly have been done by Randall or his companion. I also had an interview with the previous occupant of the house. Nothing had occurred in his time.

STATEMENT OF BRIDGET THORPE

I was a servant in the house of Mr. Nicholas Redmond, 8 Court Street, Enniscorthy. I remember John Randall coming to lodge there. It was on a Monday night he first came. On the following Friday morning I heard John Randall and George Sinnott, another lodger, talking about the clothes being pulled off the bed. On Friday night I heard the bed running about the floor in Randall's room. I was then in my own room. On the next morning I heard John Randall say that he would not sleep in the house any more. I remember going into Randall's room one night with Mr. Redmond as we heard noises; and when we went in Richard Roche, another lodger, who was there that night, was in one bed and John Randall in another. The bedclothes were all pulled through the bars at the foot of Roche's bed. Roche was very much frightened. I frequently heard rapping in Randall's room. I always thought it came from the corner of Randall's room nearest to Mr. Redmond's room. On the night that Mr. Murphy and Mr. Devereux were there I heard footsteps walking about the lobby outside the door where they were. I often heard these footsteps. The night I heard the bed running about the floor, the floor shook as if a very strong man was pulling the bed around.

(Signed) B. THORPE
Witnessed by N. J. MURPHY

It will be noticed that Randall mentions two companions in the bedroom with him. This was for a short time the case, but one of them had left when Mr. Murphy visited the house.

STATEMENT WRITTEN BY J. W. RANDALL

On Saturday, the 2nd of July, 1910, I came to work in Enniscorthy as an improver in the carpentry trade. Monday, I went to lodge in a house in Court Street. There were two other men stopping in the same house as lodgers. They slept in the same room also, but shared a different bed at the other side of the room. My bed was in a recess in the wall at the opposite side. There was one large window in the room, which opened both top and bottom. The room was about 14 feet square and 10 feet high. There was one door opening into it. The window already described was in the back wall of the house nearly opposite the door opening into the room from the top landing. There were two other doors on the same landing opening into different rooms. There was also a fireplace in the room.

THE ENNISCORTHY CASE

On Monday night, July 4th, we went to bed, and my first night in the strange house I think I slept pretty soundly. We got up at six o'clock the next morning and went to work. We left off work at six in the evening, and went to bed the same time as the night before, between 10 and 10.30 o'clock, slept soundly, and all went well, also on Wednesday.

Went to bed on Thursday night at 10.45, the three of us going as before. We blew out the light, but the room was then fairly lightsome. We had been only about ten minutes in bed when I felt the clothes being gently drawn from my bed. I first thought it was the others that were playing a joke, so I called out, 'Stop, George, it's too cold.' (George being one of their names and the other Richard.) Then I heard them say, 'It's Nick' (that is the name of the man of the house). It wasn't any of them that had pulled the clothes off me, so they thought it was Nick that was in the room, and did not mind. At this time the clothes had gone off my bed completely, and I shouted to them to strike a match. When they struck a match I found my bedclothes were at the window. The most curious part was that the same time when the clothes were leaving my bed, their bed was moving. I brought back the clothes and got into bed again. The light was then put out, and it wasn't long until we heard some hammering in the room—tap-tap-tap-like. This lasted for a few minutes, getting quicker and quicker. When it got very quick their bed started to move out across the floor, and that made us very frightened, and what made us more frightened was the door being shut, and nobody could open it without making a great noise. They then struck a match and got the lamp. We searched the room thoroughly, and could find nobody. Nobody had come in the door. We called the man of the house (Redmond); he came into the room, saw the bed, and told us to push it back and get into bed (he thought all the time one of us was playing the trick on the other). I said I wouldn't stay in the other bed by myself, so I got in with the others; we put out the light again, and it had been only a couple of minutes out when the bed ran out on the floor with the three of us. Richard struck a match again, and this time we all got up and put on our clothes; we had got a terrible fright and couldn't stick it any longer. We told the man of the house we would sit up in the room until daylight. During the time we were sitting in the room we could hear footsteps leaving the kitchen and coming up the stairs; it would stop on the landing outside the door and wouldn't come into the room. The footsteps and noises continued through the house until daybreak. We got up at nine o'clock and went to work for a three-quarter day.

That night (Friday) when we went to bed about eleven o'clock we felt a bit nervous in going. We put out the light, and in a few minutes the footsteps started again, and noises. There were also noises like chips getting chopped in the kitchen. This night passed over not near so bad as the night before, but yet we were afraid to go to sleep.

Saturday we all went home for the Sunday, but returned Sunday evening. We went to bed Sunday night, as before, and it passed over with very slight noises. On Monday night the noises started again after going to bed, and about a quarter of an hour their bed ran again. They then struck a light and I got into the bed with them. There were terrible noises everywhere; on the walls, out on the landing, and downstairs. We left the light lighted for some time, and whilst it was lighted, what added more to our fright was a chair dancing out to the middle of the floor without a thing near it. We put out the light again after moving back the bed. Immediately the light was put out the bed ran again out on the floor. Richard had the matches always ready to strike. Every time we would hear the noise and feel the bed moving, we would shout: 'Strike, Richard, strike; we're going again!' We were trembling from head to feet with fear. We left the light lighted till morning after that.

Tuesday night passed over about the same, and on Wednesday night there wasn't a stir. After hearing nothing on Wednesday night we thought it had stopped, but still we felt nervous. On Thursday night it started as bad as the first night, and several people remarked it being so bad on the night exactly a week after it had started. The bed ran out several times, and what never happened to any one of us before, George was lifted out of bed without a hand near him. He went home next day, and stopped at home for two days. So while he was away, Richard and I stopped in the room. The same noise still continued, and the bed ran also. We went home on Saturday as on the week before.

George came back again on Sunday night, and slept in the same bed with us again, and it wasn't extra bad that night. It went on about the same way every night until the following Friday night, when it was very bad. The bed turned up on one side, and threw us out on the floor, and before we were thrown out, the pillow was taken from under my head three times. When the bed rose up, it fell back without making any noise. This bed was so heavy, it took both the woman and girl to pull it out from the wall without anybody in it, and there was only three castors on it. After being thrown out of the big bed, the three of us got into my bed. We were not long in it when it started to rise, but could not get out of the recess it was in unless it was taken to pieces. It ceased about daybreak, and that finished that night's performance.

It kept very bad then for a few nights. So Mr. Murphy, from the *Guardian* office, and another man named Devereux, came and stopped in the room one night. They sat on two chairs in the room, while we lay each in our own beds. We were not long in bed when I felt a terrible feeling over me like a big weight. I then felt myself being taken from the bed, but could feel no hands, nor could I resist going. All I could say was: 'I'm going, I'm going; they're at me.' I lay on the floor in a terrible state, and hardly able to speak. The perspiration was pouring through me. They put me back in bed again, and nothing more than strange knockings and noises happened between that and morning. We slept again in the room the next night, but nothing serious happened. We then got another lodging, and the people left it also. For the three weeks I was in the house I lost nearly three-quarters of a stone weight. I never believed in ghosts until that, and I think it would convince the bravest man in Ireland.

JOHN WILLIAM RANDALL

18 Main St., Enniscorthy

I heard from Randall a few days ago (January 25th). Nothing has occurred in his new lodgings. The curious association of a particular person in a particular place at a particular time is very characteristic of all Poltergeist phenomena.

THE ENNISCORTHY CASE

FROM THE REV. CANON RENNISON

Kilpatrick Rectory, Wexford,
Jan. 27, 1911

DEAR SIR,

I have known John Randall for the past five years, and I believe him to be a thoroughly truthful and trustworthy boy. I think you may rely on any particulars he has given you about the 'haunted house' at Enniscorthy. He has always been a steady, well-conducted boy so far as I know. I am very glad to hear you are reading a paper on the whole affair.

Yours very truly,

JOHN RENNISON

My best thanks are due to Mr. N. J. Murphy, who kindly spared neither time nor trouble in assisting me in these enquiries.

THE DERRYGONNELLY CASE

I now pass on to another Irish case of which I heard soon after the disturbances broke out, and was able to visit the spot while the Poltergeist was still active, so that I was an eye-witness of many of the occurrences. I wrote a detailed account of what took place at the time, and it was published in the *Dublin University Magazine* for December 1877, under the title of 'The Demons of Derrygonnelly'. No report of this case has yet appeared in our *Proceedings*, and I can only briefly summarize it here.

In 1877 Mr. Thomas Plunkett of Enniskillen, a gentleman who has devoted much time to the geological and archaeological investigation of the County Fermanagh, wrote to tell me of some mysterious disturbances occurring in a farmer's cottage near some prehistoric limestone caves he was exploring, and asking me to visit the place, which I did.

The place was a hamlet called Derrygonnelly, about nine miles from Enniskillen, and the cottage was some two miles further on. A more lonely spot could hardly be found in this country. Across the bog that lay before us rose the huge lime-

THE DERRYGONNELLY CASE

stone cliffs of Knockmore, crowned by an escarpment of overhanging rock. The cottage itself was hidden in the hollow of a field, and no other house could be seen anywhere.

The household consisted of a grey-headed farmer who had recently lost his wife, and a family of four girls and one boy, the youngest about ten years of age, and the eldest, Maggie, round whom the disturbances arose, about twenty years old. The cottage had the usual large kitchen and dwelling-room, with earthen floors in the centre, and a smaller room opening from each side. In one of them Maggie and the girls slept on a large, old-fashioned four-post bed. The noises, rappings and scratches generally began after they had retired, and often continued the whole night through. Rats, of course, were first suspected; but when objects began to move without any visible cause, stones to fall, candles and boots repeatedly thrown out of the house, the rat theory was abandoned and a general terror took possession of the family. Several neighbours urged them to send for the priest, but they were Methodists, and their class leader advised them to lay an open Bible on the bed. This they did in the name of God, putting a big stone on the top of the volume; but the stone was lifted off by an unseen hand, and the Bible placed on top of it. After that 'it', as the farmer called the unseen cause, moved the Bible out of the room and tore seventeen pages right across. Then they could not keep a light in the house, candles and lamps were mysteriously stolen, or thrown out. They asked their neighbours' help, and here I quote the old farmer's words: 'Jack Flanigan came and lent us his lamp saying he would engage the devil himself could not steal it, as he had got the priest to sprinkle it with holy water.' 'But that', the old man said, 'did us no good either, for the next day it took away that lamp also.' They were forced to keep their candles in a neighbour's house some way off, and fetch them at night, and keep them lighted.

During the evenings I spent in the cottage, the farmer and each of his children were independently examined. He gave me a concordant account of the singular freaks of this poltergeist, and their vain efforts to put a stop to it. Those who are interested can read the story, told by the old man, which I took

THE DERRYGONNELLY CASE

down in writing, as it is published in full in my article already referred to.

My own observations were as follows: after the children, except the boy, had gone to bed, Maggie lay down on the bed without undressing, so that her hands and feet could be observed. The rest of us sat round the kitchen fire, when faint raps, rapidly increasing in loudness, were heard, coming apparently from the walls, the ceiling and various parts of the inner room, the door of which was open. On entering the bedroom with a light the noises at first ceased, but recommenced when I put the light on the window-sill in the kitchen. I had the boy and his father by my side, and asked Mr. Plunkett to look round the house outside. Standing in the doorway leading to the bedroom the noises recommenced, the light was gradually brought nearer, and after much patience I was able to bring the light into the bedroom whilst the disturbances were still loudly going on. At last I was able to go up to the side of the bed, with the lighted candle in my hand, and closely observed each of the occupants lying on the bed. The younger children were apparently asleep, and Maggie was motionless; nevertheless, knocks were going on everywhere around; on the chairs, the bedstead, the walls and ceiling. The closest scrutiny failed to detect any movement on the part of those present that could account for the noises, which were accompanied by a scratching or tearing sound. Suddenly a large pebble fell in my presence on to the bed; no one had moved to dislodge it even if it had been placed for the purpose. When I replaced the candle on the window-sill in the kitchen, the knocks became still louder, like those made by a heavy carpenter's hammer driving nails into flooring.

At midnight we drove back to Enniskillen, and next day I telegraphed to Dublin to an acute and careful observer, president of one of our learned societies, to come down to help me in the investigation. He kindly did so. It was the Rev. Maxwell Close, M.A., a man honoured in Dublin for his great learning, remarkable critical insight and singular sobriety of judgment.[1]

[1] The Rev. Maxwell Close died a few years ago; he was one of the earliest members of the S.P.R.; an obituary notice of him by the present writer appeared in the *Journal S.P.R.* for November 1903.

THE DERRYGONNELLY CASE

With him, a day or two later, we again drove over in the evening the eleven lonely miles to the farmer's cottage. In spite of the vigilance of my friends, Mr. Close, Mr. Plunkett and myself, we failed to detect the slightest attempt at imposture by any of the family, and we were each equally certain that we were not the victims of hallucination. The noises were heard as before; we searched within and without the cottage, but no cause could be found.

The following night we made another visit with the same result. When we were about to leave some two hours later, the farmer was distressed that we had not 'laid the ghost', and I asked him what he thought it was. He replied:

'I would have thought, sir, it do be fairies, but them late readers and knowledgeable men will not allow such a thing, so I cannot tell what it is. I only wish, sir, you would take it away.'

'Have you asked it to answer a question by raps?' I asked.

'I have, sir,' he said, 'as some one told us to do, but it tells lies as often as truth, and oftener, I think. We tried it, and it only knocked at L M N when we said the alphabet over.' I asked him if it would respond to a given number of raps, and he said it would. This it did in my presence. Then I mentally asked it, no word being spoken, to knock a certain number of times and it did so. To avoid any error or delusion on my part, I put my hands in the side pockets of my overcoat and asked it to knock the number of fingers I had open. It correctly did so. Then, with a different number of fingers open each time, the experiment was repeated four times in succession, and four times I obtained absolutely the correct number of raps. The doctrine of chances shows that casual coincidence is here practically out of the question, and the interesting fact remains that some telepathic rapport between the unseen agent and ourselves appears to exist, on this occasion at any rate.

Before leaving—it was now past midnight—the farmer implored us not to go without ridding him of this pertinacious poltergeist. So I asked my clerical friend to read a few words of scripture and offer up a prayer. He did so, choosing appropriate passages from our Lord's ministry to the possessed, and a suitable prayer. It was a weird scene, the children were

THE DERRYGONNELLY CASE

in bed, but not asleep, in the inner room, the farmer and Mr. Plunkett seated by the kitchen fire, Mr. Close seated on a stool at the open bedroom door, I holding a lighted candle for him, and seated just within the bedroom. The noises were at first so great we could hardly hear what was read, then as the solemn words of prayer were uttered they subsided, and when the Lord's Prayer was joined in by all, a profound stillness fell on the whole cottage. The farmer rose from his knees with tears streaming from his eyes, gratefully grasped our hands, and we left for our long midnight drive back to Enniskillen.

I am afraid this does not sound a very scientific account, but it is a veracious one.

Subsequent correspondence, and reports from Mr. Plunkett, showed that the poltergeist had fled from that night onwards, until some curious visitors, after reading my published description, had gone to the farmer's cottage, and tried to bring it back again. It came, they said, feebly and furtively, but whether genuine or Maggie's Irish desire to please the visitors, I have no means of knowing. The farmer is now dead, and Maggie, I believe, in service, but I have lost sight of them all.

In both the preceding cases the disturbances took place at night, in the next two cases they occurred in the day chiefly. The reason appears to be that only when the living radiant point, or psychic, is in a particular place, and more or less *at rest*, do the disturbances break out. The boy Randall was away from his lodgings all day at work; the girl, Maggie, was largely engaged in farm work outside, as well as housework within, and some phenomena took place in the day time when she was in the house, but were less marked until she went to bed. In the next case the psychic was evidently more powerful, a somnambulist and clairvoyant, and the disturbances arose when she was in the house, both in the daytime and at night. As in the case of dowsing, hypnosis, clairvoyance, telepathy and probably all psychical phenomena, the effect of education, the cultivation of the reasoning powers, alert consciousness, in fine, cerebral activity generally, usually diminish and ultimately inhibit the production of supernormal phenomena.

THE *ATLANTIC MONTHLY* CASE

One of the most remarkable and carefully investigated cases of Poltergeists is recorded in the *Atlantic Monthly*,[1] a leading American review, for August 1868. This case is so little known and so admirable that I will briefly summarize it.

An Irish girl, 18 years old, named Mary Carrick, went to live as servant with a family in Massachusetts soon after her arrival in America. Six weeks after she came to the family, the house bells began violently ringing without any assignable cause. This would occur at intervals of half an hour throughout the day and evening. The wires were detached from all the bells, but the ringing still continued. The bells were hung near the ceiling of the room, 11 feet high. They only rang when the girl was in the room or in the adjoining one, and were seen to ring by the family without any visible cause. The ringing was not a mere stroke of one bell, but a violent agitation of *all the bells*. A careful examination made by the writer of the article, Mr. Willis, showed that no mechanism of any kind was attached to the bells. So far the case is like the well-known 'Bealings Bells' in Suffolk, described with great care by Major Moor, F.R.S., in 1834, a full account of which will be found in Dale Owen's *Debatable Land*, p. 239 *et seq.*

But more remarkable phenomena followed in the American case. Loud and startling raps occurred on the walls, door and windows of any room where the girl was at work, and followed the girl from room to room, and could be heard in her bedroom at night when she was apparently fast asleep. A little later, chairs were upset, crockery thrown down, tables lifted and moved, and various kitchen utensils hurled about the room. This was during July. In August a careful daily record was kept. The writer of the article states that he saw the table at which the girl had been ironing suddenly lifted when no

[1] Like other articles in the *Atlantic Monthly*, the name of the author, Mr. H. A. Willis, is not given in the text, but only in the Table of Contents. As the article was published 43 years ago, it is, I fear, hopeless to obtain any confirmatory evidence at the present day; but I have written to the Editor of the *Atlantic Monthly* with this object in view. As yet no further information has been obtained.

one was near enough to touch it. This also happened when a child was sitting on the table, and when the writer and other persons tried to hold the table down.

On the 6th of August, as Mary was placing the tea tray on a heavy stone slab, $1\frac{1}{2}$ inches thick, and weighing 48 lbs., the stone slab suddenly flew up, struck the tray and upset the dishes upon it. The writer states that this happened again in his own presence when we was carefully watching the girl, who was at the moment in the act of wringing out some clothes. The slab rose and fell back with such force that it broke in two, no one touching it. Soon after one-half of the slab was pitched on the ground and the fragments thrown about. Another day a large basket filled with clothes was thrown to the floor, a stool having on it a pail filled with water ran along the floor; a washtub filled with clothes was taken off its stand and flung to the ground, and the contents thrown about.

The girl would often start in her sleep and scream in terror, the family watching the girl and hearing the violent noises.

The result of all this disturbance greatly alarmed and excited the girl, who was ignorant and superstitious; it brought on a serious attack of hysteria, and she had to be taken to an asylum. All the noises ceased in her absence. At the end of three weeks she was sufficiently recovered to return to her work. None of the movements subsequently took place, but a month later she suffered from somnambulism. Many times when fast asleep she rose in the middle of the night, dressed herself, and went about her work downstairs in the pitch darkness, even studying some lessons she was doing, and returned to bed in an hour or two.

She was also clairvoyant, and one remarkable instance of this is given by the writer of the article.

The report concludes by saying it may be justly asked why no scientific men were asked to investigate the phenomena during the ten weeks they lasted. To this the writer replies that whilst the phenomena were in full force, a statement of the facts was sent to a leading scientific man in America, with an earnest request that he would investigate and report. The request was treated with absolute contempt; they were told that such things could not happen, and that it was all trickery.

THE PORTLAND, OREGON, CASE

The writer of the article then tried some experiments himself. He conceived that the sounds might possibly be electrically produced, and made some experiments to test this idea. When the bedstead on which the girl slept was insulated on glass nothing occurred, but when the insulators were removed the noises returned as violently as ever. A daily journal of the weather and of the disturbances was kept, expecting that the phenomena would be more frequent on dry clear days, but some of the most remarkable disturbances occurred on very rainy ones. With candour the writer therefore concludes that there is some difficulty in applying the electrical hypothesis.

Electricity has to bear a good many sins on its head, but we may safely exonerate it from creating the Poltergeist phenomena. The insulation experiments, tried not only on the bed, but also on tables and chairs, certainly inhibited the disturbances, but this inhibition was more probably due to the effect of suggestion either on the girl or on her unseen tormentors. Psychic subjects are exceedingly suggestible, and this often lays them open to perpetrate fraudulent imitations, especially when the enquirer feels confident trickery is an adequate explanation of everything.

THE PORTLAND, OREGON, CASE

In the autumn of 1909 one of the leading newspapers on the Pacific coast published details of extraordinary disturbances and movement of objects which occurred in a house in Portland, Oregon. Subsequently an article on the subject appeared in the *Pacific Monthly*, and the publicity thus given to the case led to its careful investigation by Dr. Gilbert and Mr. Thacher, two most competent investigators, who were requested by the American Society for Psychical Research to make a critical and full enquiry. The results of this enquiry are given in detail in the *Journal of the American S.P.R.* for September and November, 1910.

The phenomena were associated with the presence of a boy named Elwin March, who, at the time of these occurrences, was eleven years old, and lived with his grandparents, Mr. and

THE PORTLAND, OREGON, CASE

Mrs. Sawyer, at 546 Marshall Street, Portland, Oregon. The first disturbance took place on Oct. 28th, 1909. A reporter at once got hold of the story, witnessed some of the phenomena, and next day published a full report in the principal local newspaper. The consequent notoriety was so annoying to the Sawyers that they were glad to hand the boy, Elwin, over to Dr. Gilbert, who took him into his own house in Portland, and kept his whereabouts secret for a week until the reporters again ferreted him out. Meanwhile Dr. Gilbert had obtained a detailed statement of the first disturbances from eye-witnesses, but Dr. and Mrs. Gilbert failed to obtain any satisfactory evidence of supernormal phenomena, and, in fact, were convinced that the boy Elwin was the author of the later, if not of the whole of the occurrences. I will return to this presently.

On the other hand the other investigator, Mr. Thacher, whose report, published in the *Journal of the American S.P.R.* for November 1910, is one of painstaking care, after a most searching investigation, says: practically all the eye-witnesses were convinced that the movements *were* produced by supernormal agencies, and the witnesses were numerous enough and intelligent enough to create a presumption in favour of genuine Poltergeist phenomena. Mr. Thacher remarks: 'I began to collect testimony on Oct. 29 (the day after the first outbreak) and have watched closely all developments for a period of several months. I wrote out the story immediately after the events narrated, it is in substance a diary, and reflects the mental attitude of the witnesses at the time, which gives it a certain value in the final analysis and conclusion.'

Let us now look at the evidence. A medical man, Dr. Ainley, testified on Oct. 29th, and made a signed statement next day, that he was in Mr. Sawyer's house on Oct. 28th, and standing near the door, saw the telephone fall from its stand, no one being near it but the boy, Elwin, who had come past it and was then standing near him. Shortly afterwards a chair near the telephone rose up and then fell on the floor. It was picked up, and again it was raised and fell on the floor. No one was touching it, and no one was nearer than four feet (subsequently corrected to six feet) from the chair, and the movements occurred plainly in his, Dr. Ainley's, sight. Another medical man, J. C. Ross, M.D., of Portland, also signed a declaration that he went to the house immediately after the disturbances, found the occupants frightened and bewildered, chairs, tables and pictures overturned; dishes lying broken on the floor, having by some unseen force been pulled off a sideboard. He, however, did not see any movements after he arrived.

Another witness who had been in the U.S. artillery deposed that he saw two chairs rise up and tip over in the dining-room, whilst the boy, Elwin, was in the kitchen and no one within ten or twelve feet of the chairs when they rose and fell over. Mr. and Mrs. Sawyer made very detailed depositions of the movement of various articles of furniture when no one was near them. A large glazed picture which hung on the wall, slid slowly down the wall to the floor and rested there without breaking the glass or doing any damage. Mr. and Mrs. Sawyer both saw this, and Mr. Sawyer added that the picture was lifted off the suspending hook, came slowly down, struck the ground at one corner, and then righted itself and stood leaning against the wall.

Another witness, Mr. Casson, said that, hearing of these disturbances, he went to the house and saw several knives and forks rise up an inch or two from the drain-board of the sink and fall over on to the floor. A small basket on the sink also rose up and fell over on the floor. He and Mrs. Sawyer, the only persons present in the room, were six or seven feet away from the sink, and the boy, Elwin, was in an adjoining room. Mr. Sawyer deposed to the plaster coming off the wall and pieces thrown into the room. One piece of plaster flew from the kitchen wall, hit a tailor's goose-iron which was on the table, which in its turn, though weighing over a stone, flew off the table on to the floor. Another day he saw a basket with some onions in it come off the table, and two cans of condensed milk followed it, and all fell on the floor. Then the bread can, with a pail containing some meat which stood in the pantry, fell on the floor, and a number of plates came off the shelf, and fell on the floor. Elwin, though in the room, was not near the things at the time this occurred. The basket that fell was replaced, and again thrown down; this was done several times

THE PORTLAND, OREGON, CASE

running. Many other disturbances are reported, and numerous witnesses affirmed no visible agency could have caused them.

Now let us hear the other side. Dr. Gilbert, who had taken the boy to his house, found him cheating at a game, and also saw him deliberately move some objects, when he thought he was not observed. This was some time after the original disturbances, and when nothing had lately occurred. There can be no doubt the boy did practise several tricks in December, when removed from the Sawyer's house where the disturbances broke out, and Dr. Gilbert obtained a confession from him that he did so. Moreover, though at first he denied having had anything to do with the manifestations, when they first broke out at the Sawyer's house, yet Dr. Gilbert says he was so convinced of the boy's having tricked them all along that after severe cross-examination he obtained a qualified admission from the boy that he did do some of the earlier things. Hence the conclusion arrived at by Dr. Gilbert was that the whole phenomena were fraudulent, and no supernormal agency need be assumed. On the other hand, Mr. Thacher, who made a more prolonged and searching investigation, says with considerable justice: 'Could the fact that the boy had been the centre of attention for several weeks, and that the interest was waning, together with the strong and constantly repeated wishes of the small group of persons about him that the movements without contact should be repeated, be sufficient to induce him to "fake" the phenomena, and then lie about it [the earlier ones]? Or were all the witnesses utterly unreliable, and was the immediate family all bound together in the deception?'

Now it turns out that there were two persons who influenced Dr. Gilbert's opinion, by attributing fraud to the boy at the outset; one stated that he found 38 threads fastened outside the window of the dining-room, by which the lad probably moved the objects. This evidence also led Dr. Hyslop of the American S.P.R. at first to conclude that the whole thing was fraud. However, Mr. Thacher discovered that these adverse witnesses were absolutely untrustworthy. No one saw the witness find the threads, and none were to be found; even if the threads had been there, the witness could not explain how they could move various objects within the room. Finally, this witness was found to be a rogue, so that Dr. Hyslop eventually stated his evidence was valueless. The other witness who had stated that the boy himself pulled the plaster off and threw it, turns out to be the owner of the house and anxious to discredit the whole story, as it was likely to depreciate his property; his statements were merely inferences of his own, he had seen nothing to support them, and Mr. Thacher shows they are entirely disproved, inasmuch as the plaster came from parts of the wall and ceiling which the boy, even if present, could not possibly reach.

On the one side we have two discredited witnesses, and on the other over twenty credible and disinterested witnesses who testify to these occurrences as being due to some unseen inexplicable agency. Take, for instance, Mr. Jerome Holmes's statement; he affirms in writing that when in the dining-room on October 28th in the afternoon he saw a chair, which was standing near the door, go right up in the air as much as three feet, and then, whilst it was poised in the air, it turned half over to a horizontal position, and then fell on the floor. No one was near the chair when it went up in the air. Elwin March had just gone out of the room and was outside the door when the chair rose up and fell. 'The chair was plainly in my sight, and I am sure that no person in the room touched it during its movements,' Mr. Holmes remarks, adding that when he stated what he himself clearly saw in broad daylight, people said to him, 'Well, you must be crazy.' Here as elsewhere, as regards the witnesses, it was *against* their interest to make up these stories.

That the disturbances, like other Poltergeist phenomena, are more or less attached to a place, is seen from the fact that after Elwin and his grandparents had left Marshall Street, the phenomena did not follow them; but it is asserted movements of objects without contact occurred for a short time in the neighbouring house. Two witnesses told Mr. Thacher the facts, but declined to let their names be published, as they did not wish 'to be mixed up in any spooky business'. This evidence is, therefore, of little value.

There can be no doubt that this is an important case, not only, nor perhaps chiefly, from a psychical point of view, but from a psychological standpoint.

THE PORTLAND, OREGON, CASE

We find what appear to be undoubtedly genuine phenomena passing into fraudulent imitations by the lad around whom interest chiefly centred. As a recent American writer on the 'Psychology of Child Development' says: 'A child sees an elder writing with a pencil. When he has a chance he tries it. To an observer it is a case of imitation, but to the child it is an attempt to get a new experience with a pencil through the image furnished by the adult.'

Other cases of trickery, and even confession to a part of the phenomena observed, are recorded in our *Proceedings*. In a Poltergeist case occurring in 1895 at Ham, near Hungerford, Berks., Mr. Westlake saw the twelve-year-old child, who was the centre of the disturbances, deliberately move objects. In the case of Emma Davies at Wem, in Shropshire, Mr. Hughes, who investigated the case on behalf of our Society, obtained a partial confession from Emma Davies. This led to a critical review of the case by my friend, Mr. C. C. Massey, who published a pamphlet which showed how inconclusive such subsequent confessions are, for objects jumped off tables and out of cupboards when the girl was outside the room, and under circumstances quite inconsistent with trickery. Mr. Massey remarks that it is probable the vanity of the girl was more gratified by the reputation of having duped the investigators than by that of being the medium of an unknown force.

The question then arises, are we to reject as worthless evidence of what appear to be supernormal phenomena because sometimes there are cases of subsequent imitation and trickery, and even occasionally confession of fraud? In cases of Poltergeists, children are usually the centre of disturbances, and the superficial or prejudiced observer, knowing the love of mischief among children, and that in his and nearly every one's experience objects *don't* jump about without an assignable cause, naturally comes to the conclusion that any supernormal explanation is needless and absurd. But this *a priori* argument, which satisfies the man in the street, completely breaks down when a critical and historical study of the whole subject is made.

In the numerous trials for witchcraft recorded in different countries the so-called witches freely confessed that they did

THE DALE TOWER, GEORGIA, U.S.A., CASE

quite impossible things. One of the most tragic and heart-breaking series of confessions occurred in the village of Mobra, in Sweden, where, in 1670, it is stated in the public register of the Lords Commissioners who tried the case that 71 children freely confessed that they were engaged in witchery, that they were carried away by the devil; and being 'separately and independently examined to see if their confessions did agree', the Commissioners state they 'found that all of them except some very little ones, who could not tell all the circumstances, did practically agree in the confession of particulars'. And the particulars consisted in describing the traditional devil, how they were carried through the air and down chimneys, that burning candles were stuck in their hair, but they were not burnt, that they were beaten with thorns, etc., etc. And all this upon oath, and in peril of their lives. In fact, 15 children, who so confessed, were thereupon burnt; 36 children, between 9 and 16 years old, considered less guilty, were publicly beaten once a week for a year, and forced 'to run the gauntlet'; 20 more, mere babies, were lashed with rods for three Sundays at the Church door. The number of children more or less found guilty, we are told, was 300. In addition, 70 women, all from this same village, were tried; 23 freely confessed their witchcraft and were burnt, the rest were imprisoned and afterwards executed.[1]

Obviously, therefore, we must not place too much reliance upon the confessions of children, nor of uneducated persons, who believe the superstitions of their day to be actual facts, and tacitly accept the opinion of their 'betters', when told that they have taken part in the witchery of which they are accused.

THE DALE TOWER, GEORGIA, U.S.A., CASE

One of the most recent Poltergeists has occurred in Georgia, U.S.A., and is described in the *Occult Review* for May, 1911. The narrator is a medical man, T. Hart Raines, M.D., who as soon as he heard of the occurrences began an investigation, and whilst he did not witness the phenomena himself, he inter-

[1] See Glanvil, *Saducismus Triumphatus*, the last tract.

THE DALE TOWER, GEORGIA, U.S.A., CASE

viewed the three young men who collectively saw what occurred and he personally visited the scene of the disturbance. Dr. Raines states that the young men are intelligent telegraph operators, and their veracity above suspicion: they are positive that they were not deceived or hallucinated, and they have all signed a statement certifying to the truth of the facts.

The disturbances took place in a little railway telegraph tower at Dale, Georgia, on the main line of the Atlantic coast railroad. The tower adjoins the railway track, and is the only house of any description within a quarter of a mile. During nine months in the year the tower is closed, and is opened for the tourist season from January to April. The three young men—Bright, Davies, and Clark—opened the tower on January 4, 1911, and were the sole occupants living in its two rooms, one room above the other, a trap-door closing the stair leading to the upper room. The first thing that occurred was the sudden, inexplicable flinging open of the trap-door, and the difficulty of keeping it closed. In spite of fastening it with stout nails and an iron bar, it would still fly open; mysterious footsteps were also heard on the stair, but a careful search revealed no cause for the disturbances. Then followed the raising and lowering of the window sashes in the upper chamber, in full view of the three occupants, no one being near the window. 'To assure themselves against tricksters, the trap-door leading down to the floor below was closed and securely fastened, and raised only when necessary to descend to the ground. This precaution had no effect whatsoever on the phenomena, and soon various articles began to be levitated about the room in broad open daylight in full view of all three occupants of the tower, when there was no possible chance for trickery or fraud. A can of condensed milk was seen to lift itself into the air and pass from one end of the desk to the other without the contact of a visible hand. A large dish-pan lying near the stove slowly lifted itself and rolled down the stairs and out of the tower and under it, from whence it had to be fished out with the aid of a long pole. A lantern was levitated on to the desk without having been touched, and in full view of all. On another occasion this lantern made a wild rush across the room

THE DALE TOWER, GEORGIA, U.S.A., CASE

and dashed itself into fragments against the wall. An ordinary can-opener flew wildly about the room and fastened itself in the centre of the ceiling. I [Dr. Raines] saw this can-opener, and can assure any one interested that the most expert could not perform a similar feat once in a hundred efforts. Frequently bolts and taps, such as are used in railroad construction work, would be hurled into the room, breaking a hole in the glass of the window scarcely large enough to enter through.

'On one occasion, when objects were being hurled about the room so persistently that the tower was hastily abandoned by all three occupants, a chair was dashed out of the upper window, and fell with such force that one of the rings was broken. This in broad daylight, with no one in the tower, and the only avenue of entrance or of escape guarded by the three occupants of the tower. I [Dr. Raines] saw the chair, and only a terrific blow could have so injured it.'

The young men were now in a state of panic, and one of them walked seven miles to the nearest town, to resign his position, and he assured Dr. Raines nothing would induce him again to go through the eerie experience he had suffered. The last of the strange occurrences took place a few days before Dr. Raines visited the tower and made a searching investigation of the possibility of some outside person tricking the young men. This, he says, was impossible, nor could the vibration of passing trains have caused the phenomena, and any attempt to climb the stair would have been instantly detected by the operators, one of whom was always on duty. Dr. Raines is convinced that there was no chance of deception, that the operators were perfectly truthful and were not the victims of hallucination. In fact, the whole record exactly resembles other Poltergeist phenomena in their sudden development and sudden cessation.

A recent case of Poltergeist in Surrey was reported in the newspapers and on inquiry I learned that the phenomena occurred as narrated; but I have been unable to visit the place and obtain the evidence at first hand.

THE VIENNA POLTERGEIST

In the *Journal* of the Society for May, 1907, there is a report of a typical Poltergeist occurring in a Vienna suburb. The report is sent by an eye-witness of some of the disturbances, Mr. Wärndorfer, a member of the S.P.R., living at Baden, near Vienna. Regarding this case Miss A. Johnson (Research Officer of the S.P.R.) writes to me as follows: 'Mr. Wärndorfer, whom I know personally, is an unusually cool-headed and competent observer, and a very intelligent and open-minded man. He is genuinely interested in psychical research, and would, I feel sure, be prepared to give an impartial account of anything he witnessed.' Miss Johnson adds that she believes Mr. Wärndorfer 'is not convinced of the genuineness of this case, or of any telekinetic phenomena; what it amounts to is that he investigated this case carefully, and did not discover any fraud in it'.

The principal points in the narrative are as follows. A smith named Zimmerl has a shop near Vienna (address given), where he employs two apprentices. The shop is at the end of a long court, in the *souterrain* of a large house inhabited by tradespeople, so that it is entered by going down a short, open stair. Zimmerl had had the shop some four years, but nothing unusual occurred until July, 1906, when a report appeared in a Vienna paper of the mysterious disturbances that had broken out in this smith's shop.

On July 16th, 1906, Mr. Wärndorfer visited the shop and heard from Zimmerl how tools, bits of iron, etc., had been flung about the place, and both the master and one of his apprentices had been hurt by one of these missiles. He had watched the boys, but could not detect any tricks on their part; in fact, when they were outside the shop the missiles still flew about, and from an opposite direction to where they stood, and where a solid wall intervened. The police had investigated the matter and could find nothing to account for the disturbances. The tools, etc., had to be put into boxes and moved outside, as they were afraid to work otherwise. The man was much scared, and lost customers through this mysterious annoyance. Once a pipe flew from one side of the shop to the other, and then came back and settled on the anvil in the middle of the room; another time the pipe was taken from Zimmerl's mouth and fluttered on to the lathe.

Mr. Wärndorfer made several subsequent visits, and heard still more remarkable accounts, and was able to witness many of the occurrences. On one occasion he saw more than a dozen objects thrown about, and was 'perfectly certain none of the persons present could have thrown them'; one was thrown when he happened to be alone in the shop. He never saw the objects actually fly, but heard them fall; some dropped close to him, and three struck him on the head. In reply to enquiries from the S.P.R., Mr. Wärndorfer relates five cases of inexplicable movements of objects, which he witnessed in daylight, and of which he believes 'the chances of mal-observation were very small indeed'. One of these cases was as follows. A small glazed picture which he had seen hanging on the wall a few minutes before came fluttering through the air to the middle of the shop, where it fell on the floor, but did not break; in fact, it moved like a sheet of paper. At the time he was standing about a yard and a half in front of the picture, nobody being near it, nor in that part of the shop through which it moved. He did not see it leave its place, but saw it when it was about a couple of yards from where it alighted. Mr. Wärndorfer adds that he thinks 'it would be very difficult, though not impossible, to throw or drop such a picture without its breaking'. Another incident witnessed by Mr. Wärndorfer occurred when the smith was out of the shop and the two apprentices were drilling a hole in a piece of iron. He was watching their slow work and noticed that their four hands were all engaged at their work; of this he was 'perfectly certain', when suddenly one of the boys screamed with pain; a pair of big iron compasses, which had been lying on the workbench a yard behind the boy, had flown across and hit the boy sharply on the temple, causing a swelling and a little blood. Mr. Wärndorfer saw the iron compasses ricochetting as it were off the boy's head and falling to the ground. He himself was five times hit—three times on the head, as already mentioned, and twice elsewhere, once rather severely, with pieces

THE VIENNA POLTERGEIST

of iron and steel that unaccountably flew across the room and struck him.

The disturbances continued for two months, and then ceased. One of the lads, round whom the disturbances seemed to cluster, was taken to the police court and fined, though he denied all guilt, and there was no direct evidence of his having thrown anything. The boys were, nevertheless, dismissed, and the disturbances ceased. Mr. Wärndorfer, however, does not consider that this proves anything, and he is right, for if his observations were correct the boys could not have been the culprits.

8. THE GREAT AMHERST MYSTERY

By Walter Hubbell (Brentano, New York, 1888)

Breslands, N.Y., 1888

Amherst, Nova Scotia, is a beautiful village, situated on the famous Bay of Fundy, and is reached either from Halifax, Nova Scotia, or St. John, New Brunswick, by the remarkably well managed Inter-Colonial Railway, being about 140 miles from each city. It has a population of about three thousand five hundred souls, and contains four churches, an Academy, a Music Hall, containing scenery, where dramatic and operatic entertainments are frequently given. It also has a large iron foundry, a large shoe factory, and probably more stores of various kinds than any village of its size in the Province. The private residences of the more wealthy inhabitants are picturesque in appearance, being surrounded by beautifully laid-out lawns, studded with ornamental shade trees of various kinds, and in summer with numerous beds of flowers of choice and sometimes very rare varieties. The residences of Parson Townsend, Mr. Robb, Dr. Nathan Tupper, Dr. Carritte, and Mr. G. G. Bird, proprietor of the Amherst book store, also, that of Mr. Amos Purdy, the village postmaster, were sure to attract a visitor's attention, and command his admiration during any residence in the village; and although some time has elapsed since I was last there, I doubt not but that they look just as they did then, for villages like Amherst do not grow very fast in any part of Canada; there is not the energy and push to be met with here that we have in the United States. In this little village there was on Princess Street, near Church, a neat two-storey cottage painted yellow;

it had in front a small yard extending to the stable in the rear. The tidy appearance of the cottage and its pleasant situation were sure to attract a stranger's attention and always excited the admiration of the neighbours. Upon entering the house everything was found to be so tastefully arranged, was so scrupulously clean and comfortable, that a visitor felt at home immediately, being confident that everything was under the personal direction of a thrifty housewife. The first floor of the cottage consisted of four rooms. A parlour, lighted by a large bay window filled with beautiful geraniums of every imaginable colour and variety, was the first room to attract attention, then the dining-room, with its old-fashioned clock, its numerous home-made rugs, easy chairs, and commodious table, made a visitor feel like dining, especially if the hour was near twelve, for, at about that time of day, savoury odours were sure to issue from the adjoining kitchen. The kitchen was all that a room of that kind in a village cottage should be; was not very large, and contained an ordinary wood-stove, a large pine table, and a small washstand; had a door opening into the side yard near the stable, and another into the woodshed, besides the one connecting it with the dining-room, making three doors in all, and one window from which you could look into a narrow side yard. The fourth room on this floor was very small and was used as a sewing-room; it adjoined the dining-room and parlour and had a door opening into each. Besides these four rooms, there was a large pantry having a small window about four feet from the floor, the door of this pantry opening into the dining-room. Such was the arrangement of the rooms of the first floor. The doors of the dining-room and parlour opened into a hallway leading from the front door. Upon entering the front door, at your right, you saw the stairway in the hall leading to the floor above, and upon ascending this stairway and turning to your left you found yourself on the second storey of the cottage, which consisted of an entry running at right angles with the hallway of the floor below. In about the centre of this entry was a trap-door, *without a ladder*, to the loft above, and opening into the entry, where the trap-door was, were four small bedrooms, each one of which had one small window, and one door, there being no doors between the rooms. Two of these bedrooms faced Princess Street, and the other two towards the back of the yard overlooking the stable. Like the rest of the house, all these bedrooms were conspicuous for their neat, cosy appearance, being all papered (except the one at the head of the stairs), and all painted, and furnished with ordinary cottage furniture. Everything about this little house would have impressed the most casual observer with the fact that its inmates were evidently happy and contented, if not rich. Such was the humble home of honest Daniel Teed, a shoemaker whom everybody knew and respected. He never owed a dollar to any one if he could pay it, and never allowed his family to want for any comfort that could be provided with his hard-earned salary as foreman of the Amherst Shoe Factory.

Daniel's family consisted of his wife, Olive, as good a woman as ever lived, Willie, aged five years, and George aged seventeen months. I think little Mrs. Teed worked harder than any woman I ever knew. Willie was a strong, healthy-looking lad, with a ruddy complexion, blue eyes, and curly, brown hair. His principal amusements were throwing stones at the chickens in the yard and street, and playing with his little brother. Little golden-haired George was certainly the finest boy of his age in the village, and his merry laugh, winning ways and smart actions to attact attention, made him a favourite with all who visited the cottage. Besides his wife and two sons, Daniel had, under his roof and protection, his wife's two sisters, Jennie and Esther Cox, who boarded with him. Jane, or Jennie, as she was often called, was a most self-possessed young woman, of about twenty-two and quite a beauty. Her hair was light brown, and reached below her waist when allowed to fall at full length. At other times she wore it in the Grecian style; her eyes were of that rarely seen greyish blue, and her clear complexion and handsome teeth added greatly to her fine personal appearance. To be candid, Jennie Cox was a village belle, and always had a host of admirers, not of the opposite sex alone, but among the ladies. She was a member and regular attendant of Parson Townsend's Episcopal Church, of which the Reverend Townsend had been pastor for about forty-five years. Jennie's sister, Esther, was low in stature, and rather inclined to be short. Her hair was curly, of a dark brown colour, and worn short, reaching only to her shoulders; her eyes were large and grey, with a bluish tinge, and a very earnest expression, which seemed to say: 'Why do you look at me, I cannot help being unlike other people?' Her eyebrows and lashes were dark, the lashes being long and eyebrows very distinct. Her face was what would be called round, with well-shaped features. And her teeth was remarkably handsome. She had a pale complexion, and small hands and feet that were well shaped. Esther was very fond of housework and proved a help to her sister, Mrs. Teed. In other respects, Esther Cox had an indescribable appearance of rugged honesty about her, that certainly made that simple-hearted village maiden very attractive. She had numbers of friends of her own age, which was about nineteen years, and was always in demand among the little children of the neighbourhood, who were always ready to have a romp and a game of tag with their dear friend Esther.

There were two other boarders in the cottage, John Teed, Daniel's brother, and William Cox, the brother of Mrs. Teed and her sisters. William Cox was a shoemaker, and worked in the same factory as his brother-in-law. John Teed, like his brother, was an honest, hard-working man, and had been brought up a farmer, an occupation he followed when not boarding with Daniel in Amherst.

Daniel Teed was, at this time, about thirty-five years of age, five feet eight in his stockings. Had light brown hair, rather thin on top of his well-shaped head, blue eyes, well-defined features, and what is called a Roman nose. His complexion was florid, and he wore a heavy moustache and bushy sidewhiskers. Rheumatism, of several years standing, had given him a slight halt in his left leg. He led an exemplary Christian life, had a pew in the Wesleyan Methodist Church, of which the Rev. R. A. Temple was pastor, and belonged to a temperance society. Mrs. Olive Teed had dark hair, grey eyes, and a pale complexion, and attended church with her husband. Being older than her sisters she was looked up to by them for advice and consolation when they were in trouble. Life in the household of Daniel Teed was the same monotonous existence day after day. They always dined at twelve o'clock. Shortly before that hour, Esther would generally be seen seated on the parlour floor playing with little George. Willie was frequently to be found in the yard, near the stable, in the summer. Once, I remember, he was found there tormenting a poor hen, to whose leg Mrs. Teed had tied a log of wood to prevent her from setting in the cow's stall; he however, seemed to think she had been purposely tied so that he might have the pleasure of banging her over the head with a small club, which he was doing with great persistency, when his mother came out of the kitchen, boxed his ears and sent him bawling into the house, much to the relief of the hen, who had just fallen over from exhaustion and fright. Finally, dinner would be ready, and honest Daniel would come in hungry. Jennie would be seen coming down the street from her work; she held a position in Mr. James P. Dunlop's establishment, and went to work every morning at seven o'clock. All being there they would sit down to a substantial meal of beefsteak and onions, plenty of hot, mashed potatoes, boiled cabbage, home-made bread, and delicious butter made from the rich cream of Daniel's red cow. This was the happy, innocent existence led by Daniel Teed and his family. One day was so like another that the weeks slipped away without perceptible difference, and it was while they were living thus that there occurred one of the most frightful calamities that can befall any household, Jew or Gentile, rich or poor.

To have something moving about within the atmosphere, as it did in this house, is terrible to contemplate. What was it? Where did it come from and for what purpose? were questions that not only the inhabitants of Amherst could not answer, but have been asked in vain of the scientific world. Of course there were many theories advanced, but what are theories? Often only imaginary circumstances thought out by men in an endeavour to explain mysteries when tangible facts are so elusive as to be useless. One very remarkable fact about this house was that the power within the atmosphere increased in strength. In all other haunted houses, of which I have heard, the mystery was as powerful at the first as when it had nearly ceased, or been explained away as the work of designing persons who had a specific object in view, such as an endeavour to so injure the reputation of the house, in the minds of timid persons, that its owner would rent it for half the usual rent to get it off his hands, or a desire to frighten some very sensitive person as a joke. There were no such suspicious circumstances, however, surrounding the house, of Daniel Teed. He was, in every sense of the word, a good man; paid his rent promptly, and his household was in every way highly respectable, and consequently all its members were worthy of the esteem in which they were held by all classes who knew them. Then, it must be remembered, the house stood alone on the lot, being what is known as a detached cottage. On the front was a yard opening on Princess Street, on the right side as you entered the front gate was an open lot about 100 feet deep to the next house; on the left was a cottage fifteen or twenty feet away, and on the back, the stable. I examined the cellar, and there was no subterranean passage leading anywhere. The roof was an ordinary peaked one, and so built that both sides could be seen from the front street.

The family of Daniel Teed rarely required the services of a physician, but when any member of the household was ill, Dr. Carritte was always called. Dr. Carritte is a gentleman of culture and refinement, and of very high standing in the profession of which he is such a distinguished member and ornament. It is probable that he, more than any man, except myself, can speak comprehensively of the Great Amherst Mystery. He knew of and heard this phenomenon from the commencement of its diabolical demonstration, and tried all means known to the science of medicine to frustrate its demoniacal designs, and banish it from the house, in vain. His residence in Amherst was always a delightful house to visit, and he has many warm friends in the dramatic profession, in whose members he has for many years taken a personal interest, and had an almost fatherly regard. He has, in more than one instance, corroborated my most extraordinary statements in regard to the doings of the unknown power, and I know will be only too happy to do so, in the future. For I am fully aware that there are thousands of persons who will not believe a word I have written, and to those persons I will now say, that if they will consult the

THE GREAT AMHERST MYSTERY

files of the Amherst *Gazette*, from August 28, 1878, to August 1, 1879; also the *Daily News* of St. John, N.B., of September 8, 1879, for which paper I wrote a short account of the phenomena; and the New York *Commercial Advertiser*, of January 17, 1888; or call upon any of the persons whose names appear in this narrative, they will find that all my statements are what I claim for them—simply, the Truth, which is legally sworn to in my affidavit.

THE GREAT AMHERST MYSTERY

Supper was just over. Mr. and Mrs. Teed were sitting in the parlour with Jennie, who presently went upstairs to the bedroom at the head of the stairs, where Esther was already in bed, having retired at seven o'clock. She asked Esther a question, and not receiving a reply, told her that she was going to see Miss Porter, and would soon return, remarking that the damp, foggy night made her feel sleepy too. As the night was a very disagreeable one, all retired to their rooms about half-past eight, and at about fifteen minutes to nine Jennie, having returned from her visit, also retired to the room where Esther had been in bed for some time, Getting into bed with her sister she noticed that she had forgotten to put out the lamp, which she immediately extinguished, and got into bed again, remarking that the room was very dark, as she bumped her head against the bed-post. She was nearly asleep, when Esther asked her if it was not the fourth of September, to which she replied in the affirmative, remarking that she wanted to go to sleep. The room in which the girls were in bed together was in the front of the house, in the second storey, at the head of the stairs, and next to the room occupied by Mr. and Mrs. Teed and their children, and had one window directly over the front door. They had lain perfectly quiet for about ten minutes, when Esther jumped out of bed with a scream, exclaiming that there was a mouse under the bedclothes. Her scream startled her sister, who was almost asleep, and she also got out of bed and at once lighted the lamp. They then both searched the bed, but could not find the mouse. Supposing it to be inside the mattress, Jennie remarked that they were both fools to be afraid of a little harmless mouse, 'For, see,' said she, 'it is inside the mattress; look how the straw inside is being moved about by it. The mouse has gotten inside somehow and cannot get out because it is lost. Let us go back to bed, Esther; it cannot harm us now.'

So they put out the light and got into bed again. After listening for a few minutes without hearing the straw move in the mattress the girls fell asleep.

On the following night the girls heard something moving under their bed, and Esther exclaimed,

'There is that mouse again, let us get up and kill it. I am not going to be worried by a mouse every night.'

They arose, and one of them lighted the lamp. On hearing a rustling in a green pasteboard box filled with patchwork, which was under the bed, they placed the box in the middle of the room, and were amazed to see it spring up into the air about a foot, and then fall to the floor and turn over on its side. The girls could not believe their own eyes, so Jennie again placed the box in the middle of the room and both watched it intently, when the same thing was repeated. Both Jennie and Esther were now thoroughly frightened, and screamed as loudly as they could for Daniel, who quickly put on some clothing and came into their room to ascertain what was the matter. They described what had occurred, but he only laughed, and after pushing the box under the bed, remarked that they must be crazy, or perhaps had been dreaming; and after grumbling because his rest had been disturbed, he went back to bed. The next morning the girls both declared that the box had really moved upward into the air, and had then fallen to the floor, and rolled over on its side, where Daniel had found it on entering their room; but as no one believed them, they concluded it was of no use to talk of the singular occurrence. After breakfast, Jennie went to Mr. Dunlop's to work (she was a tailoress), and the rest of the household about their daily business, as usual, leaving Mrs. Teed, Esther and the boys alone in the house. After dinner Mrs. Teed sat in the parlour sewing, while Esther went out to walk. The afternoon was delightfully cool, a pleasant breeze blowing from the bay. Walking is very pleasant when there is no dust, but Amherst is such a dusty village, especially when the wind blows from the bay and so scatters the dust of the unpaved streets, that it is impossible to walk on any of them with comfort, that Esther finding this to be the case retraced her steps homeward, stopping at the post-office and at Bird's book store, where she bought a bottle of ink from Miss Blanche and then returned home. After supper Esther took her accustomed seat on the door-step, remaining there until the moon had risen. It was a beautiful moonlight night, almost as bright as day; and while seated there looking at the moon, she remarked to Jennie, that she would surely have good luck during the month because she had seen the new moon over her shoulder. At half-past eight o'clock in the evening, Esther complained of feeling feverish, and was advised by Mrs. Teed and Jennie to go to bed, which she did. At about ten o'clock, Jennie also retired. After she had been in bed with Esther some fifteen minutes, the latter jumped with a sudden bound into the centre of the room, taking all the bedclothes with her, exclaiming:

'My God! what is the matter with me? I'm dying!'

Jennie at once got out of bed, thinking her sister had an attack of nightmare; but, when she had lighted the lamp, was much alarmed at Esther's appearance as she stood in the centre of the room with her short hair almost standing on end, her face blood-red and her eyes looking as if they would start from their sockets, while her hands were grasping the back of a chair so tightly that her finger-nails sank into the soft wood. And, truly, she was an object to be looked on with astonishment, as she stood there in her white nightgown, trembling with fear. Jennie called as loudly as she could for assistance; for she, too, was thoroughly frightened by this time, and did not know what to do. Mrs. Teed was the first to enter the room, having first thrown a shawl around her shoulders, for it was a very chilly night; Daniel put on his coat and trousers in a hurry, as did also William Cox and John Teed, and the three men entered the room at almost the same instant.

'Why, what in thunder ails you, Esther?' asked Daniel, while William Cox and John Teed exclaimed in the same breath—

'She's mad!'

Mrs. Teed was speechless with amazement; and they all stood looking at the girl, not knowing what to do to relieve her terrible agony. Suddenly, she became pale and seemed to be growing very weak, and in a short time became so weak that she had to be assisted to the bed. After sitting on the edge of bed for a moment, and gazing about the room with a vacant stare, she started to her feet with a wild yell and said that she felt as if she was about to burst into pieces.

'Great Heavens!' exclaimed Mrs. Teed, 'what shall we do with her? She is crazy!'

Jennie, who generally retained her presence of mind, said in a soothing tone, 'Come, Esther, get into bed again.'

As she could not do so without assistance, her sisters helped her in, when she gasped in a choking voice, 'I am swelling up and shall certainly burst, I know I shall.'

Daniel looked at her, and remarked in a startled tone, 'Why, the girl is swelling! Olive, just look at her; even her hands are swollen. Lay your hand on her; she is as hot as fire.'

I have asked a number of physicians if they had ever met with similar conditions in a patient, and all replied that they had not, and added, never should. Such, however, was the condition of this girl at the time. While the family stood looking at her wondering what to do to relieve her, for her entire body had now swollen and she was screaming with pain and grinding her teeth as if in an epileptic fit, a loud report, like one peal of thunder without that terrible after rumbling, was heard in the room. They all, except Esther, who was in bed, started instantly to their feet and stood motionless, literally paralysed with surprise.

Mrs. Teed was the first to speak, exclaiming, 'My God! the house has been struck by a thunderbolt, and I know that my boys have been killed,' rushed from the room followed by her husband, William Cox and John Teed; Jennie remained by Esther's bedside.

On finding the children both sleeping soundly they returned to the room and stood looking at Esther in silence, wondering what had produced the terrible sound. Going to the window Mrs. Teed raised the curtain and saw the stars shining brightly and all were then satisfied it had not been thunder they had heard. Just as she let the curtain down again, three terrific reports were heard in the room, apparently coming from under the bed on which Esther lay. These reports were so loud that the whole room shook, and Esther, who a moment before had been so fearfully swollen, and in such great pain, immediately assumed her natural appearance and sank into a state of calm repose. As soon as they were sure that it was sleep, not death, that had taken possession of her, they all left the room, except Jennie, who went again to bed beside her sister, but could not sleep for the balance of the night, through nervous excitement. The next day Esther remained in bed until about nine o'clock, when she arose, apparently herself again, and got her own breakfast. Her appetite on this occasion was not as good as usual. All she could eat was a small piece of bread and butter, and a large green pickle, washed down with a cup of strong black tea. She, however, helped Mrs. Teed with the housework, as usual, and after dinner took a walk past the post office and around the block home again.

At supper that evening the usual conversation occurred about the unearthly sounds, but as not one of them could offer an explanation they concluded it was too deep a matter for them to talk about, and all agreed to keep it secret and not inform any of their friends or neighbours what had transpired. They knew that no one would believe that such strange, unknown sounds had been heard under the bed, nor that Esther had been so singularly affected from unknown causes. About four nights after the loud reports had been heard, Esther had a similar attack. It came on at ten o'clock at night, just as she was about to get into bed. This time, however, she managed to get into the bed before the attack had swelled her to any great extent.

Jennie Cox, who had already retired, advised her to remain perfectly quiet, consoling her with the hope that if she did so the attack would in all probability pass away, and she would then be able to go to sleep without further inconvenience. Esther remained perfectly motionless as advised, but had only been so for about five minutes when, to the consternation of both, all the bedclothes, except the bottom sheet on which they lay, flew off and settled down in a confused heap in a far corner of the room. They could see them passing through the air by the light of the kerosene lamp, which was lighted and standing on the table, and both screamed as only thoroughly scared girls can, and then Jennie fainted. And was it not enough to have frightened any woman and made her faint?

On hearing the screams, the entire family rushed into the room, after hurriedly putting on some garments. There lay all the bedclothes in the corner; Esther fearfully swollen, but entirely conscious, and Jennie lying as if she were dead. Indeed she looked like a corpse as the light of the lamp, which Daniel held in his hand, fell upon her pale face.

Mrs. Teed was the first to recover her senses and, seeing that the forms of her two sisters were exposed, quickly took up the bedclothes and placed them on the girls again. She had no sooner done so than they instantly flew off to the same corner of the room, and the pillow, from under Esther's head, came flying through the air and struck John Teed in the face. This was too much for John Teed's nerves, and he immediately left the room, after remarking, 'he had had enough of it', and could not be induced to return to sit on the edges of the bed with the others who, in that way, managed to keep the bedclothes in place over the girls. Jennie had by this time recovered from her fainting spell, and William Cox went down to the kitchen for a bucket of water to bathe Esther's head, which was aching, when, just as he got to the door of the room again with the bucket of water, a succession of reports were heard that seemed to come from the bed whence the two girls lay. These reports were so loud that the whole room trembled from their vibrations; and Esther, who a moment before had been swollen, assumed her natural appearance, and in a few minutes fell into an apparently healthful sleep. As all seemed right again the entire family retired, but could sleep no more that night.

The next morning Jennie and Esther were both very weak, particularly Esther. She arose, however, when her sister did and lay down on the sofa in the parlour. At breakfast the members of the family all agreed that a doctor had better be sent for; so in the afternoon Daniel left the factory early and went to see Dr. Carritte, who laughed heartily when Daniel informed him what had occurred, and said he would call in the evening, and remain until the following morning, if necessary; but did not hesitate to say, that what Daniel told him was all nonsense, remarking that he knew no such tomfoolery would occur while he was in the house. As the hands of the clock pointed to ten that evening, in walked the doctor. Wishing everybody a hearty good-evening, he took a seat near Esther, who had been in bed since nine o'clock, but as yet had not been afflicted with one of her strange attacks of swelling, nor had any of the strange noises been heard. The doctor felt her pulse, looked at her tongue, and then told the family that she seemed to be suffering from nervous excitement, and had evidently received a tremendous shock of some kind. Just after he had given this opinion, and while he was still sitting by her side, the pillow on which her head was lying came out from under her head, with the exception of one corner, as if it was pulled by some invisible power, and straightening itself out, as if filled with air, remained so a moment, and then went back to its place again, under her head.

The doctor's large blue eyes opened to their utmost capacity as he asked in a low tone, 'Did you see that? It went back again.'

'So it did,' remarked John Teed, 'but if it moves out again, it will not go back, for I intend to hold on to it, even if it did bang me over the head last night.'

John had no sooner spoken these words than out came the pillow from under Esther's head as before. He waited until it had just started back again, then grasped it with both his hands and held it with all his strength, and he was, it must be remembered, a strong, healthy young farmer. However, all his efforts to hold it were unavailing, as it was pulled away from him by some invisible power stronger than himself, and again assumed its position under the young girl's head. Just imagine his astonishment. All the members of the family told me that they never saw any one so completely dumbfounded as John Teed was at that moment.

'How wonderful!' exclaimed Dr. Carritte.

The doctor arose from his chair; and the loud reports commenced under the bed as on the previous nights. He looked beneath the bed but failed to ascertain what had caused the sounds. He walked to the door and the sounds followed him, being now produced on the floor of the room. In about a minute after this the bedclothes flew off again; and before they had been put back on the bed to cover Esther, the distinct sound as of some person writing on the wall with a metallic instrument was heard. All looked at the wall whence the sound of writing came, when, to their great astonishment, there could be plainly read these words, 'Esther Cox, you are mine to kill.' Every person in the room could see the writing plainly, and yet a moment before nothing was to be seen but the plain kalsomined wall. I have seen this writing; it was deeply indented in the wall and looked to me as if it had been written with a dull instrument, probably a large iron spike. I say a dull instrument because the writing had a very uneven appearance, and the invisible power that wrote it was certainly neither an elegant nor an accomplished penman. It was similar in character to mysterious writing I saw during my residence in this genuinely haunted house, that was written on paper, and then either stuck on the wall with some sticky substance by the power or came out of the air and fell at our feet.

The reader can probably imagine their utter amazement at what had just taken place. There they stood around the bed of this suffering girl, each watching the other, to see that there could be no possible mistake about what they saw and heard. They all knew that marvellous things had taken place, for each had heard and seen them with his or her own eyes and ears. Still they dare not trust their own senses; it was all so strange, so different from any previous experience they had ever had, or heard of others having had; that they were all, without a single exception, awed into silence with fear. The terrible words written on the wall, 'Esther Cox, you are mine to kill.' What could their import be? Were they true? What had written them? All that was known was that they had heard the writing, had seen the letters appear, one by one upon the wall, until the sentence was complete, but there their knowledge stopped, and everything to their understanding was as blank as the wall had been before the invisible power, that threatened to commit

THE GREAT AMHERST MYSTERY

murder, had exposed upon that smooth white surface the terrifying sentence in characters nearly a foot in height.

As Dr. Carritte stood in the door wondering what it all meant, a large piece of plaster came flying from the wall of the room, turning a corner in its flight, and fell at his feet. The good doctor picked it up mechanically, and placed it on a chair; he was too much astonished to speak. Just after he had placed the piece of plaster on the chair, the fearfully loud pounding sounds commenced again with redoubled power, this time shaking the entire room and all it contained, including the doctor and other persons. All this time, Esther lay upon the bed almost frightened to death. After this state of things had continued for about two hours all became quiet, and Esther, poor girl, went to sleep. The doctor decided not to give her any medicine until the next morning, when he said he would call and give her something to quiet her nerves.

As to the sounds, and movements of the bedclothes and plaster and the mysterious writing, he could say nothing. He had heard and seen, and could not doubt his own senses; but had no theory to offer that would solve the unanswerable facts all had witnessed in the manifestations of some invisible power seeming to possess human intelligence of a very low and most demoniacal type. The next morning Dr. Carritte called, as he had promised, and was greatly surprised to see Esther up and dressed, helping Mrs. Teed to wash the breakfast dishes. She told him she felt all right again, except that she was so nervous that any sudden sound startled her and made her jump. Having occasion to go down into the cellar with a pan of milk, she came running up, out of breath, and stated there was someone in the cellar who had thrown a piece of plank at her. The doctor went down to see for himself, Esther remaining in the dining-room. The cellar stairs being directly under the stairway in the hall, the door to the cellar, of course, opened into the dining-room. In a moment he came up again, remarking that there was not any person down there to throw a piece of plank or anything else.

'Esther, come down with me,' said he.

They both went down; when to their great surprise, several potatoes came flying at their heads; and both ran up the cellar

THE GREAT AMHERST MYSTERY

stairs. The doctor immediately left the house, and called again in the evening with several very powerful sedatives, morphia being one, which he administered to Esther at about ten o'clock, as she lay in bed. She still complained of her nervousness, and said she felt as though electricity was passing all through her body. He had given her the sedative medicine, and had just stated that she would have a good night's rest, when the sounds commenced, only they were much louder and in more rapid succession than on the previous nights. Presently the sounds left the room and were heard distinctly on the roof of the house. The doctor instantly left the house and went into the street, where he heard the sounds in the open air.

On returning to the house he was more nonplussed than ever; and informed the family that when in the street it seemed as if some person was on the roof with a heavy sledgehammer, pounding away to try and break through the shingles. Being a moonlight night he could see distinctly that there was not any person upon the roof. He remained on this occasion until midnight, when all became quiet and he departed, promising to call the next day. When he had gotten as far as the front gate, the heavy poundings commenced again on the roof with great violence, and continued until he had gone about two hundred yards from the cottage, at which distance he could still hear them distinctly. Dr. Carritte told me this himself. The next week it became known throughout Amherst that strange manifestations of an unknown power, that was invisible, were going on at Daniel Teed's cottage. The mysterious sounds had been heard by people in the street as they passed the house, and several accounts had been printed in the Amherst *Gazette* and copied in other papers. The pounding sounds now commenced in the morning and were to be heard all day. Poor Esther, whom the power had chosen as its victim to kill, always felt relieved when the sounds were produced.

About one month after the commencement of the wonders, Rev. Dr. Edwin Clay, the well-known Baptist clergyman, called at the house to see and hear the wonders of which he had read some accounts in the newspapers, but was desirous of seeing and hearing for himself; and he was fortunate enough to have his desire fully gratified by hearing the loudest kind of sounds, and seeing the writing on the wall. When he left the house he was fully satisfied that Esther did not in any way produce the sounds herself, and that the family had nothing whatever to do with them. He, however, agreed with Dr. Carritte in his theory that her nerves had received a shock of some kind, making her, in some mysterious manner, an electric battery. His idea being that invisible flashes of lightning left her person and that the sounds, which every person could hear so distinctly, were simply minute peals of thunder. So convinced was he that he had ascertained the cause and that there was no deception in regard to the manifestations of the power, that he delivered lectures on the subject and drew large audiences. He always nobly defended Esther Cox and the family, when charged by unthinking people with fraud, and spoke of the affair often from the pulpit. Rev. R. A. Temple, the well-known Wesleyan minister, pastor of the Wesleyan Church in Amherst, which the Teed family attended, also witnessed the manifestations. He saw, among other strange things, a bucket of cold water become agitated and, to all appearances, boil while standing on the kitchen table.

When the inhabitants of Amherst heard that such eminent and worthy men as Rev. Dr. Edwin Clay, Rev. Dr. R. A. Temple and the genial and ever popular Dr. Carritte, took an interest in the haunted house of Daniel Teed, the shoemaker, it became fashionable for even the most exclusive class to call at the cottage to hear and see the wonders. They would come in parties and many heard the power make the sound who would not allow their names to be mentioned in connection with the affair. Often while the house was filled with visitors, large crowds would stand outside unable to gain admittance because there was not room enough inside. On several of these occasions, the Amherst police force had to be called out to keep order. Dr. Carritte, who continued to be one of the daily callers at the cottage, would have a theory one day that would seem to account for the sounds he heard and unknown power he witnessed, and the next day something would occur and upset his latest theory so completely that he finally gave up in despair and became simply a passive spectator. The power continued to manifest itself until December, when Esther, the victim of so much fear and torture, was taken ill with diphtheria and confined to her bed for about two weeks, during which period the power ceased to torment her, and all the sounds ceased. After she recovered from this illness, she went to Sackville, New Brunswick, to visit her other married sister, Mrs. John Snowdon, remaining at her house for about two weeks. The power did not follow her; and while there she was free from the torture it gave her, when moving about in her abdomen, which caused her to swell so fearfully and feel like bursting.

On returning to Daniel's cottage, the most startling and peculiar features of the power took place. One night while in bed with her sister Jennie, in another room, their room having been changed in hope the power would not follow them, she told Jennie that she could hear a voice informing her that the house was to be set on fire that night by a ghost. The voice stated it had once lived on the earth, but had been dead for some years and was now only a ghost.

The members of the household were at once called in and told what Esther had said. They all laughed and informed the girls that no such thing as that could possibly have been said, because there were no ghosts. Rev. Dr. Clay had stated that all the trouble had been caused by electricity.

'And', said Daniel, 'electricity cannot set the house on fire, unless it comes from a cloud in the form of lightning.'

To the amazement and consternation of all present, while they were talking and laughing about the ridiculous statement the girls had made, as having come from the voice of a ghost to Esther, all saw a lighted match fall from the ceiling to the bed, having come out of the air, which would certainly have set the bedclothing on fire, had not Jennie put it out instantly. During the next ten minutes, eight or ten lighted matches fell on the bed and about the room, out of the air, but were all extinguished before anything could be set on fire by them. In the course of the night the loud sounds commenced again.

It seems that about three weeks after Dr. Carritte's first visit to the cottage, Jennie stated that she believed that the power that made the sounds and lit the matches could hear and understand all that was said and perhaps could see them.

THE GREAT AMHERST MYSTERY

The moment she had finished the sentence, three distinct reports were heard; and, on Daniel requesting Dr. Carritte to ask the power if it could hear, three reports were heard, which shook the entire house. Dr. Carritte remarked at the time that it was very singular. Daniel then asked if the power could tell how many persons were in the room, and not receiving a reply, repeated the question in this form, 'How many persons are in the room? Give a knock on the floor for each one.'

Six distinct knocks were instantly made by the power; and there were just six persons in the room at the time, they being Dr. Carritte, Daniel Teed, his wife, Esther, Jennie, and William Cox; John Teed having left the room after poor Esther had buried her face in the pillow as she lay in bed, trembling with fright.

The family could now converse with the power in this way. It would knock once for a negative answer, and three times for an answer in the affirmative, giving only two knocks when in doubt about a reply.

This system of communication had been suggested by a visitor. And it was in this way that they had carried on a conversation the night the matches fell upon the bed from the ceiling.

Daniel asked if the house would really be set on fire, and the reply was 'Yes'. And a fire was started in about five minutes in the following manner. The invisible ghost that had spoken to Esther took a dress belonging to her that was hanging on a nail in the wall near the door and, after rolling it up and placing it under the bed before their eyes, but so quickly that they could not prevent the action, set it on fire. Fortunately, the dress was at once pulled from under the bed by Daniel, and the fire extinguished before any serious damage had been done to the material.

Daniel told me that when the dress was being rolled up and put under the bed, they could not see the ghost doing it. All was then quiet for the rest of the night; no one daring to go to bed, however, for fear another fire would be kindled.

The next morning all was consternation in the cottage. Daniel and his wife were afraid that the ghost would start a fire in some inaccessible place, where it could not be extinguished, in which case no one could save the cottage from burning to the ground.

All the family were now fully convinced that the mysterious power was really what it claimed to be, the ghost of some very evil man who had once lived upon the earth, and in some unknown manner managed to torture poor Esther, as only such a ghost would.

Daniel Teed explained the true nature of the torture to me, but it must be nameless here. And now to that nameless horror was added the fear of their home being destroyed by a fire kindled by this demon, with matches stolen from the match box in the kitchen, and which could not be hidden from him in any part of the house where he could not find them.

About three days after the ghost had tried to set the bed on fire by lighting it with the burning dress, Mrs. Teed, while churning in the kitchen, noticed smoke issuing from the cellar door, which, as I have already explained, opened into the dining-room. Esther at the time was seated in the dining-room, and had been there for an hour or more, previous to which she had been in the kitchen assisting her sister to wash the breakfast dishes.

They both told me, during my residence in the house, that when they first discovered the smoke on this occasion they were so terrified for the moment that neither of them could move.

Mrs. Teed was the first to recover from the shock, and seizing a bucket of drinking water, always kept standing on the kitchen table, she rushed down the cellar stairs, and in the far corner of the cellar saw a band of shavings blazing up almost to the joints of the main floor of the house. In the meantime, Esther had reached the cellar and stood as if petrified with astonishment. Mrs. Teed poured what water the bucket contained (for in the excitement she had spilled more than half on her way down) into the burning shavings, and both she and Esther, being almost choked with smoke, ran up the cellar stairs, and out of the house into Princess Street, crying, 'Fire! fire!' as loudly as they could.

Their cries aroused the entire neighbourhood. Several men

THE GREAT AMHERST MYSTERY

rushed in, and while some smothered the now burning band with rugs from the dining-room floor, others put it out entirely with water they obtained from a large butt into which the rain water ran, and was saved for washing purposes.

The Amherst *Gazette* published an account of the fire kindled by the power, and as the article was, of course, copied throughout Canada, as articles from that admirable paper always are, a tremendous sensation was created and genuine curiosity aroused.

Thousands of people who had set the whole affair down as a first-class fraud, began to think there might be something in it after all; for certainly no young girl could set fire to a band of shavings in the cellar and be at the same time in one of the rooms above, under the watchful eye of an elder sister, out of whose sight she never dared to go for fear the ghost would murder her.

The fact that both the little boys were playing in the front yard at the time the fire was started, and consequently could not have had anything to do with setting it, was also calculated to throw an air of still greater mystery around the whole affair.

The family and Dr. Carritte alone knew that the fire had been started by the ghost. The fire marshals of Amherst were of the opinion that, in some unexplained manner, Esther had kindled the fire. The inhabitants had various theories.

Dr. Nathan Tupper, who had never witnessed a single manifestation, suggested that if a strong raw-hide whip were laid across Esther's bare shoulders by a powerful arm, the tricks of the girl would cease at once.

During the following week the ghost gave as much evidence of power as ever; and the excitement in the village became intense.

[The above extract gives the most interesting facts in the Great Amherst case. After this it degenerates, nearly into farce. A few later details are to be found, however, in my Examination. Note by S. S.]

9. A POLTERGEIST CASE FROM SUMATRA

Reprinted from the Journal of the Society for Psychical Research, Vol. XII, May, 1906

The following is the account of some 'Poltergeist' phenomena witnessed by an associate of the Society, Mr. W. G. G., of Dordrecht, Holland, and discussed at the meeting of the Society on March 30th, 1906, as reported above. The account was accompanied by a number of drawings, not reproduced here. These show the construction of the house as described in Mr. G.'s letters. All the rooms were on one floor, raised above the ground by wooden piles, which passed vertically up through the floor and supported the sloping roof. The partitions between the rooms were wooden frameworks, consisting of vertical and horizontal beams, the spaces between which were covered with 'kadjang' leaves. The rooms were unceiled and the partitions between them did not reach up to the roof. Mr. G.'s native servant slept in the room next to him, there being a wooden door in the partition between the two rooms. The point in the roof from which the stones fell was approximately over this partition. Mr. G. writes:[1]

Dordrecht, January 27th, 1906

... It was in September, 1903, that the following abnormal fact occurred to me. Every detail of it has been examined by me very carefully. I had been on a long journey through the jungle of Palembang and Djambi (Sumatra) with a gang of 50 Javanese coolies for exploring purposes. Coming back from

[1] At his request we have made a few verbal alterations in those parts of the narrative where the English was slightly incorrect or not idiomatic.

THE CASE OF MR. G. IN SUMATRA

the long trip, I found that my home had been occupied by somebody else and I had to put up my bed in another house that was not yet ready, and had just been erected from wooden poles and *lalang* or *kadjang*. The roof was formed of great dry leaves of a kind called kadjang in Palembang. These great leaves are arranged one overlapping the other. In this way it is very easy to form a roof if it is only for a temporary house. This house was situated pretty far away from the bore-places belonging to the oil company, in whose service I was working.

I put my bullsack and mosquito curtain on the wooden floor and soon fell asleep. At about one o'clock at night I half awoke, hearing something fall near my head outside the mosquito curtain on the floor. After a couple of minutes I completely awoke and turned my head around to see what was falling down on the floor. They were *black stones* from $\frac{1}{8}$ to $\frac{3}{4}$ of an inch long. I got out of the curtain and turned up the kerosene lamp, that was standing on the floor at the foot of my bed. I saw then that the stones were falling through the roof in a parabolic line. They fell on the floor close to my head-pillow. I went out and awoke the boy (a Malay-Palembang coolie) who was sleeping on the floor in the next room. I told him to go outside and to examine the jungle up to a certain distance. He did so whilst I lighted up the jungle a little by means of a small 'ever-ready' electric lantern. At the same time that my boy was outside the stones did not stop falling. My boy came in again, and I told him to search the kitchen to see if anybody could be there. He went to the kitchen and I went inside the room again to watch the stones falling down. I knelt down near [the head of my bed] and tried to catch the stones while they were falling through the air towards me, but I could never catch them; *it seemed to me that they changed their direction in the air as soon as I tried to get hold of them*. I could not catch any of them before they fell on the floor. Then I climbed up [the partition wall between my room and the boy's] and examined [the roof just above it from which] the stones were flying. They came right through the kadjang, but there were no holes in the kadjang. When I tried to catch them there at the very spot of coming out, I also failed.

When I came down, my boy had returned from the kitchen

THE CASE OF MR. G. IN SUMATRA

and told me there was nobody. But I still thought that somebody might be playing a practical joke, so I took my Mauser rifle and fired 5 sharp cartridges into the jungle from [the window of the boy's room]. But the stones, far from stopping, fell even more abundantly after my shots than before.

After this shooting the boy became fully awake (it seemed to me that he had been dozing all the time before), and he looked inside the room. When he saw the stones fall down, he told me it was 'Satan' who did that, and he was so greatly scared that he ran away in the pitch-dark night. After he had run away the stones ceased to fall, and I never saw the boy back again. I did not notice anything particular about the stones except that they were *warmer* than they would have been under ordinary circumstances.

The next day, when awake again, I found the stones on the floor and everything as I had left it in the night. I examined the roof again, but nothing was to be found, not a single crack or hole in the kadjang. I also found the 5 empty cartridges on the floor near the window. Altogether there had been thrown about 18 or 22 stones. I kept some of them in my pocket for a long while, but lost them during my later voyages.

The worst part of this strange fact was that my boy was gone, so that I had to take care of my breakfast myself, and did not get a cup of coffee nor toast!

At first I thought they might have been meteor-stones because they were so warm, but then again I could not explain how they could get through the roof without making holes!

In answer to our questions, Mr. G. gave further particulars in later letters as follows:

February 1st, 1906

In the Dutch East Indies this phenomenon seems to happen pretty often; at least every now and then it is reported in the newspaper, generally concerning a house in the city. But I never gave myself the trouble to examine one of these cases, for the simple reason that it is an impossibility to control at the same moment all the people that are living around. . . .

Just because the house where I was sleeping was situated all alone, far away from other houses, I thought that this case

THE CASE OF MR. G. IN SUMATRA

might be of more interest than other similar cases. Let me repeat the following particulars of it.

(1) All around the house was *jungle*, in front, behind, to the left and to the right.

(2) There was no other soul in the house and kitchen than myself and the boy.

(3) The boy certainly did *not* do it, because at the same time that I bent over him, while he was sleeping on the floor, to awake him, there fell a couple of stones. I not only *saw* them fall on the floor in the room, but I also *heard* them fall, the door being at that moment half open.

(4) While the boy was standing *in front of me* and I shot my cartridges, at that same moment I heard them fall behind me.

(5) I climbed up the poles of the roof and I saw quite distinctly that they came right through the kadjang.

This kadjang is of such a kind that it cannot be penetrated (not even with a needle) without making a hole. Each kadjang is one single flat leaf of about 2 by 3 feet in size. It is a speciality of the neighbourhood of Palembang. It is very tough and offers a strong resistance to penetration.

(6) The stones (though not all of them) were hotter than could be explained by their having been kept in the hand or pocket for some time.

(7) All the stones without exception fell down within a certain radius of not more than 3 feet; they all came through the same kadjang-leaf (that is to say, all the ones I saw) and they all fell down within the same radius on the floor.

(8) They fell rather slowly. Now, supposing that somebody might by trickery have forced them through the roof, or supposing they had not come through it at all—even then there would remain something mysterious about it, because it seemed to me that they were *hovering* through the air; they described a parabolic line and then came down with a bang on the floor.

(9) The sound they made in falling down on the floor was also abnormal, because considering their slow motion the bang was much too loud.

The same thing had happened to me about a week before; but on that occasion I was standing outside in the open air near

THE CASE OF MR. G. IN SUMATRA

a tree in the jungle, and as it was impossible to control it that time (it might have been a monkey that did it), I did not pay much attention to it. . . .

February 13th, 1906

The construction of the house is very different from that of European houses. It is all open, as all houses in the East Indies are. There was no ceiling in the house.

The walls forming the rooms did not extend as far up as the roof, so that there was an open space between the walls and the roof. This last circumstance was the reason why I examined the phenomenon so closely and climbed up along the vertical poles of the wall up to the roof, to assure myself that the stones were not thrown over the wall through the open space.

The partition between the place where I was sleeping and the place where the boy was sleeping was continuous all around the four sides of the room, there being a closed door between us two. This partition was a wooden framework, with kadjang nailed on it, forming that way a solid wall, which did not however extend up to the roof (as just described).

The only wooden floor was formed of 2 inch boards, nailed together, there being no holes in the floor.

I am sure of the date, 1903, because in June, 1903, my sister died, and after this strange phenomenon occurred to me, I began to ponder whether there might possibly be any connection between my sister's death and the falling stones. After the phenomenon had taken place, I bought a book about spiritism, to try to find an explanation. Before the phenomenon occurred to me I had read nothing about spiritism, but I had often thought about it. I am not at all convinced that there was any connection between the falling stones and my sister's death. At the moment that the phenomenon occurred to me, I did not think about spiritism.

As I said before, one of my impressions was that the stones might have been meteor-stones, on account of their being hot. I put them in my pocket and carried them about with me for a long time, as there was a geological Professor coming to visit us and to inspect our work. I intended to have the stones inspected by him, but before he came the stones had been lost.

THE CASE OF MR. G. IN SUMATRA

I hope that my plan is plain enough to give you an idea of the way in which I watched the stones coming through the roof. I was inside the room, climbed up along the framework to the top of the wall, held on with one hand to the framework and tried to catch the stones with the other hand, at the same time seeing the boy lying down sleeping outside (in the other room) on the floor behind the door, the space being lit up by means of a lamp in his room. The construction of the house was such that it was impossible to throw the stones through the open space from outside.

I wrote before that it seemed to me that the boy had been dozing all the time after I awoke him. I got that impression because his movements seemed to me abnormally slow; his rising up, his walking around, and everything seemed extraordinarily slow. These movements gave me the same strange impression as the slowly falling stones.

When I think over this last fact (for I remember very well the strange impression the slowly moving boy made on me) I feel now inclined to suggest the hypothesis that there might have been something abnormal in my own condition at the time. For, having read in the *Proceedings* about hallucinations, I dare not state any more that the stones in reality moved slowly; it might have been on account of some condition of my own sensory organs that it seemed to me that they did, though at that time I was not in the least interested in the question of hallucinations or of spiritism. I am afraid that the whole thing will ever remain a puzzle to me.

The criticisms on the case made at the meeting of the Society on March 30th having been communicated to Mr. G., he wrote again on April 3rd, reiterating in further detail his reasons for thinking it impossible that the boy could have thrown the stones without being detected by him; viz. that three stones came through the roof while he was touching it with his left hand and looking over the top of the partition at the boy; again, while he was leaning over the boy to awaken him and facing towards the open door leading into his own room, he both saw and heard two stones falling there: also, while he was shooting into the jungle, the boy standing a

THE CASE OF MR. G. IN SUMATRA

little in front of him and to his right, so that he could see if he moved, he heard stones falling on the floor behind him. He was entirely alone in the house, but for the boy. The coolies had brought his instruments and tools there and then gone on to the bore-place, about four kilometres from the house, to which the boy also went when he ran away. On the first occasion referred to when he witnessed some stones falling and thought they might possibly have been thrown by a monkey, another servant was with him—a Soendanese native—whereas on the second occasion the boy was a Malay Palembang coolie.

10. THE WORKSOP AND WEM POLTERGEISTS

Report by Frank Podmore, reprinted from Proceedings of the Society for Psychical Research, Vol. XII, June, 1896

April 11th, 1883

At the beginning of March, 1883, the *Retford and Gainsborough Times* and other local papers gave accounts of some remarkable disturbances which had occurred in the first two or three days of the month, at the house of a small horse-dealer in Worksop, named Joe White. One or two members of the Society entered into communication with the principal persons named in the newspaper reports, and with a friend in the neighbourhood, who very kindly took some trouble in inquiring into the matter for the Society. But it soon became obvious that, as nearly all the witnesses of the occurrences related were of the humbler class, and unable, therefore, to write a connected account of what had happened, the best way to arrive at the truth of the matter was for one of us to go in person to make inquiries. Accordingly, at the request of the Haunted House Committee, I went down to Worksop on the afternoon of Saturday, April 7th, with the intention of inspecting the actual scene of the occurrences, and of personally interrogating the principal witnesses; in order, if possible, to arrive at some rational explanation of the business. I spent the Saturday evening, and the whole of the following day in my inquiries, and have, I think, obtained as intelligible and trustworthy a history of the matter as the lapse of time, the nature of the phenomena themselves, and the character of the witnesses will permit.

THE WORKSOP POLTERGEIST

I derived my information from seven principal eye-witnesses of the disturbances, whom I interrogated, with the single exception of White himself, *separately*. I wrote out the statement of each witness in full immediately after the interview, and the three most important witnesses, Higgs, Currass, and White, subsequently read through my notes and signed them. The depositions of these three persons are printed in full below. My time was too short to allow a second interview with the four other principal witnesses, and I was unable, therefore, to obtain their signatures to the depositions; but I have incorporated the statements of all the principal witnesses in my report.

Besides the seven chiefly concerned, I questioned, in presence of White and his wife, three or four other witnesses of the disturbances, viz., White's brother Tom, a bright-looking lad of 18 or 20; Solomon Wass and his wife, next-door neighbours of the Whites, the former an ordinary North countryman of the lower class, the latter a pleasant-looking intelligent woman; and George Ford (Buck Ford), a man of about 28. From these I obtained general confirmation of the various incidents, as described by White, Higgs, etc., at which they had themselves been present; but time did not permit of much cross-questioning, nor of taking down their evidence in full.

White's house has been built, according to his own statement, about seven years. He has only resided in it three years. I was unable to discover anything about the former occupants. The house stands at the end of a piece of waste land, called the New Building Ground, with another house or cottage attached; the nearest separate building being a public-house, about 100 yards off. With that exception, there are no other buildings within about 200 yards.

There is no entrance to the house by the front, the front door being locked, and the joints secured with paper from the inside. Entrance is obtained by a covered passage, open at either end, which separates the two houses, and gives access immediately to a yard, surrounded on one side by high palings, and on the other three by piggeries, stables, and the two houses. The kitchen is about 15 feet square. The upper floor is divided into two rooms, the back one, corresponding to the kitchen, being used as a bedroom for Tom and the children;

the front one as a store-house for bacon, horse-furniture, and various odds and ends. There is also a garret above this, into which I did not enter, it being at the time full of bacon in salt. The whole house, not excepting the bedrooms, is hung with bacon, the very staircase being lined with it, so that I had to draw my coat close to me in going up. A large part of the bacon, as I was told by White, had gone bad during the period of the disturbances.

The front or inner room on the ground floor was an ordinary room, like all the rest of the house half-filled with bacon and containing, besides bedroom furniture, a large beer-barrel on trestles; everything in it filthily dirty.

I looked all over the house in daylight, but could discern no holes in the walls or ceilings, nor any trace of the extensive and elaborate machinery which would have been required to produce the movements by ordinary mechanical means.

The history of the disturbances, as gathered from the various witnesses whom I interrogated, appears to be briefly as follows:

Nothing remarkable had been seen or heard in the house until about the 20th or 21st February, 1883, when, as Mrs. White was alone with two of the children in the kitchen one evening, washing up the tea-things at the table, the table tilted up at a considerable angle; the candle was upset, and the washtub only saved by Mrs. W. holding it. She positively assured me that she exerted no pressure whatever upon the table, and the whole incident struck her as very extraordinary. Her husband made light of it at the time.

On Monday, February 26th, White was absent from home until the Wednesday afternoon. On the Monday his wife allowed a girl, Eliza Rose, the child of an imbecile mother, to come into the house and share her bed at night. White returned on Wednesday night, but left on the following morning until Friday afternoon. During that one night the girl slept on the squab. On Thursday night, March 1st, at about 11 p.m., Tom White went up to bed—the children having gone up some hours before. At about 11.30 Mrs. White and Eliza Rose being then alone in the kitchen, various things, such as a corkscrew, clothes-peg, a salt-cellar, etc., which had been in the kitchen only a few minutes before, came tumbling step by step down the kitchen stairs. Tom positively and solemnly denied having thrown the articles, and the mystery was increased when, at least 20 minutes after he had gone upstairs, no one having left the room in the interval, some *hot* coals were thrown down.

On the following night, March 2nd, at about the same hour —White, Mrs. White, and Rose being in the kitchen—a noise was heard as of some one coming down the passage between the two houses, and stopping just outside the outer door. White told Rose to open the door, but she was too frightened to do so. Then they heard a surcingle and immediately afterwards some pieces of carpet thrown down the stairs. Then followed some knives and forks and other things. The girl picked them up; but they followed still faster. White then left the room to go up to Tom. During his absence one of the ornaments flew off the mantelpiece into the corner of the room near the door. Nothing was seen by the two women; but they heard it fall, and found it there. Their screams summoned White down; as he entered the room his candle went out, and something struck him on the forehead. The girl picked up the candle—which appears to have left the candlestick—and two new ones which had not been in the house previously, from the ground; and as soon as a candle was lit, a little china woman left the mantelpiece, and fell into the corner, where it was seen by White. As soon as it was replaced it flew across the room again, and was broken. Other things followed, and the women being very frightened, and White thinking that the disturbances presaged the death of his child, who was very ill with an abscess in the back, sent Tom (who was afraid to go alone) with Ford to fetch the doctor. Mrs. White meanwhile took one of the children next door. Rose approached the inner room to fetch another, when things immediately began to fly about and smash themselves in that room. After this all appear to have been absent from the house for a short time. White then returned with Higgs, a policeman, and, whilst they were alone in the kitchen, standing near the door, a glass jar flew out of the cupboard into the yard; a tumbler also fell from the chest of drawers in the kitchen, when only Higgs was near it. Both then

THE WORKSOP POLTERGEIST

went into the inner room, and found the chest of drawers there turned up on end and smashed. On their return they found Rose, Wass, and Tom White in the kitchen [? and Mrs. Wass], and all saw a cream jug, which Rose had just placed on the bin, fly four feet up in the air and smash on the floor. Dr. Lloyd and Mrs. White then entered, and in the presence of all these witnesses, a basin was seen to rise slowly from the bin—no person being near it except Dr. Lloyd and Higgs. It touched the ceiling, and then fell suddenly to the floor and was smashed. This was at 12 p.m. All then left except Tom White and his brother. The disturbances continued until about 2 a.m. when all grew quiet and the Whites slept. At about 8 a.m., on Saturday, the 3rd, the disturbances began again.

White left the kitchen to attend to some pigs; and, in his absence, Mrs. White and Rose were left alone in the kitchen. A nearly empty port wine bottle leaped up from the table about four feet into the air, and fell into a bucket of milk, standing on the table, from which Mrs. White was filling some jugs, etc.

Then Currass appears to have been attracted to the scene. He entered with White, young Wass, and others, and viewed the inner room. They had but just returned to the kitchen, leaving the inner room empty, and the door of communication open, when the American clock, which hung over the bed, was heard to strike. (It had not done so for 18 months previously.) A crash was then heard, and Currass, who was nearest the door, looked in, and found that the clock had fallen over the bed—about four feet broad—and was lying on the floor.[1] Shortly afterwards—no one being near it—a china dog flew off the mantelpiece, and smashed itself in the corner near the door. Currass and some others then left.

[1] It will be noted that there is a discrepancy between White's and Currass' version of this incident. Mrs. White, however, confirmed her husband's account; and I have little doubt that the statement in the text is substantially accurate. Currass is more likely than White to have been mistaken in his recollection of White's position at the time; and Currass' account of his own position does not differ greatly from that given by White. The material point, and one on which both witnesses are agreed, is that no one *saw* the clock fall. Currass' written statement is not clear on this point, but he told me *viva voce* that his attention was drawn to what had taken place by hearing the crash. He only then turned round and saw the clock lying on the floor.—F.P., April, 1883.

THE WORKSOP POLTERGEIST

Some plates, a cream-jug, and other things, then flew up in the air, and smashed themselves in view of all who were in the kitchen—Rose, the Whites, and Mrs. Wass.

White then lay down on the sofa; but disturbances continued during his siesta. In particular, some pictures on the wall next the pantry began to move, but were taken down at once by his brother. At about 2 p.m. a Salvation Army woman came in, and talked to White. Rose only was with them in the kitchen. A candlestick flew from the bin, and fell behind the Salvation Army woman, as she stood near the pantry door. She left the room in terror.

Other things then followed at intervals. A full medicine bottle fell without breaking. An empty medicine bottle and a lamp-glass fell and broke themselves. It was then about 4 p.m., and White could stand it no longer. He told the girl she must go; she did in fact leave before 5 p.m. After her departure nothing whatever of an abnormal character took place, and the house has remained undisturbed up to the present time.

With regard to the positions of the persons present, in relation to the objects moved, it may be stated generally that there was no possibility in most cases of the objects having been thrown by hand. It will be seen, on reference to the depositions of the witnesses which are appended, that the objects were frequently moved in a remote corner of the room, or even in an adjoining room. Moreover, the character of the movements, in many cases, was such as to preclude the possibility of the objects having been thrown.

Of course the obvious explanation of these occurrences is trickery on the part of some of the persons present. In regard to this, it seems to me a matter of very little significance that most of the educated people in Worksop believe White himself to have caused the disturbance. For most educated persons, as we know, would not be ready to admit any other than a mechanical explanation, and if such an explanation be adopted, White, the owner of the house, a man of considerable intelligence, whose record was not entirely clean, and who was himself present on the occasion of nearly all the disturbances, must obviously be the agent. But whilst believing White to be at the bottom of the matter, none of the persons with whom

I conversed were prepared with any explanation of his *modus operandi*. That he should have thrown the things was universally admitted to be impossible. And beyond this, I could discover little more than an unquestioning faith in the omnipotence of electricity. No one professed to have any idea of what mechanical means could have been employed, or how they could have been adapted to the end in view. Still less did any one pretend to have discovered any indications in the house itself of any machinery having been used. Moreover, there was a total absence of any apparent motive on White's part, supposing him to have been capable of effecting the movements himself. Whilst he was unquestionably a considerable loser—to the extent of nearly £9 as estimated by himself, though this estimate is probably exaggerated—by the articles broken, he appears to have reaped no corresponding advantage. The one motive which I heard suggested—if we disregard a report in one newspaper, subsequently contradicted in another, to the effect that White was anxious to buy the house, and to buy it cheap—was that he produced the disturbances in fulfilment of a sporting bet. But I saw no reason to regard this explanation as anything but a scholium evolved by some ingenious commentator from the facts themselves.

Again, had White himself been the principal agent in the matter, it is clear that he must have had at least two confederates, for he was not himself present during the disturbances on the Thursday night—which might, indeed, have been caused by his brother Tom—nor was either he or his brother present during some of the occurrences on the following day. Moreover, these confederates must not only have been extremely skilful, but they must have been capable of more than ordinary reticence and self-control. For it is remarkable that, with the single exception of the statements made by the girl Rose, no one professed to have heard even a hint from White himself, from his brother, or from any other, of any trickery in the matter.

Moreover, it is hard to conceive by what mechanical appliances, under the circumstances described, the movements could have been effected. The clock, for instance—a heavy American one—was thrust out from the wall in a horizontal direction, so as apparently to clear a 4-foot bedstead which lay immediately beneath it, and the nail from which it depended remained *in situ* on the wall. The objects thrown about in the kitchen moved generally, but by no means always, in the direction of the outer door. And it is noticeable that, in most cases, they do not appear to have been thrown, but in some manner borne or wafted across the room; for, though they fell on a stone floor 15 ft. or 16 ft. distant, they were often unbroken, and were rarely shivered. And it is impossible to reconcile the account given of the movements of some other objects, variously described as 'jerky', 'twirling', and 'turning over and over', with the supposition that the objects depended on any fixed support, or were in any way suspended.

Lastly, to suppose that these various objects were all moved by mechanical contrivances argues incredible stupidity, amounting almost to imbecility, on the part of all the persons present who were not in the plot. That the movement of the arms necessary to set the machinery in motion should have passed unobserved on each and every occasion by all the witnesses, is almost impossible. Not only so, but Currass, Higgs, and Dr. Lloyd, all independent observers, assured me that they examined some of the objects which had been moved, immediately after the occurrence, with the express intention of discovering, if possible, any clue to an explanation of the matter, but entirely failed to do so. These men were not over-credulous; they certainly were not wanting in intelligence; and they were not, any of them, prepossessed in favour of White. But they each admitted that they could discover no possible explanation of the disturbances, and were fairly bewildered by the whole matter.

STATEMENT OF JOE WHITE[1]

I returned home about 7 on the Friday night (March 2nd). I had been absent from home on Monday and Tuesday nights: and it was during my absence that my wife took in the girl

---

[1] A fair witness. I think that he always intended to speak the truth, but that occasionally his memory proved treacherous. In all important points, however, he was corroborated by his wife (an excellent witness), Higgs, and Currass.—F. P.

THE WORKSOP POLTERGEIST

Rose, who shared her bed in the front inner room. I slept at home on Wednesday, and the girl then slept on the squab in the kitchen. I left again on Thursday morning, and returned as mentioned on the Friday.

When told by my wife and Tom what had happened on Thursday night, I said some one must have been tricking, and didn't think much more about it. But I chaffed the lass (Rose) a good deal, for she was much frightened. About 11.30 on Friday evening, when my wife, the girl, and I were alone in the kitchen, just going up to bed, I heard a noise as if some one had come down the passage between the two houses, and were standing just outside our door. They didn't knock; but I said to Rose, 'Go and see who's there.' But she was frightened and didn't go. Then presently a lot of things came rattling down the stairs. I don't know what came first; but a lot of things came—a surcingle, bits of carpet, knives and forks, a corkscrew, etc. The girl went to pick them up, and put them on the table, and just as fast she she put them on more things came down. Then my wife said to me, 'The salt cellar came down last night, but you won't have it down to-night, for here it is on the table.' She was using it at the time for salting Tom's dinner for the next day. She had hardly said this, when the salt cellar flew off from the table, and into the corner near the outer door. Rose was in that corner, and not near the table: my wife was at the table, but certainly didn't touch the cellar. I saw the thing go, though I couldn't believe my eyes. My wife didn't see it go, but we both saw it as it struck the wall in the corner. All the salt was spilt out of it. I fairly couldn't believe my own eyes; but I couldn't help thinking it must be Tom. So I went upstairs to him, and told him to leave off. 'Thou'lt frighten our Liz to death.' He said, 'It's not me, Joe. I'll take my oath it isn't. I've never thrown nowt down.' Whilst I was still talking to him, I heard a crash downstairs; and the women screamed; and my wife cried, 'Come down, Joe.' As I was just coming into the room the candle which I held in my hand went out—I don't know how at all—and we were left in darkness, except for the firelight. Then something hit me on the forehead, and I cried out, 'Who threw that?' Then there was a crash in the corner. I found out when we had a light again, that the salt cellar had fallen again into the corner and broken itself. Then I found out that the candle was not in the candlestick, and asked where it was. I told the girl to look for it, and then she felt among the things at the bottom of the stairs and picked up *three* candles, two of them quite new. We had only had *two* candles in the house [Mrs. White expressly confirmed this.—F. P.] which had been bought just before, and both had been partly burnt. I lit the old ones and left the new ones on the table; but they disappeared afterwards, and I have never seen them since.

When the candle was lit again, I saw the little china woman jump off from the mantelpiece, and go into the same corner. It fell on its side, and then righted itself, and stood upright, unbroken. I distinctly saw it go through the air; it passed near me as I stood about the middle of the room. None of us were near the mantelpiece. I picked it up, and presently it fell into the corner again, and broke itself. Then the tea-caddy and the candlestick, all from the mantelpiece, followed. Then I went out and found George Ford ('Buck' Ford), and asked him to fetch Dr. Lloyd for the child—for they had told me that all this disturbance meant the death of the child, who was very ill with an abscess in its back.

Then I got my wife to take the little lad out, and lay him next door, he lying on the squab in the kitchen at the time. [Mrs. W. denied this, and said he was in the inner room.—F. P.] Rose went with her, and they took all the children with them. Before going, Rose had to go into the inner room, and then things began to fly about there and make a disturbance. All had been quiet there before.

I went after the others into the next house and stayed there some little time. When I came back, I found Police-Constable Higgs in the kitchen. He and I were alone there. (Rose all this time was next door.) We heard a crash in the inner room, and we went in—Solomon Wass and Tom, who had just entered, with us, and Higgs with his lantern,—and we found the chest of drawers turned up on end, and the lustres and looking-glass, and everything else that had been on it, in pieces on the floor. Then we came back into the kitchen, and we saw the cupboard door open, and a big glass jar flew out, and flew into

THE WORKSOP POLTERGEIST

the yard and broke itself. Also some things flew off the bin at the side of the door, from the end near the fire; and they pitched in the corner, and then went out in the yard. Things often pitched on the floor by the door first, and then got up again and flew out into the yard.

Then Dr. Lloyd came in with my wife, and Higgs showed him what had happened in the inner room. Then when we had got into the kitchen again, and were all standing near the door of the inner room—Higgs, my wife, and Tom, and Wass, and Lloyd—who was about six feet from the bin, and the nearest to it of our party—we all saw a basin which was lying on the bin near the door, get up two or three times in the air, rising slowly a few inches or perhaps a foot and then falling plump. [Mrs. W. corroborated this, and so did Mr. Wass, the next-door neighbour, who was also present.—F. P.] Then it got up higher, and went slowly, wobbling as it went up to the ceiling, and when it had reached the ceiling, it fell down all at once, and broke itself.[1] Dr. Lloyd then looked in the bin, saying the devil must be in the house, and then left. All the others shortly afterwards left, Mrs. W., Rose and the children stopping in the next house. Tom and I sat in the chair on either side of the fire until the next morning at 8 a.m. Things kept on moving every now and then until about 2 a.m., and then was all quiet, and we got to sleep a bit. At about 8 a.m. I had to go out to see after a pig which had been pigging, and then things began again; and a lot of folks came in to see about it. Currass came in and I went with him into the inner room and showed him the chest of drawers, he and I alone; we came out leaving the door open—I am quite sure it was open—and I was sitting near the fire, and Currass was just inside the kitchen, not far from the open door, when Wass's little lad, who was sitting at the table, said, 'There's the clock striking,' meaning the big clock which hung over our bed. I couldn't hear it, and I said it was a lie. Just then we heard a crash, and I asked what it was, and Currass looked round, and said it was the American clock had fallen right across the bed, and lay on the floor at the foot, with its bottom knocked out. Then I took it into the yard, I

[1] During this scene the room was lighted by one candle, Higgs' lantern, and a blazing fire; so that the light was pretty good.

THE WORKSOP POLTERGEIST

think—indeed, I am sure, that Coulter was *not* here when all this happened. The other clock fell and was broken, but whether before or after I cannot remember; and he may have seen that. I don't remember where the girl Rose was when the American clock fell. She may have been in the kitchen, but she certainly wasn't in the inner room; no one was in that room, I am sure. I don't remember saying just at that time, though I often did say, that wherever she went the things smashed.

After that, Currass and I and one or two others were standing near to the outer door talking, when the china dogs, or one of them, flew off the mantelpiece and smashed; and lots of things kept on flying into the corner and smashing. I saw one of the dogs leave the mantelpiece and go through the air. I don't remember exactly when Coulter came; he may have been here when the china dog was smashed, but I don't remember that he was. Then a cream jug fell off the table; it had done so four or five times without smashing. At last I filled it with milk, and had placed it on the bin, when it suddenly fell off and smashed, and the milk was all spilt.

Then I was tired, and lay down on the squab; but things kept moving. I was told some pictures on the wall began to move, but I didn't see them. At about 2 p.m., a Salvation Army woman came in and was talking to me as I lay on the squab; she stood near the inner door; Rose was near the outer door, having brought in some carpet. There were two candlesticks on the bin, at the end near the fireplace. Suddenly something dropped behind the Salvation Army woman. No one saw it going through the air; but we turned round and found that it was one of the brass candlesticks. It was half balanced on the small end where the candle goes, and was wobbling about on the end. Then the Salvation woman said, 'I must go'; and she went.

Then a little after, when Rose was going to lay down the carpet, and no one else in the room, a medicine bottle full, fell from the bin on to the roll of carpet, about three or four yards off, and was broken. A lamp-glass had fallen several times without breaking; but at last that fell and broke. Then an empty bottle flew off from the mantelpiece. That was one of the last things that happened. Well then, I couldn't stand it any

THE WORKSOP POLTERGEIST

longer. Wherever the lass seemed to go, things seemed to fly about. So I said to her, 'You'll have to go.' She began to roar. But my wife gave her some tea, and she went. That was between 4 and 5 p.m., very soon after the last disturbance. Nothing happened after she left. We sat up in the kitchen that evening, a lot of us, as the newspapers tell; but nothing happened at all.

I have been in the house three years. I think the house had been built four or five years before that. Nothing of the kind had ever happened in it before, as far as I know, except that once I thought I heard some one moving in the yard, and fancied it might be some one after the fowls; but there was no one there; and there was that strange tilting of the table when my wife was washing up the things about a week before.

The Wasses and the Willises [Mrs. Willis is Wass's sister] had lived together in the next house; but since all these disturbances, the Willises have left the house; but Mr. and Mrs. Wass are still there.

(Signed) JOSEPH WHITE

New Building Ground, Worksop
April 8th, 1883

STATEMENT OF POLICE CONSTABLE HIGGS[1]

On the night of Friday, March 2nd, I heard of the disturbances at Joe White's house from his young brother, Tom. I went round to the house at 11.55 p.m., as near as I can judge, and found Joe White in the kitchen of his house. There was one candle lighted in the room, and a good fire burning, so that one could see things pretty clearly. The cupboard doors were open, and White went and shut them, and then came and stood against the chest of drawers. I stood near the outer door. No one else was in the room at the time. White had hardly shut the cupboard doors when they flew open, and a large glass jar came out past me, and pitched in the yard outside, smashing

---

[1] A man of good intelligence, and believed to be entirely honest. Fully alive, as becomes his official position, to White's indifferent reputation, but unable to account for what he saw.—F. P.

itself. I didn't see the jar leave the cupboard, or fly through the air; it went too quick. But I am quite sure that it wasn't thrown by White or any one else. White couldn't have done it without my seeing him. The jar couldn't go in a straight line from the cupboard out of the door; but it certainly did go.

Then White asked me to come and see the things which had been smashed in the inner room. He led the way and I followed. As I passed the chest of drawers in the kitchen I noticed a tumbler standing on it. Just after I passed I heard a crash, and looking round, I saw that the tumbler had fallen on the ground in the direction of the fireplace, and was broken. I don't know how it happened. There was no one else in the room.

I went into the inner room, and saw the bits of pots and things on the floor, and then I came back with White into the kitchen. The girl Rose had come into the kitchen during our absence. She was standing with her back against the bin near the fire. There was a cup standing on the bin, rather nearer the door. She said to me, 'Cup'll go soon; it has been down three times already.' She then pushed it a little farther on the bin, and turned round and stood talking to me by the fire. She had hardly done so, when the cup jumped up suddenly about four or five feet into the air, and then fell on the floor and smashed itself. White was sitting on the other side of the fire.

Then Mrs. White came in with Dr. Lloyd; also Tom White and Solomon Wass. After they had been in two or three minutes, something else happened. Tom White and Wass were standing with their backs to the fire, just in front of it. Eliza Rose and Dr. Lloyd were near them, with their backs turned towards the bin, the Doctor nearer to the door. I stood by the drawers, and Mrs. White was by me near the inner door. Then suddenly a basin, which stood on the end of the bin near the door, got up into the air, turning over and over as it went. It went up not very quickly, not as quickly as if it had been thrown. When it reached the ceiling it fell plump and smashed. I called Dr. Lloyd's attention to it, and we all saw it. No one was near it, and I don't know how it happened. I stayed about ten minutes more, but saw nothing else. I don't know what to make of it all. I don't think White or the girl could possibly have done the things which I saw.

(Signed) WILLIAM HIGGS, G.E. 30 *April 10th, 1883*

STATEMENT OF ARTHUR CURRASS, COAL-MINER[1]

I had to go out on the Saturday morning (March 3rd) to get some swill for the pig, about 8.15 a.m. I passed by White's house, and hearing a disturbance, I looked over the railings, and White said to me, 'There's something in the house that's breaking all afore it.' I asked him what it were, and he told me to come and see. I got over the railings, and I followed White into his own house. He took me into the front place where the clock was hanging over the bed's head, and was showing me a nest of drawers, where his suit of clothes came out of the bottom drawer into the top one but one. While I was looking at the drawer, and the broken pots there was lying there, the clock by some means came from the wall, slantingwise about seven feet and dropped clear of the bed's foot on to the floor. It had been fastened up on the wall, near the bed's head, and it fell between the bed's foot and the door. I said, 'What is that?' White said, 'It's something else smashed.' I turned round and saw that it was the clock. The nail still remained in the wall. The girl Rose was coming out of the kitchen towards the inner door, but had not got quite up to it. She seemed to be much frightened. White said to me, 'It doesn't matter a damn where that lass goes, there's something smashes.' The clock was taken right away into the yard and placed on an empty cask, and there it stayed. White and I were alone in the front room when the clock fell. White and I then went into the back kitchen, and I remained about four feet from the outer door, with my face towards the fireplace. I then saw a pot dog leap from the mantelpiece, and come within five feet of the pantry door and break, passing close to me. There was nothing attached to it, and there was no one near it. I then began to move away, and just then Coulter appeared. This would be between 8.30

---

[1] A Methodist, and apparently a very steady, respectable man. Believed that White did it, but couldn't guess how it was done.—F. P.

THE WORKSOP POLTERGEIST

and 8.45 a.m. Coulter had not come before whilst I was there, and certainly had not been present when the clock and the dog were broken. The clock was in the yard when he came, and I showed it him there.

(Signed) ARTHUR CURRASS

John Street, Worksop
April 8th, 1883

I have given the evidence in this instance at considerable—perhaps tedious—length, because, of all the cases which have been investigated by representatives of the Society, it is, as it stands, one of the most difficult to harmonize with any explanation by ordinary material causes. The concordant testimony of so many honest and fairly intelligent persons certainly produced, as will have been seen from my report, a strong impression on my mind at the time. Nor do I see reason now to question my original estimate of their intelligence and good faith. If my verdict on the Worksop disturbances in 1896 differs from that which I gave in 1883, it is because many things have happened since, which have taught us to discount testimony in matters of this kind.

For it will be seen that the value of these reports, as testifying to the operation of some supernormal agency, depends wholly upon two assumptions, first, that the various witnesses —imperfectly educated persons, not skilled in accurate observation of any kind—correctly described what they saw: and, second, that after an interval of more than five weeks, during which time the experiences had been discussed and compared and gaped at by every village fireside, and in the public press, they correctly remembered what they described. But in the course of the 13 years which have passed since I wrote my report, we have received some striking object-lessons demonstrating the incapacity of the ordinary unskilled observer to detect trickery or sleight-of-hand: and we have learnt to distrust the accuracy of the unaided memory in recording feats of this kind, especially when performed under circumstances of considerable excitement.

And, indeed, if we scrutinize the account as it stands, we shall find various discrepancies and contradictions in the evi-

THE WORKSOP POLTERGEIST

dence. (1) Thus, according to White, Higgs and he went into the front room first, to see the damage done there, and on their return to the kitchen, a glass jar flew out of the cupboard. But according to Higgs' version, it was after seeing the glass jar fly through the air that White and he went into the inner room. (2) White's account is that two or three witnesses were present when the glass jar flew out; Higgs says, 'that no one else was in the room at the time'. (3) There seems to be a doubt as to whether Rose entered the kitchen during Higgs' visit. White does not mention her entrance at all. Higgs says they found her in the kitchen on their return from the inner room. (4) Currass says he was in the inner room on the morning of the 3rd when the clock fell. White says that Currass was in the kitchen. (5) Again, White cannot remember where Rose was at the time of the incident; whilst Currass says she was near the inner door. (6) White and Currass agree that Coulter was not present when the American clock fell and was smashed. Now Coulter, whom I saw, and who impressed me favourably as an honest man, stated that he was present when the clock fell, and also during the immediately succeeding disturbances in the kitchen.[1]

Such are some of the discrepancies which appear in the evidence even as prepared and taken down from the lips of the witnesses by a too sympathetic reporter. It is probable that more and more serious discrepancies and contradictions would have been found if there had been no speculation and consultation and comparison in the interval of five weeks; and if each witness at the end of that time had written an independent account of the incidents.

It would be idle, in the circumstances and at this distance, to speculate on the real cause of these disturbances. But it is to be noted that Eliza Rose—the daughter of an imbecile mother—was present, by all accounts, at most of the disturbances; that they began shortly after her entrance to the cottage and ceased with her departure; and that she was regarded by White himself as the prime cause of all that happened. And if one

---

[1] Coulter's evidence was omitted from the account given in the text, originally printed in the *Journal* of the Society, as I did not at the time sufficiently realize its importance, and came to the conclusion that the man was telling a deliberate falsehood.

THE WORKSOP POLTERGEIST

apparently honest witness could describe himself as having seen occurrences that he knew of only by hearsay; if others could be mistaken as to the sequence of important events, and the presence or absence at given times of particular persons; it is perhaps not unreasonable to conjecture that the statements made by White and others that some abnormal movements took place during Rose's absence may have been incorrect, and that Rose herself, as the instrument of mysterious agencies, or simply as a half-witted girl gifted with abnormal cunning and love of mischief, may have been directly responsible for all that took place.

In the next case we have clear evidence that some, at least, of the phenomena which puzzled those who witnessed them, and gave rise to suspicions of preternatural agency, were due simply to sleight-of-hand on the part of a young uneducated village girl.

THE WEM CASE

The subjoined extract from a daily paper gives an account of some mysterious disturbances at a Shropshire village, in November, 1883.

'A series of occurrences which have caused great excitement in the neighbourhood of Leebotwood, and no small speculation and wonder in the adjacent town of Shrewsbury, have just taken place. At a secluded farm called "The Woods", which is about a mile and a half from Toppington and nine or ten from Shrewsbury, resides a farmer named Hampson, and about four o'clock one afternoon, at the latter end of last week, the servants were in the kitchen of the farmhouse, preparing tea. On the fire was a saucepan in which were some eggs boiling, and this "jumped", as the girls declared, off the fire, while the tea things were thrown from the table and smashed. Some of the hot cinders were also thrown out of the grate, and set fire to some clothes in a basket. So far, the explosion of some material in the grate might have been sufficient to account for the occurrence; but what is said to have occurred subsequently will not bear such an explanation. On the table was a paraffin lamp, with a globe, and the globe was "lifted" off the stand

THE WEM POLTERGEIST

and thrown across the room, the lamp itself being left on the table. A mat under the lamp took fire, and the inmates of the house becoming alarmed, then ran out for the neighbours. Among others who went to the house was a Mr. Lea, an adjacent farmer, who states that when he approached the house it seemed as if all the upstairs rooms were on fire, "as there was such a light in the windows". Mr. Hampson consequently went upstairs and made an examination, but everything there was safe, and in the usual order. As things were continuing to jump about the kitchen in a manner which was altogether inexplicable, and many were getting damaged, Hampson decided to remove everything that was in that apartment outside. He accordingly took down a barometer from the wall, when something struck him on the leg, and a loaf of bread which was on the table was thrown by some invisible means and hit him on the back. A volume of *Pilgrim's Progress* was thrown or "jumped" through the window, and a large ornamental sea-shell went through in a similar fashion. In the parlour a sewing machine was thrown about and damaged, and has had to be sent to be repaired. The nurse-girl was nursing the baby by the fire when some fire leapt from the grate, and the child's hair was singed and its arms burnt. The girl was so alarmed that she set off to a neighbour's, and on the way there her clothes took fire, and had to be torn from her body. During the evening, while the girl was at the neighbour's, a plate which she touched while having her supper was apparently thrown on the floor, and the pieces were picked up by some unseen agency, and put in the centre of the table. Other occurrences are said to have taken place in the neighbour's house while the nurse-girl was there, the whole lasting considerably over half an hour. As no one could explain the cause of what they witnessed, the police were communicated with, and made full inquiries from the inmates of the house and others, the result being that they ordered the coal to be consumed in the open air, believing it to contain some explosive substance, but it burnt quietly away. Those who witnessed these occurrences tell a marvellously straightforward story, and curiously enough none of them attributed it to any supernatural cause, as might have been expected in a quiet country locality, but they say it was "something in the coal or in the air", while one or two fancy it was some electrical phenomena.'

Subsequently, the same paper states, their 'Shrewsbury correspondent telegraphs that he paid another visit to Weston Lullingfield yesterday, and was informed that on Saturday and Sunday there were more extraordinary manifestations in connection with the girl Emma Davies. Police-constable Taylor, of the Shropshire Constabulary, remained in the house until late on Saturday. During the time he was there the fender moved from the fireplace into the middle of the room, and on being replaced, came forward a second and third time. A cushion placed at the back of a chair on which the girl sat several times flew across the room, and all the stitches in her apron came undone, followed later on by the buttons upon her dress being wrenched off. Miss Maddox, the village schoolmistress, made a statement to the correspondent to the effect that she called to see the girl, a former pupil, on Saturday evening, and had not long been seated when she observed both the chair and the girl rise from the floor. She took the girl on her lap and sat in the chair herself, and immediately the girl's boots flew off, and although replaced, the circumstance was twice repeated. On Sunday a box in a bedroom was hurled across the room, and a number of cups and saucers were smashed.'

REPORT BY MR. F. S. HUGHES

December 3rd, 1883

During the first and second weeks of November, 1883, accounts were to be seen in the London and local papers of strange phenomena stated to have taken place at Wood's Farm, near Wem, and other houses in the neighbourhood.

These phenomena could not apparently be accounted for by ordinary physical laws, and it seemed therefore very desirable that the stories should be thoroughly sifted on behalf of the Society for Psychical Research.

The scene of the first series of these phenomena was Wood's Farm, and the time, the afternoon of Thursday, November 1st. A nurse-girl at the farm, named Emma Davies, was connected in some way with the disturbances by the occupiers, and she was accordingly dismissed and sent to her home at a village called Weston Lullingfield, about five miles off. Here the singular phenomena appeared shortly after her arrival, and the affair began to attract very general attention.

On Friday, the 9th, the girl, who seems to have got into a very nervous state, was taken to a branch establishment at Wem, of Dr. Corke, of Baschurch, and kept in strict seclusion, at the same time being closely watched by the housekeeper, Miss Turner.

On the following Thursday the *Daily News* and the *Daily Telegraph* both had long reports, stating that the girl had confessed to having wrought all these wonders by very ordinary sleight-of-hand.

As, however, these accounts did little to explain away the phenomena which had taken place according to the previous newspaper reports, I was asked by the Society for Psychical Research to go down to Shropshire to investigate the evidence on which the original stories rested, and to see whether they could really be accounted for satisfactorily by the girl's alleged trickery.

On Saturday, the 17th November, I proceeded to Wem and shortly after my arrival called at the doctor's house, and saw Miss Turner, Dr. Mackey, the assistant of Dr. Corke, not being at home.

Miss Turner is a lady of about 30 years of age, who appeared to be a practical, shrewd person, not at all excitable, and she gave her evidence in a very straightforward manner.

Calling again, later on in the evening, I saw Dr. Mackey, who is a young Scotchman, of about 27 or 28, and who seemed nervously anxious not to give any evidence about which he had any doubt.

I am quite confident that the girl was well treated while living with them, and was subjected to no undue influence.

I made notes of the evidence they were able to give me on the subject, and obtained their signatures to my account after they had heard it read to them.

Briefly their account is: That certain manifestations took place, similar in character to those that preceded them, and for

THE WEM POLTERGEIST

two or three days they were quite unable to detect any fraud, though no manifestation ever took place when the girl was not in such a position that she *might* have produced them by ordinary trickery.

Thus, in the presence of Dr. Mackey and Miss Turner a piece of bread jumped across the room, the girl not being actually seen to throw it. On another occasion when Miss Turner had left the room, the girl suddenly screamed, and when Miss T. returned a pair of slippers were on the sofa which had just before been seen on the hearthrug. Again, when Miss T. had just turned her back to the girl, the usual scream was heard, and turning round Miss T. saw a bucket in the air descending to the ground. A knife on another occasion was thrown across the room, being in the air when Dr. Corke's servant was entering the room.

On Tuesday morning, however, Miss Turner was in an upper room at the back of the house, and the servant of the establishment and Emma Davies were outside, Emma having her back to the house, and unaware that she was observed. Miss Turner noticed that Emma Davies had a piece of brick in her hand held behind her back. This she threw to a distance by a turn of the wrist, and while doing so, screamed to attract the attention of the servant, who, of course, turning round saw the brick in the air, and was very much frightened. Emma Davies, looking round, saw that she had been seen by Miss Turner, and apparently imagining that she had been found out, was very anxious to return home that night.

Miss Turner took no notice of the occurrence at the time, but the next morning (Wednesday) she asked the girl if she had been playing tricks, and the girl confessed that she had, and went through some of the performances very skilfully, according to Miss Turner's account.

Later on in the day she repeated these in the presence of the doctor, Miss Turner, and the two reporters from London, but Miss Turner said nothing like so well.

Dr. Mackey further gave me an account of a conversation which he had had with Emma Davies, chiefly with reference to some of the extraordinary stories that had appeared in the papers.

THE WEM POLTERGEIST

One of these stories was that after the girl's return to her father's house, she was in the habit of assisting her sister in household work. One day they were putting clothes out on the hedge to dry, but those placed by Emma Davies refused to remain on the hedge, and 'jumped over into the road'.

With reference to this, the statement of Emma Davies, as reported by Dr. Mackey, was as follows: 'They put the clothes on the hedge, and then returned to the house, nothing unusual having occurred. On going outside again, the linen was found on the ground, two little boys being seen running away.' She was quite confident that she did not see the things going off the hedge.

Several of the other stories were similarly disposed of by her. Thus, when the windows were broken at her father's cottage and farm, there were a lot of men and boys standing about outside.

The girl always denied that she had produced the various phenomena at Wood's Farm and Weston Lullingfield, but Dr. Mackey thought that she had been carefully primed not to 'let on' about this.

Dr. Mackey added that the girl's physical and mental condition was quite normal, so far as he could ascertain.

On the following morning I drove over to Wood's Farm, which is about five or six miles distant from Wem, and there obtained evidence of the following witnesses:

Mr. and Mrs. Hampson, their servant girl, Priscilla Evans, Mr. and Mrs. Lea, of a neighbouring farm, and the waggoner at Wood's Farm, Thomas Williams.

Mr. Hampson was a very intelligent man, who unfortunately was not at home at the time of the occurrences, and only had evidence on some minor details.

Mrs. Hampson was very diffuse in her account, and appeared rather credulous. She looks about 30 years of age.

The girl, Priscilla Evans, is about 16, very voluble, but gave her evidence in a very straightforward manner, giving me the impression that she was telling me what she believed to be the truth. She had an excellent character from Mr. and Mrs. Hampson; and it is mere justice to her to state that the charge of complicity with Emma Davies' trickery, brought against her

THE WEM POLTERGEIST

by the reporters of the *Daily News* and the *Daily Telegraph*—on the ground of a supposed confession of the waggoner Williams, that he had taught his fellow servants 'how to shift things about'—completely broke down under my examination. The waggoner denies that he ever said, or could have said, anything of the sort; and his denial was entirely confirmed by Mr. Belliss, the innkeeper, who drove the reporters over from Wem, and himself suggested the questions put to the waggoner which led to the reporters' mistake.

I could not regard Mr. and Mrs. Lea as good witnesses, since their firm conviction of the devil's agency in the matter rendered them too much indisposed to accept any ordinary explanation of any of the occurrences to which they referred, and they did not bring forward any cases of manifestations which took place when Emma Davies was *undeniably*, according to my opinion, in such a position that she could not have produced them.

According to Mrs. Hampson's account, the family, with the exception of Mr. Hampson, were occupying the parlour on Wednesday, October 31st, when suddenly coal was seen to be 'alive' in various parts of the room, apparently having flown out of the fire. Nothing unusual was observed that day in addition to this, the fire having been removed to the kitchen, and coke instead of coal being employed.

The next day, about four p.m., the family were about to sit down to tea, when the saucepan on the fire jumped off, and coal began to fly about. A cup and saucer 'went off' the table, by unseen agency, and they were all so frightened that Emma Davies was sent off to Lea's farm for help. Mrs. H. and Priscilla retreated to the dairy, whence, it will be seen on reference to the map, they had a full view of the kitchen table. They both state that they saw the crockery rise up off the table and fall to the ground. The articles did not go off all at once, but one or two at a time. They are quite certain that this happened while Emma Davies was absent, fetching Mrs. Lea from the neighbouring farm.

Some of the crockery, on the return of Emma Davies and Mrs. Lea, was placed on the table, but again went off. Mrs. Lea and Mrs. Hampson then deemed it desirable to go for further assistance, the girls being left behind. This ends Mrs. Hampson's evidence as regards the occurrences of that evening at the farm.

Mrs. Hampson also stated that in the morning the baby was in its cradle inside the parlour, where it had been placed to be out of range of the fire. Mrs. Hampson and the girls were in the kitchen, and Emma Davies went in to see after the baby, returning presently, screaming, saying that the baby was on fire. On the various occasions (three or four) that the baby was on fire, E. D. was always the one to discover it; and she always had time to cause the fire, according to Mrs. Hampson. Once she was seen to be shaking the child's pinafore, which was alight, although Mrs. H. had carefully warned her always to 'crush' fire out.

Further, on one occasion when E. D. was alone in the parlour, during the manifestations, a noise as of a striking match was heard, and when Mrs. H. entered the room, there was a distinct smell of brimstone, and a used match was found at the baby's head.

Priscilla Evans added some information with regard to articles found on fire, which was corroborated by Mr. Lea. Mrs. Hampson was not present, I believe, when they were discovered.

It is well to note that Emma Davies was always the person to discover anything on fire, and none of the witnesses could state positively that on any single occasion was she in the company or in sight of any one when she made the discovery.

One of the baby's caps, of a kind of woollen material, and a paper mat were found in flames, the flames being very high and white, and the articles apparently burning were very little singed when the flames were extinguished. The cap and mat, which had both been exposed to the air for some time, were shown to me, and I cut off a bit of the cap, which I dipped in paraffin, which was largely used at the farm. Lighting it, she, Priscilla E., declared it presented exactly the appearance of the former blaze, and the bit of cap was of course little singed, when the flame was extinguished. Mr. Hampson stated that the cap, when shown to him on his return, had a greasy feel.

THE WEM POLTERGEIST

The most important piece of evidence that the girl Evans contributed is, that when Mrs. H. and Mrs. Lea had left the house, the cupboard opposite the dairy door was apparently locked by one of them, but afterwards flew open, whereupon E. D. going to close it, became, as it were, rooted to the spot. Priscilla tried to pull her away, but the girl shrieked and said she couldn't move. The cupboard was well stocked with crockery, and these things proceeded to come out of the cupboard two or three at a time. Priscilla states that E. D. had her arms folded all the time, and that she, Priscilla, watched her closely, and was certain that she did not pull the things out. I should, however, point out that it must have been nearly dark at the time.

With regard to the statement that E. D. was put up to these tricks by the waggoner, there appears—as I have already said—no evidence for this, and it is almost absurd to suppose a heavy rustic capable of giving lessons in legerdemain.

Priscilla and E. D. appear to have been on rather bad terms, and none of the people at the farm gave E. D. a good character.

Continuing my journey I arrived at Weston Lullingfield, a village about five miles from Wood's Farm. I first called on Miss Maddox, a woman of about 40, who had been training the youth of Weston for the last 12 years ('come December'). She is rather excitable, and a woman who would, I think, be easily imposed upon. Her evidence is a remarkable illustration of the manner in which the sensational newspaper reports dwindle down into the commonplace.

She states that when she visited the girl, there were about 20 people standing and sitting about the room, and the girl E. D. was wriggling about on her chair in a state of great excitement. Miss M. is positive that the chair rose off the ground about a foot, but this I imagine a clever child could accomplish by a clever 'kick off'.

Miss M. then took the child on her lap, and the child's boots flew off, but whether they were securely fastened on her feet, or downtrodden at the heels, she cannot say.

The only further evidence that Miss M. had on the subject was that she saw a table (*up against a wooden partition*) moving up and down rather violently, without, she thought, any one being near. She added that the partition seemed 'bulged in', so that somebody might have been pushing it on the other side of the partition.

She gave Emma Davies a good character.

I then visited the girl's home, but could not see the girl. The father, however, came out and spoke to me, but he himself had seen nothing.

The rustics of the village, whom I afterwards interviewed, were nearly all unable to sign their names, and their evidence is hardly worth recording. One man, who was present with Police-constable Taylor when the fender performed feats, states that Taylor was sitting on one side of the fire, and E. D. on the other, but he could not say how the fender 'came forward', whether parallel to itself, or only in such a manner that the girl might have pushed it out with her foot.

All the other evidence at this place was of the same unsatisfactory nature.

The next day I drove over with Mr. Maitland to try and see Emma Davies, but she would not speak, and was taken upstairs. After the lapse of an hour she reappeared, but we could not get anything out of her.

Summing up, I consider that there is abundant evidence of some trickery on the part of the girl E. D., at Wood's Farm; but that some portion of the phenomena cannot be referred to this cause if the statements of Mrs. Hampson and Priscilla Evans as to what occurred in E. D.'s absence, and the description given by Priscilla Evans of the crockery coming out of the cupboard, can be at all relied on. Still, if the case were an isolated one, the evidence is not of so satisfactory a nature as to justify the assumption that phenomena unexplainable by trickery actually took place; but on the hypothesis that there are cases on record in which trickery and genuine preternatural phenomena were combined, this case might, with some degree of probability, be included amongst them.

FRANK S. HUGHES, B.A. (Cantab)
December 3rd, 1883

As exception has been taken to Mr. Hughes' treatment of part of the evidence in this case, on the ground that he was

THE WEM POLTERGEIST

biassed against a belief in supernormal agencies, it seems best to quote textually the two passages specially referred to.

(1) The signed statement by Miss Maddox gives the following version of the 'levitation': 'There were about 20 people standing and sitting about the room when Miss Maddox entered. The first thing Miss Maddox saw was the chair on which the girl sat wriggling about, and once rising a foot from the ground, the girl having no point of contact with the ground at the time. She was writhing about, and in a state of great nervous excitement.'

(2) The following passage is from a statement signed by Henry and James Lea: 'Emma Davies was with Mrs. Lea at the gate, a long distance off, while the noises continued and things came flying out of the window. Things came out after the place had been cleared of people.'

It will be admitted, I think, that the conditions described by Miss Maddox—some twenty people present in the room, and Emma Davies twisting and wriggling on her chair in a condition of great nervous excitement—were not specially favourable for observation. It may be added that under more favourable circumstances a phenomenon of the kind which Miss Maddox claims to have witnessed is not easy to observe with accuracy. As regards the Leas' statement that Emma Davies was at a distance from the house during the progress of some of the disturbances it will be remembered that in the Worksop case it was shown that memory is apt to be treacherous on such matters as the presence or absence of particular persons at particular times, and the precise sequence of various events. A statement of this kind would no doubt be deserving of consideration if it emanated from a first-rate witness. But Mr. Hughes' estimate of the Leas as being indifferent witnesses must be allowed to have weight.

Upon the whole, after a reperusal of the documents in the case, I cannot find that Mr. Hughes has misrepresented the evidence in any material particular. As regards the two incidents upon which he lays special stress, it may be considered that if Emma Davies was able to evade detection when closely watched for two or three days by suspicious and educated witnesses, it seems not unlikely that she might have succeeded in the easier task of eluding the vigilance of Priscilla Evans, a young rustic already mystified and excited by the marvellous manifestations which she had witnessed, and that the crockery which flew out of the cupboard in the twilight was merely propelled by the hand of Emma Davies. There remains the statement of two witnesses who saw crockery fall off the table during Emma Davies' absence. This statement, if accepted literally, is hard to reconcile with the supposition of trickery.

It should be added that though Emma Davies was regarded by the doctor who examined her as being quite normal, Mr. Hughes, in the course of his enquiries, found some evidence of unusual precocity on her part. Moreover, according to her mother's statement, while she had been a healthy child before the outbreak of the disturbances, she afterwards fell into ill-health and became subject to fits. It should be added that Miss Maddox in her signed account states that, during some of the disturbances at which she was present, Emma Davies cried out that an old woman was at her, and would not let her breathe, and called to her mother to relieve her.

INDEX

Amherst Mystery, the Great, 133, 138–44, 359–79
Atlantic Monthly case, 345–7
Auk, Great, considered as a witch, 60
Axholme, Isle of, 54–5

Bardili, Dr., 319
Barrett, Sir William, F.R.S., 135–8, 328–40
Bayswater, Moscow Road, Poltergeist of, 133–4, 298–9
Bealings Bells, 67
Bell-ringing, 67
Berlioz, Hector, 130
Bishop, Bridget, 65
Borley Rectory, Suffolk, most haunted house in England, 33
Bristow, Mr., in the Swanland case, 70
Burroughs, Rev. George, a Witch of Salem, 61
Bute, Marquess of, 127

Calvados, haunted Castle in, 131–2, 268–87
Campbell, Gilbert, 305–6
Carrick, Mary, in the *Atlantic Monthly* case, 67, 345–6
Cashen's Gap, talking mongoose of, 85, 95, 104, 107–9, 121–2
Catherine the Great of Russia, story of, 26
Chattox, Old, a Lancashire Witch 56–7
Cideville, Curé of, 17–20, 140
Clarke, T. B., the case of, 68–9

Copertino, Flying Saint of, 37–8
Cottin, Angélique, 133–4, 299–301
Cox, Esther, of the Great Amherst Mystery, 138–44, 361–79
Crowe, Mrs. Catherine, 288–327
Curé of Cideville, 17–20, 140

Dale, Georgia, hauntings in a railway telegraph car at, 69, 353–5
Davies, Emma, 352, 406–15
Demdike, Old, a Lancashire Witch, 56–7
Derrygonnelly case, the, 135–7, 340–4
Desborough, Nicholas, haunting in the house of, 63–4
Dornoch, last of the Witches burnt at, 60
Drum, the poem, by Miss Edith Sitwell, 113–18
Drummer of Tedworth, the, 113–24, 134, 214–29, 304

Emmerich, Mademoiselle, 301–2
Enniscorthy case, the, 137–8, 328–40
Epworth Rectory, 80–91, 136, 157–88
Essex, Witches of, 58, 101–3

Fischer, Carl, of Stuttgart, 303
Fives, near Lille, case at, 74
Flammarion, Camille, *Haunted Houses*, 73, 75, 131–2, 268–87

417

INDEX

Forfar, Witches of, 59

G., Mr., his adventure in Sumatra, 144–5, 380–6
Glanvil, Rev. Joseph, author of *Saducismus Triumphatus*, 113–24, 214–29
Gowdie, Isobel, the Auldearne Witch, 59
Gruppenbach case, 321

Hahn, Councillor, of Ingelfingen, 307–17
Harvard University, 61
Haxeyhood, old festival, 55
Hilton, The Cauld Lad O', 152–3
Hinton Ampner, haunting of, 126–30, 230–67
Hitler, Adolf, as potential Poltergeist, 54
Hubbell, Mr. Walter, 138–44, 359–79

Iceland, Poltergeists in, 66–7

Jobson, Mary, 322–5

Kemp, Ursley, a Witch of St. Osyth, 101–3
Keppoch case, 305
Kerner, Dr., 321
Khayn, Fraulein, governess of Catherine the Great, 26

Lang, Andrew, *Cock Lane and Common Sense*, 31–2
Liguori, St. Alphonso, 38
Livry, Emma, dancer, 40

Malking Tower, 55–6, 151
March, Elwin, 347–51
Marcinelle, in Belgium, stone throwing at, 71
Mather, Increase and Cotton, 61–3
Molesworth, Captain, 317–8
Mompesson, Mr., 113–24, 134, 214–29

Mongoose, the talking, 85, 95, 104, 107–9, 121–2
Moore, Major Edward, F.R.S., 67
Morse, William, haunting in the house of, 62
Murray, Miss Margaret, 126
Mystère, Le Parc du, 149–50

Nijinski, Vaslav, 39

Ointment, flying, 126
Osyth, St., Witches of, 58–9, 101–3

Palmisano Signar Paolo, story of, 171
Paul I, Czar, 28–30
Pendle, forest of, 55–6, 151
Peter III, Czar, 28
Phelps case, 45–54, 62, 74, 121
Pirano, luminous woman of, 34
Plotitsine, Maxime Koutzmine, 44–5
Portland, Oregon, case, 347–53
Potts, Thomas, chronicle of the Lancashire Witches, 56–7
Price, Mr. Harry, 34–6
Procter, Mr. Joseph, of Willington Mill, 91–100, 189–213

Rachilde, Madame, 149–50
Rambouillet, Poltergeist of, 134
Randall, in the Enniscorthy case, 68, 328–40
Ricketts, Mrs., the case of, 126–130, 230–67
Rieger, Barbara, 321
Ringcroft, in Galloway, Poltergeist of, 79, 84
Rossetti, Christina, Goblin Market of, 59
Ruxton, Dr. Buck, 43

Saducismus Triumphatus, 113–24
St. Vincent, Earl, 126–30
Salem, Witches of, 60–3
Saragossa Ghost, the, 107
Schlotterbeck, 306

INDEX

Schuppart, Professor, 134, 304-5
Shchapoff, Mme, case of, 74-5
Skopiți, 44-5
Stauntons, the, 42-3
Stockwell Ghost, the, 132-3, 289-98, 303
Style, Elizabeth, of Stoke Trister in the County of Somerset, 124-6
Sumatra, case from, 380-6
Swanland, near Hull, carpenter's shop at, 70-3

Tackley in Oxfordshire, hauntings at, 127
Taglioni, Marie, 39-40
Teed, Daniel, of Amherst, 359-79
Thérèse of Lisieux, St., 36
Toadpool Farm, the Poltergeist of, 65-6

Vestris, Auguste, dancer, 38-9
Vienna, Poltergeist, the, 356-8

Wärndorfer, Mr., 356-8
Weir, Major, a Witch of Edinburgh, 59
Wem, Poltergeist at, 133, 146-7, 352, 404-15
Wesley, John, a long note from his Journal, 101-2, 157-88
Wesley, Samuel, 157-88, 304
Weston, ghost at, 25-8
White, Joe, of Worksop case, 387-404
Wildin, Rosina, 320-4
Willington Mill, 91-100, 104-12, 189-213
Wincanton, the Witch of, 125-6
Worksop, Poltergeist of, 145-6, 387-404

Zugun, Eleanore, Rumanian Poltergeist, 48, 62